Fish Migration

Fish Migration

F. R. HARDEN JONES
Fisheries Laboratory, Lowestoft

Illustrated by
H. E. JENNER

Edward Arnold (Publishers) Ltd. London

SBN: 7131 2182 3

Printed and bound in Great Britain by
Spottiswoode, Ballantyne & Co. Ltd., London and Colchester

Preface

My interest in fish migrations stemmed from a meeting of the Cambridge University Natural History Society which was held in the Zoological Laboratory on 6 November 1953. The subject of the meeting was a discussion on 'How animals find their way about'. The main lecture theatre was filled, and Dr. W. H. Thorpe was in the chair. Dr. G. V. T. Matthews spoke on birds, Dr. D. M. Voles and Dr. J. S. Kennedy dealt with insects, and I made representations on the behalf of fish. The meeting was, by all accounts, a great success. But although I may have been able to deceive a proportion of the audience, the experience convinced me that I really knew very little about the subject on which I had been speaking. After leaving Cambridge for the Fisheries Laboratory at Lowestoft, I tried to learn a little more about fish migration and orientation. This book is the result of my efforts.

The book started to take shape in 1958. Progress was very slow but quickened in 1961 when I was asked to give a series of lectures in the Institute of Fisheries, University of British Columbia, Vancouver, British Columbia. The lectures were sponsored jointly by the Nuffield Foundation, the National Research Council of Canada, and the University of British Columbia. The Ministry of Agriculture, Fisheries, and Food gave me special leave of absence and early in 1962 I gave a series of ten lectures in Vancouver under the general heading of 'Problems of fish migration'. As a result of Professor N. J. Wilimovsky's initiative I was asked to repeat some of these lectures at the College of Fisheries, University of Washington, Seattle, and at the Auke Bay Laboratory of the U.S. Bureau of Commercial Fisheries in Juneau, Alaska. Finally, the whole series was repeated at the Bureau's Biological Laboratory at Woods Hole, Massachusetts. All these lectures were based on an early draft of this book, which was then revised and, I hope, improved, in the light of the criticisms and comments made by my North American audiences. I am very grateful to them for their lively response.

The final typescript reached the publishers on 1 April 1967 and papers seen after that date are not cited. Although the book is longer than was originally intended, it is not as complete as I would wish. I have tried to be selective with references but I am sure that some that should have been mentioned have been missed. As to content, there are some obvious omissions, such as, for example, the Baltic salmon, Faroe Bank cod, and tuna. The latter is a serious omission in a book on fish migrations. But the tuna literature is so large,[1] and my knowledge of it so small, that I would be faced with a further 2 to 3 years of work before feeling competent to write about the migrations of this group. It seemed wise to stop now rather than to strive after a coverage which might be beyond my powers. The book is not therefore a complete account of fish migration. I hope that it may be thought of as an interim report, and used as a kind of stock-taking. In some cases, at least, I hope that the problems have been set out clearly, and some indication given of the lines of attack that might be adopted to solve them.

[1] See 'Proceedings of the world scientific meeting on the biology of tunas and related species', FAO Fish. Rep., (6) 1: pp. 1–100, 1963; 2: pp. 101–957, 1963; 3: pp. 977–1851, 1963; and 4: pp. 1853–2272, 1964.

I could not have written this book outside the climate of the Fisheries Laboratory at Lowestoft, and it is therefore a pleasure to acknowledge my debt to the Ministry of Agriculture, Fisheries, and Food, and to my colleagues at Lowestoft. Finally I owe much to all those who have given me encouragement, advice and data and, in some cases, read part or all of the text. They are: D. L. Alverson; R. Balls; E. Bertelsen; G. C. Bolster; H. O. Bull; A. C. Burd; Rannevig Burd; W. G. van Campen; J. N. Carruthers; H. A. Cole; F. Creutzberg; D. H. Cushing; W. A. Dence; J. Eggvin; T. S. English; U. Fagerlund; R. E. Foerster; A. Fridriksson; M. Graham; C. C. Groot; J. A. Gulland; Clodagh Harden Jones; W. L. Hartman; A. D. Hasler; J. H. Helle; N. G. Heise; C. C. Hemmings; W. S. Hoar; E. S. Hobson; D. R. Idler; T. D. Iles; J. Jacobsen; K. S. Ketchen; R. T. King; P. A. Larkin; R. J. LeBrasseur; A. J. Lee; C. C. Lindsey; H. W. Lissmann; C. E. Lucas; N. B. Marshall; C. H. Mortimer; R. W. Murray; C. S. Myall; F. Neave; T. G. Northcote; B. B. Parrish; F. T. K. Pentelow; R. B. Rae; H. T. Ramsden; S. B. Saila; J. Shelbourn; J. E. Shelbourne; A. C. Simpson; F. H. C. Taylor; G. C. Trout; J. F. de Veen; N. J. Wilimovsky; H. E. Winn; P. M. J. Woodhead; J. J. Zijlstra.

The figures in this book have all been drawn by Mr. H. E. Jenner and I am very grateful to him for the care that he has taken over the work.

In many figures the outlines of charts are taken from British Admiralty, Meteorological Office or Ordnance Survey maps which are Crown Copyright and have been used by permission of the Controller of Her Majesty's Stationery Office. Figures based on material contained in Official Canadian publications are reproduced by permission of The Queen's Printer and Controller of Stationery, Ottawa. Permission to use other published material in the preparation of figures has also been given by the following: George Allen and Unwin, Ltd., London; Baillière, Tindall and Cassell, Ltd., London; California Department of Fish and Game; Deutsches Hydrographisches Institut, Hamburg; Fiskeridirektoratets Havforskningsinstitutt, Bergen; Imray, Laurie, Norie and Wilson, Ltd., St. Ives, Huntingdonshire, England; International Commission for the Northwest Atlantic Fisheries, Dartmouth, N.S., Canada; International Council for the Exploration of the Sea, Charlottenlund, Denmark; International Hydrographic Bureau, Monaco; International North Pacific Fisheries Commission, Vancouver, B.C., Canada; International Pacific Salmon Fisheries Commission, New Westminster, B.C., Canada; Kommissionen for Danmarks, Fiskeriog Havundersøgelser, Charlottenlund, Denmark; Pergamon Press, Ltd., Oxford; University Research Institute, Department of Fisheries, Reykjavik, Iceland.

F. R. Harden Jones

The Mill, Lound,
Lowestoft, Suffolk.
1967

Contents

Chapter 1

Introduction

In its normal use the word migration means to move from one place to another. When applied to animals it has a special meaning: a migration is a coming and going with the seasons, with a 'once-a-year' implication, and the most obvious examples are provided by birds. Here there are many types of migratory movement and Landsborough Thompson (1942) groups them under three headings:

1. Local and seasonal movements.
2. Dispersals.
3. True migrations.

The local seasonal movements are merely changes of ground at a particular time of the year. Some of these movements may be very small, others larger while still confined within one geographical area. An example in the British Isles is the autumn migration of starlings to the south and west, and their return to the north and east the following spring. The second group of movements are more extensive and classed as dispersals or wanderings. Only the breeding area is well defined and the movement is, ideally, an even and outward spread from this centre. The migrations of young guillemots and gannets are of this type. However, a dispersal may have a bias in one direction, and so be difficult to distinguish from a true migration. Landsborough Thompson stresses as the essential feature of a dispersal the fact that the concentration of individuals remains greatest near the breeding area, whereas in the third group, the true migrations, there is a real movement from one area to another, 'a shift in what may be called the centre of gravity of the population' (Landsborough Thompson, 1942, p. 24). Wilkinson (1952) has also made a distinction between a wandering or dispersal from the breeding quarters over a wide stretch of territory, and the more clearly defined migration where there is a movement between widely separated and well-defined areas. The former he calls diasporic migration and the latter anastrophic migration. These distinctions may be useful when applied to bird migrations but difficulties arise if attempts are made to fit the same scheme too rigidly to fish. Here it may even be more difficult to make the distinction between a dispersal and a migration in the sense that these terms are used for birds. Fish may be carried passively hundreds of miles by oceanic currents and what may be no more than a dispersal could then have all the appearance of a true migration. It should be possible to distinguish between the two if the time taken for a fish to move from one place to another is significantly different from that expected if it were carried passively by the current. In practice, this means that the times of departure and arrival of a fish must be known accurately as well as the speed of the current at the depth at which it was swimming. This is rarely, if ever, possible. Compared with birds, the collection of data on the migration of fish is a much more difficult problem. There is no great body of enthusiastic fish watchers to report and record the migrants on passage. Fisheries, it is true, change with the seasons, and much can be learned from fishermen, but what one learns may be more about the movements of fishing boats than the movements of fish. The fishermen's information is necessarily incomplete, and is only the start of the story. To go further scientists have to go to sea, to catch and to tag fish. Landing statistics have to be examined, fluctuations followed and worked out in detail. All this takes time, is expensive, and the work is slow. So the study of fish migrations has lagged behind that of birds, even though scientific interest in both fields first developed on a significant scale during the same decade, between 1890 and 1900.

I propose to adopt Heape's definition (1931, p. 16) of the term migration as 'a class of movement which impels migrants to return to the region from which they have migrated'. Heape uses the word 'impels' in the sense of biological necessity. There is no suggestion of actual force or compulsion. Migration can be contrasted with emigration, 'movements which entail change of environments, but which do not involve return to the original area of habitat'. These definitions make no reference to the means by which the migration or emigration may be brought about.

Heape recognized three types of migration: alimental migration, in search of food and water; climatic migration, to secure more suitable climatic conditions; and gametic migration, for reproduction. To these three Myers (1949) would add a fourth category, osmoregulatory migration.

The really spectacular migrations of mature adult fish are for spawning and for feeding. They breed in one area, but grow up and feed in another. Examples are provided by the cod of the Arcto-Norwegian stock and the European eel. In summer months the Arcto-Norwegian cod feed in an area roughly bounded by Spitsbergen, Bear Island, Novaya Zemlya, and the Murman coast. In October and November the older fish start to move southwards after the Arctic night has set in and four months later, in February and March, most of the mature and ripe fish arrive on their main spawning ground at the Lofoten Islands, within the West Fjord, 700 miles or more distant. In the spring and early summer the spent and larval fish return to the feeding grounds in the north.

The European eel is believed to spawn somewhere between the Bermudas and the Bahamas in an area corresponding more or less with the Sargasso Sea, where the water is warm and of relatively high salinity. The larval eels, known as leptocephali, are carried towards the European coastline where as elvers, now about two and a half years old, they enter rivers. Ten or more years later, as fully grown eels, they leave freshwater and are thought to make the return journey of over 3,000 miles back to their birthplace, to spawn and to die.

Spectacular feeding and spawning migrations are also made by plaice and herring. Then there is the example of the salmon which spawns in freshwater but spends most of its adult life in the sea. Salmon are believed to return to freshwater to spawn in the stream in which they grew up as fry.

These fish are all of economic importance. The round figures for their total world catch, in thousands of metric tons during 1965, are as follows (FAO, 1966).

Herring, *Clupea harengus*	3,942
Cod, *Gadus morhua*	2,730
Salmon, *Salmo* sp. and *Oncorhynchus* sp.	419
Plaice, *Pleuronectes platessa*	144
Eel, *Anguilla anguilla*	17

Together, the total catch of these fish amounts to nearly 7·25 million tons, an important contribution to the world catch of 52 million tons, of all species, taken that year. A detailed knowledge and understanding of their migrations is one of the essential steps towards the rational exploitation of their stocks, and the research effort that has been directed to this end is considerable.

Meek (1916a) realized the importance of the study of migrations to the fisheries and brought together a mass of material in his book *The Migrations of Fish*. Scheuring (1929, 1930) covers a wide field in his accounts.

Fish migrations are not, of course, only of economic or practical interest. They raise many problems, some of which might perhaps be thought to lie more within the field of academic zoology than of fisheries science. But here, as in other fields of research, the academic and the more practical aspects of the problem are closely related one to another and an advance in knowledge and understanding on one side often stimulates and promotes advances on the other. My interest in fish migrations centres round the problem of how fish find their way about. How do cod of the Arcto-Norwegian stock make their way to the spawning grounds at Lofoten ? How does the eel find its way back to the Sargasso Sea ? If it is true that a grown salmon returns to spawn in its parent stream, how does it find its way back ? It is no answer to say that the fish has a sense of direction and leave it at that. As Griffin (1953, p. 215) remarks, one might was well talk of a sense of honour or a sense of decency. The fish are probably responding to environmental factors, and it is to a study of these factors, and of the sensory physiology and the behaviour of the fish, that one should turn to find the answer to these questions.

There are several ways by which a fish could make a migratory movement and these may be considered under three headings.

1. By drift

Drift is used in the sense of being carried passively by water currents. A directional trend may result if the overall water movement is in one direction. While the locomotory movements of the fish make no significant contribution to the movement, it is important to remember that a vertical migration from deep to shallow water, or vice versa, would produce great changes in horizontal distribution if the water layers were moving at different speeds or in different directions. Hardy (1936) was one of the first to draw attention to this and Mackintosh (1937) has shown how the migrations and distributions of several species of Antarctic macroplankton could be brought about by a combination of passive drift and vertical movement. There may be some difficulty in accepting the idea that a migration could be brought about by drift, and this really comes down to the definition of migration. It will be recalled that Heape's definition makes no distinction between passive and active migrations and Meek (1916a, p. 19) clearly refers to the drift of eggs and larvae as a passive migration. There may, in general terms, be a difference here between adults and larvae: adults *could* drift, but in many cases larvae *must*.

2. By random locomotory movements

Locomotory movements that are random in direction can lead to a uniform distribution or to an aggregation. In a uniform environment fish released from a point will spread out equally in all directions. The fish could be considered as spreading out by diffusion and the spread from the initial point of release would be called a dispersal. This will ultimately lead to a uniform distribution. It is unusual to use the term diffusion to describe the movement of animals but is justified on occasions as it suggests that the changes in distribution which follow from random locomotory movements can be described in mathematical terms according to the laws of molecular diffusion. On the other hand, random movements could lead to an aggregation if there were differences in the environmental field, such as light or temperature, which affected their speed or the frequency of turning. In studies on animal behaviour, locomotory movements which are random in direction are called kineses (Fraenkel and Gunn, 1940).

3. By orientated locomotory movements

Orientated locomotory movements fall into one or other of two groups (Fraenkel and Gunn, 1940). The first group includes the taxes which are directed reactions: the animal turns either towards or away from the source of stimulation. The second group includes the so-called transverse orientations. Here the animal is orientated at some angle to an imaginary line running between it and the source of stimulation. It is sometimes helpful to separate the orientating or pure taxis component of the response from the swimming movements which actually move the fish in the direction in which it is heading, as the speed of swimming may vary with the intensity of stimulation. Thus the complete response could have steering and kinetic components which can be separated by experiment.

Heape (1931, p. 18) defined the home as 'the place selected for the production and rearing of the young, that is to say, the nursery of the species'. The concept of homing has been extended by Gerking (1959), who has adopted a definition of homing as 'the return to a place formerly occupied instead of going to other equally probable places'. This is a very useful definition and will be followed in this book. So far as homing to a spawning area is concerned, the precision with which a fish returns might be expected to vary according to its reproductive habits. Thus the reproductive home of a salmon, which lays its eggs in a specially constructed bed of gravel (a redd), has a specific geographical location and may be contrasted with that of the cod which lays its eggs in midwater over what may be a wide geographical area, covering 10, 100, or perhaps even a 1,000 square sea miles.

Griffin (1952, 1953) recognized three levels of homing, or navigational ability, in birds. In Type I the bird relies on 'visual landmarks, or in their absence, the search for familiar territory by means of random flights or by a more or less systematic exploration'. Type II navigation 'is the ability to fly in a particular direction, even in unfamiliar territory', and Type III 'is the ability of a bird to head for the home locality even when released in unknown territory'. Attempts have been made to apply Griffin's scheme to fish. Parker and Hasler (1959, p. 15) modified his classification as follows:

'Type I: The ability of an animal to find home by relying on local landmarks within familiar territory and the use of exploration in unfamiliar areas.'
'Type II: The ability to maintain a constant compass direction in unfamiliar territory.'
'Type III: The ability to head for home from unknown territory by true navigation.'

Adler (1963) introduced further modification. Type I becomes undirected search; Type II orientated movement, and Type III 'navigation in the full sense of the word'.

There are difficulties in using Griffin's three-type system for fish. For example, there is no room in his scheme for a fish that drifts passively in a current or for a fish that swims upstream along a path bounded by two isotherms, or depth contours, and reaches home: there is no exploration (Type I), the direction may not be constant (Type II), and the course made good may not lead directly to the home (Type III). While Griffin's levels of homing, or navigational ability, are useful within the field for which they were created, namely bird migration, there does not seem to be any purpose in degrading their meaning, or increasing their number, to cover both fish and fowl. So they will not be used here.

In this book an attempt will be made to determine whether or not enough is known about fish migrations to account for the facts, and should the facts themselves prove inadequate, to suggest what further observations and experiments are required. The argument is mainly restricted to salmon, eel, cod, plaice, and herring, as these are the fish about whose migrations most is known. As an introduction to a detailed examination of their life histories something will be said, in general terms, of the biology of fish migrations, followed by an outline of the different methods that are used in their study.

Chapter 2

Biological Aspects of Migration

INTRODUCTION

In general terms the pattern of fish migration is thought to conform to that shown in Fig. 1. The young stages leave the spawning grounds at A for the nursery grounds at B; from the nursery grounds the juveniles recruit to the adult stock on their feeding grounds at C; and the mature and ripening fish move from the feeding grounds back to the spawning grounds at A. Then as spents, they return to the feeding grounds. The migration pattern is believed to be related to that of the currents: the young stages drift with the current to the nursery ground; the spawning migration from B to C is against the current, and the spents return to the feeding ground with the current.

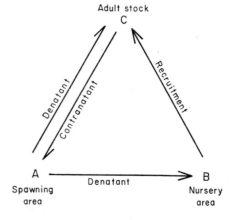

Fig. 1. Fish migrations can usually be reduced to a simple triangular pattern, with the spawning area, nursery area, and adult stock at the three corners.

Nikolsky (1963) recognized three main movements in the migratory cycle of fishes, the spawning, feeding, and wintering migrations. These are the same three movements that Heape mentions and they may be linked together in a variety of schematic diagrams. The one shown in Fig. 2 separates the cycles of the mature and immature fish. But not all the movements occur in every life cycle; the overwintering migration may be omitted, spawning and feeding grounds may coincide. The spawning season may be before or after the winter, and the immature fish may recruit to the adult stock through the feeding or wintering stage of the cycle. Nikolsky discusses the biological signi-ficance of migratory movements and argues that migration is an adaptation towards abundance; there may not be enough food on the spawning or nursery grounds to maintain both the immature and mature members of a large population. So it could be an advantage to have separate spawning, nursery, and feeding areas. If migration is an adaptation towards abundance, it would explain why the important commercial species are migratory: they are of commercial interest because they are abundant, and abundant because they are migratory. Furthermore, there would appear to be something to be gained by a species whose adults returned to spawn in an area where the environmental conditions were similar to those under which they themselves survived when young. Thompson (1959) argues the case well for salmon. Consider, for example, a fish which spawns along the length of a coastline, or in half-a-dozen tributaries of one river system. At any

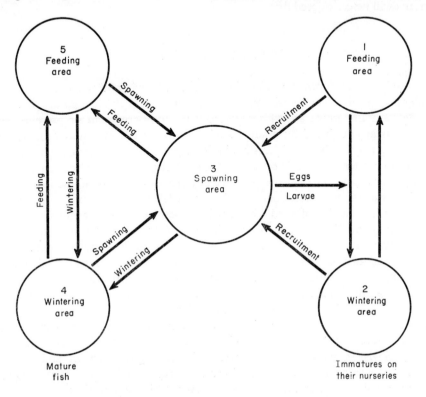

Fig. 2. The pattern of migratory movements can vary and this diagram shows the range of sequential variation. The cycles of the mature and immature fish are separated. Recruitment is shown as taking place only from the immatures' feeding or wintering areas to the spawning areas. Recruitment could also take place from either of the two nursery areas to the adult feeding or wintering areas: these arrows have been omitted to avoid confusion.

one part of the coast, or in any one of the tributaries, the environmental conditions might be particularly favourable for the survival of the eggs and larvae. A return to the parent spawning ground, or area, provides a means by which these favourable conditions may be exploited. Thus a good egg and larvae survival would lead to a greater number of spawners on a particular ground, or in a particular stream, and vice versa. As Lindsey, Northcote and Hartman (1959, p. 717) point out, a predominant return to the parent ground has the biological advantage of balancing the number of spawners against the reproductive capacity of the spawning area. On the other hand, the advantage might lie not so much in the choice of a spawning area in its own right, but for its position in relation to a favourable nursery area to which the young are carried passively by the prevailing current. In this case the spawning migrations made by the mature fish must then be related, in some way, to the drift of their young.

Bowman (1933, p. 223) puts the point this way: 'If species with pelagic eggs and larvae are to maintain their positions within a region it is obvious that the older fish must undertake at sometime active and compensatory movements in the direction opposite to that in which the pelagic stages are carried passively from the spawning grounds by the prevailing currents.' There are two factors to consider: the water currents, and the extent to which the eggs and larvae drift with them. Water currents will be considered first.

WATER CURRENTS

There are several different types of currents in the oceans. Leaving for the moment tidal currents, the remainder may be divided into drift and gradient currents. Drift currents are produced by the wind and the most important are those produced by the permanent or predominant winds. Gradient currents are produced by gradients of pressure on the surrounding masses of water. Pressure gradients may be due to differences in density, and thus dependent on the salinity and temperature of the water masses. In other cases the effect of wind may be such as to remove or bank up water near a coastline, and the pressure differences will then be due to a real difference in water level. In general, the surface currents down to a depth of 60 to 70 m are mostly dependent on the direct or indirect action of wind, density differences having a very much smaller effect. In the deeper water of the high seas, the circulation is mainly due to density differences and the velocities of the water currents are very much less than those of the surface waters.

The surface circulation in the main ocean basins is wind-driven. Munk (1955) has given a clear and simple account of the relation between wind and water movement. In the northern hemisphere the north-east trades drive the equatorial currents to the west, while in more northern latitudes the prevailing westerlies drive the water to the east. In polar latitudes prevailing easterlies again drive the water west. If these wind belts are considered as acting on a simple rectangular ocean basin, the circulation of the water resolves into several closed rings or gyrals. Close to the equator there is a narrow anti-clockwise gyral between the west-going equatorial current and the east-going equatorial counter-current; there is a broad clockwise gyral in the subtropical region between the west-going equatorial current and the east-going water at higher latitudes; and there is an anti-clockwise gyral between the east-going water and that driven to the west by the polar winds.

Reference to the surface circulation charts of the northern Pacific and Atlantic Oceans in Figs. 3 and 4 will show that this pattern can be recognized in both basins.

The west-going North Equatorial Currents turn towards the pole at the western boundaries of the oceans and carry relatively warm and saline waters into temperate latitudes. Between 30° and 40°N these currents leave the continental shores and move north-east as the Kuroshio (in the Pacific) and the Gulf Stream (in the Atlantic). South-going cold currents (Oyashio in the Pacific, Labrador in the Atlantic) mix with the Kuroshio and the Gulf Stream, which have become cool and temperate by the time they approach the eastern boundaries of the ocean. Here the two currents divide into north-going and south-going branches; in the Pacific to form the Alaska and California Current, and in the Atlantic to form the North Atlantic and Canary Current. In both oceans the south-going branch completes the great clockwise subtropical gyral, which in the Pacific is made up of the Kuroshio, Kuroshio Extension, West Wind Drift or North Pacific Current, California Current, California Extension and so back to the Pacific North Equatorial Current. The Atlantic counterparts are the Florida Current, Gulf Stream, Canary Current, and back to the Atlantic North Equatorial Current. The north-going branches carry on to form the eastern limbs of several anti-clockwise gyrals; the Alaskan, Bering Sea, and Western gyrals in the Pacific; and those in the Irminger, Iceland, Norwegian, Greenland, and Barents Seas in the Atlantic.

The surface velocities of these currents vary with wind strength and direction and fall off with depth. Velocities range from 350 cm/sec (7 knots, 168 naut. mile/day) in parts of the Gulf Stream

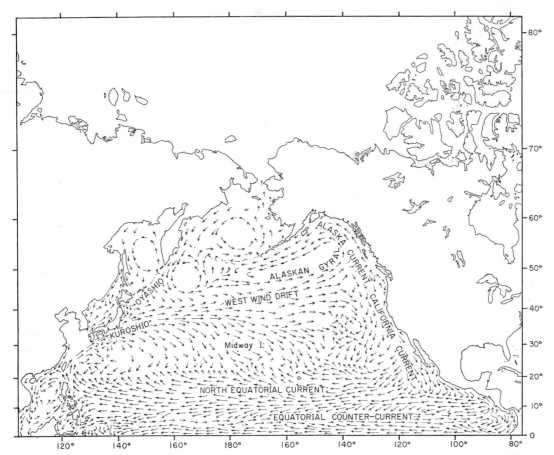

Fig. 3. The surface water currents in the North Pacific Ocean after Defant (1961) and Neave (1964). (Outline based on Admiralty Chart.)

down to 10 to 20 cm/sec (0·2 to 0·4 knots, 5 to 10 naut. mile/day) or less in the Irminger. Velocities of 6 to 18 cm/sec (0·1 to 0·4 knots, 3 to 9 naut. mile/day) have been reported for the Alaskan gyral in the north-east Pacific (Dodimead and Hollister, 1958). More detailed accounts of the surface currents and gyrals will be given when dealing with migrations in particular areas.

Below the surface currents, which may persist down to 400 m or more, there are deeper currents. These are slower than those at the surface and may move, as counter-currents, in the opposite direction. Such counter-currents are present below the Baltic outflow; below the North Atlantic

Current along the line of the Norwegian shelf; below the axis of the Florida Current on the western boundary of the Atlantic; and, as the equatorial undercurrents, below the South Equatorial currents in the Pacific and Atlantic Oceans. It is probable that there are other deep countercurrents waiting to be discovered, and likely areas are the eastern and western boundaries of the ocean basins.

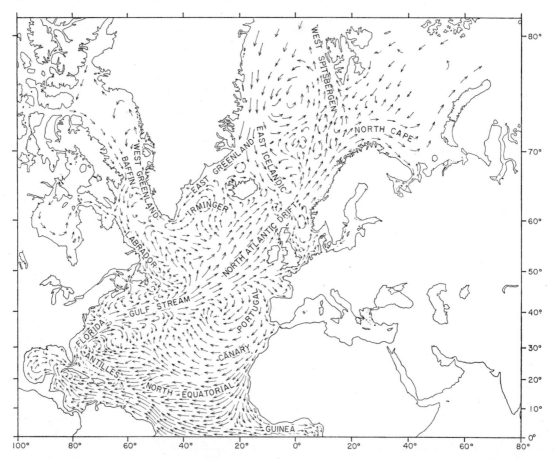

Fig. 4. The surface water currents in the North Atlantic Ocean after Alekseev and Istoshin (1959); Defant (1961); Hackey, Herman, and Bailey (1954); Lee (1963) and Stefánsson (1962). (Outline based on an Admiralty Chart.)

It is important to say something about tidal currents as opposed to oceanic currents. Water movement due to tidal action is far more marked in waters on the continental shelves than in the open sea. Tidal currents usually have no residual or overall movement, although exceptions may occur near irregular coastlines, or in certain straits such as Hecate Strait, British Columbia (Mackay, 1954). At the end of a tidal cycle the water is back where it started and if there is any residual movement in one direction or another it is due to some other factor, such as the effect of wind or an ocean current being superimposed upon an otherwise equal tidal flow. For example, in the Straits of Dover, the tidal movement to the north-east during the flood is about 12 miles, and the movement to the west is the same on the ebb. Nevertheless, there is a flow of water through the Straits of Dover to the north-east at a rate of about 2 to 3 miles every 24 hours. This residual flow is not due to the tide. It is due to Atlantic water moving up the Channel, and under conditions of strong and persistent north-easterly winds this residual flow through the Straits may be checked or even reversed.

The distinction between residual oceanic currents and tidal flow is important when considering the passive transport of fish and their reactions to water currents. Long-term passive transport, that is drift migration in the sense used in the previous chapter, will usually depend on oceanic or non-tidal currents both on the high seas and in coastal waters. But when a reaction to a water current is involved, it will, in coastal waters at least, be the tidal current that is of importance. Thus tidal currents in the southern North Sea are of the order of 1 to 2 knots (50 to 100 cm/sec), whereas the residual current is only 2 to 3 miles a day (4 to 6 cm/sec) which will be completely masked by the very much faster tide. If the fish is reacting to a water current, it will, in these waters, be responding to a tidal current that changes direction every 6 hours, but on the high seas to a more or less persistent, and generally much slower, oceanic current.

A word may be said here about the measurement of water current direction and speed. For the oceanic currents these measurements can be obtained indirectly from dynamic computations derived from temperature and salinity observations, checked, when possible, by the use of current-measuring devices lowered from an anchored ship; by tracking the movements of a free midwater acoustic target or parachute drogues; or by the use of towed electrodes. Information on the movement of the surface waters can be obtained from estimates of the drift of ships. Thus the Meteorological Office have for many years collected reports from merchant ships and this has led to the production of detailed charts of the North Atlantic current system. These charts give a fairly accurate, if generalized, picture of the main features of the circulation of the surface waters of the North Atlantic. In the shallower waters of the continental shelf a variety of current-measuring devices are available for use from an anchored ship, and there are others which can be left in the sea for days or weeks at a time unattended. Other methods include the use of surface or bottom drift bottles, a recent development being the Woodhead Sea Bed Drifter, and drift envelopes, dyes, radioactive tracers and biological indicators by which one body of water can be recognized from another. Eggvin (1940, p. 107) even used data relating to the drift of a corpse along the Norwegian coast to check on other measurements.

THE DRIFT OF EGGS AND LARVAE

Free-floating pelagic eggs are carried passively in the body of water in which they are spawned. The same fate awaits the larvae, and those from demersal eggs, when they hatch out: they too will drift with the current until they are able to detect its direction and orientate themselves to head up- or down-stream. If the larvae can swim well enough they might stem the current, or even make headway against it. When the larvae are near the bottom they may be able to take cover so as to avoid being swept away.

Freshwater eggs and larvae

As a general rule most freshwater fish produce a relatively small number of large yolky eggs which sink to the bottom. These demersal eggs are not carried away by the water currents. They may be laid under several centimetres of gravel in specially constructed beds or redds (salmon and trout), under stones (roach), or adhere in long sticky strings to stones or weeds (perch). The early larvae hide under gravel and stay close to the bottom or among weeds until they are strong enough to withstand the current.

There are, however, some examples of freshwater pelagic eggs. The eggs of the Anabantidae are often lighter than water. Many, but not all, of these fish are bubble-nest builders, such as *Betta splendens*, the Siamese fighting fish, or *Macropodus*, the Paradise fish (Forselius, 1957). The eggs float because they have a large oil globule which the larvae come to use as a buoyancy mechanism until the swim-bladder is fully developed (Peters, 1947). The larvae of some species, such as *Macropodus cerpanus*, have cement glands on the top of the head which serve as anchors (S. Jones, 1940).

An oil globule in the eggs of the goldeye, *Hiodon alosoides*, which is of some commercial importance in Canadian Lakes, is probably a flotation mechanism. Battle and Sprales (1960) have recently shown that the eggs of this fish are semi-buoyant. Their paper has a useful review of some of the literature on pelagic freshwater eggs. The eggs of the freshwater gadoid *Lota*, the burbot, are also more or less pelagic (Fabricius, 1954) and so are those of the Chinese grass carp, *Ctenopharyngodon idellus*. The grass carp is of great commercial importance in fish farming and has an extraordinary life history (Lin, 1935; Gidumal, 1958). It breeds in the West River of China. The eggs are small when laid, but swell rapidly due to the absorption of water. This increase in volume probably makes the eggs nearly buoyant and parallels the flotation mechanism in marine pelagic eggs. The larvae hatch out 30 to 40 hours after fertilization, by which time they may have been carried a 100 miles or more downstream and will drift even further unless they get into still waters near the banks.

Several migratory species of Black Sea and Caspian Sea herring belonging to the genus *Caspialosa* have pelagic eggs (Nikolsky, 1963). These fish spawn in the main river systems of the area (Danube, Dniester, Bug, Dnieper, Don, Kuma, Volga, and Ural), moving upstream for distances up to 300 miles. The eggs, which do not have oil globules, develop as they are carried downstream.

In most streams and lakes the distance covered by the mature fish to reach the spawning area may be no more than a few thousand or only a few hundred metres. It is when the young fish are carried, or move, great distances from the freshwater into the sea that the return migration becomes outstanding. The Pacific salmon (Hoar, 1959, gives an excellent account) provide the best example of a series showing the stages from a typical freshwater life history to that of an obligatory ocean dweller. Sockeye salmon may live their whole life in freshwater, when they are known as kokanee. More typically sockeye and coho salmon, like the Atlantic *Salmo salar*, live a year or more in freshwater before undergoing the morphological and physiological change from parr to smolt and taking to the sea. On the other hand chum and pink salmon show no smolt transformation and are carried or migrate out to sea soon after emerging from the gravel. In the sea-going salmon there must be a return of mature adults to freshwater to spawn. In these examples the direction of the adult migration is upstream and against the current. Lindsey *et al.* (1959) have described an exception to this general rule shown by the rainbow trout (*S. gairdneri*) in Loon Lake, British Columbia. The fish lay their eggs in the inlet and outlet streams of the Lake, the former involving a movement against and the latter a movement with the stream to reach the spawning grounds.

Marine eggs and larvae

Many marine species have pelagic eggs. The herring, which has demersal eggs, is a notable exception among commercial species in the Atlantic Ocean, and this is often interpreted as showing the freshwater affinities of the Clupeidae. In the Pacific Ocean, however, demersal eggs are quite common among species whose Atlantic counterparts have pelagic eggs. Rass (1959) argues, convincingly, that the habit of laying demersal eggs among Pacific species is an adaptation to the more rigorous environmental conditions in that ocean as compared with the Atlantic.

The buoyancy demands of the egg are far less in the sea than in freshwater and are met, not by the provision of fat droplets such as occurs in the Anabantidae, but by the adsorption of fluid produced by the follicular cells in the ovary immediately before spawning. The egg increases in volume as the fluid is taken up and its bigger displacement allows it to float in sea-water. Shelbourne (1956) regards the buoyancy mechanism of the marine pelagic eggs as a further development of the method by which all eggs are provided with a reserve of water. If this reserve is increased sufficiently the egg will float in the sea.

Pelagic marine eggs are generally small, with little yolk, and are usually produced in enormous quantities. They must hatch out in the surface 200 m if the larvae are to find the small planktonic plants and animals upon which they feed. This means that bathypelagic fish with pelagic eggs must somehow get them to the surface nursery area, either by coming up themselves to spawn or, as is suspected for the angler fish *Ceratias*, and most other midwater oceanic species, the eggs must be shed and fertilized in deep water and float freely up to the surface (Marshall, 1954). Some deep-water fish, such as the brotulids, are viviparous, and the young do not have to come right up to the surface. It is interesting to note that viviparity has also developed among some of the deep-water cottids in Lake Baikal.

When a pelagic egg hatches out the larvae can take advantage of the food supply in the productive surface waters. As the larvae feed and grow they are carried by the surface currents and this drift is something they may have to make up, or correct for, as mature adults.

A pelagic fish, with pelagic eggs and larvae living in a region covered by an oceanic eddy or gyral, and carried round passively within the system, is essentially a planktonic organism, however strong a swimmer it may be. In tropical waters it is not unreasonable to suppose that the environmental conditions could be favourable for the development and survival of eggs and larvae at all times of the year and throughout the whole region covered by the eddy. As production in the tropics is probably continuous and even a steady-state process (Cushing, 1959a), food should always be available in sufficient quantities for the larvae. Egg production could be continuous, as Qasim (1955) suggests. Eggs, larvae, young and adult fish would be found together, but possibly at different depths, and the species would have a continuous distribution throughout the region of the eddy (Fig. 5A). This sort of pattern may prove to be characteristic of tropical species, such as tunas. Under these conditions a pelagic fish may have no biological need for a definite spawning area, or season. Young fish that are carried or escape from the system would, so far as reproduction is concerned, be waste material. But difficulties arise if the eddy system extends into temperate or arctic waters, when there would be environmental differences within the region covered by the gyral. The water may change its character as regards temperature and salinity, so that while the older fish may be able to live anywhere within the system, the young stages could not do so and spawning would only be successful within a limited area. In the temperate and arctic waters the production cycle differs from that found in the tropics and food is not available in more or less equal quantities throughout the year (Cushing, 1959a). If the young are going to survive, the adult fish must not only spawn at the right place, but also at the right time. As shown in Fig. 5B egg production must be limited to a particular season and there must be an annual cycle of activity in the gonads (Qasim, 1955). The distribution of the species becomes discontinuous and it can only survive as a passive, planktonic organism if the processes of growth and maturation are geared to the circulation time of the eddy so that sufficient numbers of mature and ripe adults are brought into the spawning area at the right time. But the eddy may be opened up, or some environmental barrier, such as water temperature, may prevent the mature individuals going round the system. The older fish may take to the bottom outside the restricted area in which they spawn. In these conditions the older fish must, as Bowman says, make some compensatory movement in the direction opposite to that in which the eggs and larvae are carried (Fig. 5C and D).

Fulton (1897, p. 374) appears to have been the first to have recognized the need for the return movement of the mature fish. He showed, by a series of drift bottle experiments, that some of the plaice eggs spawned in the Moray Firth and Firth of Forth area, on the east coast of Scotland,

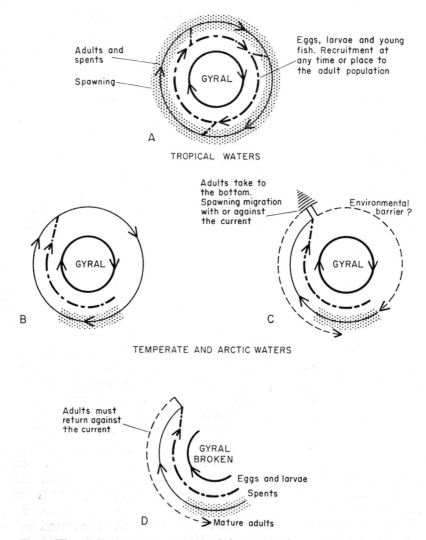

Fig. 5. The relation between oceanic circulation, production cycles and migration.

would be carried southwards along the coast, and suggested a return movement of mature plaice to the north against the prevailing residual current to make up for this. The northward spawning migration of the mature plaice was later demonstrated by tagging experiments carried out between 1910 and 1913 (Fulton, 1919).

DENATANT AND CONTRANATANT MOVEMENTS

Meek (1915*a*, p. 231; 1915*b*, p. 14) introduced these terms to describe the movements of fish in relation to the water current. Denatant means swimming, or drifting, or migrating with the current, contranatant means swimming or migrating against the current. To use the terms in connexion with the migration pattern given in Fig. 1, one would speak of the denatant migration of the pelagic eggs and the contranatant migration of the adults towards the spawning area. Now it is important to be clear as to what water current the adults are supposed to migrate against. The whole biological significance of the migration of the ripening fish is that it is in the opposite direction to the current which carries the eggs and larvae away from the spawning area. But this does not mean that the adults have to swim against a current, that is upstream, to reach the spawning area. In the sea, or even in fjords and lakes, there is always the possibility that the adults, living in deeper water than the younger stages, are moving with the stream in a counter-current lying below that in which the eggs and larvae are carried in the opposite direction. I think that such a migration should be considered as contranatant even if the adults are swimming, or even drifting passively, with a counter-current towards the spawning area. The whole point of Meek's terminology is that it recognizes the biological relationship between the migration of the eggs and larvae on the one hand and that of the adults on the other. A contranatant migration should always be thought of in this descriptive sense.

However, the term contranatant is sometimes used in an almost explanatory sense to convey the suggestion that water currents provide the directional clues used by a fish on migration. Bidder (1906, p. xxxv) drew attention to the possibility that fish might move against the currents and the matter has been discussed by Borley (1916, p. 64), Bowman (1933), E. S. Russell (1937), Tait (1952) and Hasler (1956). In reviewing the results of his tagging experiments on lemon soles, Bowman (1935, p. 23) definitely suggests a causal relationship between the direction of the prevailing bottom currents and the migration of fish. Recently, Beverton and Holt (1957, p. 156), have linked the words contranatant and orientation together. It is perhaps unfortunate that a word which well expresses the biological significance of a migration should now be used in discussing the means by which the migration is brought about. The description of a phenomenon can so easily become accepted as its explanation and there may be confusion if a migration which is obviously contranatant in the biological sense turns out to depend on some other clue or stimulus from the point of view of behaviour. Here, the term 'contranatant' will be used only in a descriptive sense to stress the biological significance of the migration, without any suggestion of an explanation as to how the movement is brought about.

THE DETECTION OF WATER CURRENTS BY FISH

The possibility of a causal relationship between water currents and the migration of fish raises the question of how fish might detect and react to them. While the problem is discussed more fully in later chapters, the following points may be made here. A fish can detect a water current if it is in sight of or in contact with a fixed external reference point, such as the bottom, when it will see or feel the background move as it is displaced by the stream. A fish in midwater, and without an external reference point, cannot detect its displacement by the stream unless there is an acceleration involved or unless the flow of water sets up some form of turbulence to which it might react. While it is physically possible to detect a water current from the electromotive force generated by the stream as it moves across the vertical component of the earth's magnetic field, there is, at the present, no evidence to show that fish can do this. Fish have never been shown to react to water flowing at a constant linear velocity unless they are close to or are in sight of the bottom, when they often head into and swim against the stream. The sensory mechanisms and thresholds for the various rheotropic responses will be considered later (p. 193).

THE SPEED AT WHICH FISH CAN SWIM

The speed at which fish can swim is of interest in connexion with their migrations and possible reactions to water currents. Much of the available information is summarized and discussed by Gray (1953), Bainbridge (1958, 1960), and Blaxter and Dickson (1959). There are two speeds to consider, the maximum speed and the maximum sustained or cruising speed. It appears that the maximum speed that a fish can reach is more or less equal to 10 times its own length per second, but this speed can only be kept up for about a minute. The maximum sustained speed is considerably less, about 3 times its own length per second, and it seems reasonable to use this, the cruising speed, when calculating distances that fish might be able to cover over a number of days or weeks. The '3 times' rule can be safely applied to fish from 10 to 100 cm in length for species such as salmon, cod and herring. Thus an 80 cm cod could cruise comfortably at 240 cm/sec (4·8 knots) and a 25 cm herring at 75 cm/sec (1·5 knots). Little, however, is known about the swimming powers of flatfish, or of eels. Blaxter and Dickson (1959) give some figures for the maximum speeds for the plaice but no accurate data are available for the cruising speed of this species. Fulton (1903, p. 42) mentions plaice swimming leisurely round a large tidal tank at a rate of about 65 cm/sec (1·30 knots) but does not give the size of the fish. These fish were probably 20 to 30 cm long, giving a cruising speed of 2 to 3 times their length per second.

Very little is known about the swimming powers of fish larvae. Bishai (1960) found that 0·7 cm herring larvae could maintain their positions for over 45 min against a water current of about 1 cm/sec. At higher speeds the larvae drift back with current, although they still swim against it. Ryland (1963) found that the cruising speed of plaice larvae was about 3L/sec.

TERMS USED TO DESCRIBE FISH MIGRATIONS

Myers (1949) has proposed some revisions and additions to some of the terms used to describe fish migrations and his suggestions will be adopted here. Myers' terms and definitions are as follows:

1. Diadromous

'Truly migratory fishes which migrate between the sea and freshwater.'

(*a*) *Anadromous*. 'Diadromous fishes which spend most of their lives in the sea and migrate to freshwater to breed' (salmon, shad, sea-lamprey).

(*b*) *Catadromous*. 'Diadromous fishes which spend most of their lives in freshwater and migrate to the sea to breed' (freshwater eels).[1]

(*c*) *Amphidromous*. 'Diadromous fishes where migration from freshwater to the sea, or vice-versa, is not for the purpose of breeding, but occurs regularly at some other definite stage of the life-cycle.'

Myers suggests that the migrations of some gobies might fall into this category.

The use of amphidromous in this sense should not be confused with the terms amphidromic point and amphidromic system, which are used by oceanographers in the description of tidal phenomena.

2. Potamodromous

'Truly migratory fishes whose migrations occur wholly within freshwater.'

3. Oceanodromous

'Truly migratory fishes which live and migrate wholly in the sea.'

Spawning area, ground, and bed are terms whose meaning should be made clear. The spawning bed is, in the case of a fish with demersal eggs, the actual site where the eggs are laid. Numerous beds may be located within a specific spawning ground, and more than one spawning ground within a spawning area. Thus the spawning area for a salmon may be the upper reaches of a particular river system, the spawning ground delimited to a specific stretch of a stream within which it has its spawning bed, called, for the salmon, a redd. Another example is provided by the winter spawning herring of the southern North Sea. Their spawning area is the Southern Bight, within which there are several clearly defined grounds, for instance, near the Gabbard, North Hinder, or Sandettié Banks. On these grounds the demersal eggs may be laid on one or more beds. Using the terms this way it is clear that fish with pelagic eggs do not have spawning beds; the eggs are released at some position, the spawning ground, within the spawning area. The Arcto-Norwegian cod may be taken as an example: the spawning area for this stock is along the Norwegian coastline from the Murman coast to Romsdal. Within this spawning area there are spawning grounds at Motovski Gulf, Lofoten, Romsdal, and other places along the coast.

[1] The freshwater salmonid *Galaxias attenuatus* is sometimes described as spawning in the sea. But it has been shown that this fish is an estuarine spawner (Hefford, 1931).

Chapter 3

Methods of Studying Fish Migrations

INTRODUCTION

Studies of fish migrations are of two kinds: those that set out to describe the migrations and those that attempt to explain them. Descriptive work deals with the overall pattern of migration as determined by marking and tagging experiments, echo surveys, the use of fishery statistics and a knowledge of the biology of the species (spawning season, growth, feeding habits, and so on). When finer detail is required the problem is often that of the recognition of races, or reproductively isolated groups of one species, and meristic, morphometric, or biochemical methods may be used to identify samples or individuals of different racial origin. Explanatory work sets out to analyse the causal mechanisms behind the patterns. Much of this work falls within the field of behaviour. In the laboratory, experiments and observations must be made to determine the responses of fish to changes in the environmental conditions and to see how these responses vary according to the physiological state of the fish. At sea the movements of fish can be determined by direct observation from land or ship, from aircraft, or underwater by divers, or with the use of cameras or television. The direction of movement can sometimes be inferred from the distribution of the catch in the net. Shoals, or individuals, can be followed with acoustic echo-ranging techniques, or by special tagging experiments. Some methods, for example acoustic techniques and tagging, can be used in both descriptive and analytical work. But all the methods have their limitations which are clear when they are examined in detail: the advantages and disadvantages of each can then be seen.

MARKING AND TAGGING EXPERIMENTS

Marking and tagging of fish started on a large scale between 1890 and 1900, at about the same time that tagging was first tried scientifically on wild birds, and one of the best ways of following the migrations of fish is from changes in the distribution of the recoveries of marked or tagged individuals. Fish are usually marked by the removal of one or more fins in such a manner and combination that the mutilation is unlikely to be confused with those naturally occurring among the population. Stuart (1958) has reported on some aspects of this problem.

A very wide variety of devices have been used for tagging fish. Nearly seventy tags are figured in the Journal du Conseil's lists (Anon, 1932, 1953), of which a third edition (Anon, 1966) has now been published. Experiments have also been made on dyeing (Kasahara, 1957) or tattooing (Hickling, 1945) fish. These were not very successful as the marks were not recognizable after more than a few weeks. Recently trials have been made with subdermal injections of coloured liquid latex (Chapman, 1957; Riley, 1966) and with metal or plastic subcutaneous tags (Le Cren, 1954; Moore and Mortimer, 1954; Butler, 1957), and these methods may prove useful for special experiments. Suggestions have also been made that fish might be labelled with radioisotopes (Pendleton, 1956; Seymour, 1958).

One new development that seems very promising is the use of natural living tags, parasites, to distinguish and sort out different stocks. The method is being tried for salmon in the Pacific. A great deal of effort has been put into this work and it seems that it may have valuable results (International North Pacific Fisheries Commission, 1961). The ideal parasitic tag is one which the salmon acquires early on in its freshwater life and which is confined to fish brought up in a particular river system. The distribution of immature or mature salmon on the high seas bearing the parasite could then be used to determine the spread of fish of a known origin and the percentage infection used to estimate mixing with other stocks. Promising results have been obtained with Bristol Bay (Alaska) and Asian sockeye, some of the former being infected with the cestode *Triaenophorus crassus* and a proportion of the latter with the nematode *Dacnitis truttae*.

The ideal mark or tag should stay in place indefinitely, be readily spotted or recoverable when the fish is caught, allow an individual fish to be identified if this is required, and should not harm or injure a fish or make it more liable to capture by predators or fishing gear. Numerous marking and tagging experiments have been made to try to find the methods best suited for particular purposes. Graham (1929a) has reviewed much of this early work. Rounsefell and Kask (1945), who give an extensive bibliography, have discussed marking and tagging techniques in some detail, while Ricker (1956) has given a shorter account as a contribution to the Ecological Society of America's 1956 symposium on 'Uses on marking animals in ecological studies'.

During the period from 1927 to 1951, member countries of the International Council for the Exploration of the Sea marked and tagged over 500,000 fish, of which 200,000 were plaice (Fridriksson, 1952). In recent years the rate of marking and tagging has increased, herring coming in for a good deal of attention, and now the total for the ICES countries alone is probably more than 750,000. Many of these experiments have been made to obtain data for the study of population dynamics. Beverton and Holt (1957, p. 184) give an authoritative account of the use of tagging in this sort of work. In May 1961 a 'North Atlantic Fish Marking Symposium' was held at Woods Hole, Mass., and the proceedings have been published by the International Commission for the Northwest Atlantic Fisheries (ICNAF, 1963). The 62 contributions presented in this volume describe many of the recent advances in marking and tagging techniques. What follows here about marking and tagging is more or less directly related to their application in the study of fish migrations.

Marks and Tags

Some fish are too small to be fitted with a tag; examples are salmon and trout fingerlings. In such cases the fish are marked by fin clipping, and some of the combinations that have been used are shown in Fig. 6. It is not easy to spot an adult salmon whose fins were clipped when it was young, and the method is only satisfactory if the total number of fish landed is relatively small, and they are handled individually, either when caught or in a cannery. Clipping is of no use for immature herring which are landed in astronomical numbers. In 1957, for example, the number of immature herring taken from the Bløden nursery ground south-east of the Dogger Bank was of the order of 14 hundred million (Cushing, 1959b). These young fish are taken in the Danish 'industrial' trawl fishery and are processed in factories for meal and oil where there is little or no chance of a marked individual being spotted. To tag these fish small bits of metal are shot into the body cavity with a gun, the fish being specially caught by a purse seine for this purpose (Fridriksson and Aasen, 1952; Aasen *et al.*, 1961). The tags are subsequently recovered by magnetic separators at some stage during the processing.

Two external tags that have been widely used are the Petersen button or disc and the Lea hydrostatic tag. The Petersen disc comprises a pair of ebonite buttons joined, like a pair of cuff links, by a silver or nickel wire, which is threaded through some part of the body of the fish. This tag is often used on plaice. The Lea tag is a small plastic cylinder containing a message printed on fine paper. The size of the tag is such that it is of neutral buoyancy in sea-water. It can be attached to the fish by a steel bridle, but nylon braid or monofilament is more generally used. Difficulties over the supply of Lea tags have led to the development of a plastic flag tag at the Lowestoft Laboratory. Fritz (1959) figures and describes this tag. This is attached to the back of the fish by a short length of braided nylon and is coming into general use for round fish such as whiting, haddock and cod.

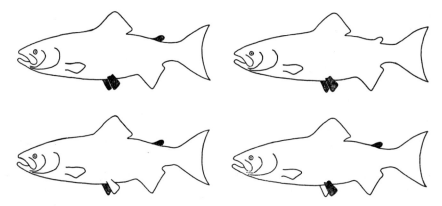

Fig. 6. Combinations of fin clippings used to mark salmon smolts at Cultus Lake, Fraser River, British Columbia. (After Foerster, 1937.)

The mortality of tagged fish and the loss of tags

In a tagging experiment, it is important to keep the mortality due to tagging as low as possible, and to be certain that tags stay on over the period during which the fish are liable to be recaptured. Neither tagging mortality nor tag loss can be completely avoided. But this is not important as long as they are kept low and it is known how great they are.

MORTALITY OF TAGGED FISH

The heaviest mortality is almost certainly due to the damage done to the fish when they are caught. Most fish have a gas-filled swim-bladder, which functions as a hydrostatic organ, making the density of the fish more or less equal to that of the water in which it is living. When the fish are brought up to the surface from deep water the reduction in hydrostatic pressure, 1 atmosphere for every 10 m of water, leads to an expansion of the swim-bladder gas. In some fish the swim-bladder is open and has a duct opening into the anterior part of the gut. Excess gas can be released through this duct which can be thought of as a sort of escape valve. Herring, salmon, and eels have open swim-bladders of this type. In other fish, such as cod, haddock, and hake, the swim-bladder is completely closed and the excess gas cannot get away unless it is reabsorbed by the blood, which is a very slow process. Cod taken from 40 to 80 m often come up completely bloated, and float help-lessly on the water. They are in a very poor condition for tagging (Graham, 1924). Surprisingly, cod caught in deeper water, down to 200 m or so, are in much better condition. This is because the pressure of the expanded gas ruptures the swim-bladder wall. The gas passes into the body cavity, tearing the body wall near the anus, and escapes to the outside (Trout, 1957, p. 28). The wound, unless it is very big, does not seem to harm the cod, but it may to some extent contribute to the mortality of those that are tagged. Cod taken from water much deeper than 200 m are usually very badly blown and the swim-bladder gas does a lot of damage before it escapes. There are severe internal haemorrhages, the stomach may be forced out through the mouth, the rectum everted. Hickling (1927) experienced the same trouble in his attempts to tag hake taken from deep water. Fish taken from deep water are usually quite useless for tagging. Plaice, like other flatfish, do not have a swim-bladder, and this sort of problem does not arise when tagging them.

Fish are often badly damaged in the trawl, seine, or drift-net itself, and this results in wounds, abrasions and, most serious of all, loss of scales. Herring are particularly difficult to tag for this reason. Finally when a good catch is made, the sheer weight on the fish in the cod end when the net comes out of the water does considerable damage, as does the knock the fish get when the cod end is opened and they fall out on deck. Trawling is a poor way of catching fish for tagging but more often than not it is the only way possible.

In spite of the importance that the condition of the fish must have on the returns from a tagging experiment, it is only recently that any effort has been made to look into the matter properly. Parker and Kirkness (1956) introduced graded tagging for chinook salmon in Alaskan waters, while similar work was carried out by Beverton, Gulland, and Margetts (1959) on whiting caught by Danish seine in the north-western part of the Irish Sea during November and December 1957. The main purpose of the whiting experiments was to assess the effect of increases in mesh size on the fishery. The fish were tagged with Lowestoft plastic flag tags and before release were graded according to the damage observed to their scales and for their general condition. The scale grading was as follows:

Only a few scratches	good
Those with less than 5 cm² of scales removed	moderate
The rest	poor

In the tagging tanks some fish floated belly up with distended swim-bladders and these floaters were classified as *active floaters* if they managed to swim down below the surface after being dis-turbed. Those fish that made only feeble and ineffective attempts to swim down were graded as *sluggish floaters*. Some fish swam comfortably around the bottom of the tanks. The swim-bladders of these fish had presumably ruptured and the excess gas escaped. These fish were classified as *sinkers*. An analysis of the returns up to 1 July 1958 is given in Table 1. It will be seen that the general condition of the fish as assessed at sea appears to have little effect on the returns, whereas the condition of the scales is clearly important, fish with good scales having a percentage recapture (21%) three times that of the fish with poor scales (7%).

The differences in the returns from different groups of fish must be mainly due to mortality resulting from tagging. If it is assumed that all the best fish (good scales, sinkers), giving the highest

percentage recapture (28%) survived, then $100 - \left(\dfrac{5 \cdot 2}{28} \times 100 \right) = 81\%$ of the group giving the

Table 1. Results of the 1957 whiting tagging experiment to show the effect of condition on the numbers of fish returned. (Beverton, Gulland, and Margetts, 1959.)

Condition of scales	Numbers of fish	Sinkers	Floaters		Totals
			Active	Sluggish	
Good	tagged	241	376	905	1,522
	returned	68	84	163	315
	%	28·0	22·3	18·1	20·7
Moderate	tagged	556	345	1,867	2,768
	returned	71	54	297	422
	%	12·8	15·7	15·9	15·5
Poor	tagged	498	189	1,223	1,910
	returned	26	15	19	132
	%	5·2	7·9	7·4	6·9
Total	tagged	1,295	910	3,995	6,200
	returned	165	153	551	898
	%	12·7	16·8	13·8	14·1

lowest returns (poor scales, sinkers) must have died. It is clear then that capture and tagging procedure can cause a high mortality, and that this sort of loss could lead to a serious under-estimate of the extent of a migration unless the tagging experiment is carried out carefully.

THE LOSS OF TAGS

With improvements in tagging techniques, it is generally supposed that tags are not shed in any significant numbers. It is true that tags have been recovered many years after they have been put on fish. Here are some examples.

Fish	Tag	Years of liberty	Author
Plaice	Petersen	6½	
Whiting	Flag tag	1½	Lowestoft Laboratory
Cod	Lea	6½	
Dogfish	Petersen	9¾	Kauffman (1955)
Sole (*Microstomus pacificus*)	Petersen	6	Best (1957)
Herring	Lea	5	Höglund (1955, p. 29)

However, these may be exceptional cases, and what is really needed is a convincing double-tagging experiment to show the loss that does take place. In this type of experiment some fish are fitted with two tags close together and the recaptured fish are carefully examined to determine the loss of a tag from one or other position. The experiment is by no means as simple as it appears to be and only one has been carried out properly so far. This was in 1947 and is described by Beverton and Holt (1957, pp. 202–18), whose account should be referred to for all the details. They worked with plaice double-tagged with Petersen-type ebonite discs, and the estimate of the loss rate was such that 'a given number of marked fish would be reduced to about 75% of their initial number during the course of a year through detachment of marks, even if no mortality of any kind occurred'.

This estimate only applies to plaice tagged in this way, but it does show that the loss of tags could be an important factor if recaptures are required over a period of years.

The interpretation of results

Tåning (1937, p. 29) raised the interesting point that the recoveries of tagged fish taken from deep water might be misleading if the fish did not return to the depths from which they were taken. Water currents at the surface and the bottom usually move at different speeds and sometimes in opposite directions. If the fish stayed near the surface they might be carried miles away from the main body whose migrations the experiments were designed to follow. However, the fact that tagged fish are often recaptured on the bottom a day after release at the depths from which they were originally taken makes it most unlikely that this happens. Furthermore, Trout *et al.* (1952) have actually followed tagged fish down to the bottom with an echo-sounder within minutes of their release.

In interpreting the results of marking and tagging experiments it is important that the movements of the fish should not be confused with those of fishing boats. Furthermore, there may be a bias due to the fishing gear used, as fish of a particular size may be more vulnerable to one method of fishing. During the Lofoten season the Norwegians catch, by purse seine, many large cod for tagging. Very few of these large fish are returned by the British trawler fleet and one reason for this may be that the bigger fish avoid capture by the otter trawl (Trout, 1958).

Trout (1958) has also shown that the chance of tagged fish being spotted by a deckhand in the fish pounds of a trawler depends on the type of tag used and that good advertising and public relations all have their part to play in making an experiment a success. The rewards for the tags have to make it worth while to take the trouble of returning them. The Ministry of Agriculture, Fisheries and Food offers rewards for the return of the tags, with an extra few shillings for the value of the fish if that is handed in as well. The rewards are as follows.

Whiting	5/–
Cod	5/–
Plaice	5/–
Herring	10/–

In America and Norway lotteries have been introduced to increase the return of tags that have been recaptured (Rollefsen, 1959; Hylen, 1963).

But the work is not finished even when the tag is returned to the laboratory. The position and the date of capture must be carefully checked. This involves a lot of trouble and takes time. My colleague Mr. George Bolster once had a herring tag returned by a Welshpool (Montgomeryshire) housewife who found it on her plate among the bones of the fish she had just grilled and eaten. She got her 10/– reward. From the housewife Bolster obtained the name of the fishmonger she bought the fish from, and from the fishmonger, his wholesaler. The wholesaler was a Hull firm and this kipper was made from a batch of herring bought for them by a salesman on Lowestoft market. The salesman was able to give the name of the drifter and the date of purchase. Finally, Bolster was able to check with the skipper of the drifter, which happened to be 'Friendly Star', where she fished on the night in question and so found out, after all this detective work, where and when this one herring was caught. It is not always as difficult as this, but this one instance does give some idea of the detail that must be gone into on the laboratory side.

When the position and the date of recapture are finally determined, it is up to the scientist to make the best use that he can of the data. One way is to plot the position of recapture on monthly or quarterly charts. If suitable corrections are made for fishing effort, should they be needed, the change in the distribution of recaptures will give a good picture of the movement of the fish. The data may also be dealt with statistically along the lines developed by Jones (1959, 1966) for the results of haddock tagging experiments off the coast of Scotland.

The track taken by the fish on migration is unlikely to be the line often drawn on a chart between the release and recapture points. It is difficult to get evidence for a migration route and data must come from several sources, such as the change in the geographical position of a succession of recoveries of tagged fish (for example, Höglund's (1955) treatment of the Swedish Skagerrak herring data, and Alverson and Chatwin's (1957) data on the movements of the Pacific petrale sole); fishery statistics; echo-sounder surveys; and general information as to the biology and distribution of the species.

THE STUDY OF MERISTIC AND MORPHOMETRIC CHARACTERS, SCALES, AND OTOLITHS

Labrador cod have an average of 55 vertebrae, those from West Greenland fewer, about 53·5 (Schmidt, 1930). This makes it unlikely that there can be any extensive migration between the two stocks. This example shows the sort of use that can be made of meristic or numerical characters for the study of migrations. Similar differences may exist between other meristic characters, such as the number of fin rays, keeled scales, or gill rakers. Other characters which can be used in a similar way are the proportional size of various body parts, such as head length to overall length, and the detailed structure of the scales and otoliths.

However, it is clear that while significant differences between samples may, by themselves, be good evidence of the separate identity of the adult stocks, the converse does not necessarily mean there is any mixing between them.

1. MERISTIC CHARACTERS

An enormous research effort has been put into the counting of meristic characters: literally millions of herring vertebrae must have been counted during the last fifty years. Ever since the 1890s when Heincke started this work, there have been arguments as to what extent the differences in vertebral counts or fin rays are genetically or environmentally determined. This, of course, may not be important to the fisheries biologist so long as the groups can be identified by their counts and that the differences are fairly constant. It is then immaterial whether the differences are inherited or due to environmental factors.

But the problem of determination is in itself an extremely interesting one and will be of importance if there are variations in the vertebral counts between the year-classes of what appears to be one stock. Schmidt's earlier work, followed by that of Tåning (1952a), who has reviewed the whole field, has gone a long way to show the important role of environmental factors. In particular, temperature variations during the early stages of embryonic development have a marked effect on the number of vertebrae and fin rays. Blaxter (1958) gives a summary of the literature, and a more recent paper is that by Lindsey (1961). Schmidt showed that quite unrelated species show a tendency towards higher meristic counts at the northern edge of their range. The Canadian data on the Pacific herring is a textbook example (Tester, 1937, 1938c). But the Norwegian spring herring show a decrease in vertebral count with latitude: the sea temperature in the coastal waters increases from south to north, under the conflicting influences of the cold

Baltic outflow and the warm Atlantic current. The normal increase with latitude is interesting as in the majority of laboratory experiments the relation between temperature and vertebral count takes the form of a V, the higher counts being related to the extremes of temperature. Lindsey (1958) suggests that other environmental factors, such as light, may be important. However, as Johnsen (1936) pointed out, Schmidt's relation between falling temperature and increasing vertebral count is only a very rough one. For strictly comparable purposes one wants representative samples of a year-class spawned at a particular locality and the water temperatures over the period when development takes places.

It is only in exceptional cases that meristic counts can be used to separate individual members of a species belonging to two or more races. The differences are usually small, and between herring samples of a hundred or so fish, amount only to a fraction of a vertebrae. Sometimes the differences are considerable; the American eel has 104–111 vertebrae, the European 111–119, and most individuals can, with confidence, be referred to one group or the other. There seems to be little doubt that the dozen or so specimens taken at West Greenland are American eels (Jensen, 1937).

2. MORPHOMETRIC CHARACTERS

The measurements of various body parts are sometimes used for statistical comparison between two different spawning groups. The work is laborious and errors due to shrinkage in preserved specimens must be avoided. For example, Vernon (1957) made such a comparison between three spawning stocks of land-locked sockeye salmon—kokanee—in Kootenay Lake, British Columbia, measuring head length, peduncle length and eye diameter from photographs of freshly caught material. Vernon's morphometric comparisons were made between samples of 52 fish collected at each spawning site. These samples are small by comparison with those that would have to be taken from herring during the spawning season and the practical difficulties of working up the mass of material would be formidable. For this reason at least large scale morphometric comparisons are rarely undertaken in Fisheries biology, and then only when the more easily determined characters, such as vertebral or fin ray counts, prove inadequate.

3. SCALES AND OTOLITHS

Scales, otoliths, and other bony parts are widely used in age determination and population studies because the growth and critical events in the life history of the fish are often reflected in the detailed structure of these parts. Scale and otolith markings can be very striking and are sometimes used to identify fish of particular origins and for this reason they are useful for the study of migrations.

Scales

DEVELOPMENT OF THE SCALE

The scales of most modern bony fish are thin, flexible, and transparent. They are formed by dermal papillae whose development is related to that of the neuromasts of the lateral line. From each primary papilla a column of fibroblasts grows out dorsally and ventrally. In the trout, these columns are inclined obliquely forward and penetrate between the dermis and its underlying generative layer, the so-called stratum germinatum. At intervals along these outgrowing columns the fibroblasts concentrate to produce secondary dermal papilla. Ultimately the rows of papillae give rise to rows of scales which grow to overlap one another, from head to tail, as tiles on a roof. The

2

details of the development of the scale from the papilla will not be gone into here. Wallin (1957) gives a comprehensive account and survey of the literature.

Scales appear at the time of metamorphosis of the post-larval stage into the young fish. There is some variation in the length, even for one species, at which the scales are first formed and the following table gives some idea of the range.

Species	Length in mm at which scales first appear	Author
Herring (*C. harengus*)	37–48	Meek (1916*b*) Lebour (1919) Paget (1920)
Plaice (*P. platessa*)	10–13	Kyle (1898, p. 234)
Salmon (*O. nerka*)	36–40	Clutter and Whitesel (1956, p. 11)
Cod (*G. morhua*)	30–50	Graham (1934, p. 70)
Eel (*A. anguilla*)	150–200	Bertin (1956, p. 38)

The eel's scales are very late in developing. They do not appear until long after larval metamorphosis into a young eel is completed, when the fish is about five to seven years old.

THE STRUCTURE OF THE SCALE

The scale consists of two parts: an outer calcified or bony layer which is ridged, and an inner fibrous plate which is partially calcified. According to Wallin's (1957) account, both the bony layer and the fibrous plate are derived from the same germ structure at the periphery of the scale.

The different parts and markings of the bony layer of the teleost scale have been given a number of names and no real attempt had been made to use a consistent nomenclature until Clutter and Whitesel (1956) took the matter in hand. Their system is a good one but it is designed for the sockeye salmon (*O. nerka*) and the structural differences between, say, the salmonid, clupeoid, and the gadoid scales make it difficult to apply, without some modification, to other types.

A typical teleost scale is represented diagrammatically in Fig. 7. The anterior field is the part lying in the scale pocket while the posterior field is exposed but partly covered by the scale in front. If spines or ctenii are present, they are carried on the posterior field. Certain terms are used to describe various features of the scales.

(*a*) *Focus*. This is a small area of the centre of the scale within the first circular ridge. Equivalents: centrum, nucleus, platelet, placode.

(*b*) *Circuli*. These are the concentric ridges that appear on the upper bony layer of the scale. Sometimes they only show up well on the anterior field. When growth is rapid the circuli, or ridges, are heavy and far apart, but they are fine and closer together when growth is slow, and the zones of crowded and fine circuli are known as annuli. The reason for the formation of the ridges is not completely known. Neave (1940) believes they are formed when the scale-forming materials are present in greater quantities than can be laid down at the growing edge. On the other hand Wallin (1957) argues that the circuli are formed as the result of pressure around the periphery of the scale pocket, which causes a pile-up of scale-forming cells. In salmonids the circuli are arranged concentrically around the focus. In most clupeoid scales the arrangement is different.

The circuli, often called striae, run across the anterior field dorso-ventrally. In the herring, only the scales taken from the back by the tail show a concentric pattern of circuli (Paget, 1920). In the cod and plaice the circuli are made up of concentric rings of discrete platelets, usually called sclerites. In the eel's scale these platelets are more bead-like and are known as loculi. For circuli it is clear that several equivalent terms are in common usage; these are striae, sclerites, and loculi; others include circular ridges, rings, and ridges.

(c) *Annuli*. These have already been referred to as zones of crowded, fine, or incomplete circuli. In the cod, the annulus can be recognized by a zone of narrow sclerites, but it is often difficult to detect unless the width of the sclerites is plotted out as a scale trace (Graham, 1926). In the herring

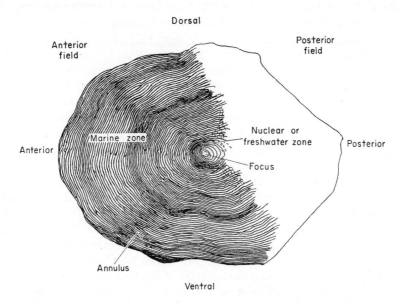

Fig. 7. Scale of a sockeye salmon showing some of the terms used in describing the teleostean scale. (After Clutter and Whitesel, 1956, Fig. 5.)

the annulus forms a distinct line due to a break, bend, or incomplete formation of the striae over-lying the last narrow winter lamella in the lower fibrous layer (Paget, 1920; Muzinic and Richardson, 1958). The annuli are interpreted as indicating a period of slow (winter) growth. Equivalents: annual winter rings, periodic rings, winter bands, winter checks.

(d) *Accessory rings* are zones of crowded or incomplete circuli which resemble annuli but are not correlated with a period of winter growth. Spawning rings [may be included here as a special type of accessory. Equivalents: accessory marks, accessory checks, false annuli, false checks.

(e) *Nuclear area*. This is a term used by Clutter and Whitesel (1956) and refers to that portion of the salmon or trout scale formed in freshwater during the period of lake or stream residence.

(f) *Radii* are groves in the bony layer and run from the centre or some distance from it (second-ary radii) to the edge of the scale. Calcification is incomplete in the radii, which are said to make the scale more flexible. In the herring radial marks appear in the lower fibrous layer as well as the upper bony layer (Huntsman, 1918).

THE ANNUAL GROWTH OF SCALES

The growth rate of individuals of a single species varies considerably from one area to another, particularly in their early years, and this depends on factors such as the date when the young hatch out, temperature conditions and the availability of food. If there is a relation between the structure and size of the scale and growth of the fish, the scale could possibly be used to identify the stock to which the individual belongs. There is an extensive literature in this field, which has been reviewed by Graham (1929c), Van Oosten (1929), and, more recently, by Colefax (1952).

The alternating bands of narrow and wide circuli occur annually. Lea (1924) proved this for the herring by following an outstanding year-class over a number of years and showing the addition of a new annulus to the scale each year. In cod, which can be tagged satisfactorily, the annual nature of the bands of wide and narrow circuli has been shown by comparing scales removed when the fish was tagged with others taken on its recapture (Winge, 1915). In the laboratory, feeding experiments with trout (Bhatia, 1931a and b; Gray and Setna, 1931; Bhatia, 1932) have shown conclusively that the formation of a large number of widely spaced circuli is related to an abundant supply of food and good growth, and fewer and narrowly spaced circuli to a poor supply of food and poor growth. Dannevig (1925) has shown the same sort of relation in the cod. Other factors besides food probably have an effect on the number and size of the circuli and Gray and Setna (1931) have discussed the ways in which temperature might act. Dannevig (1956) claims that O-group cod kept at 12°C grow well but the scales have narrow or moderately wide circuli, while other cod kept at 4°C and 8°C grow just as well but have wide circuli on the scales. There may be something in this but unfortunately the data are not presented in such a way as to make the difference between the two groups clear and convincing. Dannevig's results recall the earlier work of Cutler (1918) who studied the effect of temperature and food on the growth rate and scale structure of plaice. Cutler claimed that temperature had an effect of sclerite width (narrow sclerites at low temperature, the opposite result to Dannevig's) which was independent of the growth of the fish. His results have never gained general acceptance but no one has tried to repeat them. It would be interesting to see if annuli were formed in the scales of fish kept for long periods under constant temperature and given constant daily rations of food. Brown's (1946) work on trout might have given an answer to this question but unfortunately the frequent handling to which her fish were subjected resulted in a heavy loss of the original scales and the replacements were useless for reading (Brown, personal communication).

In *Tilapia esculenta*, a cyprinoid found in Lake Victoria (Africa), the formation of a typical annulus, where the circuli are irregular or broken, may be due to mobilization of calcium reserves and reflect temporary mineral deficiency at the time of breeding and brooding (Garrod and Newell, 1958). The partial adsorption of the scales (Van Someren, 1937) and other bony structures (Tchernavin, 1938) in salmon during their upstream migration is another aspect of the problem and a great deal of work has yet to be done, particularly on the physiological side (see Wallin, 1957) before it is fully understood.

THE USE OF SCALES AS CERTIFICATES OF ORIGIN

If it is accepted that a relation between the size and structure of the scale and the growth of the fish has been established, even if all the factors are not yet known, there is a basis for the use of the scale as a certificate of origin, or as an identity card. In salmon, there is often a significant difference in the number of nuclear circuli in the scales of downstream migrants from various nursery areas in one river system. These differences reflect the various environmental conditions in the different streams. If the adult returns to spawn in the parent stream, these differences should be maintained among the adults of concurrent lake or stream residence taken on the spawning grounds. This sort of evidence could be important in testing the validity of the Parent Stream Theory, and will be discussed later. In the cod, Thompson (1943) has used the number of circuli in the first year scale as a basis of determining the origins of the stock found in the Newfoundland area, while scale structure has been used extensively in identifying the stocks of herring, the papers of Hjort (1914) and Lea (1929b) being classical accounts.

Otoliths

THE INNER EAR

The inner ear, or the membraneous labyrinth, of fish can be divided into two parts. The upper part, the Pars Superior, consists of the three semicircular canals and the sac-like utriculus. The lower part, or Pars Inferior, which joins on to the utriculus, contains the sacculus and the lagena. The Pars Superior is primarily concerned with the maintenance of equilibrium, and muscular tonus. The semicircular canals, set more or less in three planes at right angles to one another, detect angular accelerations while the utriculus is sensitive to any acceleration and thus to both postural and positional changes. This is the part of the ear which could play the role of the sensor in a biological inertial navigation system. The Pars Inferior is mainly concerned with hearing. If it is destroyed on both sides, fish swim normally but no longer react to the full frequency range of sounds as they did before the operation.

The essential structure of the utriculus, sacculus and lagena is very similar. A bed of sensory hair cells, the macula, is in close contact with a calcareous structure, the otolith. The otolith does not lie freely on the macula but is held in place by strands of supporting tissue arising from special epithelium cells at its edge. Between the otolith and the macula itself there is a gelatinous cushion produced by the sensory cells, the so-called 'otolith membrane'. The details of the suspension and form of the macula and related structures are different in the three otolith organs and vary from species to species. Werner (1928) has described the detailed structure in a number of fish, while de Vries (1956) gives an account of the physical properties of the membrane.

In the cod, calcium compounds make up about 87% by weight of the otolith, calcium carbonate in the form of aragonite being the main constituent (E. H. Dannevig, 1956a). The density of an otolith is about 2·93 (de Vries, 1956), and Pumphrey (1950) has discussed the physical advantages that are to be gained by anchoring the hair cells to a mass with a density of this order. A fish lying in the path of a sound wave will more or less follow the movements of the medium and the otolith provides what is virtually a fixed reference point from which the fish should be able to detect the magnitude, frequency and direction of the displacements.

THE DEVELOPMENT AND OCCURRENCE OF OTOLITHS

Two of the three pairs of otoliths appear early. In the cod they can be seen on the sixth day after fertilization (M'Intosh and Prince, 1890), four days before the larvae hatch out. The otolith of the lagena appears later than those of the utriculus and the sacculus. All three otoliths increase in weight as the fish grows (Fig. 8). This is interesting and it is quite unexplained why the whole labyrinth increases in size as the fish gets older while in man, for instance, the labyrinth shows no further increase in size after the first six months of intra-uterine life (O. Gray, 1951). The membraneous labyrinth in fish is consequently relatively big, the span of the semicircular canals of a large cod exceeding the size of the complete labyrinth in an elephant or a hippopotamus.

Another interesting feature is the occurrence of the large compact calcareous otoliths themselves. They are not present in the Cyclostomes (lamprey and hagfish), the Chondrichthyes (sharks and rays), amphibians, reptiles, birds, or mammals. These groups have small calcareous

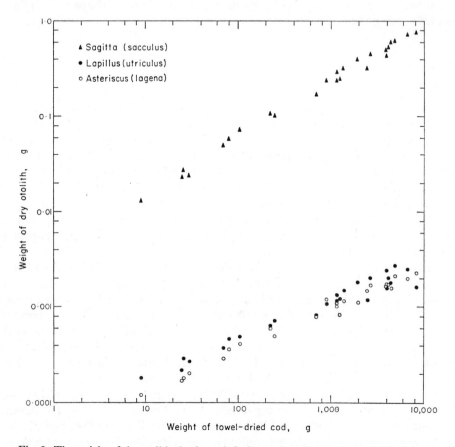

Fig. 8. The weight of the otoliths in the cod *Gadus morhua*. (Original unpublished data.)

crystals, called statoconia, which often give the macula a soft chalky appearance. The Crossopterygians (the lung fish *Ceratodus* and *Protopterus*) and the Chondrostei (sturgeons) have otoliths and statoconia (Retzius, 1881). With the exception of the sturgeons, the rest of the Actinopterygii, the surviving Palaeoniscid *Polypterus*, the Holosteans *Amia* and *Lepidosteus* and all the Teleostei, have typical compact otoliths. Carlström (1963) has completed a crystallographic study of the vertebrate otoliths and has reviewed the problem from both physical and biological aspects.

Pelagic fish must often be without visual reference points for spatial orientation and might have to rely entirely on information from the labyrinth. Groen (1956, p. 106) suggested that the size of the otoliths might be related to their importance and contrasted the massive otoliths of teleosts with their smaller counterparts in mammals. Shepherd's (1910) observations suggested that pelagic and bathypelagic teleosts might have relatively larger otoliths but the relationship between otolith size and mode of life was not always clear. Comparisons have been made between the sensory areas of the inner ear in some fish (Tomaschek, 1937; Freedman and Walker, 1942) and further work might lead to a greater understanding of any functional significance of the differences in otolith size.

THE STRUCTURE AND GROWTH OF OTOLITHS

Graham (1929c) has summarized the early work, much of which set out to justify the use of otoliths in age and growth studies. The saccular otolith, the sagitta, is the only one of the three pairs that is used extensively.

The otolith material produced early in the life of a fish forms the otolith nucleus around which layers of calcareous matter are laid down. A section through a saccular otolith of a cod shows, when viewed by transmitted light, a series of concentric hyaline and opaque bands. If the same otolith is viewed by direct light on a black background, the hyaline bands appear black and the opaque ones white. The hyaline and opaque bands are sometimes called 'winter' and 'summer' zones respectively. But the two zones can be formed in either season (Irie, 1957) and although the 'winter-summer' terminology has wide usage, it is best avoided, or used parenthetically to reduce confusion.

The alternating bands of hyaline and opaque material occur annually and Hickling (1931) showed that there is a difference between the bands, or zones, with regard to the organic constituent of the otolith. The organic constituent appears, in sections across the long axis of the otolith, as a series of concentric shells of a fibrous nature about 2 μ apart. The shells vary in thickness and there are alternate layers in which thick and thin shells predominate. The layers where thick shells predominate correspond to the opaque zones, and the layers where the thin shells are more numerous correspond to the hyaline zones. The concentric shells are bound together by stouter radial fibres among which the crystals of aragonite lie and interlock to build up the solid structure of the otolith. Hickling (1931, p. 555) himself remarked on the apparent similarity between the structure of the otolith and the nacreous layer in the molluscan shell and pearl. Dannevig (1956a) has since shown that the organic material, which is mainly concentrated in the opaque zone, is a protein, conchiolin, which is closely related to the organic material found in the shell of certain molluscs.

The difference between the opacity of the two zones in the otolith appears to be related to the relative amounts of calcium and protein that are laid down. Irie (1960) has shown that the hyaline zones are associated with a high rate of calcium deposition, and the opaque zones with a low rate of calcium deposition. When calcium deposition is low the $CaCO_3$ crystals are small and the spaces between them are filled with protein and the opacity of the zone increased. When calcium deposition is high, the crystals are larger: there is relatively less protein present and the zone is less opaque. So the otolith grows by building up alternate zones of material of differing opacity. As the otolith increases in weight as the fish grows, and the increase in otolith weight is largely due to calcium deposition, Irie's results suggest that the hyaline zones should be formed during the period when the fish is growing. But in the arctic cod, Trout (1954, Figs. 11 and 12) has shown that over three-quarters of the growth in length of the fish occurs during the period when the opaque zone is being formed. This anomaly has yet to be resolved. Environmental factors could affect zone formation in the otolith and Molander's (1947) aquarium experiments suggest that temperature is important. Molander found that plaice kept in cold water (4–6°C) had well-developed opaque zones and narrow hyaline zones, whereas those kept in warmer water (about 14°C) had well-developed hyaline zones and narrow opaque zones. But as Graham (1929*c*, p. 42) remarked, 'growth-rate, scale-structure, otolith-structure and temperature are sometimes observed to be in the same phase and yet seem sometimes to be out of phase. That is, they seem all to be connected to Something, but not to each other.' Nearly forty years later we are really no wiser as to what the 'Something' might be.

Relatively little is known about the way in which otoliths grow. Irie (1960) found that the calcium deposited on the otolith was largely derived from the sea-water, rather than the food, although deposition was faster in well-fed fish. In flatfish and goldfish, analysis of the endolymph has shown a seasonal increase in protein concentration at the time of opaque zone formation (Mugiya, 1964) and a corresponding decrease in endolymph calcium (Mugiya, 1966). A seasonal change in endolymph calcium also occurs in arctic cod (Harden Jones and Woodhead, unpublished data). The form of the saccular otolith (Frost has a long series of papers on the form of the teleostean saccular otolith in the *Annals and Magazine of Natural History*, 9th series, volume 15 for 1925 *et seq.*) is quite distinct for a particular species but the means by which this is determined is unknown. If the otoliths are removed they are, after a period of months, reformed, but the form and size of the new structure is quite different from the normal otolith (Schoen and Holst, 1950).

THE USE OF OTOLITHS AS CERTIFICATES OF ORIGIN

As with scales, the detailed structure of the otolith can sometimes be used as an identity card, otolith structure reflecting environmental differences. For example, both herring (Raitt, 1961) and plaice (de Veen and Boerema, 1959) which spawn in the Southern Bight of the North Sea have a first hyaline (winter) otolith zone which is wide when compared with that found in the otoliths of Dogger spawning herring and German Bight spawning plaice respectively. It is almost certain, as Raitt (1961) argues for herring, that the differences in otolith structure reflect the conditions on a common nursery ground at different times of the year or, as in the case of the plaice, different nursery grounds at the same time of the year. In these two cases otolith structure, in terms of a narrow or wide first hyaline (winter) zone for herring, and in terms of the width of the first year's growth ring, equivalent to the width of the first hyaline (winter) zone, for plaice, can be used to assign fish to different spawning groups. Similarly, attempts have been made to separate summer-, autumn- and winter-spawned herring by the appearance (Einarrson, 1951) or size (Postuma and Zjilstra, 1958) of the otolith nucleus. Rollefsen (1934*b*) has been able to separate coastal from Arcto-Norwegian cod of Lofoten by differences in otolith structure, and Trout (1957) has used the structure of cod otolith in working out the migration patterns of the cod in the Barents Sea.

ANALYSIS OF FISHERY STATISTICS

Graham (1924) found the main spawning areas of cod in the North Sea from a study of market statistics. The task was made possible by the introduction of a new system for tabulating the catches of fishing boats. In 1920 the old area system, based on depth, was replaced by a rectangular grid dividing the North Sea into a large number of so-called 'statistical' rectangles, each one covering

1° of longitude by ½° of latitude. Every fishing boat returned details of the catch made in a particular rectangle during her voyage. From these statistics it was possible to build up, month by month and so throughout a year, a picture of the distribution of cod in the North Sea. The high landings from February to April of roes with a large proportion of ripe eggs fixed the spawning season. From the landings per 100 hours fishing of the trade category 'large', previously shown to be mature cod, it was possible to plot the concentrations of fish in each statistical rectangle during the spawning season. This gave the spawning area, and special cruises of the research ship for egg and larval surveys served to delimit the areas even further. It is obvious that commercial statistics only provide information for those areas where the boats are working, and for those fish captured by the gear used, and analyses of this type need to be checked by special cruises of research ships. With these safeguards, Graham's method is an excellent one and has been successfully applied to other fish, as, for example, the hake (Hickling, 1927). Similarly, the movements of herring in the Norwegian Sea have been inferred from changes in distribution shown by the catch statistics of the Russian drifter fleet (Marty, 1959).

More recently Trout (1957) has described the seasonal change in depth of the Arctic cod using data largely derived from catch and depth reports by trawlers. Alverson (1960), carrying this approach even further, has used commercial data to outline the migrations of several important species of Pacific ground fish. Alverson's paper could serve as a model for further work in this field.

Statistics must be used properly and critically. For example, the migration of cod between Greenland and Iceland is believed to be associated with climatic changes so that the movements of the cod are reflected in the yields of the commercial fisheries in different areas over a number of years. This may well be true. Now the abundance of fish can be measured in terms of the catch-per-unit-of-effort, such as hundredweights of cod per hours trawling, or hundredweights of cod per days absence from port. Over the last thirty years the fishing power of trawlers has increased considerably. The modern trawler is bigger, more powerful, and with navigational aids such as radar, decca, and echo-sounders, a more efficient machine for catching fish than its 1930 counterpart. It is obvious that if catch and effort statistics are to be compared over a number of years, corrections must be applied to take into account changes of fishing power, whether these are due to bigger or better ships (the catching power of a motorship is 1·4 times greater than that of a steamship of the same gross tonnage), or improvements in gear, such as the change from the otter trawl to the Vigneron-Dahl modification with bridles. Gulland (1956) has dealt with the question of the fishing effort in the English demersal fisheries and derives, for trawlers, the best expression of catch-per-effort as cwt/ton hour fishing, thus taking into account the size of the fishing boat. Bell and Pruter (1958) have critically examined the use of fishing statistics in relation to climatic changes. Between them, these two papers mention most of the pitfalls to be avoided when trying to correlate one change with another, and should be read carefully by anyone interested in problems of this sort.

BIOCHEMICAL METHODS

The morphological and morphometric characters used to identify fish originating from different groups are to some extent, at least, subject to environmental influences. It seems reasonable to suppose that reproductively isolated groups of one species might develop biochemical as well as morphological differences. Of particular interest is the study of blood sera and their reactions.

Systematic serology is based on three assumptions (Sindermann, 1961): (a) that biochemical characters are as valid in systematics as are morphological and morphometric characters; (b) that biochemical differences are often genetically determined; and (c) that sub-populations may be distinguishable by the quantitative differences in the frequency of occurrence of particular genes. Biochemical methods offer two main lines of attack:

1. The use of blood characteristics in the antigen-antibody reactions of (i) blood serum proteins and (ii) blood cells.

2. Differences in the amino acids found in muscles.

1. Blood characteristics

The antigenic properties of blood serum proteins have been used for a number of years to demonstrate the affinities between one group of animals and another. Gemeroy (1943) and O'Rourke (1959) have applied this technique to fish and more recent work (Nyman, 1965) suggests that the polymorphic variation in serum proteins has a genetic basis and may be of practical use at an intraspecific level.

Intraspecific differences have been found in the antigenic properties of the red blood cells, characters known more simply as blood types. Individual differences have been demonstrated in goldfish (Hildemann, 1956), tuna (J. E. Cushing, 1956), salmon (Ridgway, Cushing, and Durall, 1958; Ridgway and Klontz, 1961), herring (Sindermann and Mairs, 1959a and b) and redfish (Sindermann, 1961). J. E. Cushing (1964) reviews the whole field. Blood types are, by analogy with mammalian work, genetically controlled, and the fact that intraspecific differences do exist in fish suggests that serology may become as important as vertebral counts in problems involving racial analysis. Another serological character likely to be of use in racial analysis is haemoglobin polymorphism, which Sick (1961) has examined by zone electrophoresis to show that intraspecific differences are present among whiting, cod, sole and eel-pout. The work is now being extended in more detail to cod (Sick, 1965, 1966).

2. Muscle amino acids

Farris (1957) has discussed the application of paper chromatography in systematics, with particular reference to fish, and it is clear from E. H. Dannevig's (1956b) work that differences can be shown between the amino acids in the muscles of different species of fish and in members of the same species taken from different areas. For example, the paper chromatographs of cod from the Skagerrak are very different from those of Lofoten. This may be related directly to feeding and it is not clear, at the moment, to what extent the method may be useful in identifying individuals from particular localities and thus establishing the origins of individual fish.

DIRECT OBSERVATIONS

1. From land or ships

Unlike birds, the direct observation of fish on migration is seldom possible. Exceptions are almost entirely confined to shallow water and, in particular, rivers, where the fish are at or near the surface in such numbers as to draw attention. The upstream migration of elvers and salmon are well-known examples. Another example, but not so well known, is the early spring movement of three-spined stickleback (*Gasterosteus aculeatus*) up river on their return from the sea where many of them winter. Lowestoft drifters have sometimes landed several boxes of three-spined stickle-backs which have been foul meshed in the drift nets. In the 1880s the stickleback migration up the River Welland (in Lincolnshire, England) was on such a scale that a fishery developed for them. Sticklebacks were caught by the hundredweight and rendered down for oil, manure and poultry food.

At sea, direct observations of fish on the move are very few. Hansen (1949) saw large shoals of cod feeding on sand eels (*Ammodytes lancea*) moving northwards off the West Greenland coast in August 1931. 'The weather was calm, the sea like a mirror. The migration was going on right at the surface with the dorsal fins of the cod in many cases showing above the water. Everywhere as far as one could see, the dorsal fins projected from the water and one could observe distinctly, that the shoals were moving northward' (Hansen, 1949, p. 41). Marty (1959, p. 45) records the presence of numerous herring shoals at the surface in the Norwegian Sea, and Hasler (1960, p. 112) reports on the movement of salmon seen at the surface during the night in the Pacific. de Veen (1963) has reported that fishermen sometimes see sole (*Solea vulgaris*) at the surface during the night in the Southern Bight of the North Sea. The sole are most commonly seen in the spring when the inshore spawning migration is under way (see p. 242).

2. From aircraft

Direct observations of fish have also been made from aircraft and Joubin (1918) was one of the first to suggest their use for spotting fish shoals. Heldt (1921) followed up this idea with some success. He flew in an airship and an aeroplane along the coast of Brittany in August and September 1921 and was able to identify shoals of sardines—young pilchards—and horse mackerel swimming above the bottom, which was at about 14·5 m (8 fathoms). Hardy (1924*b*) made two flights in a seaplane off the East Anglian coast during the herring season and two more in March off the Cornish coast towards the Scilly Isles looking for mackerel. Hardy had rather bad luck as he never got a combination of the four conditions probably necessary for success, a calm surface, clear water, strong sunlight with few cloud shadows, and fish. Wood and McGee (1925) were more fortunate.

Aircraft have been used fairly successfully in other areas. Spotting from a seaplane seems to have been some help to the fishery for menhaden—*Brevoortia tyrannus*—in Chesapeake Bay on the Atlantic seaboard of America (Anon, 1921, p. 10; Harrison, 1931, p. 105). Cushing *et al.* (1952) and Hardy (1952) have given some details of the use of aircraft in the Icelandic herring fishery. Here aerial scouting is used to increase the searching efficiency of the fleet. Seaplanes and helicopters are also used in tuna fishing in the Pacific and aerial spotting appears to be coming into its own in the fishery for the Pacific sardine, *Sardinops caerulea*, off the Californian coast. There are many reports of aerial surveys in the Commercial Fisheries Reviews from 1954 onwards. The shoals are clearly visible from a height of 500 to 1,000 feet and their position is reported over the radio to the purse seiners. Over half the fleet appears to depend on spotting planes to locate the sardine shoals (Anon, 1955*a*). Squire (1961) gives a recent account of spotting fish from aeroplanes. But it seems as if the straightforward use of aircraft in this way depends on the fish shoals being at or near the surface: there is little chance of seeing them if they are more than a few metres down. Recently attempts have been made to tow an echo-sounder transducer through the water at speeds up to 30 knots from a helicopter (Anon, 1957), thus extending the high-speed search to the bottom.

As yet little use has been made of aircraft in fisheries research. Blackburn and Tubb (1950) used aerial observations for survey work on pelagic fish in Australian waters. Kelez (1947) has tried to count salmon spawning in rivers and lakes of western Alaska by the examination of aerial photographs and attempts are also being made to estimate the abundance and density of shoals of the Pacific sardine from aerial observations (CCOFI, 1956). Rivas (1954) used a low flying aircraft to follow shoals of giant blue fin tuna, *Thunnus thynnus*, migrating to the north through the straits of Florida. Their swimming speed over the ground was estimated at 3·5 knots (1·75 m/sec), which agreed well with other observations made from ships.

3. Underwater observations

Although there have been numerous underwater observations of fish made by divers, from bathyscaphes, and with underwater television sets, there are few descriptions or reports of fish on migration. Ellis (1961, 1962) has made some preliminary underwater observations on migrating sockeye and coho salmon in the Somass River system, Vancouver Island, British Columbia. For sea-going work submarines with viewing ports, infrared equipment or high resolution acoustic gear might enable answers to be given to some of the problems connected with the movements of fish in deep water.

MOVEMENT OF FISH INFERRED FROM THE CATCH IN THE NET

A stow net is a fixed bag set across the line of the current to catch fish moving downstream. If two stow nets could be set so that one opened upstream and the other dowstream, and the first net caught many fish and the second a few, it would be reasonable to conclude that the fish were moving downstream. The same conclusion would follow whenever there is a marked and consistent difference between the number of fish caught on either side of any fixed net set across the stream. But it is important to note that the direction in which the fish are thought to be moving is given relative to the fixed net and not relative to the water. A fish would still be carried downstream if its speed through the water when heading the current was less than that of the water over the ground. So a greater catch on the upstream side of a fixed net gives information concerning the relative motions of the fish and net but not on the orientation of the fish; whereas a greater catch on the downstream side would only be possible if the fish were swimming upstream and was orientated against the current.

Johansen (1927, p. 15) suggested that the direction in which herring were moving could be determined from the side of the drift net on which they were caught when the fleet was shot across the tide. Huntsman (1936, p. 5), Barnaby (1952), Hartt (1962), Johnsen (1964), and Larkins (1964) have extended the same arguments to salmon caught by drift net and purse seine. Both drift net and purse seine are assumed to move passively with the water so that there is no flow of water across the meshes of the net or into the bag of the purse. Fish meshed in the net, or caught in the bag, must therefore have been moving relative to the water, and it has been thought that the direction of movement could be determined by reference to the side of the net in which they were caught, or to the direction in which the mouth of the purse was open.

But for the drift net, at least, this seems too naive an interpretation. Fish are caught in a drift net because they swim into it. Some of these fish may have swum headlong into the net, which they failed to detect, and others may have swum into the net which they detected, but failed to avoid: a drift net probably catches a proportion of the fish which come within a critical range of a few metres. In the most simple case, both net and fish drift passively with the tide, and random swimming movements take some fish close to the net and a proportion of these are caught. The absence of fish meshed on one side or the other could simply indicate that there were no fish on one side of the net. But when the force of the wind on the drifter is sufficient to overcome the resistance of the hull and the nets to movement through the water, the drifter and her nets will be carried downwind. If a fleet is shot across a south-going tide and the wind is from the south-west, the nets will drive north-east across the tide, and the relative movement between the net and fish carried passively south will be $V \sin \theta$, where V is the velocity of the net through the water at an angle θ to the line normal to the tide. Under these conditions more fish will be caught on the north side of the net, not because the fish are moving south (they are, but passively, and not relative to the water), but because the net is moving north. The point is that the movement of the fish relative to the water, that is their direction of movement or orientation, cannot be inferred from the distribution of the drift net catch, or from the set of a purse or ring net, unless critical data are available concerning the movement of the net relative to the water: only when the wind is very light can it be assumed that there is no relative movement between them.

Creutzberg (1961) tried to find out if elvers were swimming actively inshore by comparing tow-net catches made with and against the tide on the ebb and the flood. He towed a 1 m² ring net at constant speeds through the water within the range of 3 to 5 km/h (83 to 140 cm/sec). If the elvers were swimming inshore, more should be caught in the off-shore hauls. If they swim at a cruising speed of 25 cm/sec (2·5 L, see p. 16), the off-shore and inshore catches should have differed in proportion to the relative speed of elver and net; that is $(83 + 25)$ to $(83 - 25)$, an increase of 86% at a towing speed of 83 cm/sec, and $(140 + 25)$ to $(140 - 25)$, an increase of 44% at a towing speed of 140 cm/sec. The flood tide hauls always caught more elvers and the off-shore hauls, on both ebb and flood tides, were usually higher. The results of the 1957 trials gave off shore and inshore catches of 0·5 and 0·3 elvers/km on the ebb, and 4·0 and 3·5 elvers/km on the flood, increases of 67% and 14% respectively (Creutzberg, 1961, p. 270, Table III). But these results were not statistically significant, the paired hauls being few in number and the catches variable.

ECHO-RANGING TECHNIQUES

1. Working principles

Echo-ranging (or sonar) techniques were developed as navigational aids for recording depth. The principle behind them is simple enough. Short pulses of sound waves are sent out from the ship into the water and the time interval between the moment of transmission and the return of the echo from the sea floor is measured. As the speed of sound through water is known, the depth of the bottom can be calculated. The sound waves used in echo-ranging have frequencies within the range of 10 to 500 kHz. These frequencies cannot normally be detected by the human ear, whose upper threshold lies between 10 and 20 kHz, and they are well above the threshold for those fish that have been tested, very few of which respond to frequencies above 2,000 Hz (Kleerkoper and Chagnon, 1954; Tavolga and Wodinsky, 1963).

There are two sorts of echo-ranging devices, echo-sounders and asdics. The difference between them is that while the echo-sounder's oscillators are fixed to the hull of the ship and the pulses are sent out vertically down to the bottom, asdic oscillators can be rotated beneath the ship in a horizontal plane. An echo-sounder is therefore restricted to receiving echoes from targets more or less directly below the ship, whereas an asdic can be used to search for targets around the ship, in the case of fish shoals up to ranges of 1,000 m under good conditions.

Some asdic and echo-sounder transmitting and receiving oscillators are made of numerous thin nickel rings or plates, and work on the magnetostriction principle, whereby high frequency vibrations can be induced by discharging a suitable voltage through a low impedance winding surrounding the pack. Other transducers make use of the piezzo-electric effect originally discovered by the Curie brothers and applied to echo-ranging by Langevin (1932). Wood (1941) gives a full account of the application of magnetostriction phenomena to echo-ranging, and Sparling (1945) gives details of echo-sounder engineering practice.

Most echo-ranging devices have a recording unit installed on the bridge, which, in the case of an echo-sounder, provides a permanent picture of the contours of the sea floor below the ship. The recording chart is usually made of absorbent paper soaked in starch-iodide solution. When a direct current is passed through the paper iodine released from the positive electrode combines with the starch to form a blue mark which rapidly turns brown. The negative electrode is a plate behind the recording paper while the positive electrode is attached to a rotating arm. When the rotating arm starts to cross the paper, a signal is sent out by the transmitting oscillator. The pulse length of the signal is of the order of a millisecond and its acoustic output several hundred watts. As the signal leaves the transmitter it is picked up by the receiver, and the electrical effect is amplified and passed on to the electrode attached to the radial arm, to produce a mark on the paper corresponding to the outgoing signal. When the echo from the sea floor is picked up by the receiver the arm has moved further across the paper so that the outgoing signal mark and the echo returned from the sea floor are separated by a distance proportional to the depth of water beneath the transducer. Knowing the speed at which sound travels through sea-water, and the speed at which the radial arm crosses the recording paper, a scale can be set up across the latter so that the depth of water can be read directly. The paper moves forward all the time so that each mark is partly superimposed on the preceding one to form a continuous picture. If fish are present to return an echo this appears on the recording paper between the transmission mark and the bottom. Time marks are usually made on the paper every minute, so the actual distance represented by a length of paper can be worked out if the speed of the ship is known. In some types of echo-sounders the paper record is supplemented by a cathode-ray tube presentation which increases the instrument's sensitivity; recent development is leading to greater resolution in order to pick out and recognize small individual targets.

With asdic the oscillators can be set to scan an arc in a horizontal plane around the ship and there is no need to watch the paper recorder all the time if the instrument has a sound repeater. The search for fish proceeds as in a submarine hunt. However, the interpretation of an asdic chart is not so easy as that of an echo-sounder, and may be very difficult when working in shallow water, of 20 to 30 m, if there are rocky outcrops on the bottom. The reason for this is that the sound beam spreads out after it leaves the ship and the lower part of the beam soon hits the bottom in shallow water. Bottom echoes may then be received at the same time as those from targets in midwater and considerable experience is required to distinguish between them.

2. Identification of echoes: target classification

The successful use of echo-ranging in fishing and research work largely depends on the identification of the targets that are returning the echoes. A considerable amount of work has been done along these lines, important papers being those of Hodgson (1950*a*) and Cushing (1957*a*). Other work is referred to in the reviews of Cushing *et al.* (1952) and Hodgson and Fridriksson (1955).

Identification may be difficult as sound energy will be reflected by any target whose acoustic properties differ sufficiently from those of surrounding medium. Echoes may be returned by swarms of the smaller zooplankton, single euphausids, small fish, and probably by sharp temperature discontinuities.

There are two lines of approach to the problem of identification. The first is based on the appearance of the echo trace on the recording paper: this depends on the relative movement between the ship and the fish shoal, and the size and shape of the latter in relation to that of the sound beam. In one area particular types of traces can be associated with catches of different species of fish and in this way it is possible to build up a scheme of identification. One might call this the biologist's approach and for certain areas, and at certain times, it works well enough. But different species sometimes give identical echo-sounder traces, or one species may give several types, depending, for example, on the size, shape and packing density of fish within the shoal, and the depth at which it is lying. Cushing (1957*a*, 1963), discusses some of these difficulties in detail.

The second approach, call it that of the physicist, will almost certainly give the more reliable identification in the long run. This depends on increasing the resolution of the echo-ranging device so as to be able to detect and deal with single targets. If the acoustic properties of different targets are known, some sort of identification can be made from the amplitude of the returned signal at one or at different frequencies. For this method it is better to use a cathode-ray tube presentation on which echoes from single targets can be resolved and their amplitude measured by comparison with an injected signal.

A series of measurements made on the strength of the echo returned by single cod at 37 kHz serves to illustrate this method (Harden Jones, 1959). Dead 70 cm cod were hung below the ship at different depths. Measurements showed that the amplitude of the echo returned by the fish varied with depth according to the inverse square law, as was expected. The next step was to determine the amplitude of the echo returned by different sizes of cod at one depth. From these two sets of data it is possible to calculate the amplitude of the echo expected from different sizes of cod at different depths. With this information a rough estimate can be made of the size of a target returning an echo of known amplitude from a given depth. This does not enable one to distinguish between echoes returned by cod, haddock, or coalfish of a similar size, but it is a small step in the right direction and it is along such lines that the problem of identification may be solved. But the problem is a difficult one. Knowledge of the acoustic properties of different targets, target strengths and scattering cross-sections (a full discussion of these concepts is to be found in 'The Physics of Sound in the Sea', Summary Technical Report of Division 6, NDRC, 8, 1946, Washington, D.C.) is needed and this information can only be obtained by carefully controlled experiments. Smith (1954), Harden Jones and Pearce (1958), Cushing *et al.* (1963), and Midttun and Hoff (1962) have done work of this sort. Haslett (1964) gives an up-to-date account of recent research in this field.

3. The use of echo-ranging for studying migration

There are two ways in which echo-ranging techniques can be put to use for studying migrations. The first is by following single or small groups of fish more or less continuously until they are lost, and the second by carrying out surveys to show changes in the distribution of fish over a period of days or weeks.

TRACKING SINGLE OR SMALL GROUPS OF FISH

The success of this method depends on how long one can keep track of a particular target A modern echo-sounder can pick up a 70 cm cod at a depth of 180 m quite easily but following a single fish is not practicable with a conventional sounder. Furthermore, fish lying very close (0·3 m) to the bottom cannot be recognized as such with much confidence. Echo-sounding is of no use for plaice, dabs, or other bottom-living species. Following a single fish with asdic is a very much more difficult task than following a submarine. The beam target strength of a small-sized submarine is of the order of +30 db (NDRC, 1946), while that of a 20 cm perch is about −35 db (Harden Jones and Pearce, 1958), nearly 2,000 times less. Attempts have been made to track a single fish by fitting it with a miniature transducer. This so-called 'sonic tag' emits a high frequency signal and this is picked up by an automatic tracking device which aims an asdic at the target. Trefethen (1956) and Trefethen, Dudley, and Smyth (1957) have described the construction and use of this tag, which was tried on 45 to 75 cm salmon. The tag was an aluminium capsule weighing 2 g in water, containing a 15 V battery with a life of 10–100 hours, depending on its size, a transistor, and a crystal operating at 132 kHz with a repetition rate of 450 pulses per second. Tags were attached to salmon which were returned to the water and followed for ranges up to 250 m. Johnson (1960) has described some attempts to follow salmon in the Columbia River, using this technique. Bass and Rascovich (1965) have designed a much larger sonic tag for use with sharks and tuna.

With normal echo-ranging gear it is more practicable to follow groups of fish than individuals. Harden Jones (1957a, 1962) has tracked herring shoals for several hours in the English Channel and followed their movements in relation to the tidal streams. There is little doubt that asdic would probably be better for this sort of work, but trials have shown that the use of asdic brings its own problems, particularly in shallow waters, and when there is any traffic about, wakes cause a lot of trouble.

A further development of asdic for following fish shoals is provided by a sector-scanning sonar in which a beam is swept by electronic means over a wide sector at high speed (for a simple account of a delay-line system, see Tucker, 1959; for modulation scanning, see Voglis and Cook, 1966). The cathode-ray tube presentation displays range against bearing. When working from an anchored ship, the movements of fish shoals across the sector can be filmed, analysed and related to measurements of the velocity of the tidal stream measured below the ship. These new developments have proved themselves in sea trials (Harden Jones and McCartney, 1962; Voglis and Cook, 1966; Cushing and Harden Jones, 1966) and will give important results.

It is of interest to note the use which is now being made of radar to track migrating birds, which have almost certainly been identified as the cause of the so-called 'angels', whose appearance on radar screens has long been both a mystery and nuisance to operators (Harper, 1958; Tedd and Lack, 1958). Ornithologists are fortunate to be able to make use of a system that can follow flocks up to ranges of a 100 miles and more. The attenuation of radiowaves is so great (Liebermann, 1962) that radar cannot be used underwater. Biologists must look forward to the day when acoustic echo-ranging systems with performances to match those of radar are available for tracking fish shoals in the open sea.

THE USE OF ECHO AND ASDIC SURVEYS TO SHOW CHANGES IN THE DISTRIBUTION OF FISH

The Norwegians were probably the first to make use of asdic to follow fish in the open sea. In the winter the research ship 'G.O. Sars' makes regular asdic surveys for the Norwegian spring herring in the Iceland-Faroes area and the information is passed on to the fishing fleet. Quite apart from the practical value of these surveys, they are claimed to provide data on the route taken by these herring on their spawning migration towards the Norwegian coast.

Cushing (1952) made a major step forward by introducing a quantitative approach in echo survey work by counting, on the paper record, the number of transmissions returned by shoals over a given distance and contouring the results on a survey grid. Alternatively, the results may be presented as so many millimetres of fish trace per mile of the ship's survey track. This method has been used for surveys of herring (Cushing, 1955a), pilchards (Cushing, 1957b) and cod (Cushing, 1959c). A further development of this technique is to use banks of dekatron counters set at different amplitude levels to count the echoes returned by fish lying close to the bottom (Mitson and Wood, 1961) and this method has been successfully used for survey work on Arctic cod. During the East Anglian herring fishery, the Ministry of Agriculture, Fisheries and Food's research vessels based on Lowestoft used to carry out regular echo surveys over the route taken by the herring moving through the Southern Bight to spawn on the Channel grounds. The information obtained on these surveys was passed on to the drifter fleet every day. Tungate (1958) has summarized some of the results. In addition, regular surveys were made by selected British Railways passenger and ferry boats whose routes took them over the migration track (Harden Jones, 1957b).

Care must be taken in the interpretation of echo and asdic surveys when continuity is lost during or between cruises. While there may be a clear change in the distribution of the echo patches, it does not necessarily follow that they are the same ones. And, of course, there is always the problem of the identity of the targets. It is clear that surveys have their limitations; nevertheless, they could be valuable in showing what is going on when supported by evidence of identification provided by fishing, either by the fleet or the research boat.

Chapter 4

Salmon and Trout

INTRODUCTION

Members of the salmon family, the Salmonidae, occur naturally off the coasts and in rivers and lakes of the North Temperate zone. They have, however, been introduced to other areas, such as South America and New Zealand. Salmonids breed in freshwater. When young, many migrate downstream to the sea where the greater part of their growth takes place. Later they return to fresh water to spawn. But this habit of running down to the sea is very variable. Some members of a particular species do so while others do not. Differences even exist among the population of a single stream, as for instance among steelheads in Fall and Beaver Creeks, Klamath River, California (Taft and Shapovalov, 1938). Landlocked stocks of salmon are well known. There is the kokanee, a landlocked sub-species of the Pacific sockeye salmon, in Canadian Lakes (Ricker, 1938). In Lake Byglandsfjord, southern Norway, there is a dwarf form of the Atlantic salmon called the 'belge' (Dahl, 1928). In the South Island of New Zealand there appears to be a freshwater form of *S. salar* in Lake Te Anav, which does not migrate to the sea although there is no serious obstruction to prevent it from doing so (Calderwood, 1927). All salmonids seem to show some migratory tendencies. While the sea-going forms return to freshwater to spawn, the landlocked or freshwater forms return to their head rivers. It is believed that the fish return to spawn in the very same stream or tributary in which they grew up. This is the essential point of the 'Parent' or 'Home Stream Theory'. It is not only of great interest as an academic problem but is, as Rich (1939) has emphasized, of far-reaching importance in working out practical measures for the conservation and management of the salmon fisheries.

Classification

Before going on to consider the Parent Stream Theory, something should be said about the systematic arrangement of the Salmonidae. This is a matter over which authorities differ and there is even a certain amount of confusion as to the common names of some species. Opinions, arguments and discussions on these topics are given by Tate Regan (1914, 1929), Tchernavin (1939), and Hildebrand (1957). There is little to be gained by going into details. What is important here is to know which particular species is being discussed and those to which reference will be made are in the Table opposite.

The literature

A great amount of research has been carried out on the biology, migration and conservation of the Atlantic and Pacific salmon. Some of this is summarized in *The migration and conservation of salmon* published by the American Association for the Advancement of Science and edited by Moulton (1939), while other papers dealing more with problems of homing and migration are

Genus	Species	Common name
Salmo	*S. salar*	The Atlantic salmon
	S. trutta	The migratory sea trout and the fresh-water brown trout (*S. fario*) are the same species.
	S. gairdneri	The North American steelhead trout is considered to be the same species as the rainbow trout, *S. irideus* (Snyder, 1940).
Oncorhynchus (Pacific salmon)	*O. nerka*	Sockeye, red, quinault, or blueback salmon
	O. gorbuscha	Pink or humpback salmon
	O. keta	Chum or dog salmon
	O. kisutch	Coho or silver salmon
	O. tshawytscha	Chinook, King, quinnat, spring, or tyee salmon
	O. masu	Masu salmon (Japan only)

reviewed by Scheer (1939) and Shapovalov (1941). More recently the literature on the Atlantic salmon has been listed and briefly reviewed by Pyefinch (1955). J. W. Jones' book (1959) covers the details of the life history of *S. salar*, and Bergeron (1962) has compiled a bibliography. There are three reviews of work done on the different species of Pacific salmon in the International North Pacific Fisheries Commission's Bulletin No. 1. Of these the one by Foerster (1955) alone refers to over 200 original papers and reports. Finally, Wilimovsky and Freihofer (1957) have produced a comprehensive guide to the literature on the biology of the Pacific salmon. There is then a wealth of information available. In this account the problems of homing raised by the migrations of salmon and trout are going to be put in their simplest possible form, and only work that has a direct and significant bearing on the main issues will be considered in any detail.

Life history

The main facts of the life history of the salmon are well known. Apart from certain landlocked stocks which spend their whole life in freshwater, salmon are anadromous, spending much of their adult life at sea and only returning to freshwater to spawn. Spawning takes place in the autumn and winter. The eggs are laid in gravel beds, the redds, in lakes or streams and take about 60 days to hatch, according to the temperature. The fry, or alevins, grow up into parr. Finally, as smolts, the salmon migrate down to the sea in the spring and summer. The time that the young salmon spend in freshwater varies considerably. In the Atlantic salmon the period of freshwater residence may be from 1 to 6 years, although 2 to 3 years are more usual. Among the Pacific salmon, the pink and chum go down to the sea in their first spring, soon after emerging from the gravel beds.

In the sea, the salmon enter into a period of heavy feeding and growth. The mature fish usually return to spawn in freshwater after two or more winters, although some return after only one winter in the sea. This is not unusual and in both the Atlantic and Pacific species these precocious fish, which are generally males, are known as grilse or jacks. While some Atlantic salmon survive to spawn a second or third time, the Pacific salmon does so only once and dies in freshwater after its first and only spawning.

The hypothesis that salmon return to spawn in the stream in which they grew up raises two questions:

1. What evidence is there to show a return to the parent or home stream, and if this does occur, what is the probability that this return is something more than might be expected by chance?

2. When salmon go down to the sea, do they wander far away from their river's zone of influence? And if they do go far away, what proportion of them get back?

The two questions concern slightly different aspects of salmon migration. The first deals simply with the question of homing and, if there is a case to answer, must lead on to the factors involved in the recognition of the parent stream. The second concerns the fate of salmon in the open sea. If they do reach the sea, is it just chance that brings them back to the parent stream, or is there more to it than that?

Salmon and trout migrations have always aroused great interest and these problems are still a field for observation, experiment and controversy. Some of the credit for this must go to A. G. Huntsman, formerly Consulting Director, Fisheries Research Board of Canada, whose uncom-

Table 2. 1964 catch, in thousands of metric tons, of Pacific and Atlantic salmon. (Data from FAO, 1966.)

Pacific salmon
Total catch 383,000 tons

Species	Country				Totals
	Canada	USA	Japan*	USSR	
Chinook	5·5	13·0	—	1·4	20
Chum	10·8	29·9	81·1	26·5	148
Coho	13·0	17·3	—	1·2	32
Pink	16·5	73·6	38·9	14·7	144
Sockeye	10·4	26·0	—	3·1	40
Totals	**56·2**	**159·8**	**120·0**	**46·9**	**384**

* In the FAO statistics the Japanese catch of chum includes chinook, coho, and sockeye.

Atlantic salmon
Total catch 13,000 tons

Country	Catch
Canada	2·1
Scotland	1·9
Norway	1·9
Denmark	1·7
Greenland	1·5
Ireland	1·4
N. Ireland	0·6
Finland	0·6
Sweden	0·6
Poland	0·4
W. Germany	0·3
Iceland	0·2
England and Wales	0·1
Total	**13·3**

promising and critical approach to the subject in the late 1930s aroused a great deal of interest and discussion. Huntsman may, as he has said, have 'suffered the fate of a heretic' for questioning the orthodox theories of salmon migration and homing. But no one who has followed the details of the controversy he aroused, which was always enlightening and entertaining, can doubt that it was high time that someone did ask some plain and simple questions, or that there is, perhaps, a moral to be drawn when a generally accepted theory is shown to rest rather more on what distinguished scientists of the day believed to be true than on the firmer basis of established fact.

There are, then, these two questions to deal with, but in spite of the very extensive literature on the biology and migrations of salmon and trout, the critical evidence which has a significant bearing on them is rather limited. Much of what there is comes from American and Canadian work. This is not because European workers have been particularly idle. As can be seen from Table 2, the North American salmon fisheries are of far greater economic importance than those in Europe. This difference is naturally reflected in the research effort, which is much greater, and generally very much better, in the New World than in the Old.[1]

There could be three lines of evidence to support the theory that salmon return to the stream in which they grew up.

1. The return to the parent stream of marked downstream migrants.
2. The return of downstream migrants hatched from transplanted eggs.
3. The existence of local stocks among neighbouring streams which could only be maintained by a consistent return to the parent stream.

The return to the parent stream of marked downstream migrants

There have been quite a number of experiments in which young salmon migrating downstream have been marked by fin clipping and a watch kept for their return as adults in the parent stream in later years. Rich and Holmes (1929) were among the first in this field. In their experiments with fingerlings derived from autumn runs of chinook salmon to the Little White Salmon and Big White Salmon Rivers (Fig. 9) both tributaries of the Columbia River, 174,000 downstream migrants were marked (experiment nos. 3, 8 and 12). Of the 504 recoveries, 99 were caught at the hatcheries at which the young were reared and liberated; 5 fish strayed to near-by tributaries; the rest were taken in the commercial fishery.

However, the return of a few marked fish to the parent stream does not constitute critical evidence for the Parent Stream Theory. Out of all the experiments that have been done only a few appear to be reasonably critical and significant. The series that are going to be considered in detail here are those done at Cultus Lake by Foerster, at McClinton Creek by Pritchard, at Duckabush River Hatchery, Washington State, and at Snake Creek, Olive Cove, Alaska, by Davidson, and at Scott and Waddell Creeks and the Klamath River, California, by Taft and Shapovolov.

CULTUS LAKE EXPERIMENTS

These experiments were done with *O. nerka*, the red or sockeye salmon. Cultus Lake (Figs. 9 and 84) has one outflow to the Fraser River and this, together with certain other advantages, led to it being developed from 1924 onwards as a centre for detailed and careful investigations into its

[1] In 1964 the United Kingdom catch of salmon (2,000 tons) fetched a first sale price of £1.7 million (FAO, 1966). In the same year United Kingdom imports of canned salmon (44,000 tons) were valued at £29 million, the greater part (£18 million) coming from Japan (MAFF, 1965).

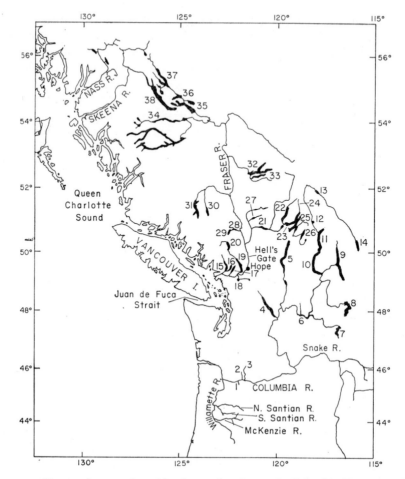

Fig. 9. Place names of interest in connexion with salmon migration on the Columbia, Fraser, and Skeena Rivers, north-west Pacific coast of America and Canada.

KEY

Columbia River. 1 Herman Creek; 2 Little White Salmon R.; 3 Big White Salmon R.; 4 L. Chelan; 5 L. Okanagan; 6 Grand Coulee; 7 Coeur d'Alene L.; 8 Pend Oreille L.; 9 Kootenay L.; 10 Lower Arrow L.; 11 Upper Arrow L.; 12 Revelstroke; 13 Kinbasket L.; 14 Columbia L.
Fraser River. 15 Pitt L.; 16 Alouette L.; 17 Stave L.; 18 Cultus L.; 19 Harrison L.; 20 Lillooet L.; 21 Kamloops L.; 22 Adams L.; 23 Shuswap L.; 24 Seymour R.; 25 Eagle R.; 26 Mabel L.; 27 Loon L.; 28 Seton L.; 29 Anderson L.; 30 Taseko L.; 31 Chilko L.; 32 Quesnel L.; 33 Horsefly L.; 34 Francois L.; 35 Stuart L.; 36 Trembleur L.; 37 Takla L.
Skeena River. 38 Babine L.
(Place names from an International Pacific Salmon Fisheries Commission map. Coastal outline from an Admiralty Chart.)

natural salmon runs. The outlet was screened and fenced so that all the fish leaving and entering the lake would be enumerated and sampled. In the spring of 1927 and 1928 a proportion of the downstream migrants was marked by fin clipping. Some of these young salmon were expected to return to spawn in the lake during the autumn 1, 2, or 3 years after they had left. The results of the 1927 and 1928 experiments will be considered first and these are summarized in Table 3. Some of the marked salmon did return to the lake but there were no reports of marked fish being recovered from other streams or hatcheries. It will be seen that the proportion of unmarked fish returning to the lake was greater than that of the marked fish. Assuming that there had been no confusion between the two due to fin regeneration, the difference may have been caused by one, or all three, of the following factors:

(i) infiltration of unmarked fish,
(ii) straying of marked fish being greater than that of unmarked fish,
(iii) an increased mortality among the marked fish.

Table 3. Cultus Lake marking experiments in 1927 and 1928.

Year	Downstream migrants		Adults returning to Cultus Lake		Proportion of adults returning as percentage of downstream migrants		Author
	Unmarked	Marked	Unmarked	Marked	Unmarked	Marked	
1927	158,100	91,600	3,930	804	2·49	0·88	Foerster, 1934
1928	236,000	99,700	7,549	1,340	3·2	1·34	Foerster, 1936

The 1930 and 1931 experiments (Foerster, 1937), when all the downstream migrants were marked, will be considered in more detail. Sockeye salmon normally leave Cultus Lake in the spring of their second year, but some may stay for an extra year and leave in their third. The majority of the second year migrants return in their fourth year, two and a half years later. But some, mostly males, return a year earlier as precocious grilse or jacks in their third year, and a few stay an extra year in the sea to return in their fifth year. To make this quite clear, the life history of a typical Cultus Lake sockeye, leaving the lake in its second year and returning in its fourth is summarized as follows:

Years of life	1st year	2nd year	3rd year	4th year
Year	1929	1930	1931	1932
Winter	hatched	in lake	at sea	at sea
Spring	in lake	migrates	at sea	at sea
Summer	in lake	at sea	at sea	at sea
Autumn	in lake	at sea	at sea	returns to spawn

There are two important features in the life history of a salmon, the year of life in which it matures and that in which it leaves freshwater. It is customary to express these by two numbers, one in large type for the year of life at which it matures, the other in small type, to the right and below, for the year of life in which it left freshwater. For example, a fish that leaves freshwater in its second year and returns to spawn in its fourth is referred to as a 4_2.

Going back to the marking experiments, it is clear that the second year downstream migrants in 1930 will be expected to return mainly in their fourth year (4_2) in 1932, but that third year fish (3_2) might turn up in 1931 and fifth year fish (5_2) in 1933. Among the downstream migrants in 1930 there will have been some third year sockeye which had stayed in the lake for an extra year. These will return two and a half years later in their fifth year (5_3) in 1933. The expected returns to the lake from 1931 to 1934 can be summarized as follows:

Year of downstream migration	Year of return of adult							
	1931		1932		1933		1934	
1929 unmarked	4_2	5_3	5_2	—	—	—	—	—
1930 all marked	3_2	—	4_2	5_3	5_2	—	—	—
1931 all marked	—	—	3_2	—	4_2	5_3	5_2	—
1932 unmarked	—	—	—	—	3_2	—	4_2	5_3

So in 1933 the only unmarked fish expected to return to the lake would be small 3_2s of the 1932 downstream migration. If any other unmarked fish returned they could only be migrants that had escaped marking or infiltrators from other areas. From 1931 to 1934 considerable efforts were made to ensure the recovery of marked sockeye taken by the autumn commercial salmon fishery on the grounds traversed by the sockeye returning to the Fraser River. The grounds are wide-spread and arrangements were made to have the returns made from the canneries at which the fish were landed. In 1932 and 1933, when the bulk of the returns were expected, Hatchery Officers and Fishery Guardians throughout the Fraser River watershed were warned to be on the lookout for marked sockeye.

The results of the experiments are summarized in Table 4. Leaving for a moment the question as to whether there is an increased mortality among marked fish, the results show that about 3·5% of the original migrants were recovered and well over half of these, 65%, were taken in the commercial fishing areas. No recoveries of stray marked fish were reported from other creeks or hatcheries. So out of every 1,000 downstream migrants, 35 returned, and of these the commercial fishery took 23, leaving 12 to get back to Cultus Lake. But the real significance of the returns to Cultus Lake appears to depend on what happened to the 965 missing fish. Did they die or did they stray?

Table 4. Cultus Lake marking experiments in 1930 and 1931 (Data from Foerster, 1937, Table 1.)

Year	Number of downstream migrants marked	Marked adults returning to Cultus Lake		Marked adults taken in the commercial fishery		Total recovery of marked fish	
		Number	% Downstream migrants	Number	% Downstream migrants	Number	% Downstream migrants
1930	104,061	1,835	1·76	1,986	1·91	3,821	3·67
1931	365,265	3,160	0·87	9,572	2·62	12,732	3·49

Something more must now be said about infiltration and the possibility of increased mortality among marked fish as errors here could lead to an over-estimate of the number of missing fish. In the 1927 and 1928 experiments when only a proportion of the downstream migrants was marked, the returns to Cultus Lake gave a higher proportion of unmarked fish than marked fish. Foerster (1937) did not consider this to be due to infiltration of unmarked fish or straying of marked fish. He interpreted the results as showing a higher mortality among the marked fish. However, marked migrants show no immediate effects of fin clipping (Foerster, 1937) although held under observation for three weeks. Similarly Pritchard (1939) could detect no ill effects of fin clipping among much smaller pink salmon migrants held for 3 to 4 months. In 1933, there should have been no unmarked adults entering Cultus Lake other than the 1932 3_2 migrants and those which had escaped marking in 1930 and 1931. Foerster (1937, p. 34) gives the total sockeye run for 1933 as 3,471 individuals, whereas the total number of marked fish is 2,864 (his Table 1). Thus there were 607 unmarked fish among the 1933 run but most of these proved to be 3_2s. Even if the remainder are all taken as infiltrators, the numbers are so small compared to the total run that they do not have any significant effect on the proportional returns of marked and unmarked migrants. So there does appear to be an extra mortality, of about 50%, among the marked fish. If this is true the recoveries from the 1930 and 1931 experiments should be doubled in estimating the probable return of salmon from the sea, that is 70, not 35 fish, would have returned out of every 1,000 that migrated downstream. But there are still 930 missing fish.

The fact that the Fraser River salmon are not caught in local waters until the late summer or autumn of the year of their return to freshwater suggests that part of their life may be spent in the open sea. Evidence for this will be considered later. If a large proportion of the missing fish survived their life at sea and were available to make the return journey, the few recovered in the fishing area and at Cultus Lake suggest that a great number were lost on the way back.

Allowing for a higher mortality rate among the marked fish, it seems as if 7% of the downstream migrants get back into home waters from Johnstone Strait in the north to the Juan de Fuca Strait in the south. Of those that do return, 65% are taken in the commercial fishery. An error could come in here if marked fish were missed, but the estimate of fishing intensity, 65% of the sockeye available, is high, not unreasonable, and agrees well enough with other estimates. Even allowing for an underestimate of 5 to 10% in the return of marked fish from the canneries, 900 fish out of every 1,000 are still unaccounted for, have never been found anywhere else and are apparently lost at sea. The results can be summarized this way:

Downstream migrants to the sea	'Lost at sea'	Return to home waters		
		Total	Taken by fishing boats	Return to Cultus Lake
1,000	900	**100**	75	25

The apparent return from the home waters to the Cultus Lake seems fairly good evidence for the Parent Stream Theory. There is a return to the parent stream, there may be some infiltration, and although there were no authentic recoveries or marked fish straying, it is unreasoanble to assume that this does not occur. As will be seen, other experiments with pink salmon show that straying does in fact take place. The Cultus Lake experiments also raise the problem of the fish that are apparently lost outside the home waters. This apparent loss, however, is no discredit to the Parent Stream Theory and will be further considered when dealing with the return of fish from the sea to their home waters.

MCCLINTON CREEK EXPERIMENTS

McClinton Creek runs into Masset Inlet, on Graham Island, the most northerly of the Queen Charlotte group (Fig. 10). There are good runs of pink salmon (*O. gorbuscha*) to McClinton Creek in the even years, the odd years being barren. The cause of this phenomenon is not yet understood.

Pink salmon migrate seawards as fry (35 to 40 mm long) in their first year and those that return to fresh water do so in the autumn of their second. Pritchard (1938) has suggested, as a possible explanation of the barren or 'off' years, that a severe freshet one autumn might have washed all the eggs out of the gravel beds, leaving a permanent blank every other year as there would be no spawning stock left.

In 1930 McClinton Creek was selected as a permanent centre for a study of the life history of the pink salmon. Screens and fences (Pritchard, 1944*a*) were set up so that counts could be made of the

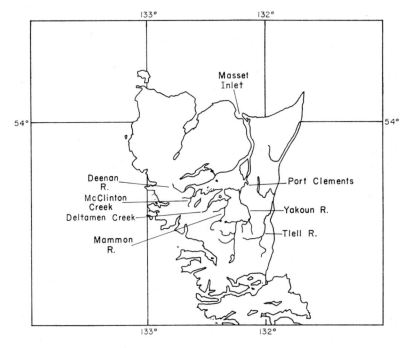

Fig. 10. Graham Island, the most northerly of the Queen Charlotte group, Pacific north-west. Place names of interest in connexion with Pritchard's (1948*a*) experiments with pink salmon in McClinton Creek. (Outline from an Admiralty chart.)

downstream migrants and adults returning to the creek to spawn. As with the Cultus Lake experiments, fin clipping the downstream migrants was expected to throw some light on the problem of homing to the parent stream.

In 1931, 1933, and 1935 (Pritchard, 1939) a proportion of the downstream migrants were marked by fin clipping, returns being expected in 1932, 1934, and 1935. To illustrate this the life history of the 1931 migrants may be considered:

1930   Autumn spawning run
1931   Spring migration of the fry to the sea
1931   Barren year; no autumn run
1932   Barren; no spring migration, river empty
1932   Autumn spawning run of the 1931 downstream migrants

One point worth noting is that there are no young salmon in McClinton Creek before the start of the spawning runs in the even years.

The results of the marking experiments were as follows:

Year	Downstream migrants		Adults returning next year to McClinton Creek			
			Unmarked		Marked	
	No. unmarked	No. marked	No.	% migrants	No.	% Migrants
1931	5,200,000	185,557	15,504	0·30	96	0·05
1933	2,150,000	107,949	152,255	7·08	2,941	2·72
1935	12,500,000	85,634	52,277	0·42	35	0·04

As with the Cultus Lake experiments, it was found that the proportion of unmarked fish entering McClinton Creek was greater than that of the marked fish. Collection facilities were poor for returns in 1932 and 1936, and it is the 1934 returns of the 1933 migrants that are claimed to show that the majority of fish return to spawn in the stream in which they were hatched. In 1934, 2,941 marked fish were taken in McClinton Creek, a further 324 in the Masset Inlet fishery and 11 others elsewhere. Of these 11, 7 were taken late in the season and so far away from McClinton Creek as to make it unlikely that they would have returned there to spawn. Of the recoveries, it will be seen that 90% were taken in the parent stream, McClinton Creek. But the total return to the creek in 1934 amounted to only about 7% of the migrants that left it in 1933, leaving, as in Cultus Lake, over 90% of the migrants unaccounted for.

In a later paper, Pritchard (1948*b*) examines more closely the discrepancy in the proportional returns of unmarked and marked fish. Here again the problem is much the same as Foerster came up against at Cultus Lake. Pritchard (1939) found no evidence of increased mortality among marked fry held for one to three months as compared with controls. As to wandering, that is, the infiltration of McClinton Creek by unmarked fish, or the straying of marked McClinton spawners to other creeks, attempts were made to estimate the extent to which this occurred. These results are extremely important for their bearing on the Parent Stream Theory. Marking was continued and in 1940 a search was made for marked pink salmon in four major rivers close to McClinton Creek.

Counts at McClinton Creek showed a return of 781 marked fish among a total run of 35,521, a ratio of 50 marked fish in every 2,274 spawners. On this basis, an estimate was made of the number of marked fish likely to be recovered from the samples taken in the other rivers if the returns were in the same ratio as those found in McClinton Creek. The results were as follows:

River	No. of pinks examined	No. of marked pinks found	Marked pink salmon	
			Most likely no. on McClinton ratio	Lowest no. expected on McClinton ratio
Yakoun	1,847	0	41	26
Mammon	3,400	1	75	55
Deltamen	400	1	9	3
Deenan	275	0	6	2
Total	**5,922**	**2**	**131**	**86**

On the basis of the McClinton Creek ratio, the best estimate of the recovery of marked pinks in the samples from the other four rivers is 131 and it is most unlikely that less than 86 would have been found. Comparison of these estimates with the 2 actually found, leaves little doubt that most of the marked pinks were returning to the parent stream.

Further confirmation of this is that the proportion of marked fish taken in different areas in Masset Inlet increases with the approach to McClinton Creek. The 1940 returns for instance were as follows:

Area of returns	Marked fish per 1,000
Port Clements and SE. Masset Inlet	0·8
McClinton Bay	15·3
McClinton Creek	22·0

It is clear that the proportion of marked fish becomes greater as one approaches the parent stream.

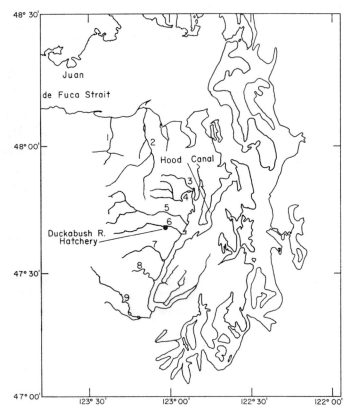

Fig. 11. Davidson's (1934) pink salmon marking experiments at Duckabush River Hatchery, Hood Canal, Washington State.

KEY

1 Morse Creek; 2 Dungeness R.; 3 Little Quilcene R.; 4 Big Quilcene R.; 5 Dosewallips R.; 6 Duckabush R.; 7 Hamma Hamma R.; 8 Lilliwaup Creek; 9 Skokomish R. Pink salmon spawn in the Hamma Hamma, Duckabush Dosewallips and Dungeness Rivers and in Morse Creek. (Outline from an Admiralty chart.)

Some marked McClinton Creek fish were taken in fisheries outside Masset Inlet. Many of these might have returned to the parent stream had they not been caught. But the fact that a certain amount of straying of McClinton Creek fish to other streams does occur, and that it is reasonable to suppose that infiltration of other fish takes place to McClinton Creek, is not inconsistent with the conclusion that these experiments and observations provide very good evidence that the majority of marked McClinton Creek fish that came into Masset Inlet did return to the parent stream to spawn. But it must be pointed out that this conclusion is a little different from Pritchard's which states (Pritchard 1948*b*, p. 128) that it is 'beyond reasonable question that the great majority of pink salmon do in fact return to the parent stream'. On the contrary, both the Cultus Lake and McClinton Creek experiments show that the great majority of salmon do not, in point of fact, return at all. What they do show is that it seems very probable that of those adults that do return to home waters, a striking and significant proportion get back to the parent stream.

DUCKABUSH RIVER AND SNAKE CREEK EXPERIMENTS

Davidson (1934) marked pink salmon (*O. gorbuscha*) in two widely separated areas. The first was at the Duckabush River hatchery, State of Washington, to the south of the Juan de Fuca Strait, the second at Snake Creek, Olive Cove, Alaska. The location of these areas is shown in Figs. 11 and 12. While the experiments were neither as extensive nor as conclusive as those carried out at Cultus Lake and McClinton Creek, they are of interest in connexion with straying. There are streams with natural runs of pink salmon close to the Duckabush, whereas Snake Creek is more or less isolated. Davidson found evidence of straying of Duckabush spawners to the nearby streams

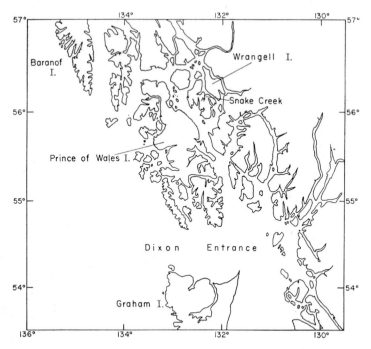

Fig. 12. Snake Creek, Olive Cove, Alaska, where Davidson (1934) carried out marking experiments with pink salmon. (Outline from an Admiralty chart.)

(in 1931 there were 8 returns of marked pinks to Duckabush, 1 to Hamma Hamma and 1 to Dosewallips) but this was not observed at Snake Creek, where the nearest run taking place at the same time was at a stream 20 miles away. The results suggest that straying may take place more readily among salmon from nearby streams than between those which are more separated. As in the Cultus Lake and McClinton Creek experiments, Davidson found a return of adults, marked as downstream migrants, to the parent stream, but the results need not be considered in detail.

MARKING EXPERIMENTS WITH STEELHEAD TROUT

Taft and Shapovalov (1938) carried out two series of marking experiments with steelhead trout, *Salmo gairdneri*, in Californian rivers.

(i) The first series was carried out in Scott and Waddell Creeks, Santa Cruz County, California (Fig. 13). The distance between the mouths of these small creeks is about 5 miles. The details of these experiments are summarized in Table 5. The number of fish marked by fin clipping each year is given by Shapovalov (1937). The results show a clear return to the parent stream but there is a small amount of straying between the two creeks.

Table 5. Marking experiments with steelhead trout carried out at Scott and Waddell Creeks. (Data from Taft and Shapovalov, 1938, and Shapovalov, 1937.)

Stream	Season marked	Number marked	Returns to Waddell Creek				Returns to Scott Creek			
			1933/34	1934/35	1935/36	1936/37	1933/34	1934/35	1935/36	1936/37
Waddell Creek	1931	924	3	3	—	—	0	0	—	—
	1933/34	2,452	—	66	63	15	—	1	1	0
	1934/35	1,013	—	—	17	39	—	—	0	0
	1935/36	3,118	—	—	—	27	—	—	—	3
Scott Creek	1932/33	9,826	0	0	0	—	9	39	4	—
	1933/34	10,504	—	0	1	0	—	38	79	10
	1934/35	5,608	—	—	1	5	—	—	197	177

(ii) The second series of experiments was carried out in the headwaters of the Klamath River, California (Fig. 13). Marked steelheads were liberated in Fall and Beaver Creeks and the returns to the parent and nearby creeks recorded. Not all steelheads descend to the sea but those that do can be picked out by the details of their scale markings. The returns of the marked steelheads that did run to the sea are given in Table 6. As in the first series of experiments, the results show a good return to the parent stream and give evidence of a certain amount of straying.

Table 6. Klamath River experiment: returns of marked sea-run steelhead trout. (Data from Shapovalov, 1937.)

Stream of liberation	Season marked	Number marked	Returns in 1936–37			
			Beaver Creek	Fall Creek	Cottonwood Creek	Bogus Creek
Beaver Creek	1934	23,280	70	1	1	1
Fall Creek	1934	12,650	0	45	0	0

THE RETURN OF ATLANTIC SALMON KELTS

Some Atlantic salmon spawn more than once. While the proportion of previous spawners in a run is generally low, say 5 to 10%, Went (1947) argues that as a proportion of the calculated escapement, that is, those salmon that are allowed to spawn, 10 to 20% of the fish return to spawn a second time. But the returns of tagged kelts are low, Went (1964) giving a figure of 794 recoveries from over 33,682 kelts tagged in Ireland (2·4%): tagging mortality appears to have been high. The

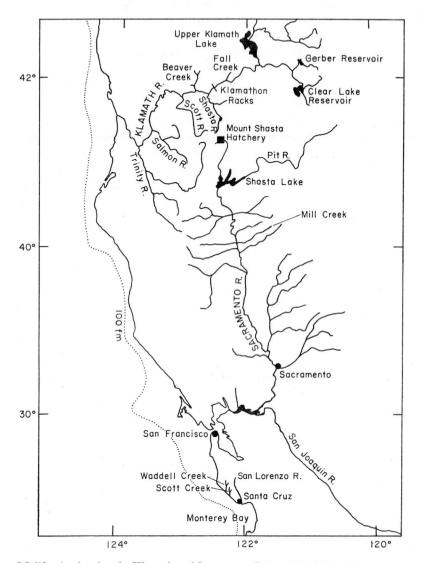

Fig. 13. Part of California, showing the Klamath and Sacramento Rivers, Waddell and Scott Creeks. (Place names from Snyder, 1931, and Taft and Shapovalov, 1938.)

kelts were tagged in the rivers and their estuaries. Of those that were recaptured in freshwater, a very high proportion (718 out of 724 fish, 99%) are said to have been taken in the same river (or corresponding estuary) as that in which they were tagged.

The return of migrants hatched from transplanted eggs

Eggs have been moved from one stream to another for hatching and rearing of the young. Marking experiments have shown that migrants raised from transplanted eggs do not return to the original parent stream from which the eggs were taken. There is evidence to show that adults derived from transplanted eggs will return to the adopted stream. On the other hand there are cases where transplantation experiments have failed. Details of some of the more striking cases of success and failure in transplantation experiments are as follows:

FAILURES

(a) McClinton Creek, Queen Charlotte Islands

Pink salmon only return to spawn in McClinton Creek, Masset Inlet, in the even-numbered years. Pritchard (1938) tried to establish runs during the odd-numbered years with eggs taken from the Tlell River, some 30 miles distant (Fig. 10). Transplantations were carried out in 1931, 1933, and 1935. Unfortunately, the 1933 transplantation was a failure as a heavy November snow-fall, followed by rain in the New Year, caused unprecedented freshets in the creek and washed most of the eggs out. From the planting of 540,000 eyed eggs in October 1933, only five fry were taken at the counting fence the following spring. The 1931 and 1935 plantings gave the following returns:

Year of planting	Downstream migrants in the following spring	Returns of adults Tlell R.	McClinton Creek
1931	Unmarked, 753,646	—	1
	Marked, 124,002	0	0
1935	Unmarked, 397,657	—	2
	Marked, 108,200	0	4

In 1933, 40 returns were made of pink salmon, bearing apparently legitimate McClinton Creek 1931 fin-clipping scars, from the commercial fishery in the vicinity of the Fraser River, some 300 miles to the south. No such returns were made from the 1935 experiments.

(b) Eagle River (Fraser River, No. 25 in Fig. 9), British Columbia

Foerster (1946) has summarized the unsuccessful attempts to restock the depleted sockeye salmon run to Eagle River, on the Upper Fraser. Plants were made of eggs taken from Cultus Lake, which is on the Lower Fraser, and Adams River (below Adams Lake), on the Upper Fraser (Fig. 9, Fraser River Nos. 18 and 22). These experiments, made from 1929–1933, may be summarized as follows:

Origin of eggs	No. of fingerlings marked and released in Eagle R.	Recoveries Fishing areas	Cultus Lake	Adams R.	Eagle R.
Cultus Lake	417,301	12	—	—	—
Adams River	559,391	147	—	—	10

Foerster rightly draws attention to the fact that very few fish released in the Eagle River were taken in the commercial fishery as compared with the returns from his earlier experiments at

Cultus Lake. The Eagle River recaptures ranged from only 0·01% to 0·04% of the marked fingerlings whereas the returns were 1·9% and 2·6% for Cultus Lake. It seems likely that the marked Eagle River fingerlings could have:

(i) suffered heavy mortality,
(ii) wandered to other rivers along the coast on their return to freshwater,
(iii) remained in Lake Shuswap into which the Eagle River flows.

Whatever the explanation, it is evident that these transplantation experiments failed.

SUCCESSES

(a) Rich and Holmes' Columbia River transplantations

Rich and Holmes (1929) were about the first to carry out extensive transplantations from one stream to another. The area in which their experiments were made is shown in Fig. 9. In their two most successful experiments (Nos. 6 and 7), chinook salmon eggs were taken from the Willamette, McKenzie and Santian Rivers and hatched and reared at Herman Creek on the main branch of the Columbia River. From these eggs 85,000 marked migrants were released. Subsequently 51 adults were recovered. Only 4 of these reached the adopted stream. None were taken in the parent streams from which the eggs were taken. An interesting point about these experiments is that the chinook salmon runs to the Willamette, McKenzie, and Santian Rivers take place in the spring, adults being caught early in May and June. On the other hand, the branch of the Columbia to which the eggs of the spring runs were transplanted is characterized by autumn fish: they do not appear till late July, August, and September. The dates on which Rich and Holmes' returns were taken show that the adults derived from the transplanted eggs returned in the spring and not in the autumn. The transplants did not take up the habits of the salmon characteristic of the adopted stream.

(b) Transplantation experiments between the Klamath and Sacramento rivers

Snyder (1931) has brought together the results of several years work on the chinook salmon in the Klamath and Sacramento rivers, California (Fig. 13). In the course of this work marking and transplantation experiments were carried out to determine the ocean range of the chinook and to test the Parent Stream Theory. Two transplantation experiments were carried out:

Year	1919	1922
Source of eggs	Mill Creek, Sacramento R.	Klamathon Racks, Klamath R.
Yearlings transplanted to	Fall Creek, Klamath R.	Mt. Shasta hatchery, Sacramento R.
No. of marked migrants	25,000	15,000
Returns		
Klamath R.	50	0
Sacramento R.	0	0
At sea	10	4

The 1919 experiment had some measure of success; that of 1922 must be considered to have failed.

(c) The Apple River experiments

Apple River is a small stream in Cumberland County, Nova Scotia (Fig. 14). It empties into Chignecto Bay, in the Bay of Fundy. The river is partly tidal and has East and West Branches.

3

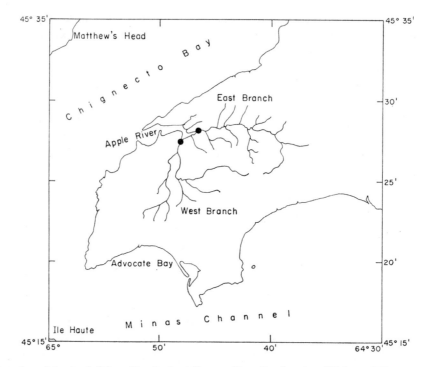

Fig. 14. Branches of the Apple River, Cumberland County, Nova Scotia, where White and Huntsman carried out transplantation experiments with salmon. Solid circles indicate the position of traps. (After White, 1936. Outline from a Canadian Department of Mines and Technical Survey chart.)

Both branches used to have runs of Atlantic salmon but in the 1870s a dam was built across the head of the tide on the East Branch and the run of salmon to that branch stopped. The dam was taken out in the 1920s but up till 1931 there had been no return of the natural runs to the East Branch. The Apple River salmon are autumn running or late fish. The young salmon spend two years in the river before migrating to the sea in the spring of their third year. In the autumn of the following year the majority return to spawn, as grilse, in their fourth year. In July 1932, 25,000 fry, believed to be Restigouche salmon, were planted in the East Apple River. The Restigouche empties into Chaleur Bay and so into the Gulf of St. Lawrence. Restigouche salmon are typically early running and spend three years in the river and a further two or three years at sea before returning to spawn. The results of this transplantation experiment are given by White (1936) and White and Huntsman (1938). There are three points to note.

(i) The returns. From the 25,000 fry planted in the East Branch in 1932 there were 3,252 migrants to the sea in 1934. These were marked by fin clipping. The 1935 and 1936 returns of marked fish were distributed among the two branches of the Apple River as follows:

	1935 Grilse	Virgins	1936 2nd spawners
West Branch	6	1	1
East Branch	92	4	19

There appears to have been a good return to the adopted stream with little straying to the nearby West Branch.

(ii) The Restigouche fry behave as Apple River fish, spending only two years in the river and the majority of those that returned did so as grilse after only one year at sea. This result may be contrasted with those obtained by Rich and Holmes (1929), experiments 6 and 7, who found that Willamette-McKenzie River fish transplanted to Herman Creek retained the behaviour characteristic of the parent stream and did not follow that of the adopted stream.

(iii) Although there had been no natural runs to the East Apple river in the 10 years previous to the transplantations carried out in July 1932, adult salmon entered and spawned in that branch in the autumns of 1932, 1933, and 1934. White (1934) has interpreted this as a consequence of the introduction of young salmon to the stream.

(d) *Attempts to transplant Pacific salmon to foreign waters*

Davidson and Hutchinson (1938) have reviewed the attempts made between 1872 and 1930 to introduce Pacific salmon to foreign waters. Transplantations have been made to the Eastern United States, Eastern Canada, England, Ireland, France, Holland, Germany, Italy, and Finland; Chile, Argentina, Australia, Tasmania, New Zealand, and Hawaii. On the North American continent transplantations were successful in establishing natural runs only in the States of Maine and provinces of New Brunswick and Ontario. The only other transplantations which have led to the development of natural sea-going populations were those made to Chile and to the south island of New Zealand. In New Zealand transplantations of chinooks (*O. tshawytscha*) were successful after efforts were concentrated in one river system, the Waitaki. From this river chinooks have spread to other rivers of the South Island.

The varying successes of these transplantation experiments seem to have depended very largely on the environmental conditions, particularly temperature and salinity, that the salmon met in their new surroundings. Natural sea-going runs have only been developed where the temperature and salinities lie within the range experienced by the Pacific salmon in their native waters. The most recent transplantations are those begun in the Soviet Union in 1956. Millions of pink and chum salmon eggs have been transplanted to the Kola peninsula and the young released as fry (1957–58) or fingerlings (1959). The 1960 return of 70,000 pink salmon from the 1959 release (Isaev, 1961) suggests that these transplantations may be successful in building up self-propagating stocks. In the meantime steps are being taken to secure international agreement for their protection until the numbers are sufficient to stand exploitation.

The existence of local stocks

It is well established that there are differences between the salmon of one river and those of another. Indeed, there are differences between the runs to lakes or streams within one river system. These differences may, for example, be in the size of the spawning fish; in the size of the mature eggs; in the number of vertebrae or fin rays; in the number of pyloric caecae and in the details of the scale markings. There are other differences and for a further account and guide to the literature, Rich (1939) and Scheer (1939) may be referred to for *Oncorhynchus*, and Dahl (1939), Menzies (1939*a*), and Pyefinch (1955) for *Salmo*. The main point of interest here is to decide to what extent these differences may be regarded as evidence for the Parent Stream Theory. Rich (1937*b*) argues that such differences could not be maintained unless the fish returned to their parent stream to spawn, and he concludes that each river system and tributary has its own local race or stock. However, Huntsman (1939) rightly points out that while consistent differences between the adults spawning in various streams show that there is some order in the return, they do not necessarily imply a return to the parent stream. For instance, the salmon returning to a particular stream might consist of more or less constant proportions of individuals born in several different streams. So differences between the adult runs themselves cannot be held as evidence in support of the Parent Stream Theory. Scheer (1939) apparently failed to appreciate this. In his review there are some tables showing differences between the salmon running to the different Canadian river systems which are presented in such a way as to suggest they are evidence for the Parent Stream Theory. While they are not inconsistent with it, they are certainly not positive evidence for it.

However, the problem is in theory, at least, a very simple one. It may be possible to show that there are differences between the downstream migrants, the smolts, from various streams. If the survivors do later return to freshwater to spawn in the parent stream, the same differences should be apparent in the adults on their spawning grounds. Unfortunately, in spite of all the work that had been done on local races, or stocks, of both the Pacific and the Atlantic salmon, complete and rigorous proof along these lines does not seem to have been obtained. There is, however, a little evidence that does go some way towards it and this may be looked at in detail.

LOCAL RACES OF THE SOCKEYE SALMON IN THE FRASER RIVER

The best work has been done on the Fraser River sockeye. This was started by Gilbert (1914) who summarized his research in a series of ten annual reports on the life-history of the sockeye. Later Gilbert gave this work up to investigate the Alaska salmon fisheries but the series was continued and is still running today. Gilbert made a particular study of scales and his earlier work is recognized as being fundamental to the successful management of the Fraser River sockeye salmon. His pioneer work has now been established on a firmer basis (Clutter and Whitesel, 1956; Henry, 1961).

Scales appear on sockeye salmon during their first spring when they are 30 to 40 mm long, and the inner nuclear area of the scale corresponds to their life and growth in freshwater. It is the nuclear area of the scale which is of interest in racial studies. Gilbert (1916) argued that the range of temperature, food, and general conditions for growth on the spawning beds in the Fraser River basin might be expected to show up in the detailed structure of the nuclear zone of the scales. He was able to show differences in the number of nuclear circuli in the scales of yearling migrants from different tributaries and in the nuclear area of scales of adult fish taken on their spawning beds (Gilbert, 1918, 1919). However, he did not show that the differences between migrants were maintained among the adults of concurrent lake or stream residence on their return to spawn in freshwater.

Clutter and Whitesel (1956) give some comparisons along these lines and their results are summarized in Table 7. Of the 9 samples, it will be seen that in 7 instances the number of nuclear rings is greater in the returning 4_2 fish than in the smolts taken as downstream migrants. In 6 of these cases the differences are said to be significant. Henry (1961, p. 14), who has carried on this scale work, suggests that the difference is due to a higher marine mortality among the smaller downstream migrants with the lower nuclear circuli counts. Henry's own work with scales shows that nuclear circuli counts can be used to identify local stocks of the Fraser River sockeye; this is of great practical value in relation to management and conservation.

Table 7. A comparison between the mean number of nuclear circuli in the scales of one-year smolts and returning 4_2 adults of concurrent lake residence. (From Clutter and Whitesel, 1956.)

Lake	Year of Lake residence	Smolts		4_2 Adults		Difference between adult circuli count and smolt circuli count
		No. in sample	Mean No. circuli	No. in sample	Mean No. circuli	
Chilko	1949	1,239	10·6	310	11·8	+1·2
	1950	117	11·5	187	12·5	+1·0
	1951	159	13·3	762	14·0	+0·7
	1952	144	12·5	184	13·3	+0·8
	1953	358	12·2	181	13·1	+0·9
Cultus	1951	189	12·7	216	12·6	−0·1
Francois	1950	116	19·3	187	19·0	−0·3
Shuswap	1952	184	14·0	164	14·2	+0·2
Stuart	1950	190	16·8	100	18·0	+1·2

Summary of the evidence for a return to the parent or home stream

The main points from the evidence that has been considered can be summarized quite briefly as follows:

(a) Experiments involving the marking of downstream migrants of Pacific salmon have shown that of those fish that are recovered a high proportion make their way back to the parent stream. There is evidence of infiltration and of straying.

(b) Tagging experiments with the kelts of the Atlantic salmon shows that the majority of the fish which return a second time to freshwater are recaptured in the river, or its estuary, into which they were released.

(c) Adults which are reared from transplanted eggs return to the stream in which they grew up and not to the stream in which the eggs were laid. While some transplantation experiments have failed, others have succeeded and these successful experiments are good evidence in support of the Parent Stream Theory.

(d) There is a good deal of evidence, particularly from the point of view of management and conservation work, that local populations of salmon exist and it has been supposed that they are maintained by the return of the fish to the parent stream.

(e) There seems to be little doubt that the body of evidence leads to the conclusion that those salmon which survive their stay in the sea and return to freshwater try to get back to the stream in which they grew up. The Cultus Lake experiments stand out as the most convincing set of data. There can be no question at all that there is a case to answer: how do the spawning migrants recognize their parent stream?

THE RETURN OF SALMON FROM DISTANT PLACES IN THE SEA

There have been differences of opinion as to whether salmon move far away from the zone of influence of the river by which they reached the sea. The matter was raised by Huntsman (1937a) who wrote that 'On inquiry and examination of the literature I have failed to find a clear case of a salmon returning to its natal river from a distant place in the sea, that is, away from the neighbour-hood of the river mouth. Admittedly this is a difficult thing to prove, since we must be sure of three things for the individual fish: (1) which is its natal river? (2) where it has been in the sea, and (3) that it is again in its river. Perhaps some one may be able to produce such evidence.' No doubt Huntsman had his tongue in his cheek when he wrote this. Neither in the ensuing controversy (Rich, 1937*a*; Huntsman, 1937*b*; Rich, 1937*b*; Calderwood, 1937; Huntsman, 1938; Dahl, 1939; Huntsman, 1939) nor, in the papers and discussion presented at the Ottawa symposium (Moulton, 1939), was a clear case brought forward.

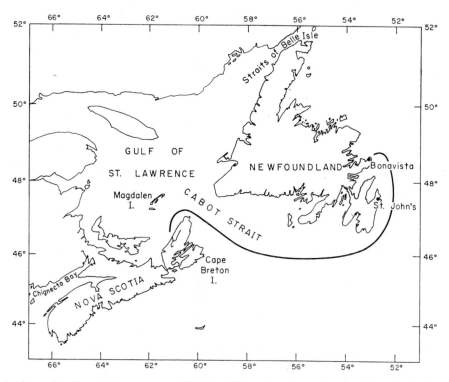

Fig. 15. A salmon, fin-clipped in the north-east Margaree River, Cape Breton, was caught and tagged at Bonavista and subsequently recovered in the north-east Margaree. The travels of this fish are indicated by the line linking the clipping and tagging areas. (Outline from an Admiralty chart.)

Ironically enough, it was Huntsman (1942) himself who was the first to report the return of a marked salmon from a distant place. In 1938 a number of Atlantic salmon smolts were marked by fin clipping during their descent of the north-east Margaree River, Cape Breton. In June 1940 one of these fish was caught, tagged and released 550 miles away at Bonavista, on the east coast of Newfoundland. In September of the same year the fish was caught again, this time back in the north-east Margaree River where it was originally marked as a smolt. The travels of this particular fish are shown in Fig. 15.

Pritchard (1944*b*) has reported two more cases. In the spring of 1942 pink salmon, *O. gorbuscha*, were marked as fry during their seaward migration from Morrison Creek, Puntledge River, on the east coast of Vancouver Island. In August 1943, two of the marked pinks were caught and tagged, one 45 miles to the north of Morrison Creek, the other 115 miles to the south as shown in Fig. 16. In October 1943, the two salmon, marked and tagged, reached the counting weir of the home stream. So there are three cases, each of which fulfils Huntsman's requirements, for there can be no doubt at all that these fish did, as adults, move far away from any possible influence of the parent river, to which they did, nevertheless, return.

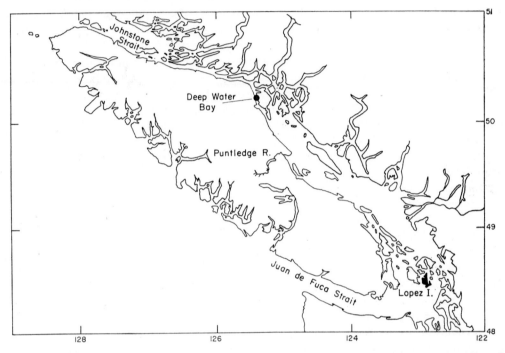

Fig. 16. Two pink salmon originally marked in the Puntledge River were caught and tagged at Deep Water Bay and near Lopez Island, and subsequently recovered in the home stream. (Outline from an Admiralty chart.)

Atlantic salmon

It is by no means clear how far one can generalize on the strength of these three returns. Salmon living in the rivers that empty into the Baltic Sea appear to migrate to a feeding area in its southern part and later return to the rivers to spawn (Alm, 1934, 1958). But nobody really knows where the rest of the European stocks of salmon go when they reach the sea. It is true that salmon and sea trout are sometimes taken at sea by trawls, seine or drift nets, by lines, or are found in the stomach contents of sharks. Balmain and Shearer (1956) have summarized the records available from 1888–1954, which concern 78 salmon and 160 sea trout. Most of these were returned from the North Sea.

Tagging experiments have shown that salmon may cross from Norway to Scotland or from Scotland to Norway (Dahl, 1937). These returns are of great interest on their own account but they do not, of course, give any information as to where the bulk of the salmon go when they have reached the sea. Menzies (1939b, p. 24) concludes that the results of the tagging experiments as a whole are not inconsistent with the hypothesis that all the European salmon have a feeding ground 'at some indeterminate distance to the west of Norway and Great Britain from which an easterly migration takes the fish to the coasts after their feeding period is finished'. This may well turn out to be true. Marty (1959) records that young salmon have been caught by herring drifters in the eastern part of the Norwegian Sea. Large salmon have been caught in the Celtic Sea (50°N., 8° 30′W.) in mackerel nets (Layrle, 1951). J. W. Jones (1959, p. 60) has suggested that the salmon that return as grilse have feeding grounds comparatively near the coast, while those that return after 2, 3, or 4 years' absence go to more distant grounds. The problem can only be resolved by fishing in the North Atlantic and the feeding grounds probably lie within the area bounded by the 50°–65°N. parallels and 15°–49°W.

On Canada's Atlantic seaboard salmon have been taken a hundred miles or more from the point at which they were tagged (Huntsman, 1939). One salmon from the Annapolis River, Nova Scotia, turned up two years later in Ramah, northern Labrador, 1,900 miles away (Huntsman, 1948). Huntsman (1939, 1950, 1952) is of the opinion that these movements are of a passive nature, the fish being more or less carried where the water currents take them and that, in general, salmon do not go far from the zone of influence of their rivers. For the Canadian Atlantic seaboard at least, there may be something to be said for his view (Huntsman, 1938) that the soundest thing to do is to believe the salmon to be principally where they are caught, rather than in the open ocean where only an occasional one has been found.

But recently there have been several reports of Canadian and European tagged salmon being recaptured on the West Greenland banks.[1] Saunders, Kerswill, and Elson (1965) summarize the data. The Greenland salmon fishery has increased from 55 metric tons in 1960 to over 1,100 metric tons in 1964 and few of these fish are thought to be of local origin. The 1964 catch is only a little less than the average taken in English, Welsh, and Scottish waters. The Greenland tag returns lend support to Menzies' original suggestion of a Western Atlantic feeding ground, and it is probable that salmon originating from both European and Canadian waters feed together in this area. But the Greenlanders may only be exploiting that fringe of the ocean-dwelling population which extends on to the West Greenland banks. From the point of view of management and conservation it is important to know if this is the case, and what proportion, if any, of the West Greenland fish return to spawn in Canadian and European waters.

Pacific salmon

Pacific salmon have been recovered in rivers hundreds of miles away from the sea area in which they were tagged. While this does not prove that they are returning to the parent stream (which is unknown unless the fish were marked as migrating smolts or can be identified in some other way), it does show that there are long-distance movements of fish in the sea. The results of some of the earlier experiments are summarized by Clemens, Foerster, and Pritchard (1939), while more recent ones are described by Milne (1957). The results of one of Milne's 1957 tagging experiments with coho salmon are shown in Fig. 17. The coho were maturing fish caught and tagged in the summer of 1951 and those recovered were taken in the commercial fishery the same autumn. It seems as if the fish were returning to freshwater to spawn and that they would have entered rivers which were, in many cases, a considerable distance from the tagging area. The general circumstan-

---

[1] It is of interest to note that there are earlier reports of salmon at West Greenland. Scudder (1883, p. 192) refers to good prospects for seine-net fishing and French trawlers had good catches in the area in 1930 (Beaugé, 1931). There was an increase in the abundance of salmon at West Greenland during the thirties (Jensen, 1939, p. 17).

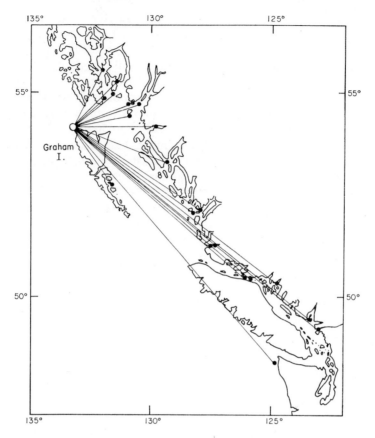

Fig. 17. Maturing coho salmon were caught, tagged and released at a position off Graham Island in the summer of 1951 and some of these salmon were recaptured in the commercial fisheries in the autumn. (From Milne, 1957. Outline from an Admiralty chart.)

tial evidence leads to the conclusion that the young smolts had previously moved the opposite way, well away from the influence of the parent stream, to which survivors nevertheless returned as mature adults to spawn.

Pacific salmon on the high seas

Milne's tagging experiments were carried out with fish taken in coastal waters within 50 miles or so of the shore and in water no deeper than 100 fathoms. One question of great interest is whether the salmon ever leave the coastal waters and go right out into the Pacific Ocean. Fortunately, quite a lot is known about the distribution of salmon out in the Pacific. This is because the Japanese have had, for many years, a high seas drift net fishery for salmon in the Pacific.

The Japanese fishery started in 1932. It is a mother-ship fishery, each with an attendant fleet of catcher boats which return to the mother-ship daily to hand over their catch for salting and canning Most of the Japanese canned salmon was exported and about 87% of the total catch went to Great Britain. Some details of the Japanese salmon industry are given by Anon (1955*b*) and Broadbent

(1947). At its peak the fishery extended over a wide area of the North Pacific and plans were made
to extend it to Bristol Bay, Alaska. These were abandoned in 1938 in the face of strong American
protests. In 1940 Japan had 4 cannery ships, 5 mother-ships and 230 catcher boats working drift
nets in the Pacific from late May until the middle of August. All but one of the cannery and mother-
ships were sunk in the war and the fishery did not get underway again until 1952. The fishing area
covered by the fleet in 1954 is shown in Fig. 18. At the beginning of the season the fishery lies to
the east, south of the Aleutian Islands, and later on moves to the west to reach the waters off
Kamchatka. The salmon are caught at depths of about 30 to 50 m. They make diurnal vertical
migrations, swimming a little deeper by day than by night. These movements have been recorded
by echo-sounding (Hashimoto and Maniwa, 1956). The fishery is usually slack until the latter part
of June when dense shoals of salmon are said to appear. From then on the fishery moves rapidly

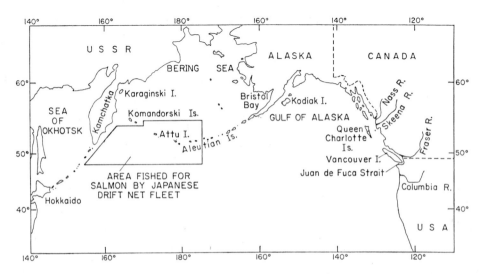

Fig. 18. Place names in the North Pacific which are of interest in connexion with salmon migration. The area
fished by the Japanese drift net fleet (from Fukuhara, 1955) is also shown. (Outline from an Admiralty chart.)

westwards, the drift nets being set from north to south when possible, and over 90% of the salmon
being taken on the east side of the net, that is, with the head facing to the west. Sockeye, chum, pink,
coho, and chinook salmon are all taken in this fishery.

Pre-war tagging experiments suggested that there might be an intermingling of Asiatic and
North American salmon in the Pacific. It is clearly a matter of great concern to the inshore fisheries
that the stocks on which they depend shall not be depleted on the high seas. In 1953, Canada,
Japan, and the United States established the International North Pacific Fisheries Commission
to look into the conservation of the fisheries of the North Pacific Ocean. As a result a great deal of
research effort is now being put into the study of the distribution and freshwater origin of the
salmon out in the Pacific. Preliminary accounts of the work have appeared in the International
North Pacific Fisheries Commissions Annual Reports. Salmon are probably distributed all over
the North Pacific and Bering Sea within a surface temperature range of 2–11°C, that is between
45°N. and 65°N. The high-seas distribution of the various stocks are not yet fully known, but
tagging experiments and a study of the parasites acquired during the period of freshwater residence

show that there are areas of overlap between fish of Asiatic and North American origin. Data relating to the off shore distribution of the North Pacific salmon stocks are appearing in the recent INPFC Bulletins.

The proportion of salmon that returns from the sea

It is clear that some of the Pacific salmon go out onto the high seas where they lead a pelagic life, most probably in the surface 50 to 60 m. What one would like to know is whether a significant proportion of these fish ever get back to the coast to find their way home to their parent streams. Hartt (1962) has reported on the American tagging experiments carried out in 1956–58, mainly in the central Aleutian area. The overall annual returns of mature tagged fish are low (sockeye, 5·3–17·1%; chum, 3·5–7·0%; pinks, 0·4–2·7%). The high returns for the sockeye occurred in 1958 when a large proportion of the fish (61%) were tagged near the Pribilof Islands, close to Bristol Bay. It could be argued that both the Pribilofs and the Aleutian chain are part of the home or local area so far as the Bristol Bay sockeye are concerned, and that Hartt's results do not give data that are relevant to the problem of the return of salmon from distance places in the sea.

A more critical and valuable experiment from the point of view of migration would be the recovery of fish tagged in the Gulf of Alaska, where the fish are well away from the coastal waters and, presumably, from any influence of the parent river. The Canadians have tagged salmon in the Gulf, (unpublished results, Biological Station, Nanaimo) but the percentage returns from inshore fishing areas and spawning streams is low (sockeye, 10%; pinks, 6·0%; coho, 5·5%; chum, 1·5%). It seems reasonable to conclude that a return of 10% of the mature fish tagged on the high seas is the best that has been obtained with present methods.

It is difficult to assess the significance of these results. The proportion of the fish that appears to reach the coast is surprisingly low. The Canadians caught their fish by longline so there is unlikely to have been a high mortality due to the method of capture. Some might have died as a result of tagging, others from natural causes (predation or disease). On the other hand, the freshwater origins of tagged fish were unknown and they may have returned to parts of the coast where the fishing intensity was low. The results are also consistent with the hypothesis that most of the tagged fish failed to reach the coast because they were literally 'lost' at sea. If this were so, the proportion of returns would be expected to increase the closer the tagging stations were to the areas where the fish were caught. There are no critical data to demonstrate this at sea such as would be provided by a series of releases in areas 8c–13c, along the line of the 50°N. parallel (see Hartt, 1962, p. 15, Fig. 4). Nevertheless, the returns from the high seas taggings are 5 to 10%; those from Milne's (1957) Queen Charlotte and Vancouver Island releases 8 to 20%; and those from fish released between the Juan de Fuca Strait and the Fraser mouth 52% (Verhoeven and Davidoff, 1962). While such comparisons are certainly not critical, or perhaps even fair, it is interesting to note that the figures do at least run the right way. The 1962 Canadian experiments have also given rather low overall returns for salmon tagged on the high seas (sockeye, 9·3%; coho, 7·6%; pinks, 6·1%). The recovery rate showed a sharp increase among fish released towards the end of the tagging period. 'A possible explanation would be that late in the season on the average maturing sockeye, pink and coho salmon were tagged closer to their spawning areas than earlier, and so experienced a higher survival after tagging.' (unpublished results, Biological Station, Nanaimo.)

The experiments carried out with downstream migrants have shown that only a small proportion return to freshwater. In the Cultus Lake experiments the returns did not exceed 10%, and they were not more than 5% in the best year at McClinton Creek. Henry (1961) has calculated the marine survival, the proportional return of the downstream migrants to freshwater, for the 4_2 sockeye in the Chilko River, one of the most important of the Fraser runs. There is a significant positive regression between survival and the first-year marine scale growth. Thus good growth in the first summer at sea, and presumably good feeding, appear to be related to a relatively high return to freshwater. McAllister (1961) has shown that zooplankton are more abundant in the British Columbian coastal waters than at the mid-gulf Ocean Weather Station 'P'. Henry's relation between marine survival and marine growth appears to be consistent with the following hypothesis. Fish with a good first year's growth remain within the coastal waters during the first summer and their centre of distribution during the period of marine residence lies nearer to the coast than that of those fish with poor growth whose centre of distribution lies in the off-shore and mid-gulf areas. If this were true, marine survival might be related to the distance between the feeding grounds and the spawning grounds.

But there may be other factors affecting marine survival. In the Cultus Lake experiments 900 out of every 1,000 downstream migrants were unaccounted for after two years in the sea. If the apparent mortality rate was constant during these two years, it seems that 70 to 80% of the salmon die each year. But there may be a very high mortality among the smolts during the first few months of their life in the sea, when predation might be an important factor. At the moment there are no data available from which it is possible to decide the cause of the low marine survival, which could be due to a high mortality, or a large proportion of the mature fish being unable to find their way back to the coastal waters, or a combination of the two.

Chapter 5

The Eel

INTRODUCTION

The term 'freshwater eel' is itself something of a misnomer as Schmidt (1925, p. 312) has pointed out. The various species of *Anguilla* are undoubtedly oceanic fish which leave the sea to pass their period of growth in freshwater and return to the sea to spawn. The details of the life histories are not known for every species but they probably conform to the same general plan. Freshwater eels spawn in warm saline water at depths of 400 to 700 m, but over very deep water. The eggs are pelagic and develop into leaf-like leptocephali larvae, which are carried by the ocean currents towards the coast. The length of the larval life varies from species to species and this is one of the most remarkable features of their life histories and plays an important part in the distribution of the fully grown eels. The leptocephali metamorphose into elvers which swim up the estuaries and rivers and so into freshwater where the eels grow. When the adults mature, several years later, they leave freshwater and run down to the sea. They are believed to return to their parent spawning area, to spawn once and die.

Fourteen of the sixteen species of freshwater eels are found in the Indo-Pacific region and their distribution suggests a tropical origin of the genus. There are no freshwater eels on the Pacific coast of North and South America, and south of the equator they are absent on the east coast of South America and the west coast of Africa. Freshwater eels are found in countries bordering both sides of the North Atlantic. Schmidt (1906, 1913) was the first to show clearly that they could be assigned to one or other of two groups by counting the number of vertebrae. Samples of freshwater eels taken in the western part of the Atlantic (south-west Greenland, Labrador, Canada, the United States, Panama, West Indies, the Guianas, and Bermuda) have a mean vertebral count of 107, while those from the eastern part (Murman coast to North Africa, Iceland, the Azores, Madeira, and the Canary Islands, the Baltic and Mediterranean countries, the Black Sea, Sea of Azov, Red Sea, and occasional specimens from East Africa) have a mean vertebral count of 114. Two species of Atlantic eels are recognized on the basis of the differing vertebral counts, the Americal eel, *A. rostrata*, to the west, and the European eel, *A. anguilla*, to the east. Ege (1939) gives the following figures for the two species:

Species	Number examined	Range	Mean vertebral count	Standard deviation
A. rostrata	962	103–111	107·2	±1·2
A. anguilla	2,775	110–119	114·7	±1·3

Fig. 19, based on Ege's (1939) data, shows the frequency distribution of the vertebral counts in the two species. The overlap is very slight and there should only be a few individuals in a sample

The Eel

which could not be assigned definitely to one species or the other. It is, however, important to note that difficulties do occur. Hornyhold (see Bruun, 1937, p. 26) found an elver with a vertebral count of 108 (*A. rostrata*) at San Sebastian, North Spain, Petersen (1905) an elver with a vertebral count of 113 (*A. anguilla*) at Biloxi, Mississippi. Are these individuals to be regarded as strays, or as European and American eels with exceptionally low and high vertebral counts respectively ? The vertebral count is the only anatomical character that can conveniently be used to separate the two species, although there are a number of other numerical and morphometric differences between them (Bruun, 1963, p. 140, Table 1).

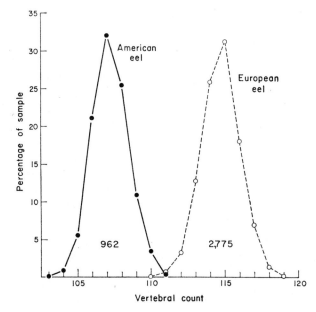

Fig. 19. The vertebral count distributions of eels caught in America and Europe. The percentages have been calculated from the data given by Ege (1939).

The American eel does not have the same economic importance as the European eel. In 1965 the catch of the American eel only amounted to about 1,000 metric tons, while that of the European eel was about 17,000 metric tons. Details relating to the European catch are given in Table 8.

Denmark has always had a great economic interest in eels and it is fitting that Danish biologists, under the leadership of Johannes Schmidt, should have found out most of what is known about their biology. Schmidt came to study eels as part of his duties as biologist to the Danish Commission for the Investigation of the Sea. Grassi's hypothesis that eels bred near the coasts in deep water won general acceptance in the early 1900s. Schmidt began to have some doubts as to the truth of Grassi's account when, in 1904, he captured an eel larva at the surface between Iceland and Faroes. In 1905 and 1906 larvae were taken all over the surface waters of the Atlantic between the Hebrides and Spain. The research vessel 'Thor' was too small to work in the open waters of the Atlantic so the cruises were continued in the Mediterranean from 1908–10. The similarity of the adult eels taken from different parts of Europe, the absence of very early larvae in European waters, and the fact that small larvae were found in the western and not the eastern part of the Mediterranean, led

Schmidt to the conclusion that the European stock was derived from a common breeding ground in the west. Hjort's (1910*a*) capture of much smaller larvae on 'Michael Sars' in the Central Atlantic led him to suggest that the spawning ground lay between the Azores and the Bermudas.

Table 8. The catches, in thousands of metric tons, of European eels taken by various countries in 1965. (Data from FAO, 1966.)

Country	Catch
Denmark	3·2
Italy	3·0
Netherlands	2·7
France	1·7
Spain	1·7
Sweden	1·7
Poland	0·9
N. Ireland	0·8
Norway	0·5
W. Germany	0·4
Morocco	0·3
Ireland	0·2
Total	**17·1**

This development was of considerable practical importance. If Grassi's hypothesis was correct, there were likely to be problems of over-fishing if too many eels were trapped on their way to the sea, the implication being that each river was supplied by elvers derived from a local spawning ground. This idea of a return to the restaurant river, is the parent stream hypothesis in reverse. But if the rivers were supplied from a common breeding stock, the downstream migrants could be fished hard, and the natural elver runs to one river supplemented by transplants from another without fear of failure. It is probably not generally realized that Schmidt's work had such practical implications, and that this is the reason why he was encouraged by the Danish authorities.

Not having a research vessel suitable to explore the Western Atlantic, Schmidt enlisted the help of the Danish Mercantile Marine who carried out net hauls along their normal routes, in the years 1910–1915. Small larvae were captured between 25°–41°N. and 18°–53°W. For practical purposes this was sufficient, and between 1910 and 1914 millions of elvers were taken from the Severn to supplement the natural runs of European rivers. In 1912 the International Council recognized Schmidt as the outstanding authority on eels when it appointed him to direct their eel investigations (ICES, 1913, p. 62). From then on the work developed into a systematic search for yolk sac larvae, first from the ill-fated 'Margrethe' in 1913, then by the cruises of 'Dana I' and 'Dana II' after the years of war.

Schmidt's solution to the eel problem is well known. He tracked down the limits of the distribution of the smallest larvae of the American and European eels to two areas in the Sargasso Sea. Here the two species appeared to spawn in warm saline water at depths of 200 to 400 m and the larvae, reaching the shallower layers, are carried by the currents of the Atlantic Ocean to the continental shelves of America and Europe. The larval eels must in some way be sorted out so that *A. rostrata* (vertebral count 103–111) end up in the New World and *A. anguilla* (vertebral count 110–119) in the Old. Schmidt's explanation of this was a difference in the larval growth rate between the two species. The American leptocephali complete their growth and metamorphose into elvers in about one year, whereas the European leptocephali take about three years, by which time they have been carried well away from the American coast. The elvers of both species ascend rivers and the young eels grow up in freshwater until they mature. Then, several years later, as silver eels, they run down to the sea and return to the Sargasso to spawn. This, in brief, is Schmidt's classical hypothesis which, after an early rebuff in 1912 when one of his papers was turned down by the Royal Society,[1] gained very widespread acceptance and held the field unchallenged until Tucker (1959) put forward a new interpretation of the facts.

Tucker's hypothesis, is, in his own words:

'1. That the European eels need not and do not succeed in returning to the ancestral spawning-area, but perish in their own continental waters.

'2. That the American and European eels are not distinct species, but merely eco-phenotypes of *Anguilla anguilla*, their apparent distinguishing characters being environmentallly determined (in the manner of numerous precedents) by demonstrable differences in temperature conditions encountered during the ascent from different parts of the American eel's spawning area to the surface, and their distribution by demonstrable coincident differences in the subsequent transport of the surface water-masses.

'3. That the populations of the so-called "European" eels, *A. anguilla*, are therefore entirely maintained by reinforcements of larvae of American "*A. rostrata*" parentage.'

Here indeed is a real controversy, as good as ever Huntsman raised over the salmon, and with as lively a correspondence (D'Ancona and Tucker, 1959; J. W. Jones and Tucker, 1959; Deelder and Tucker, 1960). Harden Jones (1961) and Bruun (1963) have criticized Tucker's arguments. In this account only a few of the main points will be dealt with and the discussion can be made under four headings: the spawning, the dispersal, freshwater life, and the return. One point might, perhaps, be made straight away. No fully grown mature European (or, for that matter, American) eel has, to date, been captured at sea away from the continental shelf. It is clear that Tucker's hypothesis must collapse if evidence comes to hand which shows that European eels do reach the spawning area.

THE CLASSICAL ACCOUNT

Spawning

Schmidt tried to delimit the spawning areas of the American and European eels by the size of the leptocephali taken at different stations in the Atlantic, the leptocephali being assigned to one or other species on the basis of their vertebral or myomere counts. The station positions have been published (some 'Thor' 1904–05 stations in Schmidt, 1912; 'Margrethe' 1913 stations, and Danish merchant and naval vessels 1911–15 stations in Schmidt, 1919; 'Dana I' 1920–21, and 'Dana II' 1921–22 stations in Schmidt, 1929) but the full details of the size, myomere or vertebral counts and numbers of larvae caught at each station have never appeared, although details for some of the catches are given in various papers of Schmidt's. This makes reference to particular catches a little tedious, but it has been thought best to quote the source of the data down to the page number or figure caption so that the interested reader can go straight to the original. One point that may

---

[1] Tate Regan (1933) remarks that 'no better example could be given of the fact that the system of refereeing scientific papers has its imperfections'.

be noted here is that the depth of a catch is usually referred to in terms of metres of wire paid out. In the case of a horizontal tow an approximation to the true depth can be obtained by dividing the length of wire out by 3 or 4.

THE EUROPEAN EEL

Spawning area. One hundred and thirty-five larvae between 5 and 10 mm in length were taken in April 1921 at 'Dana I' stations 935–948 (Schimdt, 1922, p. 197, Fig. 7). The positions of these stations are given by Schmidt (1929). Some of these larvae, the so-called protoleptocephaline stages, still had remnants of the yolk sac visible (Schmidt, 1922, footnote on p. 193). Schmidt (1925, p. 307, Fig. 13) figures a 6 mm larvae. These larvae must have been recently hatched and cannot have been carried very far away from the spawning area, which is taken as being centred round a position 26°N., 55°W. (Schmidt, 1932, p. 2, Fig. 1), very close to 'Dana II' station 1331.

Spawning season. It should be possible to fix the spawning season by noting the months during which the small protoleptocephali are caught. The important area is that bounded north and south by the 30° and 20°N. lines of latitude, and on the west and east by the 60° and 50°W. lines of longitude (Fig. 21). The months during which the Danish ships have worked stations within the rectangle are given in Table 9, together with the number of stations.

Table 9. Stations worked by Danish research, merchant and naval vessels within the rectangle bounded north and south by 30°N. and 20°N. latitude and west and east by 60°W. and 50°W. longitude. Bold underlined italic numerals indicate capture of small protoleptocephali.

Month	Number of stations worked by research ships				Number of stations worked by Danish merchant and naval vessels 1911–15
	'Margrethe' 1913	'Dana I' 1920	'Dana I' 1921	'Dana II' 1922	
January	—	—	—	—	3
February	—	—	—	—	5
March	—	—	15	—	8
April	—	3	***7***	3	2
May	—	2	—	***12***	***8***
June	—	12	—	5	7
July	—	4	—	—	4
August	—	—	—	—	1
September	—	—	—	—	4
October	9	—	—	—	8
November	—	—	—	—	1
December	8	—	—	—	2

Numerous hauls were made at the stations occupied by the research ships and the cover during the months when they were within the area is probably adequate. But the month by month coverage throughout the year is hardly satisfactory. The very small larvae of the European eel were found by 'Dana I' in April 1921 (Schmidt, 1922, p. 197, Fig. 7), and by 'Dana II' in May 1922 (Schmidt, 1925, p. 307, Fig. 13). Two were taken by a merchant ship in May 1914 (Schmidt, 1922, p. 191), and Schmidt (1922, p. 194) implies that others were found by another merchant ship in 1915 and by 'Dana I' in 1920. Details are not given. Schmidt (1922, p. 190) concluded that the eels did not spawn throughout the year: if they did, 'Margrethe' should have caught some proto-leptocephali during the autumn and early winter of 1913. He says (p. 206) that spawning starts in early spring and goes on well into the summer.

THE AMERICAN EEL

Small larvae, less than 10 mm in length and identified as *A. rostrata*, were caught in April 1921 by 'Dana I' at station 948 (22° 14′N., 67° 22′W.). Schmidt (1925, p. 308, Fig. 14) gives the size distribution of the catch. He also refers (Schmidt, 1922, p. 203) to 7 to 8 mm larvae of *A. rostrata* taken in February, presumably by 'Dana I' in 1922, and therefore at one or other of stations 901–905. It is clear that there is very little information available to fix the area or season in which the American eel spawns. As to the area, Tucker (1959) argues that it is probably due south and contiguous with that of *A. anguilla*, and his argument is quite reasonable. In the absence of detailed larval surveys it will be assumed that the spawning of the American eel is under way in February.

THE DEPTH OF SPAWNING

Eggs identified as belonging to the American and European eel have never been taken. Schmidt (1922, p. 206; 1929, p. 16) says that the young stages of the leptocephali are taken deeper than the older stages, at about 200 to 500 m. This makes it probable that the eels spawn at 400 to 700 m and that the pelagic eggs, like those of many oceanic species, float up to the surface where the larvae hatch out and feed.

TEMPERATURE CONDITIONS IN THE SPAWNING AREA

Tucker (1959) has drawn attention to the differences in the vertical temperature gradients that an egg, rising from 400 to 700 m to the surface, will encounter in the northern and southern regions of the *Anguilla* spawning area. Iselin's (1936) Haiti-Bermuda section ('Atlantis' stations 1208–1219, 7–13 April, 1932) shows, at the northern limit, a steady increase in temperature from about 12°C at 700 m to 20°C at 50 m. At the southern limit the temperature change is more rapid in the surface 200 m, increasing from 10°C at 700 m to 20°C at 200 m, and then to 25°C at 50 m. Tucker suggests that the steeper gradient in the south may arrest the development of the larvae and curtail the number of myomeres to 103–111, the number characteristic of *A. rostrata*. Iselin's section probably is, as Tucker claims, a fair picture of the hydrographic structure of the area at that time of the year. There is no doubt that marked differences in temperature do occur between the northern and southern limits: 'Dana II' hydrographic stations 1319 (26 April, 1922, 22° 43′N., 61° 43′W.) and 1335 (8 May, 1922, 28° 02′N., 62° 26′W.) show this very well (Schmidt, 1929). While Tucker is correct when he points out that the steeper temperature gradients and higher absolute temperatures occur in the south of the *Anguilla* area, D'Ancona (1959) rightly draws attention to the fact that there are, apparently, no sharp differences in the steepness of the vertical gradients from north to south. The vertical gradients gradually become steeper, and the temperature of the surface water gradually increases towards the south. The different conditions at the northern and southern limits of the *Anguilla* spawning area might produce, from one phenotype, the vertebral counts typical of the two eels. But the interesting question is, why are there so few eels with vertebral counts of 109, 110, 111, and 112? If there is one common spawning area, and the two extremes of temperature lead to high and low vertebral counts, the intermediate conditions of temperature might be expected to lead to the intermediate vertebral counts. It is clear from Fig. 19 that these intermediate vertebral counts are not found. If Tucker is correct, there may be a critical temperature, or rate of change of temperature in time, below which myomere development proceeds to give a larva with a high vertebral count, and above which myomere development is arrested at a low vertebral count. Only experiment can decide this point.

Growth, drift and metamorphosis

GROWTH

Direct evidence for the growth rate of the leptocephali could be given by length measurements of larvae of known age. But their age cannot be determined by reference to scale structure as the scales do not usually appear until the fourth year after metamorphosis, when the eels are 16 to 18 cm long (Tesch, 1928). Ehrenbaum and Marukawa's (1913) interpretation of the structure of

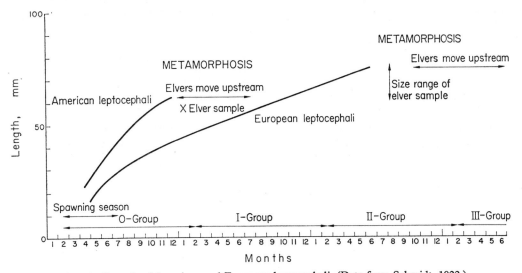

Fig. 20. Growth of American and European leptocephali. (Data from Schmidt, 1922.)

the leptocephalus otolith, which might give some clue to age, has never been used in length-for-age studies.

Small larvae caught in the summer and autumn near the spawning area clearly belong to the O-group but difficulties arise when dealing with the larger larvae taken in other months and at stations well away from the spawning area. Eels appear to spawn over a period of several months and it might be hard to separate the slow-growing and late-spawned larvae of one season with the quick-growing and early-spawned larvae of the following season. At some stations the catch of leptocephali shows a wide range of sizes, suggesting the presence of two or more age groups in the sea, which is confirmed by the differences in the mean length of larvae taken in the same month but at stations hundreds of miles apart. Schmidt (1922) constructed a growth curve for the larvae of the European eel by plotting the mean lengths of his monthly samples in such a way as to give a regular curve. Bruun (1937) used essentially the same method for the larvae of the deep-sea eel *Synaphobranchus kaupi*. Schmidt's graph, together with the growth curve for the American eel drawn from his data, is reproduced in Fig. 20. It is clear that the larvae of the American eel grow faster and metamorphose at an earlier age and smaller size than those of the European eel.

DRIFT

The European leptocephali take about 2·5 years to grow to 70 to 80 mm and during this time they drift in the surface waters of the North Atlantic. The younger stages may feed on diatoms for Schmidt (1925, p. 309) noted the remains of what appeared to be Coccolithophoridae in the guts of the protoleptocephali. The food of the older larvae is not known. There is some evidence to show that the older larvae undergo a diurnal vertical migration, as greater numbers are caught at the surface during the night than during the day (Schmidt, 1909*a*, p. 14) but this may be an effect of net avoidance. Schmidt (1922) gives the June distribution of the age groups and their average length as follows:

Age group	Central position	Average length in mm.
O	West Atlantic	25
I	Central Atlantic	52
II	Off Europe	75
III	Fresh and brackish waters of Europe	Elvers metamorphosed

Schmidt (1923, p. 54) says that eels enter the Mediterranean as unmetamorphosed larvae when between one and a half and two years old (I–II group). Strubberg (1923, p. 21) gives the eastern limit of the occurrence of fully grown II-group larvae in the Mediterranean at about 15°E. This is very nearly the longitude of the Straits of Messina, where Grassi and Calandruccio caught their leptocephali. To the north, unmetamorphosed larvae have been taken in August at about 3°W. in the Faroe-Shetland channel (Schmidt, 1927). It is clear that Schmidt and Strubberg regard the fully grown leptocephali taken in the summer near the Shetlands, on the edge of the continental shelf south-west of Ireland, and in the Mediterranean as far as 15°E., as II-group larvae, members of the same year-class, and of about the same age.

METAMORPHOSIS

The European leptocephali start their metamorphosis in their third summer, when they are about 2·5 years old. Schmidt (1906, p. 168) recognized 6 main stages, starting with the pelagic transparent leptocephali (Stage I) and finishing with the bottom-living pigmented elvers (Stage 6). Some of the stages have been subdivided (Schmidt, 1906, p. 249; Strubberg, 1913). Schmidt (1906, p. 174) concluded that the complete metamorphosis took about a year; Stage I to Stage 5a (pelagic glass eels) 9 to 10 months, and Stage 5a to Stage 6b a further 2 to 3 months. The larvae lose weight and show a reduction in length during the metamorphosis. Schmidt (1909*a*) compared Stage I leptocephali caught by the 'Thor' in June 1905 with glass eels (Stages 5 and 6) taken the following winter and spring at south-west Ireland, and showed a change in mean length from 75·21 mm to 71·12 mm, an overall reduction of 4·09 mm. Strubberg (1913) kept Stage 5b larvae in a salt-water aquarium at 15 to 21°C from 4 April to 28 June, when they had reached Stages 6a, III and IV. The elvers showed a reduction in length of 3·5 mm. Strubberg did not feed his elvers. Schmidt (1909*a*, p. 10, footnote) remarks that Stage 5b elvers feed on copepods so that part, if not all, of the reduction in length observed by Strubberg may have been due to starvation.

The pelagic glass eels are the first stages to arrive in coastal waters. In October, November and December they appear at south-west Ireland, the Basque coast, Portugal, Spain, Italy, and the Nile. In February they start to run up the Severn, in March they arrive at the Netherlands and the river Alpheios in Greece. In Denmark the ascent starts in April, and during this and the following months fully metamorphosed larvae reach the Baltic. It is clear, as Strubberg (1923) and Bertin (1956) point out, that time of arrival of the elvers, in Western Europe at least, is related to the distance of the country from the continental shelf: the further to the east they are the later they arrive. Similarly the time of ascent of the American elvers varies from place to place (Bigelow and Welsh, 1925, p. 80). They arrive at Woods Hole in March, but in Canadian waters during the summer.

One further point may be mentioned. It has often been observed, both in the Mediterranean and in Western European waters, that there is a decrease in the size of the elvers during the season. The first elvers to ascend the rivers are the largest, the later ones are smaller. This phenomena is not to be confused with the apparent decrease in size of the elvers during metamorphosis. Strubberg (1923) has brought much of the data together and discusses the problem.

This concludes the classical straightforward account of the dispersal, growth, and metamorphoses of the leptocephali of the European eel. It is not, however, so simple as it looks and there are two points that might be examined in a little more detail.

The delimitation of the spawning grounds

Vladykov (1964) has commented on the presence of adult American eels so far south as Trinidad and the Guianas. As the South American coast is swept by the north-going equatorial current, it is difficult to see how leptocephali could reach the area from the supposed spawning grounds lying 800 to 900 sea miles to the north. Vladykov suggests that the true spawning area of the American eel could be much further south than Schmidt supposed. If this was true, Schmidt's growth rate hypothesis to account for the separation of the American and European eels might have to be recast. Vladykov's point is a good one, and would be strengthened by the discovery of any great numbers of American leptocephali in the waters of the North Equatorial Current. Schmidt (1909b) noted the presence of American eels in British and Dutch Guiana but never appears to have taken up the problem of how they arrived there. The pattern of surface currents in the Antillean-Caribbean basins (Wüst, 1964) makes it unlikely that any large number of eel larvae hatched north of the West Indies could be carried to Guiana, although some of those that cross the Yucatan Channel between Cuba and Mexico could possibly be carried to South America in a series of coastal eddies. Another possibility is that the adult eels reached Guiana overland from Mexico.

The drift of leptocephali across the North Atlantic

It is of interest to see how the velocity of the surface currents of the North Atlantic fit in with the supposed drift of the leptocephali. While the protoleptocephali are found at depths of 200 to 500 m, the later stages are found nearer the surface, from 50 to 100 m. This shows up quite well in Hjort's (1910a) catches on 'Michael Sars'. It seems very reasonable to assume that most of the larvae are in the surface homogeneous layer of the North Atlantic (Lumby, 1955, has calculated its quarterly depth), so that their movements will, very largely, be those of the surface currents. The surface current system of the North Atlantic is well known, and there have been several series of drift bottle experiments from which it is possible to estimate speeds (Albert, Prince of Monaco, 1932; Winge, 1923). But the most convenient estimates are those compiled by the Meteorological Office from observations made over a period of 29 years by British merchant and naval ships. These have been published (Meteorological Office, 1945) as a series of charts and the appropriate ones for the present purpose are those giving the quarterly vector means of the surface currents.

These charts have been used to plot the drift of two patches of leptocephali, both hatched in March, one in the Northern '*A. anguilla* area', the other in the southern '*A. rostrata* area'. The results of the plots are shown in Fig. 21. There are several points to note.

1. The larvae from the northern patch arrive over the continental shelf south-west of Ireland as II-group fish, about 2 years 9 months after hatching. The time taken over the drift, as calculated from the surface current vector means, fits remarkably well with Schmidt's estimate of 2·5 to 3 years based on the larval growth curve.

2. The months in which the larvae should drift on to the western European coastline agree with the months in which the ascent of the elvers gets under way. There are, however, several anomalies.

(a) The first is the time it takes the larvae to get into the Mediterranean. According to the surface current charts, the larvae which pass through the Straits of Gibraltar in early summer are III-group fish, in their fourth year. Some of these larvae will reach the Eastern Mediterranean to

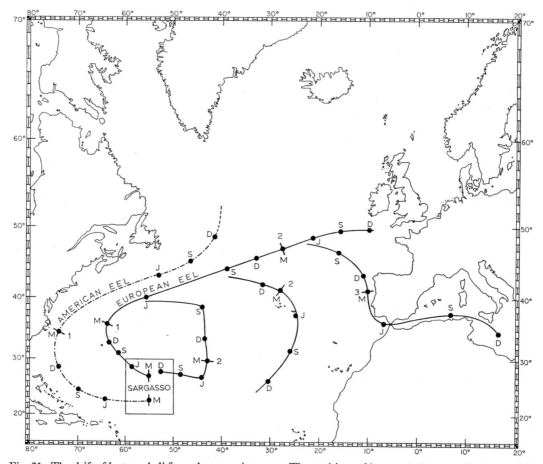

Fig. 21. The drift of leptocephali from the spawning areas. The positions of leptocephali hatched in March (M) in the two spawning areas are plotted at quarterly intervals: June (J), September (S), December (D) and March (M). The drift of the leptocephali has been worked out from the Meteorological Office charts showing the quarterly vector means of the surface currents (Meteorological Office, 1945). (Outline from an Admiralty chart.)

ascend the Nile the following winter. They will, therefore, be one year older than the elvers which ascend the rivers of Western Europe. It is true that Schmidt (1924) caught leptocephali in the Straits of Gibraltar in October ('Dana II', 1921), and that he considered these larvae as II-group fish which would enter freshwater the following spring. On the other hand, the estimates of larval drift suggest that they are the last of a batch of III-group fish, which started to pass through the Straits of Gibraltar in June, and that the next batch of larvae destined to reach the Mediterranean are still far to the north-west, as II-group fish, three hundred miles or more off Cape Finisterre. There is no easy way of resolving the anomaly. The larvae might take a more direct route than the charts indicate, or the strength of the surface currents may have been underestimated. But it does seem unlikely that any error here can be very great. The return of one of Prince Albert's floats may be mentioned. Released some 480 miles NW. of Cape Finisterre it was recovered on the north coast of Tunisia about 21 months later (float 599, see chart I in Albert, 1932). Perhaps the best way of tackling the problem would be to compare the otoliths of leptocephali taken in the Mediterranean with those of larvae taken near the continental shelf of Western Europe.

(b) The eels in the Azores present another aspect of the same problem. There is no doubt that these are European eels (Schmidt, 1909*b*) but the drift charts show that the larvae must pass the Azores when they are about 2 years old. It would be interesting to know the age of the Azores elvers. If they are 2 years old, they must be fast-growing European eels that happen to be ready to metamorphose when they approach the Azores; if they are 3 years old, they must be eels that have got left behind the main batch of their year-class, which will be hundreds of miles to the east. There is a real problem here: do the elvers which make up the annual runs in the Severn, in the Azores and the Nile belong to the same year-class ? If this is so, can the fact be reconciled with the surface drift, or should one reconsider the possibility that the Mediterranean elvers are hatched very much further to the east, and those of the Azores further to the west and south, than Schimdt's hypothesis allows ?

3. It is quite clear, from the surface current charts and the recoveries of drift bottles, that there is no hydrographic reason why larvae hatched in the southern '*A. rostrata* spawning area' should not end up in Europe. As these larvae do not appear to do so in any significant quantity, there must be a biological reason to prevent them. Schmidt's explanation was the higher growth rate and earlier metamorphosis of the American leptocephali and there seems little doubt that he would have regarded this as a real inherent genotypic difference between the two species. Tucker, on the other hand, attributes the difference in growth rate to the same factor, temperature, as he believes is responsible for the difference in vertebral count. Larvae hatched in the northern '*A. anguilla* area', where the temperature gradients and absolute values are lowest, have a high vertebral count and low growth rate; those hatched in the southern '*A. rostrata* area' have a low vertebral count and high growth rate. But as American and European leptocephali have been caught in the same net haul, it appears that they can live together in water of the same temperature, and still grow at a different rate. This suggests that differences in temperature conditions which they may have experienced earlier have had a permanent effect on their growth. Marckmann's (1958) work on the effect of temperature on the respiratory metabolism of developing sea trout is of interest here. Marckmann showed that a sudden increase in temperature was accompanied by an increase in respiratory metabolism but that the latter fell back to its previous value when the temperature was restored to normal. So far as these results go, they show that a sudden increase in temperature has no permanent effect on the metabolic rate.

However, it must be remembered that temperature cannot be the only environmental factor determining the growth rate. The availability of food must be of equal, if not greater, importance.

Clearly there is more to be learned about the growth and metamorphosis of the leptocephali. Not only are there the conflicting hypotheses of Schmidt and Tucker, but there are difficulties in Schmidt's original hypothesis. There is no doubt that Schmidt himself appreciated most, if not all, of these difficulties, as is obvious from reading Strubberg's (1923, p. 26) discussion on the 'decrease-in-size-of-the-elver-problem'. But Tucker has done well to draw attention to these questions, particularly that of extended pelagic phases (see J. W. Jones and Tucker, 1959). Then there is the time taken over the metamorphosis itself. Schmidt (1906) clearly believed that the change from Stage I (leptocephalus) to Stage 5a (pelagic glass eel) takes 9 to 10 months. These observations were based on the comparison of samples taken in different months and years. On the other hand, the aquarium observations of Grassi (1896) and Scott (1899) leave little doubt that these stages can be passed through in as short a time as a month.

FRESHWATER LIFE

Eels grow up in freshwater, and this period of their life is well documented. Bertin (1956) gives a good account. Their freshwater life is of little interest to the migration problem and will not be dealt with here. One point may be noted. Eels often stay in the Baltic for several years before moving up into freshwater. As Bertin (1956) says, the Baltic is like an enormous estuary where the greater part of their growth takes place.

THE RETURN TO THE SPAWNING AREA

On approaching sexual maturity the eels undergo a series of physiological and physical changes which culminate in the transformation of the freshwater yellow eel into the sea-going silver eel. It is as a silver eel, with enlarging eyes with a retinal pigment characteristic of deep-sea fish (Carlisle and Denton, 1959), that the European eel migrates downstream to the sea in the autumn months. Silver eels have been tagged and followed in the Baltic (Määr, 1947) but these experiments are of little interest in connexion with the supposed return of the European eels to their spawning area in the Sargasso. Very few European or American silver eels have been taken out in the open sea.

Tucker (1959) gives several arguments against the hypothesis that European eels do return, which have been countered by D'Ancona and Deelder. It is doubtful if there is anything to be gained by going into the details. What it all amounts to is this: Tucker supports the null hypothesis that European eels do not get back to the Sargasso Sea, and this hypothesis stands until it is disproved by conclusive evidence that they do. This could be provided by the capture of an eel itself, and if the eels are there they will be caught only if the correct fishing method is used (high-speed midwater trawl, pelagic long lines, or deep-water gill nets). It may not be necessary to capture an eel. If differences of otolith structure exist between the American and European eels, the recovery of European-type otoliths from the bottom deposits of the Sargasso would be conclusive evidence for the return. The method is worth looking into. Jensen (1905) was the first to use it and he recovered identifiable otoliths of various gadoids from depths of over 2,000 m in the Norwegian

Sea. Furthermore, if it could be shown that there were genetically determined serological differences between the adult American and European eels, it would be fair to conclude that the European eel does return to the spawning area.

DISCUSSION

The 'eel problem' is not settled. The really important point seems to be whether the differences in vertebral counts between the two species of Atlantic eels are environmentally determined or not. One wonders what Schmidt would have thought of Tucker's hypothesis, and on reading his 1915 paper, the 'Second report on eel investigations', it seems astonishing that he does not come to a similar conclusion himself. At the end of this paper Schmidt compares the European eel with *Zoarces*, the viviparous blenny. He contrasts the similarity of the vertebral counts of eel samples taken from widely separated areas with the variation to be found between the vertebral counts of *Zoarces* samples. *Zoarces* has a vertebral count whose range (99–126) exceeds that of *A. anguilla* and *A. rostrata* combined, and from the comparisons with the European eel Schmidt concludes that the northern population of *Zoarces* is divided up into numerous local stocks, whereas all the European eels belong to one single stock. He goes on to say that the 'relation between two samples of *Zoarces* will thus be comparable, not with that between two samples of European eels, but with that between the European eels as a whole and the American in like wise. Since the two last named, are classed as distinct species, *Anguilla vulgaris* and *A. rostrata*, it would be equally correct statistically speaking, to regard for instance, two of the most widely differing stocks of *Zoarces* as distinct species also' (Schmidt, 1916, p. 21). But Schmidt does not do this; he considers the European *Zoarces* to be divided into a large number of local races, characterized by numerical proportions and distribution, and in a later paper (Schmidt, 1917, p. 316) he clearly states that the American, European, and Japanese eels can be considered as races comparable with those of *Zoarces*. And as to the cause of the races, he asks, 'Is the fact that the stock of *Zoarces* in one locality differs from that of another with regard to average values of number of vertebrae etc., due to genotypic differences in such two communities, or merely to the effect of varying external conditions, or possibly to a combination of both factors?' (Schmidt, 1916, p. 23).

Schmidt's (1920) own work with *Zoarces* in the Ise Fjord-Roskilde Fjord area, Sealand, Denmark, show the importance of heredity in determining the vertebral counts. The working area is shown in Fig. 22. Schmidt's results are worth looking at in some detail. At station 31 the average vertebral number was 113·2. Schmidt first showed that this average was maintained in successive year-classes. The second step was to compare the number of vertebrae in mothers taken at this

Table 10. Transplantation experiment with *Zoarces*. Vertebral counts of the offspring of mothers transplanted from station 34 to station 31, with data for the controls at station 31. (Data from Schmidt, 1920).

Station	Average at station	Transplanted from Stn. 34 to Stn. 31		Controls at Stn. 31	
		Mothers	Offspring	Mothers	Offspring
34	107·768 ± 0·468	107·0	108·3		
31	113·101 ± 0·447			113·1	114·8

The Eel

station with that of their offspring. The results, shown graphically in Fig. 23, leave little doubt that the vertebral count is largely genotypically determined.

Schmidt then went on to a transplantation experiment from station 34 (average vertebral count 108·0) to station 31 (average vertebral count 113·2). About 300 specimens were caught at each

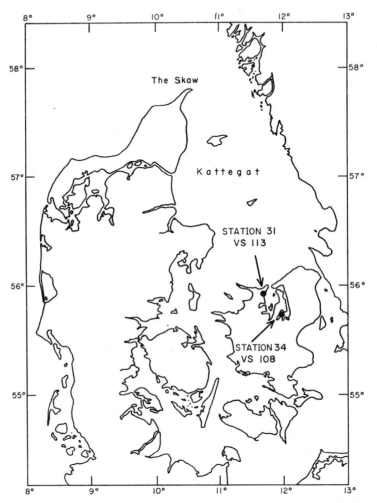

Fig. 22. Schmidt's (1920) transplantation experiments with *Zoarces* from the Ise Fjord-Roskilde Fjord area, Sealand, Denmark. The positions of stations 31 and 34 are shown, with the mean vertebral count of the local resident *Zoarces* populations. (Outline from an Admiralty chart.)

station and kept in wooden boxes at station 31 so that pairing and development took place under the same environmental conditions. If the cause of the differences of about 5 vertebrae between the populations found at the two stations was a direct action of the environment, it would be expected to disappear if the young were reared under similar conditions. The results summarized in Table 10 show, quite clearly, that the differences are maintained. This transplantation experiment has a familiar ring about it. It is almost as if Schmidt forestalled Tucker's suggestion of experimental work on the eel, but because of practical difficulties, worked on two *Zoarces* stocks with vertebral counts similar to those of the American (107) and European eels (114).

It is difficult to believe that Schmidt never considered the possibility that the differences in vertebral counts between the American and European eels were environmentally determined. Surely he must have done so. Another transplantation experiment, this time a comparison between two samples of the *Zoarces* populations at station 31, developed under different environmental

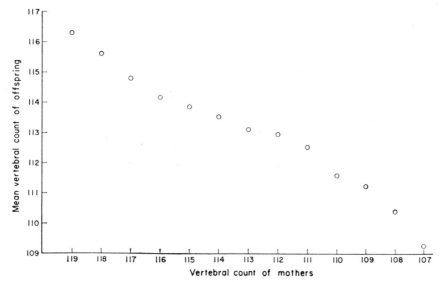

Fig. 23. The mean vertebral count of *Zoarces* at station 31 was 113·2. Schmidt (1920) compared the number of vertebrae in mothers captured at this station with that of their offspring. The results suggest that the number of vertebrae is determined genotypically.

conditions (Schmidt, 1920, p. 6), showed clearly the importance of external factors. But the difference was small, 114·535 ± 0·493 against the control of 113·251 ± 0·372. Schmidt's view was, without much doubt, that racial differences between stocks were primarily genotypic and that environmental effects were only of secondary importance (Schmidt, 1917, p. 350). But he never committed himself to an opinion one way or another about the Atlantic eels, unless a paragraph on p. 344 (Schmidt, 1917) could be interpreted as showing that he believed the differences to be of genotypic origin.

Tucker's hypothesis is that the American eel, whose mean vertebral count is 107, will give rise to young with a count within the range of the European eel (110–119), unless the egg is subjected to a shock-effect (sudden temperature change) during the supersensitive period. The hypothesis is based on some of Tåning's experiments with trout. Tåning did produce, as Tucker says, means of 56·86 and 60·06 vertebrae in batches of young from the same parents, and the difference (3·20 in a mean control of 58·84, 5·4%) is proportionally similar to that between the two eels (7 in 114, 6·1%). I have made the point (Harden Jones, 1961) that Tåning's shock-effect is quite different from Tucker's. Tåning (1952a, p. 182) transferred his 3°C eggs to 15·3–17·7°C, and then back again to 3°C (experiment 1 in Fig. 24), and his 12°C eggs to 2·3–3·0°C and back to 12°C again (experiment

2 in Fig. 24). Each sample was affected twice, once by the change from warm to cold, or cold to warm, and secondly by going back to the original temperature. This is not the sort of treatment Tucker postulates for the eel, which is an abrupt increase of only 4°C. The correct comparison is with the experiments Tåning describes on p. 178 of his *Biological Review*. Tåning's words may be quoted in full: 'If samples intended to hatch at lower temperatures are exposed to a heating influence in this period' (he is referring to the supersensitive period) 'we normally do not get a rise in

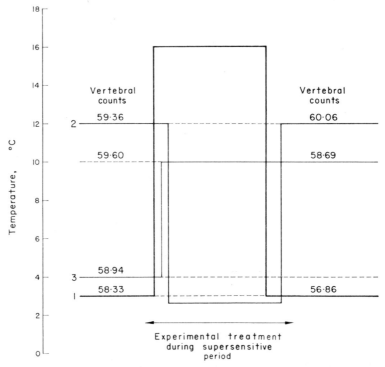

Fig. 24. A diagram showing the results of some of Vedel Tåning's experiments on the effects of temperature changes on vertebral count in trout. Experiments 1 and 2 involve two sudden temperature changes, experiment 3 only one change. Experiment 3 is the one which is of interest in connexion with Tucker's eel hypothesis.

the number of vertebrae, as might be expected from the results of the experiments with constant temperature, but a fall, and still more remarkable, usually a fall below the value which the control sample for the low temperature gives (see (a) in examples below.).' His example (a), shown in Fig. 24 as experiment 3, is as follows:

Heat-treated sample

Average of vertebrae in control sample at 4°C.	58·94
Average of vertebrae in control sample at 10°C.	59·60
Average of vertebrae in sample transferred in supersensitive period from 4°C to 10°C.	58·69

This experiment seems convincing enough, but the small drop in vertebral count (0·4%) is hardly of the order required to give support to Tucker's hypothesis.

Serological techniques have not yet given conclusive evidence of genetic differences between the American and European eels. Their haemoglobin patterns as determined by agar-gel electrophoresis appear to be the same (Sick, Westergaard, and Frydenberg, 1962). Although Gemeroy and Boyden (1961) found clear differences between the blood sera of the two species with reciprocal precipitin tests, these results cannot be considered as conclusive evidence of genetic difference, and the matter is still unresolved.

It would be interesting to compare the Atlantic eel problem with those that exist in connexion with the life histories of the other species of the genus. Jespersen (1942) has discussed some of these points but the fact of the matter is that too little is known to go into details here. The Japanese eel, *A. japonica*, is the best species to compare with those from the Atlantic. Its spawning area is somewhere to the south of Japan, on to whose shores the leptocephali are carried by the Kuroshio current. But it is only recently that a leptocephalus of *A. japonica* has been captured (Matsui, 1957) and that maturing eels have been taken out at sea.

Arguments over the eel problem will probably continue until conclusive evidence is produced to show that European eels do get back to the Sargasso. In my opinion, and opinions are worth very little in such matters, it may turn out that Schmidt was correct. Any hypothesis that sets out to account for the observed facts of fish migrations must provide some explanation of the return of the American eel to the Sargasso, and, quite probably, that of the European eel as well.

Chapter 6

The Herring

INTRODUCTION

In 1965 the total landing of Atlantic and Pacific herring was about 4·7 million metric tons. Figures for individual countries are given in Table 11.

Table 11. World catch, in thousands of metric tons, of Atlantic and Pacific herring in 1965. (Data from FAO 1966.)

Pacific herring		Atlantic herring	
Country	Catch	Country	Catch
Russia	496·6	Norway	1,078·6
Canada	201·4	Iceland	762·9
Japan	50·2	Russia	701·8
United States	16·1	Denmark	344·8
Philippines	5·7	Sweden	288·7
		Canada	183·5
Total	**770·0**	Poland	125·6
		W. Germany	115·4
		United Kingdom	99·7
		Netherlands	87·9
		Finland	45·9
		Faroe	35·6
		United States	34·2
		France	26·4
		Ireland	10·7
		Belgium	0·8
		Total	**3,941·5**

The Pacific herring differs from the Atlantic herring in the form of scales on the underside of the body, the so-called ventral scutes. In the Atlantic species *Clupea harengus* Linn. the ventral scutes are keeled both in front and behind the pelvic fins, whereas in the Pacific *C. pallasi* Cuv. and Val. the ventral scutes in front of the pelvic fins are not keeled (Tate Regan, 1916). This appears to be the only clear-cut anatomical difference between the two species: the other differences are biological.

Clupea harengus is found on both sides of the Atlantic within the North Boreal zone. On the European side it ranges from Spitsbergen to the Bay of Biscay, from Iceland to the White Sea. In American waters it is found at Greenland, off Northern Labrador, and to the south as far as Cape Hatteras. *C. pallasi* is distributed throughout the Arctic zone and the North Boreal zone of the

Pacific. Both species have demersal eggs and pelagic larvae. The Atlantic herring may spawn in winter, spring, summer or autumn, and often does so on shingle or gravel beds in depths from 40 to 200 m, sometimes on banks far from the shore. The Pacific herring spawns only in spring and comes right inshore to lay its eggs on seaweeds in depths which lie between the tide marks. Rass (1959) suggests that the use of the littoral zone for spawning by the Pacific herring is an adaptation to severe winter conditions: this is the part of the sea which is the first to thaw and it is here that production first gets under way.

This account mainly deals with the migration of *C. harengus* in the north-east Atlantic. Le Gall (1935) divides the herring of this area in seven main groups as follows:

1. Atlanto-Scandian ⎫ Atlantic herring
2. Hiberno-Caledonian ⎬
3. Channel
4. North Sea
5. Skagerrak, Kattegat, Sound and Belts
6. Baltic
7. Estuarine, Fjord or local stocks

The last group includes several more or less isolated stocks found in certain fjords and estuaries. The distribution of the six remaining groups is shown in Fig. 25. There is some interchange between them, but by and large the individuals of one group do not mix freely with those of another. A single group, however, is not necessarily homogeneous and may comprise several spawning stocks. The Atlanto-Scandian group includes Icelandic spring and summer spawners and Norwegian, Murman, Faroe, Shetland, and Viking spring spawners. The North Sea group includes Scottish north-east coast summer spawners, Dogger autumn spawners (the Bank stock), Southern Bight winter spawners (the Downs stock) and some spring spawners.

One of the problems facing the Fisheries Biologist engaged in herring work is to determine the effects of fishing on a particular stock[1] and the problem becomes easier if the movements and migrations of a stock are known throughout the area occupied by the group to which it belongs. Recent changes in the yield of certain north-east Atlantic herring fisheries have led to an increase in the attention being given to the biology of the herring, with particular emphasis on the Atlanto-Scandian and North Sea groups. Attempts have been made to determine the pattern of the migrations of the different stocks within these groups and to understand the factors which control the course and timing of their movements. As the Atlanto-Scandian and North Sea herring have received the most attention, what follows will be largely restricted to these two groups.

The literature on the herring is extensive. Le Gall's (1935) paper is still worth reading, while Hodgson's (1934, 1957) two books are very readable accounts of the biology and fishery of the Atlantic herring. Scattergood's (1957) bibliography lists most of the important papers up to 1956. Parrish (1962) gives an account of the North Sea herring while Blaxter and Holliday (1963) have reviewed the physiological literature of the clupeoids in general and the herring in particular. Parrish and Saville (1965) have reviewed the biological aspects of the north-east Atlantic herring populations.

---

[1] The stock is, for the Fisheries Biologist, the unit of management. The unit stock has been defined as "a relatively homogeneous and self-contained population whose losses by emigration and accessions by immigration, if any, are negligible in relation to the rates of growth and mortality" (Anon, 1960a, p. 8).

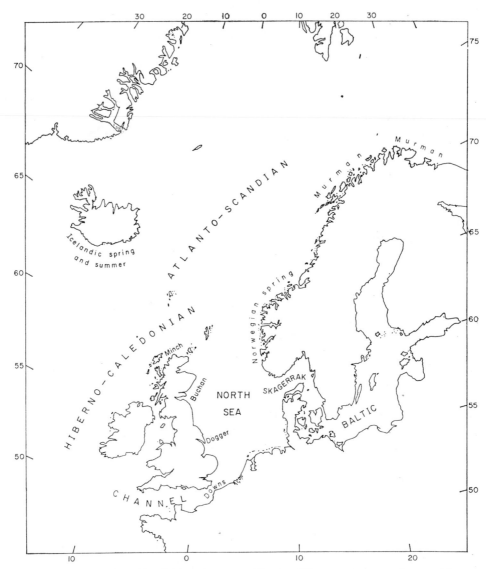

Fig. 25. The distribution of six of Le Gall's main groups of herring. The spawning areas of some of the component spawning groups are indicated (Atlanto-Scandian: Icelandic spring and summer, Norwegian spring and Murman spring spawners; North Sea: Buchan, Dogger and Downs spawners). (Outline from a Meteorological Office chart.)

LIFE HISTORY

Spawning season

Herring spawn in the spring, summer, autumn or winter. Confusion results when biologists cannot agree when one season ends and another begins and the following calendar scheme will be adopted here:

Spring	March, April, May
Summer	June, July, August
Autumn	September, October, November
Winter	December, January, February

In a ripe herring the gonads make up about 20% or more of the wet weight of the fish. Different stocks may spawn at different times of the year but the physiological burden of reproduction is such that it is unlikely that an individual herring would spawn more than once a year, and the maturation cycles of the different stocks are almost certainly geared, in some way, to those of organic production in the areas where the fish live.

Maturation stages

Certain conventions are used in describing the maturation stages of the gonads in herring. In 1930 the International Council decided to adopt, with certain modifications, the scale set out by Hjort (1910b). The 1930 scale provided eight stages (Ehrenbaum, 1931), but was not used by all the participating countries (see Bowers and Holliday, 1961). In 1962 an ICES Herring Committee Working Group on 'Methods used in the North Sea Herring Investigations' recommended the use of the scale of maturities put forward by the Atlanto-Scandian Working Group which had previously met in Bergen. The Bergen scale follows that of Heincke and Johansen in that Stage II is for virgin herring with developing sexual organs, whereas in Hjort's scale Stage II includes virgins and recovering spents. The Bergen scale is as follows:

Stage

I. Virgin herring. Gonads very small, thread-like, 2–3 mm broad. Ovaries wine-red. Testes whitish or grey-brown.

II. Virgin herring with small sexual organs. The height of ovaries and testes about 3 to 8 mm. Eggs not visible to naked eye but can be seen with magnifying glass. Ovaries a bright red colour; testes a reddish-grey colour.

III. Gonads occupying about half of the ventral cavity. Breadth of sexual organs between 1 and 2 cm. Eggs small but can be distinguished with naked eye. Ovaries orange; testes reddish-grey or greyish.

IV. Gonads almost as long as body cavity. Eggs larger, varying in size, opaque. Ovaries orange or pale yellow; testes whitish.

V. Gonads fill body cavity. Eggs large, round; some transparent. Ovaries yellowish; testes milk-white. Eggs and sperm do not flow, but sperm can be extruded by pressure.

VI. Ripe gonads. Eggs transparent; testes white; eggs and sperm flow freely.

VII. Spent herring. Gonads baggy and bloodshot. Ovaries empty or containing only a few residual eggs. Testes may contain remains of sperm.

VIII. Recovering spents. Ovaries and testes firm and larger than virgin herring in Stage II. Eggs not visible to naked eye. Walls of gonads striated; blood vessels prominent. Gonads wine-red colour. (This Stage passes into Stage III.)

From an accurate assessment of the stage that a fish has reached in its maturation cycle it may be possible to assign an individual to a particular spawning group. This is useful when two spawning groups share a common feeding ground. However, little is known about the duration of the different stages. Aasen's (1952) work on the Lusterfjord herring, where the duration of a stage is estimated according to the length of time it predominated in the monthly samples, is not entirely satisfactory. Iles (1964) has re-examined the problem and made estimates of the duration of the maturation stages in a number of spawning groups. Iles suggests that both winter and spring spawners reach a high maturation stage several months before spawning. If this is true, Stage V fish may not necessarily be going to spawn as soon as has been thought, which raises problems with the separation of autumn and winter spawners caught towards the end of the summer. Greater accuracy in the

4

assessment of spawning time might be possible if the macroscopic appearance of the gonad reflected more detailed histological changes. Bowers and Holliday (1961) and Polder (1961) have shown that there is some relation between maturation stage and histological structure. It remains to be seen if such refinements of technique will help in judging the spawning season of an individual with greater accuracy than conventional staging.

Sex ratios

Relatively little information on sex ratios in herring is available and Table 12 includes unpublished data filed at the Fisheries Laboratory, Lowestoft. The Lowestoft Hinder samples show a significant predominance of females. Inspection of the original Lowestoft data shows that there are significantly more males than females among the 2- and 3-year-olds sampled at East Anglia ($\chi^2 = 14$, and 8) and among the 3-year-olds sampled at the Hinder and Cap Gris Nez grounds ($\chi^2 = 22$ and 5). Females outnumbered males among the 4-year-olds sampled at East Anglia 2,395 to 2,239, $\chi^2 = 5\cdot25$). Many of the Belgian herring samples taken in the Southern Bight and eastern Channel fisheries also show a significant preponderance of females (for example, Gilis, 1959, 1960).

Table 12. Sex ratios in herring samples examined at the Fisheries Laboratory, Lowestoft (unpublished data).

Area or source of sample	Years of sampling	Numbers of fish		χ^2
		Males	Females	
East Anglia	1955–60	8,491	8,434	0·2
Hinder	1956, '57, '59, '60	1,309	1,180	6·5
Cap Gris Nez	1955–59	1,469	1,370	3·385

Fridriksson (1944) gives figures which show a 1:1 ratio of males to females among 11,627 herring taken in the north Icelandic fishery, but notes that females, the proportion of which is higher among the older fish, probably recruit later than males. The data that are available suggest that some males mature a year earlier than females, and Liamin (1959, p. 177) has noted this in the Icelandic summer spawning herring. But the tendency is less marked than in cod and plaice, where the early maturity of the males is partly responsible for the marked predominance of females among the older age groups.

Arrival on the spawning grounds

In some stocks the older and larger herring spawn before the younger and smaller ones. This has been shown for spring and autumn spawners at Grande-Rivière, Bay of Chaleur, Québec, by Jean (1956); for Norwegian spring spawners (Runnström, 1941a, p. 32); and for Scottish north-east coast summer-autumn spawners (Wood, 1930, p. 44, Table 23; 1934, p. 24). Critical data are not available for the Dogger spawners. The Downs herring pass East Anglia in October and November, the younger fish appearing before the older (Hodgson, 1927, p. 70; Wood, 1936, p. 50). Ancellin's (1951) age compositions of the Dyck-Sandettié and Group-I spawners in 1949–50 show that the young fish do spawn first in this area.

Spawning grounds and behaviour

Herrings lay demersal eggs which stick on stones or gravel. Adhesion is maintained by an ovarian secretion from the granulosa cells (Polder, 1961). Spawning beds are small and it is not known what makes one locality suitable for spawning rather than another. Off the Norwegian coast, loose stones and rock appear to be the favoured substrate (Runnström, 1941*b*, p. 24). Bolster and Bridger (1957) surveyed a spawning area near the Ruytingen Bank, off Calais, and found the greatest concentration of eggs on a flint and gravel bed, 3,200 m long and only 300 to 360 m wide. The long axis of this narrow strip lay in the line of the tide. Parrish *et al.* (1959) surveyed a spawning bed in the Firth of Clyde and found that the boundary of the egg patch coincided with a change from gravel and small stones to large stones and rock. Fridriksson and Timmermann (1951) found eggs of Icelandic spring spawners on a bottom made up of black sand and gravel. Holliday (1958) showed that herrings kept in a tank laid eggs over gravel and weed rather than large stones.

Ewart (1884) and Holliday (1958) have described the spawning behaviour of herring in tanks. The female deposits the eggs in ribbons, which sometimes collect in small conical heaps. The male releases milt into the water around the female; there is no evidence of pairing. Unlike cod, sound does not appear to play any part in the reproductive behaviour of herring, and no sounds have been heard on hydrophones lowered into or close to shoals on the spawning grounds (Harden Jones, unpublished).

Holliday (1958) suggested that a herring could shed its eggs in 2 to 4 hours. Bowers and Holliday (1961) found that all the eggs appear to be released from their follicles simultaneously—which suggests rapid ovulation—and this fits in with the earlier suggestion of a quick spawning. However, Polder (1961) believes that ovulation proceeds rather slowly and the size of egg samples taken by a Petersen grab led Runnström (1941*b*, p. 30) to the conclusion that the female deposits them 'little by little'. With demersal eggs, a herring does not have to provide the amounts of water required by the pelagic eggs of fish such as the cod and plaice, and spawning can probably proceed fairly quickly on this account.

Hatching and drift of larvae

Herring eggs hatch in about two weeks, depending on the temperature. Ewart (1884, p. 72) observed that herring larvae hatched in aquaria stayed near the bottom until they were four days old. The larvae are pelagic and may be carried some distance by water currents during this phase, which lasts three to six months. Thus many of the larvae hatched from the spring and summer spawnings to the south and south-west of Iceland are carried round to the north-west, north, and east coasts (Johansen, 1927; Liamin, 1959). Larvae hatched in spring on the south-western part of the Norwegian coast are carried northwards and settle down between Bergen and Finmark. Those spawned on the Lofoten and Vesterålen grounds may be carried to West Spitsbergen, the Murman coast, Novaya Zemlya or into the White Sea (Marty, 1959). In the northern North Sea, the larvae of the spring and autumn spawnings are carried south or west towards the Scottish north-east coast or south-eastwards towards the Skagerrak (Clark, 1933), while those hatched on the Dogger in the autumn and on the Channel grounds in the winter are carried to the east and north-east into the German Bight and to the nursery grounds off the Danish coast (Bückmann, 1950).

The immature herring

Post-larval metamorphosis into the juvenile herring takes place when the larvae are about 3 to 5 cm long, and it is then that the scales appear. Many young herring spend part of their first year in shallow coastal waters. The littoral phase is not necessarily characteristic of all stocks and the Murman herring are an exception (Marty, 1959, p. 17), and there are a number of observations of

O-group Norwegian spring herring well out in the open sea over deep water (Devold, 1951*a*, p. 126). The young herring move into deeper water, and away from the coast, as they grow bigger. Immature herring form the basis of several meal and oil (so-called industrial) fisheries of which the best known are the Norwegian small and fat herring fisheries, the Scottish halflin fisheries in the east coast firths and the Danish Bløden (=soft ground) fishery near the Dogger Bank in the North Sea.

Recruitment

As with other fish (Alm, 1959; Nikol'skii, 1962), many of the important events in the life history of the herring are related to feeding and growth. Runnström (1936*c*) has shown that the immature herring which grow up in the Norwegian coastal waters leave for the open sea when they reach a length of 16 to 18 cm and enter the oceanic stage of their life history. The change from coastal to oceanic life depends on length and not on age. Within a year-class, the faster growing members are the first to leave. Similarly, individuals of the same year-class do not come to their first maturity at the same age. Recruitment takes place over a number of years and the age at which the herring first spawn varied from 3- to 8-years-old, the faster growing individuals reaching maturity earlier than the slower growing ones (Runnström, 1941*a*, p. 64). Burd (1962) has shown a similar relationship for the herring of the southern North Sea. Here the young herring move off shore at a length of 9 to 10 cm. They move out over deeper water towards the centre of the North Sea and at a mean length of 15 cm arrive on the Bløden ground to the east and south of the Dogger Bank. The immature fish leave the Bløden at a length of about 20 cm, the first maturation cycle starting when the herring have reached a length of about 22 cm. As with the Norwegian herring, the age at recruitment to the spawning shoals depends on growth, the faster growing fish recruiting one or two years earlier than the slower growing members of the same brood. Burd (1962, p. 25) has carried the argument a step further and suggested that the stock to which an individual herring recruits will depend on its growth during the first two years of its life and the time of the year at which it approaches a critical length. Jean (1956) made a similar suggestion for the herring in the Bay of Chaleur, Québec.

Feeding

The guts of herring larvae contain a variety of diatoms, flagellates, small copepods, and metazoan larvae (Hentschel, 1950; Bhattacharyya, 1957). The size of the food increases as the herring grows, and adults will take *Calanus*, *Temora*, *Pseudocalanus*, euphausids (*Meganyctiphanes*), amphipods, *Oikopleura*, and small sand eels (*Ammodytes*). In the middle North Sea *Calanus* is the most important food organism for herring (Savage, 1937). During the summer feeding season the movements of the herring are probably related to the abundance of their food. Cushing (1955*a*) has shown that herring aggregate on to and disengage from patches of *Calanus*. Pavshtiks (1959) has shown that the northward movement of the spent herring across the Norwegian sea tends to keep the feeding fish within the area of biological spring where there are pre-spawning concentrations of *Calanus* and euphausids.

Herring appear to feed all the year round so long as food is available. Rudakova (1959) records Stage V Atlanto-Scandian herring feeding on euphausids, but in the southern North Sea the Stage V fish usually have empty stomachs. Herring are not filter feeders but catch their prey (Hardy, 1924*a*). Bhattacharyya (1957) found that post-larval herring do not feed at night. Mužinić (1931) showed that herring caught on the Fladen ground and at Brucey's Garden in September and October took most food between 0300–0600 hr and 1700–2100 hr. Laboratory work (Battle *et al.*, 1936; Blaxter and Holliday, 1958) confirms the importance of light in feeding. But it is not clear to what extent changes of light intensity, the availability of food, and an endogenous feeding rhythm interact under natural conditions.

Diurnal vertical movements

Herring are believed to stay near the bottom or in deep water during the day and to come up towards the surface during the night. This is the behavioural basis for bottom trawling for herring during the day and for drift net fishing near the surface at night. Both Graham (1931) and Balls (1951) have discussed this and other aspects of herring behaviour. Echo-sounders can give information as to changes in the vertical distribution of traces, but the real problem is to identify the traces as herring. Brawn's (1960b) account is probably the most complete, and is based on the analysis of Bendix echo-sounder records collected over a period of 11 years in Passamaquoddy Bay, New Brunswick, Canada. The case for identifying the traces as herring is a general one in that immature herring (9 to 20 cm) are the only schooling fish present in quantity in the bay, and that herring were caught in the same areas as those in which the fish traces were present (Brawn, 1960b, p. 702). A midwater trawl is said to have been used (her p. 707) but no details are given. The picture that emerges from Brawn's analysis is a rise towards the surface at sunset, a midnight sinking, and a dawn rise, followed by return to deeper water during the day, the pattern being essentially the same as that found in many species of planktonic crustacea (Cushing, 1951). There are other echo-sounder observations which go to confirm the diurnal vertical movements of herring. An upward movement towards the surface has been described by Sund (1937), Runnström (1941b), Tester (1943), Richardson (1952), and Dragesund (1958a). Richardson (1952) observed a dawn rise above the night-time level, and the descent to the bottom has been seen by Tester (1943), Richardson (1952), and Dragesund (1958a). The diurnal pattern of vertical movement is important in connexion with fishing, and has been discussed in relation to seining by Tester (1938a), to drifting by Balls (1951) and to trawling by Richardson (1960). The vertical movement is probably causally related to changes in light intensity and its biological significance may be concerned with feeding. The extent of the movement appears to be related to temperature. Brawn has shown that the immature Passamaquoddy herring go deeper during the day when temperature is lower than 4 to 7°C, and Postuma (1960) has shown that the level to which the herring rise at night in the North Sea is related to the thickness of the homogeneous surface layer of water.

There is some evidence to suggest that the pattern of diurnal vertical migration is related to the gonad maturation cycle. Wood (1930, p. 17) noted that drift nets catch few ripe or spawning herring, and suggested that these fish did not rise so high in the water as spent or immature fish.

Homing

Opinions differ as to whether a herring spawns in the same season as that in which it was born and whether or not it returns to spawn on the parent ground. Storrow (1920, p. 29), Hodgson (1929, p. 65; 1934, p. 26), Jean (1956), and Graham (1962) suggest that herring do not always spawn in the season of their birth, with the implication that there may not necessarily be a return to the parent ground. On the other hand Runnström (1941a, p. 94), Zijlstra (1958), and Marty (1959, p. 19) have said that herring do return to spawn on the parent ground at the season in which they were born. When opinion is so divided the evidence must be examined carefully.

One fundamental point is the reliability with which one can say where and when a particular individual, or sample of herring, was spawned.

SOME OF THE DIFFICULTIES THAT ARISE IN DECIDING WHEN AND WHERE A HERRING WAS SPAWNED

Examination of the gonads can give some indication as to when a herring is going to spawn. But it is more difficult to say when and where a herring was spawned. This is important, for example, when trying to find out if autumn-spawned fish become autumn spawners and if they remain so throughout their lives. The presence of autumn-spawned fish, spawning out of season on a winter spawning ground, would be difficult to reconcile with the hypothesis that herring return to spawn on the grounds where they were born. The problem would be relatively simple if autumn- and winter-spawned herring could be separated by some distinct and clear-cut feature that was characteristic of one group and not of the other.

Marking and tagging

The problem could be tackled by marking young herring known to have been spawned on a particular ground and keeping watch to see where and when these fish spawned when they reached their first maturity. In the North Sea, where the autumn- and winter-spawned fish mix on a common nursery ground, the fish would have to be marked or tagged soon after hatching and no technique has as yet been devised to do this. If mixing were delayed until the fish were large enough to mark or tag, these techniques might give useful results. For example, the young herring which grow up on the Norwegian coast are almost certainly Norwegian and not Icelandic born. The two stocks are unlikely to mix to any significant extent until the Norwegian fish leave the coastal waters as fat herring 16 to 18 cm long. Recoveries of ripe or spawning herring previously tagged as I- or II-group fish in Norwegian and Icelandic coastal waters should give evidence of mixing between the two stocks. The Norwegian-Icelandic herring problem is a case where tagging would be of help. In other instances attempts have been made to use natural marks as certificates of origins. Spawning groups may differ in the mean number of vertebrae (VS) or in the mean number of keeled scales (K_2) between the pelvic and anal fins. There may be differences in otolith and scale structure, and in growth patterns. Reference has already been made to the value of these characters in migration studies and their use in herring work will now be examined in more detail.

Vertebral counts

The number of vertebrae in a herring ranges from 52 to 59, but most individuals have counts of 55, 56, 57, or 58. The difference between the mean counts of spawning stocks is small and is usually less than one. Unlike the eel (p. 69), individual herring cannot be assigned to a particular spawning group and comparisons must therefore be made between samples. Counts are best made on Stage VI (spawning) fish and comparisons should, as Lea (1929b, p. 21) suggested, be made by year-classes. The vertebral count provides information as to the composition of the spawning shoals but not necessarily as to the origins of the spawners. The data could give direct support to the hypothesis that fish return to spawn on the parent ground if differences in vertebral count reflected genetic differences between the two groups. Huntsman (1939) made a similar point in connexion with salmon. But work on the genetical aspect of the problem is still in its early stages (Hempel and Blaxter, 1961).

It is well known that meristic characters are influenced by environmental factors, particularly temperature. There are sufficient experimental (see p. 24) and observational data to associate low temperatures on a spawning ground with high larval vertebral counts, and high temperatures with low larval vertebral counts. The number of vertebrae could therefore be used to give some indication as to the temperature on the spawning grounds and thus where and when a particular sample of herring may have been spawned.

Icelandic spring and summer spawning herring may be taken as an example. Spring-hatched eggs develop in water temperatures of 5 to 7°C as compared with 7 to 9°C for summer-hatched eggs (Einarsson, 1956*b*). Spring spawners have a higher vertebral count than summer spawners, 57·21 as compared with 56·96 (Einarsson, 1951), which would be expected if the fish were returning to spawn on the grounds on which they were born. If the hypothesis of homing is correct, it should be possible to show that the vertebral count distribution of a year-class of spring spawners does not differ significantly from that of the larvae collected on the spring spawning grounds in the year of their birth. A similar argument applies to the summer spawners. If there is no correspondence between the larvae hatched on a particular ground and the survivors of the year-class that recruit to spawn, the hypothesis of homing should be suspect. Care must be taken in determining the vertebral count of the larvae. Buckmann's (1950) work in the southern North Sea suggests that there is a differential mortality which affects the larvae with the smaller number of vertebrae, as the mean VS is greater in the higher length groups.

Age determination and growth

Scales and otoliths are used for age determination and it is common practice to age a herring according to the number of completed summer growth zones. Thus a herring taken in the Shields spring fishery with two summer zones in the scale (the outer zone bounded by a winter annulus) is two years old and is about to enter its third summer. A few weeks later a scale from the same fish will show a distinct summer growth zone outside the second annulus (winter ring) and the herring is described as a 2+. Later in the year the same fish may be caught at East Anglia on its way down to the channel to spawn. The summer growth zone will be completed and the fish classed as a three-year-old, although the third winter annulus is not yet formed. Confusion can arise as it is the Scottish custom to refer to the number of winter annuli rather than to the number of completed summer zones and the fish would, by this method, be called a 2-ringer both at Shields and at East Anglia. Any doubts can be resolved if both the number of summer growth zones and winter annuli are given.

There are problems in the age determination of herring that do not arise in the case of fish, such as the plaice, which have a relatively short spawning season. Herring spawn in spring, summer, autumn and winter. Considering the scales, and the same is true for otoliths, difficulties arise, as Einarsson (1951, p. 56) points out, due to 'the circumstance that summer and autumn hatched herrings do not form a winter ring in the scales during their first winter of life, while the first winter ring in the scales of spring spawners is formed during the first winter. Herring of spring stock and summer or autumn stock, with the same number of winter rings in the scales, do not belong to the same year class'. The summer-spawned fish are about 6 to 8 months older than those spawned the following spring, but they both have the same number of annuli (winter rings) on the scales. However, Einarsson's views as to the formation of the first winter annulus in spring and summer-spawned fish are not shared by Liamin (1959, p. 167) and this will be discussed later. The point here is that routine methods of age determination are sometimes of little help in deciding the calendar year, let alone the season, when the fish was spawned.

One way of separating herring into summer, autumn, winter and spring-spawned fish does follow from Einarsson's remarks. Taking the two extremes, summer-spawned fish would be expected to have grown more than fish spawned the following spring before the formation of the first winter annulus in the scale. So the length of the fish when the first winter annulus is formed, the l_1 which can be determined by the proportional relationship between scale size and fish length, could provide a means of separating individuals spawned during the two seasons.[1] Icelandic summer spawners do have a slightly higher mean l_1 than Icelandic spring spawners (Einarsson, 1951, p. 58, Fig. 2; Fridriksson, personal communication); similarly Whitby and Dogger autumn spawners have a slightly higher mean l_1 than southern North Sea winter spawners (Zijlstra, 1958; Burd, 1962). There is, however, considerable overlap between the l_1 distributions for the different spawning groups. This is not unexpected as Clark (1933) has shown that slow-growing autumn larvae may be caught up by quick-growing spring larvae before the end of their first summer. Tesch (1937) suggests a similar overlap between autumn- and winter-spawned fish in the Channel. It is clear that the l_1 cannot always be used to separate fish spawned at different seasons as it may be impossible to make a distinction between, for example, slow-growing summer-spawned fish and quick-growing fish spawned the following spring.

Einarsson (1951) turned to otolith structure as an indicator of the environmental conditions, and thus of the season, during which the herring spent their larval and post-larval life. The clear (winter) zones in the otolith are formed from August to May, the opaque (summer) zones from May to July. The larvae of spring spawners, hatching at a time when food was abundant, would be expected to have opaque (summer) nuclei to their otoliths, the summer-spawned fish clear (winter) nuclei. Einarsson (1952b) was able to show that Icelandic spring and summer spawners differ in this respect and that otolith structure was of value in separating members of two spawning groups during those months when the gonad maturation stages were thought to be unreliable. Parrish and Sharman (1958) have extended the technique to the summer-autumn and winter-spring spawning stocks in the northern North Sea.

Postuma and Zijlstra (1958) have shown that there are differences in the radius of the clear (winter) nuclei of Dogger, Sandettié and Channel spawning herring, the early spawners having the wider nuclei. Their results are as follows:

Spawning area	Time of spawning	Mean radius of otolith centre in mm
Dogger	September–October	0·275
Sandettié	November	0·257
Channel	December–January	0·231

[1] A note of explanation should be made of the notation L_1 and l_1 so frequently used in fisheries biology. It was introduced by Lea (1910) who used L as a symbol for the total length of the fish, and L_1, L_2 and L_3, etc., as the total lengths at the formation of the 1st, 2nd, and 3rd, etc., winter annuli in the scale. Similarly l_1, l_2, and l_3, etc., represent the length of the fish at the formation of the 1st, 2nd, and 3rd, etc., winter annuli in the scale as determined by back-calculation from the formula

$$l_1 = L \frac{v}{V}$$

where L is the total length of the fish, V the linear dimension of the scale and v the linear dimension of the scale within the 1st winter annulus. The L and 1 notation is now used in growth studies involving both scale and otolith work.

They have suggested that the size of the otolith nucleus could give some indication of when the fish were spawned, the earlier spawned fish having the bigger otolith nucleus. But the problem is the same as that raised by the use of l_1's, namely, the difficulty of separating slow-growing (small otolith nucleus) Dogger-spawned fish from fast-growing (big otolith nucleus) Sandettié- or Channel-spawned fish.

Vertebral counts, or the detailed structure of the otolith, are probably the most useful criteria for establishing when a herring was spawned. The number of vertebrae and the structure of the otolith nucleus are influenced by the environmental conditions to which the egg and larvae are subjected during the early stages of development and may be used as natural marks. Their value in migration

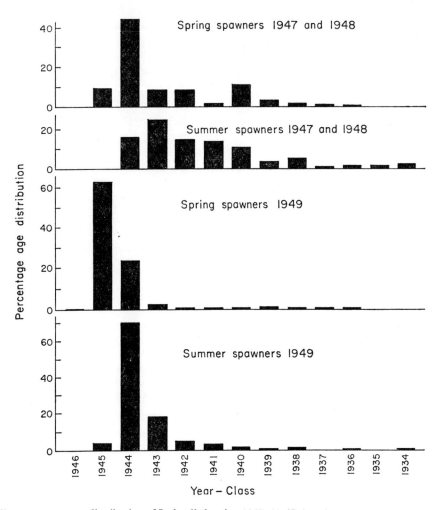

Fig. 26. The percentage age distribution of Icelandic herring 1947–49. 'It is quite evident that during 1947–1948 and again during 1949 there is a distinct correlation between the strength of the year-classes of spring spawners and summer spawners respectively. The relative strength of a year-class of summer progeny corresponds to the relative strength of a year-class of spring progeny the following spring.' (Einarsson, 1952a, p. 63, and p. 64, Fig. 1.)

work, particularly in problems of homing, depends on the difference in the environmental conditions between two spawning grounds.

A digression. Winter annulus formation in spring- and summer-spawned herring and parallelism in year-class strength

Contrary to Einarsson's (1951) view, Liamin (1959, p. 167) believes that many of the summer-spawned Icelandic herring do form a recognizable scale annulus during their first winter. Dahl (1907, p. 10), Hodgson (1927, p. 47), and Andersson (1946) made a similar suggestion for late summer- or early autumn-spawned herring in the North Sea.

If Einarsson believes that summer-spawned fish do not form an annulus in their first winter, he will put them into the wrong year-class if they really do form a first winter annulus. This is of interest in connexion with the parallelism of the year-class strength problem (Einarsson, 1952a), where the relative strength of a summer year-class at Iceland appears to correspond to the relative strength of the year-class born the following spring (Fig. 26). Spring spawners can always be put into the correct year-class: the 1945 year-class sampled in 1949 will have 4 winter annuli (45/46; 46/47; 47/48; and 48/49). But a summer spawner with 4 winter rings will, according to Einarsson, belong to the 1944 year-class, as a fish spawned in the summer of 1945 would not form a 45/46 winter annulus, and would only have 3 winter annuli when sampled in 1949. If, as Liamin claims, some Icelandic summer-spawned fish do form an annulus in their first winter, this could provide an explanation of the parallelism. Should the factors which make for a good year-class also make for good growth, in a good year more summer-spawned fish might form a winter annulus (because they have grown more before the onset of winter) than in a normal one. In a normal year some fish spawned in the summer of 1945 might be split among the 1944 and 1945 year-classes. But in a good year many of the summer-spawned 1945 brood (forming an annulus in the 45/46 winter) would be incorrectly assigned to the 1944 year-class, thus producing the 1944 summer and 1945 spring parallelism. Iles and Johnson (1962) have recently shown that a similar mechanism would account for a year-class split in North Sea sprat populations.

ATLANTIC HERRING

The Atlantic herring include the Atlanto-Scandian and Hiberno-Caledonian groups. The Atlanto-Scandian herring lie to the north of the Wyville-Thompson and Faroe-Shetland ridges, the Hiberno-Caledonian herring to the south. Included among the Atlanto-Scandian herring are the Icelandic, Faroe, Shetland, Viking Bank, Norwegian, and Murman spring spawners, and the Icelandic and Faroe summer spawners. Only the more northerly components of Le Gall's (1935) Hiberno-Caledonian group are of interest here and these include the spring and autumn spawners in the coastal waters of the Hebrides (The Minch) and those herring which spawn further to the north and west, nearer the edge of the continental shelf.

Bottom topography

The bottom topography of the area is shown on the chart in Fig. 27. The basins of the Green-land, Iceland and Norwegian Seas (following Stefánsson's (1962) nomenclature) are separated by a series of ridges which run north-east, south and west from Jan Mayen. The north-eastern ridge is

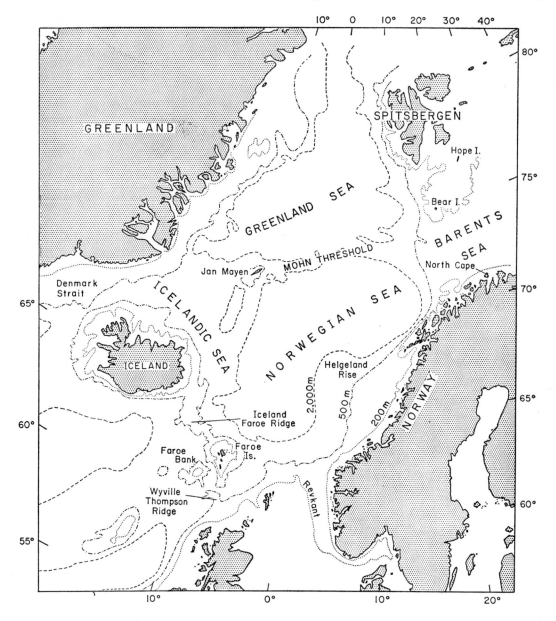

Fig. 27. Bottom topography of the north-east Atlantic Ocean. (Depth contours from Laktionov, 1959, and Stocks, 1950, and following Stefánsson's 1962 nomenclature. Outline from a Meteorological office chart.)

sometimes called Mohn's Threshold (Alekseev and Istoshin, 1959). Other important features include the Iceland-Faroe Ridge; the Wyville-Thompson Ridge; the Norwegian Rinne along which the Baltic outflow reaches the Norwegian Sea; and the Helgeland Ridge (or Rise) to the west of the Norwegian coastal plateau.

Water currents

The hydrographic regime of the north-east Atlantic is dominated by the warm Atlantic current and the cold East Greenland current. Alekseev and Istoshin (1959) give the most recent account of the circulation in this area on which the chart in Fig. 28 is based. The Atlantic current moves northwards through the Faroe-Shetland channel and divides into several branches, some of the water moving east and south into the North Sea between the Shetlands and the Norwegian Coast. The

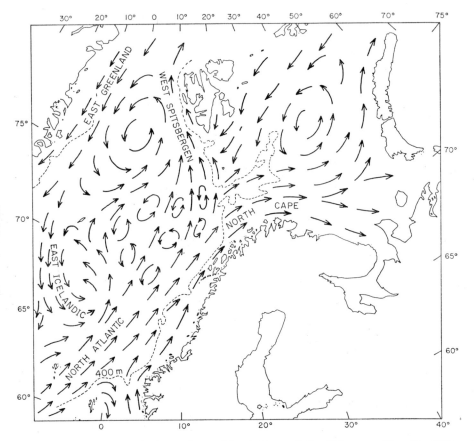

Fig. 28. The surface-water currents in the north-east Atlantic Ocean. (After Alekseev and Istoshin, 1959, and Lee, 1963. The 400 m contour is taken from Stocks, 1950. Outline from a Meteorological Office chart.)

main body of water reaches the Norwegian Sea where it splits up under the influence of the bottom topography. The most easterly branch moves up parallel to the Norwegian coast and mixes with the colder and less saline water of the Baltic outflow which loses its identity along the Møre coastline. This branch of the Atlantic current crosses the Helgeland Ridge and divides into two main streams, one of which becomes the North Cape current and enters the Barents Sea, while the other moves along the edge of the shelf, past Bear Island, towards Spitsbergen and the Greenland Sea.

A western branch of the main Atlantic stream is deflected along the southern slope of the Helgeland Ridge towards Jan Mayen. A series of eddies is formed where this branch meets the eastern side of the cold East Icelandic current. The East Icelandic current runs south-eastwards between Iceland and Jan Mayen, to the west of the line of the Iceland-Jan Mayen Ridge which divides the basins of the Iceland and Norwegian seas. The areas where cold and warm waters mix are the so-called polar fronts. The cold East Icelandic current has areas of mixing on its western side between Iceland and the Faroes and on its eastern side in the south-western part of the Norwegian Sea.

Other areas of mixing occur along Mohn's Threshold, the submarine ridge which separates the Norwegian Sea from the Greenland Sea; and between Spitsbergen, Bear Island, and Novaya Zemlya, where the Atlantic water meets the cold polar water from the north-eastern part of the Barents Sea.

Alekseev and Istoshin's (1959) and Stefánsson's (1962) accounts show that there are four cyclonic (anti-clockwise) circulations, or gyrals, in the north-east Atlantic; in the Irminger, Iceland, Greenland, and Norwegian Seas. These are formed by the interaction of the bottom topography and the two great current systems, the warm Atlantic and the cold East Greenland. The two currents dominate the biology of the herring in these waters. There is a direct effect brought about by the dispersal of young fish from the spawning grounds; the position of the polar fronts vary seasonally and from year to year; and finally the grounds on which the herring spawn may change from year to year depending on local hydrographic conditions as on the Norwegian coast in 1931.

The speeds of the surface currents in the area have been estimated by direct measurements, dynamic computations and drift bottle experiments. Along the Norwegian coast speeds of 9 to 17 miles a day (0·4 to 0·7 knot, 20 to 35 cm/sec) have been reported (Helland-Hansen and Nansen, 1909; Helland-Hansen, 1934). Hermann and Thomsen's (1946) drift bottle experiments indicated average speeds of 4 to 5 miles a day (0·16 to 0·21 knot, 8 to 10 cm/sec) between Jan Mayen and the Faroes in the East Icelandic current, and 6 to 10 miles a day (0·25 to 0·4 knot, 12·5 to 20 cm/sec) from the Faroe-Shetland area to the Møre-Trondelag district on the Norwegian coast. These speeds are all average values and the surface currents could be much faster under the influence of strong winds.

Spawning groups

Greenland

There are not many herring off Greenland. They are found on the west and east coasts and in the Denmark Strait (Runnström, 1936a and b). Spawning occurs in August and September; spring spawners have not been found (Tåning, 1936b). Many of the locally spawned fish must grow up in Greenland waters and there are no records of Greenland tagged herring turning up in other areas (Nielsen, 1960). The herring populations of Greenland and Iceland are possibly related one to another, as are those of the cod: the herring which spawn at Greenland are said (Tåning, 1936b) to be identical with the Icelandic summer spawners. A spring spawning stock may have been unable to establish itself in Greenland waters on account of the environmental conditions.

Iceland (see Fig. 29)

Spring spawners: spawning appears to be concentrated at the Selvogsbanki area during March and April, in depths from 75 to 150 m (Einarsson, 1956b). The larvae take 19 to 24 days to hatch in water with bottom temperatures between 5 and 7°C.

Summer spawners: spawning takes place off the south-west, south, and south-east coasts from July until the middle of August. There are probably three main spawning centres, at Faxafloi,

Selvogsbanki, and Hornafjordur (Einarsson, 1956*b*), Some fish spawn in depths of less than 50 m, others between 75 and 150 m. The larvae should hatch in 15 to 19 days at bottom temperatures between 7 and 9°C.

Both spring- and summer-spawned larvae must, to some extent, be carried clockwise round Iceland and some must drift away in the Irminger current towards east and south-west Greenland. No data are available from which one can estimate the loss of larval herring from Iceland. There is no regular large scale fishery for juvenile herring at Iceland, and the young fish appear to grow up in the fjords and bays, particularly on the west and south-west coasts.

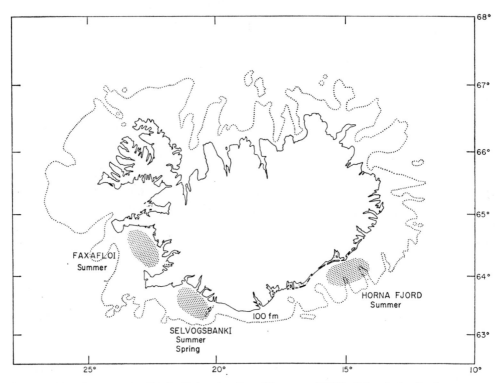

Fig. 29. Spawning grounds of Icelandic herring (from Einarsson, 1956*b*). Other Icelandic place names are given in Fig. 54. (Outline from an Admiralty chart.)

The Faroes

Herring spawn in the spring in March and April, to the south and south-east of the Faroes, at depths between 100 and 200 m (Judanov, 1960), in warm Atlantic water, bottom temperatures 5–7°C, salinity 35·15–35·35‰ (Tåning, 1936*a*). Larvae of a summer or autumn spawning stock have not been found, although there are records of ripe herring being taken in Faroese waters in the summer. Many of the spring-hatched larvae may be carried well away from the Faroes (Tåning, 1936*a*), and some may reach south-east Iceland (Liamin, 1959, p. 172). Young herring are found in various local fjords (Hjort, 1910*b*), but these probably represent a small proportion of the survivors of the spawning which takes place on the banks. While no quantitative data are available, Tåning's (1936*a*, p. 17) view that the local stock is of little importance to the fishery in Faroese waters may well be correct. Faroese spring spawners do not appear to differ significantly from Icelandic or Norwegian spring spawners in meristic characters (Johansen, 1921).

Hiberno-Caledonian components

There are spring and summer spawning herring in The Minch (the channel between the Outer Hebrides and the west coast of Scotland, comprising the Sea of the Hebrides, Little Minch, and North Minch, as described in the *West Coast of Scotland Pilot*, Admiralty, London). Baxter (1958) gives the most recent account of the composition of the stocks and indicates the location of the spawning grounds. The *West Coast of Scotland Pilot* mentions a north-going current of variable strength in The Minch and this could carry some of the newly hatched larvae towards and beyond Cape Wrath. But many of the young fish probably grow up in the innumerable lochs and bays which are a feature of this coastline and the majority of the recruit spawners are likely to be of local origin. Baxter (1958) says that the spring spawning in The Minch takes place in water whose temperature is greater than 7°C and whose salinity is more than 34·5‰.

Herring also spawn on the continental shelf some way from land. Hickling (1928, p. 72) records the presence of herring spawn in the stomach of coalfish (*Gadus virens*) taken at a position some 80 miles west of the Shetlands. Clark (1936) found clupeoid larvae to the south of the Wyville-Thompson Ridge and suggested that they were hatched near the Flannan Isle. There are more recent suggestions of herring spawning in the shelf region, adjacent to the Hebrides (Yudanov, 1962, p. 170). It is not known whether these larvae are the products of the spawning of a hitherto unfished stock, or if they represent strays from the spawning grounds nearer the coast. At all events these larvae must be carried considerable distances to the north in the Atlantic current and the young fish that survive must grow up in areas which are far removed from those in which they were spawned.

Shetland, Orkneys, and Scottish coast

There are spring spawning herring grounds to the north and west of the Shetlands, to the west and east of the Orkneys, and off the Sutherland and Caithness coasts. There are other grounds off Fife ness and Berwick. Wood (1936) gives the temperatures on the spawning ground as between 5 and 7·5°C. Some of the larvae hatched in Shetland waters will be carried to the north by the Atlantic drift. Survivors of those spawned off the Scottish coast probably grow up in coastal nursery grounds and there are clockwise eddies in the Moray Firth and Firth of Forth which will tend to keep the juveniles in these waters. At all events, spring-spawned herring do make up part of the industrial halflin fishery for I- and II-group herring in the Firths. The proportion of spring-spawned herring is generally low but varies from year to year (McPherson, 1957).

The banks of the northern North Sea plateau (see Fig. 30)

Spring spawning herring are sometimes found on certain banks at the north-eastern edge of the North Sea plateau, on the western side of the Norwegian Rinne. The Norwegians call this area the Revkant. The Viking Bank (Runnström, 1936*a*) and the Otterbank (Schubert, 1954) are grounds where spawning herring are caught. The intensity of spawning varies from year to year and this may be related to the hydrographic conditions along the Norwegian coast. In 1931 there was a heavy spring spawning on the Viking Bank and in that year the coastal banks were covered by water of low salinity and the herring did not spawn on the usual grounds (Eggvin, 1940, p. 115). When the bank water (salinity 33–34‰, 4–6°C) is replaced by Baltic (salinity below 30‰) or more saline Atlantic water (salinity $> 35‰$), the herring appear to leave the coastal areas and spawn further out to sea, possibly on the Revkant banks. Yolk-sac larvae have been found in this area (Runnström, 1941*a*, p. 24) but their drift in the currents has not been followed.

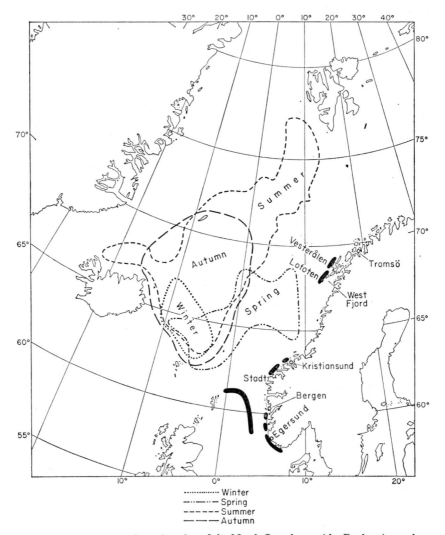

Fig. 30. Herring spawning grounds along the edge of the North Sea plateau (the Revkant), south-west Norway, and at Lofoten and Vesterålen (from Runnström, 1941*a*). The seasonal distributions of herring in the Norwegian Sea are also shown, based on observations made during the 8 years 1951–58. (From Fridland, Osetinskaya, and Bernikova, 1960, p. 380, Fig. 1. Outline from a Meteorological Office chart.)

The Norwegian spring herring (see Fig. 30)

The Norwegian spring herring spawn off the south-western coast of Norway, south of 63°N. The full fish reach the Norwegian coast between Bergen and Stadt about 5 to 6 weeks before they start to spawn (Aasen, 1962) and they form the basis for the Large herring fishery. Spawning commences in February and goes on until early April. There are two main spawning regions: one between Egersund and Bergen, south of the Large herring district, the other to the north between Bergen and Kristiansund. The hydrographic conditions show an increase in temperature and salinity from south to north as the cold and low salinity Baltic outflow mixes with the warmer and more saline Atlantic water. Thus the bottom temperatures increase from 5 to 6°C off Egersund to 7 to 8°C off Ålesund (Runnström, 1941*a*, p. 82).

After hatching, some of the larvae will enter local fjords and bays, while others will be carried northwards in the surface current. Very few of the larvae are likely to be carried round North Cape as the outer arm of the West Fjord acts as a natural trap across their drift path. The young fish settle down in the coastal waters between Bergen and Finmark but some may be carried out to sea as there are records of O-group herring being taken in July and August several hundreds of miles from land in the Norwegian Sea (Devold, 1951*a*; Wiborg, 1957).

The Murman spring herring (see Fig. 30)

The Murman spring herring spawn off the northern coast of Norway. There are spawning grounds off Lofoten and Vesterålen, at Malangen, and to the east of North Cape along the Murman coast (Runnström, 1936*c*, 1941*a*; Rass, 1939; Marty, 1959, p. 12). At Lofoten and Vesterålen spawning takes place in March and April but is delayed until May–August in the easterly regions. On the Lofoten-Vesterålen grounds the water has a temperature of 5 to 6°C and a salinity of 34·41 to 35·06‰ (Rass, 1939).

The larvae are carried round North Cape into the Barents Sea. Some may settle down in the fjords along the Murman Coast but the majority are believed to drift toward the Kanin and Goose Banks and spend their winter out in the open sea (Rass, 1939; Marty, 1959; and Dragesund, 1961, 1962*a*, who records the presence of O-group herring in the Barents Sea).

Many of the larvae from the various Atlantic herring groups must be carried a long way from the spawning grounds, particularly on westerly coastlines exposed to the influence of the North Atlantic drift. Where do the survivors grow up and feed; what are their annual movements and migrations; do they spawn in the parent area or on the parent ground? The discussion will be restricted to the movements and migrations of the Norwegian spring spawners because the life history of this group is the most well known.

Movements and migrations of the Norwegian spring herring (for place names see Figs. 27, 30, 33, and 48)

THE IMMATURE FISH

Many of the young herring spend their first year in the fjord or coastal waters between Bergen and Finmark, depending on their drift while only a few months old. The fjord and coastal herring live at winter temperatures lower than those which must be experienced by herring growing up in more open waters warmed by the Atlantic current. The former have sharply defined winter annuli (as if drawn by a fine pencil) when compared with the more diffuse annuli (as if drawn by a chalk) in the latter. The two types were originally described by Lea (1929*a*, *b*) and have been called 'Northern' and 'Southern' (abbreviated to N and S) types respectively, a description justified by Runnström's (1936*c*) analysis, which showed that 80 to 100% of I-group herring taken in northern Norway (Finmark, Troms, Nordland) had a sharply defined winter annulus compared with 7% to 8% among those taken in southern Norway (Hordalund, Rogalund). But it is clear from Runnström's (1941a, p. 68) later paper that the scale type depends more on the water in which the young fish winter (cold or warm) than on whether they grew up in the north or further to the south. Lea (1929a, p. 27) wrote that the terms 'must not be understood in a too literally geographical sense'.

Several categories of herring are recognized in the Norwegian statistics and the more important ones are as follows.

Maturity state	Length in cm	Category English	Norwegian
Immature		I-group	Bladsild
	7–19	Small	Smaasild
	19–26	Fat	Fetsild
Mixture of recruits and fat herring			Forfangstsild
Mature full fish	>26	Large } Winter	Storsild } Vintersild
Spawning fish	>26	Spring	Vaarsild

The small and fat fisheries for immature herring take place in the fjords and coastal waters between Ålesund and Finmark. Immature herring with S-type scales have a greater length-for-age than N-type fish. The difference in growth splits a year-class into several spawning classes. The larger members of a year-class are found further from the shore but they come into the coastal waters during the summer months, when they are caught in the fat herring fishery. Within the coastal waters tagging experiments show a northward movement in the summer followed by a southward movement in the late autumn (Dragesund, 1956, 1958b, 1959a).

The on- and off-shore movements are repeated each year until the immature fish reach a certain critical length, which may decrease with age. Then they leave the coastal waters and do not return until they are ready to spawn. The one or more years spent in the open sea independent of the coastal waters constitute the oceanic intermediate stage, originally predicted by Lea (1929a) before immature herring had been caught in the Norwegian Sea. There are four main lines of evidence to support his hypothesis.

1. There is no body of herring in Norwegian coastal waters from which the recruit spawners could, from considerations of age, length and sexual maturity, be directly derived (Lea, 1929a, p. 20).

2. The recruit spawners have one or more winter scale annuli which differ in appearance from the N-type and, to a lesser extent, from the S-type (Runnström, 1936c, p. 19). This winter annulus is believed to be formed under oceanic conditions and is known as the oceanic or X annulus.

3. Wilson (1958) records the oceanic recapture of a fat herring tagged off the Lofoten Islands.

4. Immature herring are found all over the Norwegian Sea, particularly in the eastern part and to the south-east of Jan Mayen (Fedorov, 1960). The area within which they are found decreases with the onset of their maturity and in the winter months they are closer to the spawning grounds, in the south-eastern part of the Norwegian Sea.

The faster growing members of a year-class (S-type) enter the oceanic intermediate stage several years before their slower growing brothers and sisters (N-type). The faster growing fish recruit to the spawning shoals in their fourth year (3 winter annuli) and 80% of these fish have S-type scales. The slower growing members of the year-class may not spawn until their sixth or seventh year (5 or 6 winter annuli) and nearly all these fish have N-type scales (Runnström, 1936c; Telkora, 1961). The recruit spawners are the last to spawn as shown by the change in the age composition during the Norwegian spring herring fishery (Lea, 1929a).

THE MATURE FISH

Information on the movements and changes in the distribution of herring in the Norwegian Sea come from four main sources.

1. Fridriksson's racial analysis of the herring caught in the Icelandic summer fishery.
2. Icelandic and Norwegian (see Table 13, p. 108), and Russian tagging experiments.
3. Russian data derived from the catch statistics of their high seas drift net fishery.
4. Norwegian sonar surveys.

The larger fish are the first to spawn and the first to leave the spawning grounds. Recoveries of spring herring tagged on the spawning grounds have been made in the Skagerrak, North Sea, and at Iceland in the year of tagging. But most of the spents move west and north-west into the Norwegian Sea where they feed heavily on zooplankton. The larger fish reach the polar front in June and July and some cross into the cold water. The limit of the summer feeding migration extends from Spitsbergen, the Mohn Ridge, and Jan Mayen in the north, to the eastern and western borders of the East Icelandic current in the south. The July size compositions of herring caught in different areas given by Marty (1959, p. 33, Fig. 4) and Marty and Wilson (1960, p. 334, Fig. 3) show that the smaller fish do not move so far to the north and west.

The area over which the fish feed contracts during the autumn when the herring are found in the south-western part of the Norwegian Sea along the borders of the East Icelandic current. The ripening herring winter in an area to the north of the Faroes. In December and January the pre-spawning concentrations move towards the Norwegian coast. The fish move about 1,800 miles (60°N. to 75°N. and back) during the year. Fig. 30 summarizes the seasonal changes in distribution.

(a) The feeding migration

Fish tagged off the Norwegian coast have been recovered off Iceland (see Table 13) and a proportion of the herring caught in the summer fishery off the north-east Icelandic coast have Norwegian-type scales (Fridriksson, 1958a). These observations have confirmed Fridriksson's (1944) earlier suggestion of a relation between the north coast Icelandic herring and the Norwegian spring spawners.

Runnström (1936c, p. 90) and Fridriksson (1944, p. 336) suggested that the spring spawners keep within the cyclonic current system of the Norwegian Sea. Runnström supposed the migration to be largely directed by the current. According to such a hypothesis the spent fish leave the Norwegian coast and move west and north-west, riding the western branches of the Atlantic stream. Later in the year they return along the boundaries of the east-going East Icelandic current towards the spawning grounds.

The spring and summer movements of the herring may be governed by the seasonal changes in the production and distribution of their food. Biological spring spreads north and north-west across the Norwegian Sea along the line of the finger-like branches of the Atlantic current (see

Fig. 31). Pavshtiks (1959) suggested that the larger herring, the first to leave the spawning grounds, move from region to region feeding heavily on the pre-spawning concentrations of *Calanus finmarchicus* and Euphausiacea to reach the polar front at the time of biological spring when *Calanus hyperboreus* is abundant in the cold water. So the direction and speed of the feeding migration may be primarily related to the availability of food and only indirectly to the current system. Marty (1959, p. 34) notes that the herring swim downstream at a speed faster than that of the current but he does not give any evidence to support this statement.

Table 13. Release and recapture data of Atlanto-Scandian herring tagged with internal magnetic tags. Within-season recaptures in the release areas omitted.

Tagging area	Tagging data Years	Number tagged	Recoveries to 1962 NE. Iceland	SW. Iceland	Norway
Norway	1948–61	262,029	240	8	2,802
NE. Iceland	1948, 1951–61	107,882	2,491	472	2,679
SW. Iceland	1953–61	46,397	465	612	5

Sources of data

Tagging.   Dragesund (1964) *Annls biol., Copenh.*, **19**: Table 31, p. 130.
Jakobsson (1961) *Rit Fiskideild.*, **2**: (10) Table 3, p. 9.
Jakobsson (1963) *Annls biol., Copenh.*, **18**: Table 11, p. 147.

Recaptures.   Dragesund (1959b) *Annls biol., Copenh.*, **14**: Table 13, p. 158.
Dragesund (1962b) *Annls biol., Copenh.*, **17**: Table 18, p. 169.
Dragesund (1964) *Annls biol., Copenh.*, **19**: Table 31, p. 130.
Fridriksson (1953) *Annls biol., Copenh.*, **9**: p. 167.
Fridriksson (1954) *Annls biol., Copenh.*, **10**: p. 147.
Fridriksson (1956) *Annls biol., Copenh.*, **11**: p. 118.
Fridriksson (1957) *Annls biol., Copenh.*, **12**: Table 9, p. 162.
Fridriksson (1958b) *Annls biol., Copenh.*, **13**: Table 10, p. 176.
Fridriksson (1959) *Annls biol., Copenh.*, **14**: Table 8, p. 154.
Fridriksson (1960) *Annls biol., Copenh.*, **15**: Table 7, p. 130.
Fridriksson (1961) *Annls biol., Copenh.*, **16**: Table 8, p. 167.
Fridriksson (1962) *Annls biol., Copenh.*, **17**: Table 11, p. 165.
Fridriksson and Aasen (1952) *Rit Fiskideild.*, (1).
Jakobsson (1961) *Rit Fiskideild.*, **2**: (10) Table 3, p. 9.
Jakobsson (1963) *Annls biol., Copenh.*, **18**: Table 10, p. 147.
Jakobsson (1964) *Annls biol., Copenh.*, **19**: Tables 18 and 19, p. 124.

(b) Summer distribution

During the summer the herring are in the surface 30 to 40 m (Devold, 1952a, p. 106; Tåning, 1951, 1952b; Marty, 1959, p. 45) where they are caught by drift net and purse seine. The shoals do not appear to make extensive diurnal vertical movements at this time of the year. This is not surprising as north of the 68° parallel there is no true night from the middle of April to the last week in August. In June, July, and August, the herring concentrate in the region of the polar front where conditions are said to be particularly favourable for a high level of production. Sonar surveys have provided some information on the distribution of herring shoals in relation to hydrographic conditions in the area, the data appearing piecemeal in the Norwegian *Fiskets Gang* and the International Council's *Annales Biologiques*. Most of the fish stay above the thermocline on the warm side of the 3 to 5°C transition area between the Atlantic and Arctic waters (Aasen, 1958,

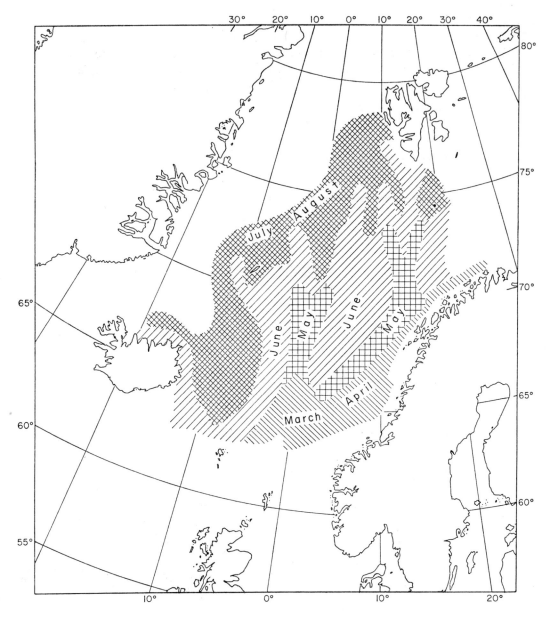

Fig. 31. The north and north-west spread of biological spring in the north-east Atlantic Ocean. (After Pavshtiks, 1959. Outline from a Meteorological Office chart.)

Fig. 8; 1959; Devold, 1951*a*, Fig. 4; 1952*a*; 1953*a*, Fig. 7; 1955; Devold *et al.*, 1961, Fig. 7; Østvedt, 1960*b*; Tåning, 1951, 1953, 1957, Fig. 13). Scattered traces are found in the polar water (Tåning, 1957; Devold *et al.*, 1961) and herring are caught there when food is particularly abundant, as in the summer of 1954 (Marty, 1959, p. 46; Pavshtiks, 1959, p. 117).

(c) The return migration

Russian experiments (see Fig. 32) have shown that herring tagged during the summer on the Mohn Ridge and in the north-western part of the Norwegian Sea are recaptured to the south-west later in the year and off the Norwegian coast the following spring. Similar Norwegian recoveries have been made from herring tagged off the north coast of Iceland.

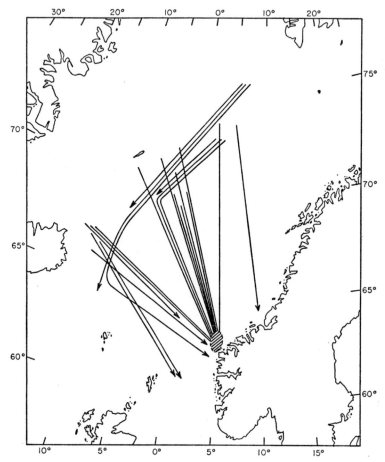

Fig. 32. Movements of herring tagged in the open sea in the summers of 1954–56 and recovered in the autumn and spring immediately following tagging. (From Marty and Wilson, 1960, p. 336, Fig. 4.) The lines joining the positions of release and recapture are unlikely to represent the routes taken by the fish. (Outline from a Meteorological Office chart.)

The return migration along the western edge of the Norwegian Sea starts between the middle of August and the middle of September (Tåning, 1956; Marty, 1959, p. 41). In October and November dense concentrations of herring are found between Iceland and the Faroes around the borders of the East Icelandic current. During December the herring are north of the Faroes. They reach the Norwegian coastal waters off Møre in January.

The distribution and movements of the shoals recorded by sonar during this part of the migration are discussed by Aasen (1958, 1959), Devold (1951a, p. 127; 1951b; 1952b; 1953a, p. 171;

1953*b*; 1954*a*; 1954*b*; 1956*a*, p. 120; 1956*b*; 1957, p. 170; 1959; 1960; 1962), Østvedt (1960*a*, 1962) and Tåning (1952*b*, 1953). Unfortunately, none of these accounts gives all the information which is essential to build up a picture of what the shoals are doing and details concerning identification of the traces are seldom presented. It is said that the shoals make extensive diurnal movements, from 300 to 400 m in the day towards the surface water at night. So the herring may be in cold water (3 to 4°C) during the day and in warm water (5 to 7°C) by night. No data have been published from which it is possible to assess the speed at which the fish move eastward. For example, Devold (1963) gives speeds of 6 miles a day (0·25 knots, 12·5 cm/sec) in the cold water and 30 miles a day (1·25 knots, 62·5 cm/sec) in the warm water, but neither in this nor in any other account does he give details of the observations from which these estimates are derived.

The full herring arrive off the Norwegian coast between Bergen and Stadt where they form the basis for the Large herring fishery. There is a delay of about 5 to 6 weeks between the arrival of the herring and the onset of spawning (Aasen, 1962) which could be thought of as an assembly (see p. 204) before they move on towards the spawning grounds, most of which, at present, lie north and south of the Large herring district between Kristiansund and Egersund. The herring approach the spawning grounds in long 'streaky' shoals (Runnström, 1941*b*, p. 42) and according to Runnström (1941*a*, p. 24) they come in along the line of deeper ridges or the seaward extension of fjords. But as has already been indicated, hydrographical conditions play some part in deciding where the fish will spawn and they appear to avoid the inshore grounds if they are covered by cold water.

This completes the description of the annual migration of the Norwegian spring herring. The movements of the other spawning groups of Atlantic herring are not so well known, but Liamin's (1959, 1960) accounts have added to our knowledge of the Icelandic summer spawners and Rass (1939) deals with the movements of the Murman herring in the Barents Sea.

The evidence for homing in Atlantic herring

Icelandic and Norwegian spring spawners have different spawning areas. There are two main spawning grounds off the Norwegian coast; off the Møre coast north of Stadt and between Bergen and Egersund. Within each of these two grounds there are a number of localized beds on which the eggs are spawned. Homing can therefore be considered at three levels: (a) a return to the parent area; (b) a return to the parent ground; and (c) a return to the parent spawning bed. The problem that is common to all three is that of being able to determine the area, ground, or bed where a fish was spawned.

1. THE RETURN TO THE PARENT SPAWNING AREA

(a) Some of the herring spawned in the spring at south-west Iceland, the Faroes, Hebrides, Orkneys, Shetlands, and Viking Bank, must be carried a long way from the parent area. It is not known if these fish spawn in other areas as there are no natural marks or tags by which they can be identified.

(b) Herring that grow up in different regions may develop characteristic scale patterns. If it is assumed that different regions act as nursery grounds for specific spawning areas the scale patterns may be regarded as birthmarks. The assumption is probably valid when considering the Icelandic and Norwegian spring spawning areas whose nursery grounds will be Icelandic and Norwegian coastal waters respectively. Fridriksson (1950) has used the scale pattern to separate Norwegian spring, Icelandic spring, and Icelandic summer spawners. Unfortunately, the scale pattern differences used in the separation have never been defined and described. While the N_N and $I_{summer\ scale}$

patterns are probably clear, an inexperienced worker might have difficulty in distinguishing between the N_s and I_{spring} patterns. There do not appear to be any records of fish with Norwegian N_N scale patterns spawning at Iceland. As can be seen from Table 13 there have been only 8 recoveries at south-west Iceland of herring tagged on the Norwegian coast, and 5 Norwegian recoveries of herring tagged at south-west Iceland. Some of the south-west Iceland tagged fish recovered at Norway may have been recovering spent summer spawners, whose occasional presence in the Norwegian catch was reported by Rasmussen (1940). The 8 Norwegian tagged fish recovered at south-west Iceland factories were all returned in 1962 (Jakobsson, 1964).

Herring of Faroe, Orkney, Shetland, or Viking Bank origin may drift into Norwegian waters and develop scale patterns typical of the region. So the presence of spawners with Norwegian-type scales on these grounds could indicate homing or straying. It seems unlikely that Southern Bight spawned fish would reach the Norwegian nursery grounds so that herring with Norwegian-type scales that appeared in the 1949 East Anglian fishery (Hodgson, 1950b; 1957, p. 124) were almost certainly strays.

(c) The Icelandic spring and summer herring spawn, on Selvogsibanki at least, on the same ground, but a different times of the year. Einarsson (1951, p. 63) holds that 'a herring hatched in spring also spawns in spring and a herring of summer progeny also spawns during summer'. If true, this might suggest, but not prove, that the spawning season was genetically determined. In the North Sea the summer, autumn, and winter herring spawn in different areas, and here if the spawning season is predetermined for an individual, this must be associated with a return to the parent spawning area. It is therefore of some interest to examine Einarsson's data as his problem is one which is relevant to homing in other areas. Data relating to otolith structure, vertebral count, and maturation stages have been given to support his hypothesis. Einarsson (1951) found that that the nucleus of the otolith of Norwegian spring spawners differed from that of Icelandic summer spawners. Norwegian spring spawners had opaque nuclei, the Icelandic summer spawners clear nuclei. There were several different types of nuclei within each group which were classified as follows:

Norwegian spring spawners (number of fish in sample = 390)

Proportion %	Type	Description
85·6	VA	Opaque nucleus
11·5	VB	Small hyaline centres
2·1	VC	Hyaline nucleus conspicuous
0·8	S	Hyaline nucleus very conspicuous and resembling that of a summer spawner. Fish with these otoliths may be spents from Iceland.

Icelandic summer spawners (number of fish in sample = 290)

Proportion %	Type	Description
67·6	SA	Well-defined hyaline nucleus
16·9	SB	Hyaline nucleus smaller
11·4	SC	Hyaline nucleus a narrow transverse groove
4·1	SD	Hyaline nucleus not visible, transverse groove present

The Norwegian analyses were carried out on four samples of spring spawners, whose mean VS ranged from 56·830 to 57·220. The Icelandic samples were immature herring (Stage I), judged to be summer spawners by their mean VS count of 56·86.

Einarsson found the VA and SA types were easy to distinguish, but that confusion was possible between VB and SC, and VC and SB. The difference in otolith type was attributed to environmental conditions: spring spawners were spawned in the spring and the larvae grew up under conditions that were good for growth, the opaque nuclei corresponding to the opaque 'summer' zone in the otolith of older fish. Similarly, the summer spawners were summer-spawned and the larvae and post-larvae grew up under relatively poor conditions, the clear nuclei corresponding to the clear 'winter' zones.

The study was then extended to 5,500 Icelandic herring (Einarsson, 1952*b*) collected in two periods, the first between 13 August and 18 October 1950, and the second between 11 November 1950 and 5 January 1951.

1. *The first period.* 13 August to 18 October 1950

(a) A maturation stage split showed that Stage II fish had a VS typical of summer spawners (56·81), Stages III to IV fish had a VS typical of spring spawners (57·22–57·35), and Stage VIII fish had an intermediate count (57·06), indicating a mixture of the two groups.

(b) An otolith split into spring and summer spawners gave spring spawners (mean VS 57·23) in maturation Stages III to IV and VIII, and summer spawners (mean VS 56·93) in Stages VII–VIII and VIII.

(c) When the otolith types (summer SA, SB, SC, SD; spring VA, VB, VC) were examined for vertebral count, they all gave values typical for their spawning group.

2. *The second period.* 11 November 1960 to 5 January 1951

(a) A maturation stage split gave Stages IV and V fish with a VS typical of spring spawners (57·24 and 57·23), and Stage VIII fish typical of summer spawners (56·95).

(b) When the collection was split by otolith type, the spring spawners were in maturation Stages IV and V, with VS's of 57·24 and 57·23, the summer spawners in Stage VIII, VS 56·95. It is clear that there is complete agreement between the spawning groups indicated by maturation stage and otolith type during this period.

(c) When the otolith types were examined for VS they gave values which were typical of those to be expected for the appropriate spawning groups.

The conclusion that can be drawn from these results is that a separation of the collections on the basis of otolith types gives two groups whose maturation stage and mean vertebral count are consistent with those of the spring and summer spawners. Einarsson (1952, p. 182) carries the argument a stage further, using the unambigious SA otolith type: 'If the spring spawners are heterogeneous, i.e. consist of herring hatched during spring and summer, we should encounter herring with otoliths of the SA type in maturity stage IV or V during the period November to January. This would indicate that the herrings had been hatched during the summer, but were going to spawn in spring.' Einarsson lists 216 SA type otoliths from the November to January collection and only one of these was in Stage IV or V. But it is difficult to see how this can be construed as supporting a hypothesis of homing when there is no evidence to show that SA types are summer-hatched. This could be provided by an examination of the otolith types in samples of young herring known to have been spawned in the summer or the spring. But this does not appear to have been done.

While Einarsson fails to prove that Icelandic spring and summer spawners return to spawn in the season of their birth, the circumstantial evidence suggests that the hypothesis is correct. The following data support it. Einarsson (1956b, p. 8) gives the vertebral count for a sample of larvae spawned in the summer of 1947. Dr. Fridriksson (personal communication) has very kindly given me some further details concerning the vertebral counts of the 1947 year-class of spring and summer herring, particulars of which have already been published (Fridriksson, 1958a). The following comparison can be made:

No. of vertebrae	Icelandic herring, 1947 year-class					
	Summer larvae		Summer adults		Spring adults	
	No.	%	No.	%	No.	%
55	4	0·6	—	—	—	—
56	124	18·6	13	19·7	3	7·5
57	442	56·3	42	53·3	27	67·5
58	92	13·8	9	13·6	10	25·0
59	5	0·7	2	3·4	—	—
Totals	667	100·0	66	100·0	40	100·0
Mean VS	56·955		57·000		57·198	

The vertebral count distribution of the summer larvae is closer to that of the summer spawners than that of the spring spawners. This is consistent with the hypothesis that the herring spawn in the same season as that in which they were born.

Further support for the hypothesis could come from a study of the fecundity of the two spawning stocks. The summer spawners have the higher fecundity, and produce a greater number of smaller eggs which Liamin (1959, p. 186) has suggested is an adaptation to compensate for a relatively high mortality of the larvae during their first winter. The high mortality of summer-spawned larvae has not been demonstrated, and the extent to which the difference in fecundity between the two spawning groups depends on environmental or genetic factors has not been determined. If genetic factors could be shown to be the more important this would support Einarsson's hypothesis.

2. THE RETURN TO THE PARENT SPAWNING GROUND

Runnström (1941a) tried to find out if there were separate spawning grounds along the Norwegian coast. Material collected from 1932 to 1936 showed that the vertebral counts of O-group herring taken in the coastal waters decreased from south to north and that the same pattern was evident among samples of spring herring. The data are summarized below, the corresponding districts being shown in Fig. 33.

District	Runnström's (1941a) data on vertebral counts	
	Table 20 O-group	Table 3 Spring herring
North 4	57·187	57·247 – 57·267
3	57·198	57·202 – 57·394
2	57·352	57·246 – 57·306
South 1	57·524	57·305 – 57·463

Runnström (1941*a*, p. 66) suggested that the fry were spawned in the district in which they were caught. Both series of vertebral counts show the same trend with latitude which suggests that there must be some order in the return of the spring herring to the districts. Further analysis showed that there were differences in vertebral counts between samples taken from different grounds within a district which led Runnström (1941*a*, p. 38) to suggest that there were 'different independent runs to the different spawning grounds'. Evidence for a return to a parent ground could

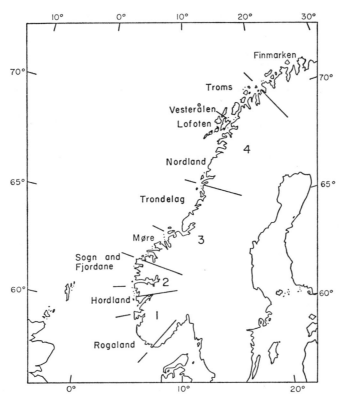

Fig. 33. Norwegian districts. (From Runnström, 1936*c*, Fig. 1; 1941*a*, p. 27. Outline from a Meteorological Office chart.)

KEY

1. Rogaland, S. Hordland; 2. N. Hordland, Sogn and Fjordane; 3. Møre, Trondelag; 4. Nordland, Troms.

have been obtained by comparing, within a district, the vertebral count of the fry with that of the survivors of the year-class who returned as spring herring. This was not done and the work has not been followed up.

Some of the spring herring sampled in Runnström's district 4 must belong to the Murman spring spawning group, for example those taken at Troms and Vesterålen, with vertebral counts of 57·247 and 57·263 (Runnström, 1941*a*, Table 3). Most of these northern spawners have N-type scales (Runnström, 1941*a*, Table 22). If Murman spring spawners were to spawn on the Norwegian spring herring grounds, Norwegian N-types might be expected to have a lower vertebral count than Norwegian S-types. This does not appear to be true (Runnström, 1941*a*, Table 22; Østvedt, 1958,

Table 1), the S-types having the slightly lower mean. This suggests, but does not prove, that the Murman spring spawned fish do not spawn on the Norwegian spring grounds.

3. THE RETURN TO THE PARENT SPAWNING BED

There is no evidence to show that herring return to spawn on the bed on which they were hatched.

4. SUBSEQUENT SPAWNING

It is of interest to know whether a herring always spawns in the same area or on the same ground of its first spawning, which may have been the true or an adopted home. Direct evidence could be provided by tagging spawning fish and noting where they were recovered during subsequent spawning seasons. Indirect evidence could be provided by a study of vertebral counts, scale or otolith structure; unless there are wanderers from other grounds, the features that are characteristic of a year-class should remain constant from year to year.

The following points are relevant:

(a) Norwegian spring herring tagged on their spawning grounds are recovered at Norway year after year (Table 13). The 8 Norwegian tagged fish recaptured at south-west Iceland in 1962 were recovered in the summer fishery and there are no data to support Fridriksson's (1944, p. 337) suggestion that some of the Norwegian spring spawners found off north-east Iceland during the summer spawn at south-west Iceland the following spring. There is no evidence of Icelandic fish spawning at Norway.

(b) Some Norwegian spring herring may stray to other areas. Fridriksson and Aasen (1952, p. 29) record the recapture of a Norwegian spring herring in the Skagerrak and remark on the possibility that the spawning ground may differ from year to year. But there is no evidence to show that a significant proportion of herring that have spawned once on the Norwegian coast go to other areas in subsequent seasons.

(c) The Norwegian tagging results are not presented in a way which would allow one to draw any conclusions concerning the possibility that Norwegian spring herring return to the south-west coast but spawn on different grounds each year. A ground may not be used if the local hydrographic conditions are unsuitable. Runnström's (1941b, p. 38) observations that a particular spawning ground to the north of Haugesund is mainly visited by recruits could be significant. If this is true the survivors may go to another ground the following year.

(d) An editorial footnote in Rass's (1939, p. 110) paper records that recruits to the Murman spring group mainly spawn between Malangen Bank and Söröy. If this is true, they may go to a different ground in their second spawning season.

(e) Baxter (1958) has concluded that the majority of spring spawners in The Minch only spawn there once after which they leave the area and do not return. This conclusion is based on the age composition of the spring spawners. In 1954 and 1955 over 90% of the spawning population were 3 and 4 years old. Emigration could account for the absence of the older fish but the possibility that mortality (fishing or natural) is the cause has not been excluded.

NORTH SEA HERRING

There are three main spawning groups of herring in the North Sea; the Scottish north-east coast or Buchan spawners; the Dogger or Bank spawners; and the Southern Bight or Downs spawners.

The three groups spawn in different seasons (summer, autumn, and winter) on different grounds. From the point of view of management and conservation it is important to know if the progeny of a particular spawning recruit to the parent group and the extent to which the immature and mature fish are mixed at other times of the year.

Fig. 34. Place name chart of the North Sea and adjacent coastal waters. The depth contours are at 10, 20, 30, 50 and 100 fathoms. In some areas the contouring has been simplified to avoid overcrowding the chart. The Southern Bight area is shown in greater detail in Fig. 35. (Place names and other details from various Admiralty charts and the North Sea Fishing Chart (Imray, Laurie, Norie, and Wilson, Ltd.). Outline from an Admiralty chart.)

Bottom topography

The North Sea is a rectangular basin whose depth decreases from north to south in three broad steps (see Fig. 37). These roughly correspond to lines joining Buchan ness with Karmoy on the Norwegian coast, and Hartlepool with Hantsholm on the Danish coast, so dividing the basin into three, the northern, middle and southern North Seas. A bathymetric chart of the North Sea is given in Fig. 34, which includes a number of the more important place names. The position of the 20 fm contour should be noted. North of Flamborough Head, it is close to the British coastline and there is only a narrow strip of shallow inshore water, in contrast with the situation further south and off the continental coastline where the shallow area is more extensive. The northern North Sea is bounded by the continental shelf to the north and the edge of Norwegian Rinne to the east. Within the area important place names are those of the Bressay and Fladen grounds, the Viking Bank, the Patch, Utsire ground and Egersund ground. To the south the bottom rises relatively steeply between 57° 30' and 58° 30'N., the line of demarcation between the northern and middle sections.

The middle North Sea is 20 to 40 m shallower than the northern basin. The Coral, Ling, and Fisher Banks lie to the east, and in the middle of the basin there are two deeper areas, the Gut and Devil's Hole. The Gut is a shallow depression which connects with the northern basin through the Swatchway. Important localities in the western middle North Sea are the Turbot, Aberdeen, Montrose, Berwick, and NE. Banks.

The southern North Sea is relatively shallow. The Dogger Bank is less than 40 m deep and is bounded on its south-western and southern sides by a channel of deeper water, Skate Hole, the Outer Silver Pit and the Clay Deep. A number of important fishing grounds lie along the northern edge of the Dogger. From east to west these include the Monkey Bank, Tail End, Outer, Middle, and NW. Rough, Brucey's Garden, SW. Patch, the Dogger Bight and SW. Spit. In the German Bight the White Bank is part of the so-called Bløden Ground, the centre of an industrial fishery for immature herring. The Southern Bight includes that part of the southern North Sea which lies between the Straits of Dover and 53°N. A tongue of deep water enters the Southern Bight through the Straits. To the east and west the deep water is bounded by a series of sand ridges which, along the continental shore, extend from the Dutch coast down to Dieppe. The more important ridges are named in Fig. 35.

Tidal currents

The tidal impulse that reaches the Southern Bight through the Straits of Dover is small and its effect does not extend beyond Texel on the Dutch coast. So far as the tides are concerned, the Southern Bight is part of the English Channel. But the North Sea receives, through its northern opening, a strong tidal impulse from the North Atlantic which maintains a standing oscillation in the basin. The dimensions of the North Sea are such that there should be two nodal lines which would be transformed into amphidromies of no tidal range by the rotation of the earth. Defant's (1961) account of the North Sea tides is the most recent summary of theory and observation. The fastest streams are found on the east coast of Great Britain and in the Southern Bight where the flow may reach 2 knots (100 cm/sec) or more at spring tides.

Residual currents

Water enters the North Sea from the Atlantic in the north, the English Channel in the south, and the Baltic in the east. Freshwater is contributed from the British Isles and the continent. Laevastu

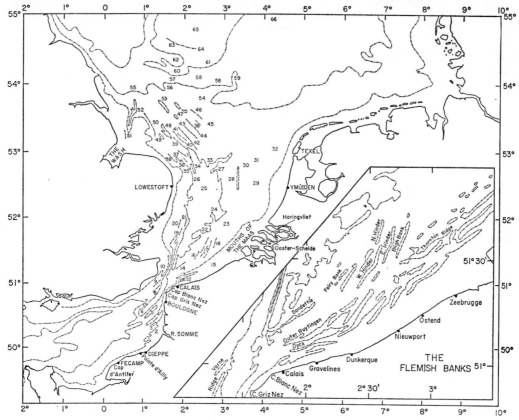

Fig. 35. Place names in the Southern Bight of the North Sea of interest in connexion with herring and plaice migrations. The insert shows the Flemish Banks in more detail. The depth contours are at 10, 20 and 30 fathoms. (Place names and other details from various Admiralty charts and the North Sea Fishing Chart (Imray, Laurie, Norie and Wilson, Ltd.). Outline from an Admiralty chart.)

KEY

1 Ridin de Dieppe	23 Schouwen Ground	45 Leman Ground
2 Bassurelle de la Somme	24 East Deep Water	46 Indefatigable Banks
3 Battur	25 Knoll Flat	47 Coal Pit
4 Bassure de Baas	26 Knoll Deep	48 Haddock Bank
5 Vergoyer	27 Winterton Shoal	49 Cromer Knoll
6 Bassurelle	28 Brown Ridge	50 Outer Dowsing
7 Bullock Bank	29 Broad Fourteens	51 Inner Dowsing
8 Ridge	30 Brown Bank	52 Inner Silver Pit
9 Varne	31 Egmond Ground	53 Haddock Bank
10 Goodwins	32 Texel Ground	54 Markham's Hole
11 Riden de Calais	33 Winterton Twenties	55 Off Ground
12 Dyck	34 Smith's Knoll	56 Well Bank Flat
13 Outer Ruytingen	35 Hearty Knoll	57 Skate Hole
14 Sandettié	36 Winterton Ridge	58 Great or Outer Silver Pit
15 Flemish Banks	37 Hammond Knoll	59 Cleaver Bank
16 Fairy Bank	38 Haisborough Sand	60 SW. Spit
17 N. W. and E. Hinder Banks	39 Leman Bank	61 Hospital
18 Bligh Bank	40 Ower Bank	62 Dogger Bight
19 Galloper	41 Inner Bank	63 Western Shoal
20 Inner Gabbard	42 Well Bank	64 SW. Patch
21 Outer Gabbard	43 Broken Bank	65 Easternmost Shoal
22 Hinder Ground	44 Swarte Bank	66 Clay Deep

(1962) has summarized the water budget for the North Sea and gives the following estimates for the annual inflow.

Source	Inflow in km^3 each year
North Atlantic	20,000
English Channel	1,800
Baltic	200
Freshwater British Isles	5
Freshwater Continent	120

If it is assumed that precipitation balances evaporation, the greater part of 22,000 km^3 must leave the North Sea each year through the Norwegian Rinne. This is a little under half the volume of the North Sea which Sverdrup *et al.* (1946) give as 54,000 km^3.

The inflow of Atlantic water into the northern North Sea increases during the autumn to reach a maximum during the winter and then declines to a minimum during the summer. The autumn increase may be related to a seasonal increase in the volume transport of the north Atlantic drift, which, as measured across the Faroe-Shetland channel, is at a maximum in the autumn and winter (Tait, 1957). Steele (1957) has suggested that cooling in the northern North Sea forms a core of dense water which finally curtails the inflow towards the end of the winter. These changes are reflected in the monthly mean positions of the 35‰ and 34‰ isohalines, the available data for the period 1905–54 being summarized in the ICES (1962) charts.

The pattern of the residual surface currents of the North Sea results from the interaction between the northern and southern Atlantic inflows, the Baltic outflow, bottom topography, and the relatively persistent cores of cold bottom water (see p. 122). The currents have been charted from salinity data (Böhnecke, 1922), drift bottle recoveries (Carruthers, 1925; Tait, 1930, 1937), and direct observations with meters (for example, Carruthers, 1936). The chart in Fig. 36 gives a generalized picture of the main features of the circulation. The swirls or gyrals numbered 1 to 9 are of particular interest, and 9 corresponds to Tait's Great Northern North Sea eddy. The positions of the swirls change with the seasons: in summer the SW. Dogger swirl (4) is displaced to the south, and the NE. Dogger swirl (6) and that off Lindesness (7) unite (Böhnecke, 1922). The residual surface currents show seasonal variations in speed and are faster in the northern North Sea. Tait gives maximum speeds up to 10 to 12 miles a day (say 0·5 knot, 25 cm/sec), while values of 3 miles a day (0·125 knot, 6 cm/sec) are more representative of normal conditions in the Southern Bight.

The bottom currents of the North Sea are not well known but the general features of the circulation are similar to those of the surface layers although the bottom water moves slower. The widespread use of Woodhead seabed drifters is leading to a greater understanding of the bottom circulation. For example, Ramster (1965) found that the normal east-going current running round the south-western edge of the Dogger is reversed in early summer. This phenomena may be related to the seasonal shift in the position of the south-west Dogger surface swirl.

Stratification in the North Sea

The depth, bottom topography, and tidal currents in the North Sea have a great influence on the hydrographic structure of the basin. The fastest tidal streams are found close to the east coast of

Great Britain and in the southern North Sea. These are also the shallower areas and the vertical turbulence is sufficient to prevent thermal stratification during the summer, which produces an area of homohaline water close to the British coast and occupying most of the southern North Sea.

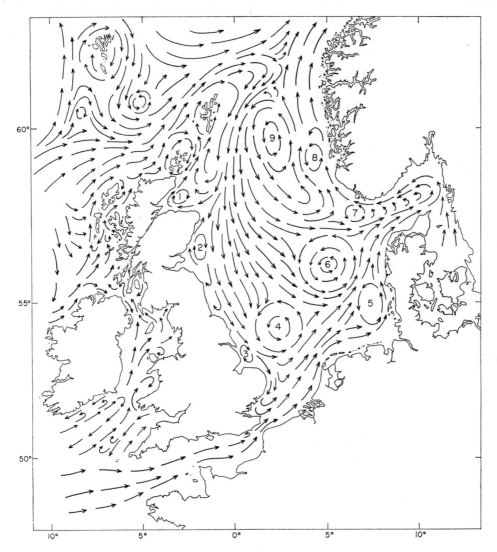

Fig. 36. Surface-water currents of the North Sea and adjacent areas. (After Böhnecke, 1922, Carruthers, 1925, and Tait, 1937.) The major North Sea swirls are numbered as follows: 1 Moray Firth; 2 Firth of Forth; 3 Inner Silver Pit; 4 SW. Dogger; 5 German Bight; 6 NE. Dogger; 7 Lindesness; 8 Stavanger; 9 Tait's Great Northern North Sea. (Outline from an Admiralty chart.)

The boundary of this water closely follows that of the 40 m contour (Dietrich, 1950, p. 59, Fig. 10). During the spring thermal stratification develops over the northern and middle North Sea and the thermocline persists until the autumn. The thermal stratification maintains three cores of cold

5

bottom water, one on the Fladen Ground, a second in the middle North Sea north of the Dogger, and a third in the deeper water south-east of the Dogger. This is shown in Fig. 37. The division between the two northern cores coincides with the 'step' between the northern and middle North Sea basins and the southern edge of Tait's Great Northern North Sea eddy and is maintained by the eastward movement of relatively warm water from the east coast of Scotland (Dietrich, Sahrhage and Schubert, 1959; Rogalla, 1961). The depth, thickness and gradient of the summer thermocline differs in the three areas, as the following summary shows (from Rogalla, 1961, p. 38, Fig. 38).

Area of North Sea	Northern	Middle	Southern
Latitude	59°	56° 30′	54° 30′
Depth of top of thermocline in m	30	30	20
Vertical extent in m	30	15	5
Range t°C	12 – 7	13 – 7	13·5 – 9
Gradient t°C/m	0·16	0·4	0·9

Vertical gradients can be steeper than 0·9°C/m, Dietrich *et al.* (1959) recording values of 2 to 3°C/m south of the Dogger.

In the winter the surface temperatures increase with the distance from the coast, while the opposite holds during the summer. The horizontal temperature gradients are usually small and the isotherms tend to run along the lines of the residual currents. The steepest gradients occur during the summer and autumn at depths of 20 to 40 m on the boundaries between stratified and unstratified water masses. The gradients are probably of the order of 0·001°C/m.

Thermal stratification breaks down over the greater part of the North Sea in the late autumn when the vertical mixing increases due to wind action, but some stability is maintained in the Norwegian Rinne where there is a surface layer of cold and low salinity Baltic water. Steele (1961)

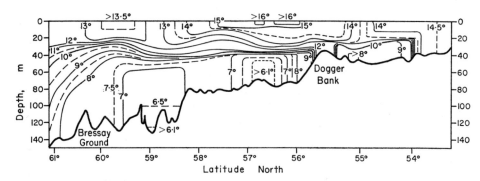

Fig. 37. Temperatures (°C) on a north-south section of the North Sea (Rogalla, 1961; Figs. 37 and 38, pp. 38–9). The section runs from the north of the Bressay Ground to end to the north-west of Texel. The line of stations lies to the east of the Fladen and the Gut and, crossing the Dogger Bank between the Middle and Outer Roughs to the north, and the Tail End to the south, continues to skirt the western edge of the Clay Deep and Bløden Ground. Place names are given in Fig. 34. The stations were completed over the period 27 June–23 July 1959. Note the step-like features of the sea-bed north of the Dogger (see p. 118), and the three cores of cold water, one near the Fladen (58°–59° N.), the other two north and south of the Dogger (see p. 120). The thermoclines lying over and around the domes of cold water are sometimes sharp.

has suggested that there is sufficient stability in this layer to allow production to start early in the year.

THE SPAWNING GROUPS

Spring spawners are not very numerous and, apart from local estuarine stocks, are restricted to the northern North Sea. These herring have already been mentioned in connexion with the Atlanto-Scandian group and their presence in the northern North Sea represents the southern edge of their distribution. They can be separated from the other North Sea groups by their maturation stage, high VS (greater than 57·00) and low K_2 count (13·90–14·20). The other North Sea groups are the Buchan, Dogger, and Downs spawners. These fish are also referred to as the northern North Sea, central North Sea, and Southern Bight spawners respectively. There appear to be consistent differences between the groups with regard to a number of meristic and growth characters (VS and K_2, length-for-age and l_1; otolith structure).

Buchan or northern North Sea summer-autumn spawners (see Fig. 38)

Relatively low VS, 56·40–56·48, but higher in recent years; high length-for-age, high l_1. Buchan ness is a rocky peninsula a few miles south of Peterhead and the Buchan herring spawn, in August and September, close to the Banffshire and Aberdeenshire coasts. According to Wood (1930) spawning is most intensive between 10 and 40 fm. There are spawning grounds off Copinsay (Orkney), on certain banks in the Moray Firth, and on the Turbot, Aberdeen, Montrose, and Berwick Banks. During the spawning season the bottom water temperatures in the area are between 9 and 12°C (Tomczak and Goedecke, 1962). The spawning grounds are close to Tait's Moray Firth and Firth of Forth eddies, which must carry many of the larvae into the Scottish firths. Others will be carried down the north-east coast beyond Berwick and some must drift out into the middle of the North Sea and into the Great Eddy, or if they are carried towards the south-east, into the Skagerrak and on to the Danish and Norwegian coasts. Clark (1933) and Saville (1960) record the presence of larvae, which are probably of northern North Sea origin, to the east of the Greenwich meridian at 57°N. The Buchan-spawned larvae have not been followed further eastward but there is nothing to prevent them reaching the Danish coast, where they would mix with larvae from the Dogger and the Southern Bight. Some of Tait's drift bottles were stranded on the Danish coast. Bückmann and Hempel (1957) have suggested that 40 mm larvae caught in the Jade estuary in February and March were spawned during the summer in the western part of the middle North Sea: they could have come from the Buchan grounds. Jensen (1960) identified autumn-spawned O-group herring of the Buchan stock in the Skagerrak during the summer of 1958.

Dogger or Bank or central North Sea autumn spawners (see Fig. 39)

Intermediate VS, 56·40–56·58, high l_1's; a high proportion of otoliths with a narrow first 'winter' zone. This group spawns in September and October. There are spawning grounds on the NE. Bank; off Whitby and Scarborough; at several places on the Dogger Bank (Middle Rough, NW. Rough, Dogger Bight); on the southern side of the Great Silver Pit towards the Cleaver Bank; off the Humber and the Wash (Outer and Inner Dowsings); and the north-east coast of Norfolk (Cromer Knoll and Winterton Ridge). Spawning tends to start first in the north and then spreads south. Larval surveys (Bückmann, 1942) show that the Dogger Bight ground is the most important.

During the spawning season the bottom water temperatures in the area are between 10 and 14°C (Tomczak and Goedecke, 1962). Some of the larvae hatched on the NE. Bank, Whitby, Scarborough and Norfolk coast grounds may be carried to the inshore waters between Flamborough and Cromer. In years of strong north-west winds some larvae may reach the Thames estuary. But under normal conditions the majority of the Bank-spawned larvae will be carried eastward to reach the Skagerrak, Danish coast, and coastal waters of the German Bight by March and April.

Downs or Southern Bight winter spawners (see Fig. 40)

High VS, 56·42–56·77, high K_2, usually more than 14·80; low length-for-age; low l_1; a high proportion of otoliths with a wide first 'winter' zone. The Downs herring spawn on grounds between the Gabbard Light Vessel (off the East Anglian coast) and Pointe d'Ailly. The capture of yolk-sac larvae (Bückmann, 1942) has shown that there are spawning grounds near the North Hinder Light Vessel, to the south-west of the Sandettié Bank and between Cap Gris Nez and Cap d'Antifer, within 10 to 20 miles of the French coast. Spawning starts in the Hinder area at the end of October, and at Sandettié in November. The latter spawners form Le Gall's (1935) Dyck-Sandettié group (VS 56·42–56·65). Spawning occurs between Cap Gris Nez and the mouth of the Somme in December and January (Le Gall's Group 1), and south of the Somme, between Dieppe and Fécamp, in January and, perhaps, February (Le Gall's Group 2, VS 56·51–56·77). The Group 2 spawners are often referred to as Ailly herring, Pointe d'Ailly being a series of white vertical cliffs a few miles south of Dieppe. Bottom temperatures throughout the area fall rapidly from November to February. The November larvae may be hatched in water of about 11°C; temperatures are down to 8·5 to 10°C at Sandettié in December; and to 7 to 8°C south of the Somme February. The November–December hatched larvae are carried into the German Bight and reach the coastal waters in March, April, or May. Bückmann and Hempel (1957) express some doubts as to whether the larvae spawned in January and February always reach the German Bight, as the vertebral counts of the smaller larvae arriving in April and May are not as high as might be expected if they had been hatched in relatively cold water on the grounds near the mouth of the Somme. But larvae with high mean vertebral counts have been caught in the Haringvliet and the Ooster-Schelde (Dutch coast) during the spring. Tesch (1929, 1937) identifies them as 'Channel Herring'. Samples of O-group herring with a relatively high VS (up to a mean of 56·75) have been taken on the English east coast (Wood, 1959), and immature herring taken in the Southern Bight have a higher VS than those taken in the German Bight (56·72 as against 56·44–56·60 in 1960, Schubert, 1962, p. 203, Table 56). Postuma and Zijlstra's (1958) work on the radius of the otolith centres in Dogger, Sandettié and 'Channel' (=Ailly) spawners fits in with these observations. The mean radius of the otolith centre in spawners from each of the three groups are shown in the table below. These results, together with those from samples of O-group herring, summarized below, suggest that the Ailly-spawned fish grow up on the Dutch coast, Sandettié fish in the German Bight, while the Lysekil sample could be a mixture of fish of Dogger and Sandettié origin.

Spawning area or ground	Mean radius of otolith centre in mm
Dogger	0·275
Sandettié	0·257
Ailly	0·231

Area of O-group sample	Mean radius of otolith centre in mm
Lysekil (Skagerrak)	0·272
Horns Reef	0·263
Wilhelmshaven	0·257
Ijmuiden	0·237
Zeeland	0·226

Spawning grounds and larval drift summarized

The main summer, autumn and winter herring spawning grounds in the North Sea are shown in Figs. 38, 39 and 40. The drift of the larvae from the three spawning areas to the inshore waters may be summarized as follows.

1. *Buchan-spawned fish.* Some are carried into the Scottish firths; others drift south and may reach the Lincolnshire coast when there are strong northerly winds. Larvae that are carried south-eastwards may reach the Skagerrak, Danish and German coasts.

2. *Bank-spawned fish.* Some larvae may be carried on to the east coast of England and as far south as the Thames estuary. The majority drift eastwards into the German Bight towards the N. Frisian islands. Others may reach the Dutch coast to the south of Norderny.

3. *Downs-spawned fish.* Some of the November–December larvae (Dyck-Sandettié Group) are carried on to the English and Dutch coasts bordering the Southern Bight. Others drift north-eastwards towards the German Bight but the centre of their distribution along the continental coast probably lies further to the west and south than that of the Bank larvae. The larvae spawned in January and February (Group 2) are not carried so far to the north-east and may stay within the Southern Bight. Some should reach the coastal waters on the Dutch coast. When there are persistent and strong south-westerly winds in the first four months of the year, a larger proportion of the larvae may reach the German Bight.

THE IMMATURE HERRING

In 1912 Hjort started to collect data on immature herring in the North Sea. Bjerkan (1918) worked up the material and other collections were made by Hodgson (1925) and Wood (1936). Postuma, Zijlstra, and Das (1965) give the most recent account. Much of the information comes from the following sources:

(a) The earlier reports by Bjerkan, Hodgson, and Wood.
(b) Cushing (1962) refers to some recent German, Scottish, and Dutch data.
(c) Danish reports on the industrial fishery (*Annales Biologiques*).
(d) German herring-catch statistics (*Annales Biologiques*).
(e) The ICES herring tagging experiments (Aasen *et al.*, 1961) which give some data on the distribution and movement of immature fish in the Bløden area.

O-group

Very small herring are found in all the inshore waters surrounding the North Sea and are particularly abundant close to the German and Danish coasts, and in the Scottish firths. Larval metamorphosis takes place at a length of 30 to 50 mm. The scales appear at this stage, but only a few of the summer- or autumn-spawned fish are big enough to form a recognizable scale ring or otolith zone during the winter. The young fish move off shore to deeper water when they reach a length of 9 to 10 cm. A proportion of the brood reaches this size before the end of the summer growth period and the off shore movement starts in July and August. O-group herring appear on the Bløden ground in the autumn and as 14 to 16 cm fish may contribute significantly to the industrial fishery (as in 1955, Bertelsen and Popp Madsen, 1957). These fish winter in an area which may be 3–4°C warmer than the inshore grounds occupied by the smaller members of the brood.

I-group

At the start of the following spring the distribution of the I-group is probably similar to that of the O-group during the previous autumn. Hodgson's (1925, p. 5, Table 1) March samples from the Dogger Bank show the relation between the size of the I-group and their distribution according to depth: the bigger fish are in deeper water.

The off shore movement starts again when growth picks up, the smaller fish leaving the inshore areas, the bigger fish spreading out over deeper water.

I-group herring are most numerous in the southern North Sea, particularly in the area south and east of the Dogger Bank. The Danish spring fishery lasts from January to May. It usually starts in the White Bank-Clay Deep area and moves westwards into the Silver Pit by the end of the season. The bulk of the catch is made up of I-group fish, but the proportion of II-group may be higher towards the end of the season when the fishery is to the west (as in 1953, Bertelsen and Popp Madsen, 1954). In the autumn, I-group fish, average size 18 to 21 cm, accounts for 60–80% of the Danish and German industrial fisheries. The area where the fishery takes place is related to a pocket of cold bottom water over which the warmer water forms a marked dome. This region of thermal stratification south-east of the Dogger has already been mentioned (p. 122). In the autumn the cold water retreats northwards towards the Monkey Bank. The stratification is finally broken down during the autumnal gales.

The catches of the industrial fisheries show that the I-group herring are abundant in the southern North Sea. They have also been caught north of the Dogger during March and April, in the Skagerrak, and on the Ling and Great Fisher Banks (Schubert, 1962); to the north and west of the Dogger by Hodgson, Wood, and Bjerkan; and by the research vessel 'Anton Dohrn' north of the Middle Rough (Cushing, 1962). In late spring the centre of gravity of the group lies south-east of the Dogger; by the following autumn the fish have spread out east, north and west, the largest members lying north of the Dogger, from the NW. Rough to the Fisher Banks and along the edge of the Rinne to the Ling Bank. There is no evidence of a clearly defined winter ground for immature I-group herring. In the northern North Sea, I-group herring are rarely found away from the coast. At the end of the year they make up over 90% of the catch of the halflin fishery in the Scottish firths.

II-group

The II-group herring lie to the north of the Dogger. In March they are in the Gut, and on the Fladen, Ling, and Egersund Banks (Schubert, 1962). They enter the North Shields summer fishery in May (Hodgson, 1925) and the summer fishery off the Scottish north-east coast in May and June. While the immature II-group herring are probably spread out all over the middle North Sea, they are not found, according to Wood (1937, Chart 2), in the deeper part of the northern

North Sea. During the year a proportion of the II-group fish come to their first maturity and recruit to one or other of the three spawning groups. The remainder, the slower growing members of the brood, probably spend the winter in the deeper water of the middle North Sea.

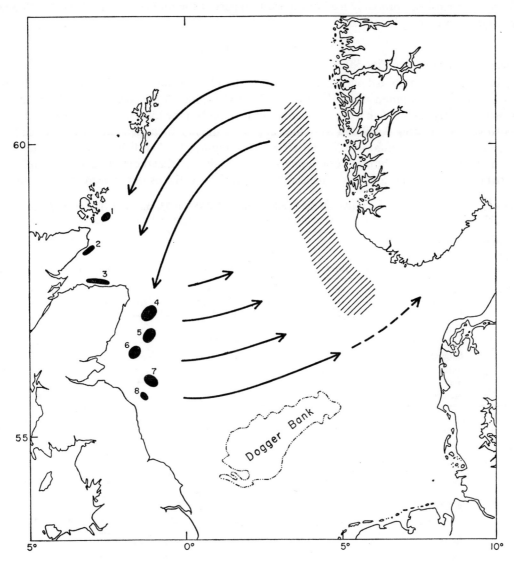

Fig. 38. The migrations of adult Buchan spawning herring. Note that the migration is anti-clockwise in the direction of the residual currents. The herring spawn to the west (spawning grounds black and numbered) and winter to the east (diagonal shading).

SPAWNING GROUND KEY

1 Copinsay; 2 Caithness; 3 Banff; 4 Turbot Bank; 5 Aberdeen Bank; 6 Montrose Bank; 7 Berwick Bank; 8 NE. Longstones.

The spawning grounds in Figs. 38, 39 and 40 are positioned according to information given by Wallace (1924), Hodgson (1928), Wood (1930), and Ancellin and Nedelec (1959). (Outline from an Admiralty chart.)

III-group and older immature fish

Most of the remaining immatures recruit to the spawning shoals the following year as III-group fish. The very slow-growing members of the brood may not do so until their fifth or sixth year (IV- or V-group), and probably feed in the western part of the middle and northern North Sea, and winter more towards the east.

THE MATURE HERRING

Buchan spawners (see Fig. 38)

Wood (1930, 1937) worked out the movements of the adults, using catch statistics and analysing samples for age, maturation stage, VS, and K_2. After spawning off the north-east coast in August and September, the spent fish move eastwards and are found on the Fladen in September, October, and November. During April and May they appear in the north-eastern part of the North Sea, in the Bressay Bank, Patch, and Viking areas. The summer Buchan fishery starts in May and June and continues until the middle of September. Wood showed that the summer fishery exploited a mixture of Buchan, Dogger, and southern North Sea fish. As the fishery moved from east of the

Table 14. The returns of herring tagged off the Shetlands in 1951, 1952, 1953, and 1954. The monthly recoveries from different areas are separated according to the month of tagging. (Data from Parrish, personal communication.)

Month of tagging	Recovery area	Month of Recovery											
		May	June	July	Aug.	Sept.	Oct.	Nov.	Dec.	Jan.	Feb.	Mar.	Apr.
May	Shetland	—	—	—	—	—	—	—	—	—	—	—	—
	Scottish NE.	—	—	—	1	—	—	—	—	—	—	—	—
	Fladen	—	—	7	4	1	1	—	—	—	—	—	—
	Gut	—	—	—	—	—	—	—	—	—	—	—	—
	English NE.	—	—	—	—	—	—	—	—	—	—	—	—
	Dogger	—	—	—	—	—	1	—	—	—	—	—	—
	Smith's Knoll	—	—	—	—	—	—	—	—	—	—	—	—
	Sandettié	—	—	—	—	—	—	—	—	—	—	—	—
	Skagerrak	—	—	—	—	—	—	—	—	1	1	—	—
June	Shetland	—	1	1	—	—	—	—	—	—	—	—	—
	Scottish NE.	—	—	1	1	—	—	—	—	—	—	—	—
	Fladen	—	2	29	28	4	3	—	—	—	—	—	—
	Gut	—	—	1	2	—	—	—	—	—	—	—	—
	English NE.	—	—	—	—	—	—	—	—	—	—	—	—
	Dogger	—	—	—	1	2	1	—	—	—	—	—	—
	Smith's Knoll	—	—	—	—	—	—	—	—	—	—	—	—
	Sandettié	—	—	—	—	—	—	—	—	—	—	—	—
	Skagerrak	—	—	—	—	—	—	—	—	1	1	2	—
July	Shetland	—	—	—	—	—	—	—	—	—	—	—	—
	Scottish NE.	—	—	—	—	—	—	—	—	—	—	—	—
	Fladen	—	—	2	5	3	—	—	—	—	—	—	—
	Gut	—	—	—	—	—	—	—	—	—	—	—	—
	English NE.	—	—	—	—	—	—	—	—	—	—	—	—
	Dogger	—	—	—	—	—	—	—	—	—	—	—	—
	Smith's Knoll	—	—	—	—	—	—	—	—	—	—	—	—
	Sandettié	—	—	—	—	—	—	—	—	—	—	—	—
	Skagerrak	—	—	—	—	—	—	—	—	—	—	—	—

Shetlands towards the Scottish coast, the Dogger and southern North Sea components were separated from the ripening Buchan spawners which moved further to the west towards their spawning grounds, where they were joined by recruits from the Scottish firths and the middle North Sea. Wood (1937, p. 46) drew attention to the correspondence between the movement of the adult stock and that of Tait's anti-clockwise gyral in the northern North Sea between 57° 30′N. and 61°N.

The migration path of the recruited Buchan stock is circular, the fish spawning off the north-east coast of Scotland, moving east to winter on the edge of the Norwegian Rinne between Egersund and the Viking Bank, and feeding in the northern North Sea in the spring and summer. The following points are relevant.

1. The returns for the 1951–55 Scottish north-east coast and 1951–54 Shetland tagging experiments (Wood, Parrish, and McPherson, 1955) are summarized in Tables 14 and 15, which Mr. B. B. Parrish has prepared for me to show the recoveries in different areas by months. There

Table 15. The returns of herring tagged off the Scottish NE. coast in 1951, 1952, 1953 and 1955. The monthly recoveries from different areas are separated according to the month of tagging. (Data from Parrish, personal communication.)

Month of tagging	Recovery area	Month of recovery											
		May	June	July	Aug.	Sept.	Oct.	Nov.	Dec.	Jan.	Feb.	Mar.	Apr.
May	Shetland	—	1	—	—	—	—	—	—	—	—	—	—
	Scottish NE.	7	2	9	1	1	—	—	—	—	—	—	—
	Fladen	—	4	28	23	5	1	—	—	—	—	—	—
	Gut	—	—	1	4	2	—	—	—	—	—	—	—
	English NE.	—	2	1	5	1	—	—	—	—	—	—	—
	Dogger	—	—	1	5	5	5	—	—	—	—	—	—
	Smith's Knoll	—	—	—	—	—	—	1	—	—	—	—	—
	Sandettié	—	—	—	—	—	—	—	—	1	—	—	—
	Skagerrak	—	—	—	—	—	—	1	—	—	1	—	—
June	Shetland	—	—	—	—	—	—	—	—	—	—	—	—
	Scottish NE.	—	29	4	3	—	—	—	—	—	—	—	—
	Fladen	—	2	49	33	9	—	—	—	—	—	—	—
	Gut	—	2	—	3	2	—	—	—	—	—	—	—
	English NE.	—	—	2	2	1	—	—	—	—	—	—	—
	Dogger	—	—	—	1	3	4	—	—	—	—	—	—
	Smith's Knoll	—	—	—	—	—	2	—	—	—	—	—	—
	Sandettié	—	—	—	—	—	—	—	1	—	—	—	—
	Skagerrak	—	—	—	—	—	—	—	—	3	—	—	—
July	Shetland	—	—	—	—	—	—	—	—	—	—	—	—
	Scottish NE.	—	—	19	2	—	—	—	—	—	—	—	—
	Fladen	—	—	61	25	3	—	—	—	—	—	—	—
	Gut	—	—	1	5	—	2	—	—	—	—	—	—
	English NE.	—	—	—	1	—	—	—	—	—	—	—	—
	Dogger	—	—	—	3	2	—	—	—	—	—	—	—
	Smith's Knoll	—	—	—	—	—	—	1	—	—	—	—	—
	Sandettié	—	—	—	—	—	—	1	—	—	—	—	—
	Skagerrak	—	—	—	—	—	—	—	—	—	2	—	—
	Patch	—	—	—	—	—	—	—	—	—	—	—	1

is a clear change in the distribution of the recoveries from the north-east coast grounds in June and July to the Fladen in August and September. It is uncertain whether Buchan fish reach the Skagerrak (see below). The Dogger and Southern Bight recoveries indicate the presence of Bank and Downs spawners in the northern North Sea during the summer and Bank fish do enter the Skagerrak after spawning. So the recoveries from the Skagerrak could be Bank spawners and it may be significant that no fish tagged in the Skagerrak have been recaptured in the Scottish drift-net fishery (Höglund, 1955, p. 26).

2. Stage II herring are caught by bottom and pelagic trawl along the edge of the Rinne between Egersund and Viking Bank from January to April. German statistics (Schubert, 1963) show that these fish have VS and K_2 counts typical of autumn spawners. In March and April more than half of the herring caught in the north-eastern part of the North Sea by the Scottish 'boxing' fishery are summer-autumn spawners (Parrish and Craig, 1957; Parrish et al., 1960, 1961, 1962). Not all of these fish may be Buchan spawners; it is very likely that a proportion of them are Dogger spawners. Sometimes a year-class that is predominant on the edge of the Rinne in early spring can be followed through the Shetland, and north-east coast fisheries to the Fladen. This happened with the VIII-group herring in 1951(Wood et al., 1952) which supports the suggestion that the eastern region of the northern North Sea is the wintering ground for the Buchan spawners. Buchan spawners may reach the Skagerrak, as spents, in the winter. Andersson (1950) made a comparison between the age composition of the autumn spawners on the Fladen and that of the autumn spawners in the Skagerrak in 1944–50. Andersson's histograms show that the outstanding year-classes of 1939 and 1941 can be followed from the August–September distributions on the Fladen to the Skagerrak in the following spring and back to the Fladen in August–September. The changes in the age distributions are consistent with a movement of fish from the Fladen to the Skagerrak and back to the Fladen. So far as the limited sampling of the Buchan spawners go, the 1941 year-class stands out in the percentage age compositions of 1947 and 1948 (24·4% and 31·3%), and was still contributing 21·7% of the catch in 1949 (Parrish, personal communication). According to the Belgian October (=Dogger spawners) data, the 1941 year-class accounted for 20% of the catch in 1948 and 6·2% of the catch in 1949 (Gilis, 1949, p. 72; 1950, p. 186, Table 10). These comparisons suggest that many of the 1941 year-class observed as spents in the Skagerrak may have been Buchan spawners.

Dogger or Bank spawners (see Fig. 39)

Johansen (1924) showed that herring that spawned on the Dogger in autumn were caught in the Bohuslan Skagerrak fishery the following spring. Cushing (1955b) figured the complete migration pattern as an anti-clockwise movement round the middle and northern North Seas, which can be broken down to wintering, feeding and spawning migrations as follows:

(a) a wintering migration from the autumn spawning grounds on the Dogger to the winter ground in the Skagerrak;
(b) a feeding migration in early spring from the Skagerrak northwestwards along the western edge of the Rinne into the northern North Sea;
(c) a spawning migration in the late summer from the northern North Sea, through the Fladen and the Gut, to the spawning grounds. At this stage the recruits from the north-east English coast grounds and the middle North Sea join the adult fish.

There are several independent lines of evidence to support this hypothesis. Wood (1937) found late autumn or winter spawners in the pre-spawning Buchan fishery, and the Scottish tagging

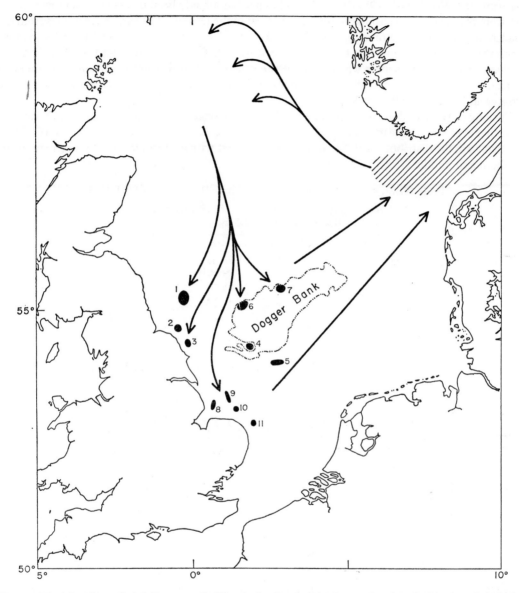

Fig. 39. The migrations of adult Dogger or Bank spawning herring. Again note that the migration is anti-clockwise in the direction of the residual currents. The herring spawn to the west (spawning grounds black and numbered), and winter to the east in the Skagerrak (diagonal shading).

SPAWNING GROUND KEY

1 NE. Bank; 2 Whitby; 3 Scarborough; 4 Dogger Bight; 5 south side Great Silver Pit; 6 NW. Rough; 7 Middle Rough; 8 Inner Dowsing; 9 Outer Dowsing; 10 Cromer Knoll; 11 Winterton Ridge. (Outline from an Admiralty chart.)

experiments (Wood *et al.*, 1955), to which reference has already been made, show a movement of fish from the north-east coast to the Fladen and then to the Dogger. The earlier recoveries from the Fladen may have been autumn spawners. Wood *et al.* (1955) go on to suggest that these fish move south through the Gut and that there is a reverse migration in the eastern part of the North Sea during the winter and spring when some of the fish reach the Skagerrak. A limited number of Danish returns (Bertelsen, 1955) from tagging on the Fladen, shows a movement towards the Dogger and on to the Skagerrak.

Cushing (1955*b*) used the results of Höglund's (1955) Dogger and Skagerrak tagging experiments as further evidence for the migration pattern. Höglund's results are summarized in Table 16. There is a change in the distribution of the recoveries consistent with an anti-clockwise movement in the northern and middle North Seas.

Table 16. Swedish herring tagging experiments. (Data from Höglund, 1955.)

A Herring tagged in February–May in the Skagerrak 1949–53.
Recoveries by months and areas.

Place of recovery	Month of recovery				
	July	Aug.	Sept.	Oct.	Nov.
Egersund Bank	—	5	2	—	—
Fladen	1	8	4	—	—
Gut	—	—	4	1	—
Dogger	—	—	16	22	4
Off Whitby	—	—	3	1	—
West Hole	—	—	—	—	1
Sandettié	—	—	—	—	3
Off Hanstholm	—	—	—	1	—

B Herring tagged in September–October on the Dogger 1952–53.
Recoveries by months and areas.

Place of recovery	Month of recovery							
	Sept.	Oct.	Nov.	Dec.	Jan.	Feb.	Mar.	Aug.
Dogger Bight	2	4	—	—	—	—	—	—
Winterton Shoal	—	—	2	—	—	—	—	—
Sandettié	—	—	3	1	—	—	—	—
Skagerrak	—	—	—	—	1	4	1	—
Fladen Ground	—	—	—	—	—	—	—	1

It is worth noting how a series of independent tagging experiments at key positions and dates (Scottish north-east coast, early summer; Fladen, late summer; Dogger, autumn; and Skagerrak, winter) have given a distribution of recoveries in time which almost completes the migration track for the Bank group. But there is a gap to be filled by tagging herring on the edge of the Rinne in the spring. Relatively few fish have been tagged in this area (Scottish Coral Bank experiments, Wood *et al.*, 1955). Nevertheless, the overall movement is obviously anti-clockwise, and Cushing (1955*b*) has drawn attention to the correspondence between the direction of the migration and that of the residual swirl in the middle and northern North Sea.

Downs spawners (see Fig. 40)

The main spawning grounds of the group lie off the continental coast between Dunkirk and Fécamp. After spawning the spent fish move north-eastwards into the Southern Bight and there is a spent fishery off the French, Belgian and Dutch coasts up to the edge of the minefield north of Texel. The fishery lasts until April. There used to be a fishery off Lowestoft for spent herring from March until May (Hodgson, 1929, p. 12). There seems to be little doubt that the Ailly (Group 2) spawners enter the Southern Bight as the mean VS of the Belgian spents increases from December to January and February, which is interpreted as indicating an influx of 'Channel spawners' into the Southern Bight (see Gilis' reports on the Belgian fisheries in *Annales Biologiques*.)

There is very little data to show whether the spent fish leave the Southern Bight to the west or east of the Dogger. Spent herring are not caught on the Bløden spring fishery, and there have been no Skagerrak recoveries of herring tagged on the Southern Bight and Channel spawning grounds (Ancellin and Nedelec, 1959). What is probably more significant is the small number of Höglund's Skagerrak tagged fish that were recovered at Sandettié, 3 as compared with 42 from the Dogger in the 1949–53 experiments. In terms of the German landings from the two grounds, about 10 times as many tags per ton of fish caught came back from the Dogger (Cushing and Burd, 1957, p. 6), which is consistent with the hypothesis that very few Downs fish reach the Skagerrak.

Bolster (1955) reported the March recaptures in the Outer Silver Pit of two herring tagged the previous December off Cap Gris Nez. Gilson (1939) found that spent fish taken in the Silver Pit in February and March had an age composition similar to that of the spents caught in the winter fishery off the French and Belgian coasts. For the pre-war years 1926–38 Burd (1962) has shown significant correlations between the catch of II-group (2 'winter' rings, 3 years old) herring at East Anglia and the catch of III-group herring (3 'winter' rings, 4 years old) at North Shields the following year; and significant correlations between the catch of III-group (3 'winter' rings, 4 years old) herring at East Anglia and the catch of IV-group (4 'winter' rings, 5 years old) at North Shields the following year. The monthly correlation coefficients are as follows:

	Correlation coefficient r	
	3-year-olds East Anglia against 4-year-olds at North Shields the following year	4-year-olds East Anglia against 5-year-olds at North Shields the following year
May	+0·336	+0·835*
June	+0·711*	+0·507
July	+0·672*	+0·443
August	+0·641*	+0·078
September	+0·511*	+0·144

*Significant at 5% level.

The results suggest that the East Anglian fish return to the north-east coast grounds the following year, the 5-year-olds arriving at Shields in May before the 4-year-olds which appear in June. The monthly changes in the value of r suggests that the 5-year-old fish pass quickly through the area covered by the Shields fishery while the 4-year-olds do not do so.

It is almost certain that some of the Downs fish go on into the northern North Sea. Wood (1936) found maturing herring off the Scottish north-east coast in May, June, and July, which had slightly higher VS and much higher K_2 counts than those characteristic of Buchan spawners. Fish

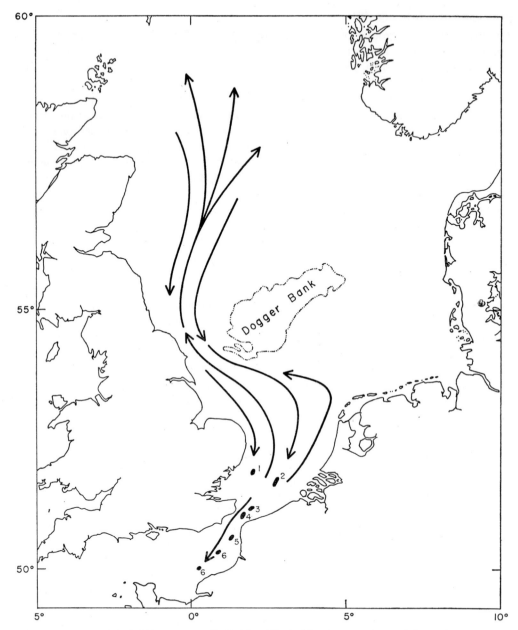

Fig. 40. The migrations of adult Downs spawning herring. The herring spawn to the south (spawning grounds black and numbered) and winter in the Southern Bight (not shaded to avoid confusion). The Downs herring feed in the middle and northern parts of the North Sea, and in the latter area it is certain that Buchan, Bank and Downs fish share a common feeding area.

SPAWNING GROUND KEY

1 Gabbard; 2 North Hinder; 3 Sandettié; 4 Cap Gris Nez; 5 Vergoyer; 6 Ailly grounds. (Outline from an Admiralty chart.)

with similar VS and K_2 counts appeared on the Fladen and the Gut in August and September. Wood suggested that they were a mixture of Dogger and Downs spawners. Comparison of the age compositions supports this view. Wood (1937) found that the age compositions of the Buchan pre-spawning, Fladen, and East Anglian fisheries were similar, having in common age groups which made no important contribution to the Scottish spawning shoals. There is only one tagging return to show the movement of Downs fish from the Channel to the northern North Sea. Ancellin and Nedelec (1959) record the recapture in August, on the Fladen or Farn Deep, of a herring tagged at the Vergoyer (Group I spawning ground) the previous November.

Wood (1936) concluded that the autumn and winter spawners left the northern grounds in August and September and moved south to spawn. The south of Dogger recoveries from the Scottish north-east coast tagging experiments show that Downs spawners are present in these waters. The Downs fish pass through the Shields fishery on the way south. For the pre-war years Burd (1962) has determined the relation between the II-group (2 'winter' rings, 3 years old) and the III-group (3 'winter' rings, 4 years old) at Shields and then at East Anglia the same year. The correlation coefficients are as follows:

	Correlation coefficient r	
	3-year-olds at Shields against 3-year-olds at East Anglia, same year	4-year-olds at Shields against 4-year-olds at East Anglia, same year
May	+0·277	+0·654*
June	+0·169	+0·808*
July	+0·064	+0·614*
August	+0·623*	+0·279
September	+0·561*	+0·515*

*Significant at 5% level.

The 3-year-old herring at Shields are first time spawners and the significant values of r in August and September indicate the presence of Downs recruits in the Shields area during these months. In the pre-war years, and from 1946–50, the East Anglian 4-year-olds included two components: one group that had already spawned once, and a second group coming into the spawning shoals for the first time. The values of r are significant for all months except August, when the presence of Bank spawners on the north-east coast grounds could mask the correlation. Burd's two sets of data (East Anglia/Shields following year; and Shields/East Anglia same year) are consistent with the hypothesis that Downs fish return to the north-east coast grounds in the summer after spawning and that they are present on the same grounds in the summer before spawning.

Since 1950 the Shields samples have been examined more closely, and winter spawners separated by maturation stages from autumn spawners. Burd (1962) has obtained a marked relation between the 'winter' 3-year-olds at Shields in July and the 3-year-olds the same year at East Anglia. These 3-year-olds will be recruits, which will have come from the south and east of the Dogger into the middle North Sea the previous autumn or spring.

In September and October the Downs fish move into the Southern Bight to reach the Smith's Knoll area in the middle of October. Hodgson (1957, p. 185) has suggested that a proportion of the recruit spawners joins the spawning migration direct from the Bløden ground at this stage. Early in November the first spawners have reached the Sandettié grounds and they are south of the

Somme in the first week of January. Tesch (1934) has shown that there is a change in the vertebral count distributions among samples taken from Smith's Knoll during the season which he interpreted as showing that the Ailly spawners (Group 2), with the higher mean VS, are the last to

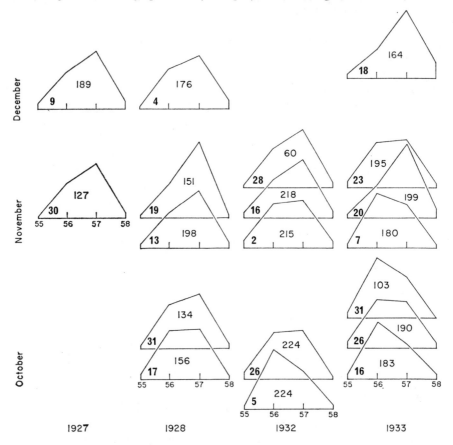

Fig. 41. The change in the percentage frequency of vertebral counts among successive samples of herring taken at Smith's Knoll. The dates of each sample are in bold type, and the number of fish in each sample indicated. There is a shift of the peak distribution from 56 to 57 vertebrae during the season. (From Tesch, 1934, p. 46, Fig. 1.)

come down the Southern Bight (see Fig. 41). Although Hodgson (1927) has shown that the older herring predominate in the second half of the East Anglian fishery, there is no evidence to show that these herring have the higher vertebral counts, nor is there any evidence to show that the older fish of the Downs stock spawn at Ailly. There is some evidence to show that there are differences in the age composition of the herring caught at Sandettié and at Ailly (Zijlstra, 1958), but this may be an effect of year-class strength rather than the older fish tending to spawn on a particular ground.

HOMING IN THE NORTH SEA HERRING

Recruitment to the parent spawning group

There are differences in meristic characters (VS or K_2), growth (length-for age, l_1), otolith type, and age distribution between the three main spawning groups. A Working Group report summarizes the available data (ICES, 1965). Table 17 shows, for the vertebral count data, that some of the differences are consistent. For example, the Ailly spawners always have a higher mean VS than Sandettié or Dogger spawners, and in 11 out of 13 years, the Ailly mean VS is higher than that of the Buchan spawners. These differences are consistent with, but do not prove, the hypothesis that when a herring comes to first maturity it joins the spawning group to which its parents belonged. It is implicit in such a hypothesis that the recruits spawn in the same season and in the same area as that in which they were born.

Table 17. The frequency with which the mean VS of Stage VI fish taken in different spawning areas or on different grounds (vertical column), was greater or less than the mean VS of Stage VI fish taken in other areas or on other grounds (horizontal row). Comparisons are made between 13 year-classes (1946/47–1958/59 inclusive), the original mean VS date being given in Table 8a of the ICES (1965) North Sea Herring Working Group Report.

Spawning area or ground	Buchan	Dogger	Sandettié	Ailly
Buchan	—	+ 7	+ 4	+ 2
	—	− 5	− 8	−11
Dogger	+ 5	—	+ 3	+ 0
	− 7	—	−10	−13
Sandettié	+ 8	+10	—	+ 0
	− 4	− 3	—	−13
Ailly	+11	+13	+13	—
	− 2	− 0	− 0	—

Hodgson (1925, 1929, 1934) has argued that herring do not necessarily spawn during the season in which they were born. He showed that the l_1 distributions of the Bank and Downs spawners were polymodal and identified the modes, at 8, 10, and 12 cm, with the progeny of winter-, autumn- and summer-spawned fish respectively (Hodgson, 1929, p. 55). In the Downs herring, fish with small l_1's are the most numerous, while the Dogger and Buchan groups have a greater proportion of fish with the larger l_1's. Hodgson maintained that the variability in l_1's showed that a year-class was not homogeneous but made up of fish derived from different spawnings. Davis (1936), Convener of the 1935 meeting of Herring Experts at Lowestoft, carried the argument further. As the East Anglian herring do not all come to their maturity in the same year of life, he suggested that 'the range of acceleration or retardation of first maturity can be at least a year, and presumably may embrace variations which, being a fraction of one year, will bring the onset of first maturity outside the modal season.' Individuals which came to maturity outside the season for their parent group would join another community, but Davis assumed that the numbers involved would be too small to influence the numerical or growth characteristics of the adopted group.

A recruitment mechanism which would account for this has been developed by Burd (1962) who suggested that growth was the dominant feature of the biology of the herring. Recruitment to an adult spawning group takes place at a 'critical length', irrespective of age. The fish with the higher l_1's would be expected to reach the critical length sooner and spawn earlier in the season than those with low l_1's. Thus fish with high l_1's are potential Bank, and those with low l_1's, potential Downs recruits. Polymodality in the l_1 distributions of the two spawning groups is attributed to acceleration or retardation of growth after the first 'winter' ring had been laid down. Cushing

(1962) has suggested that polymodality could be generated by the recruitment mechanism itself when there is partial recruitment of a brood at two or more age groups.

According to Burd's hypothesis, the spawning group to which the immature fish recruit 'will depend on their growth rate in the first two years and on the time of year at which they approach the Critical Length at the onset of sexual maturity' (Burd, 1962, p. 25). But he goes on to make the point that the 'maintenance of a consistently low mean vertebral count in fully recruited year classes of Bank herring would be unlikely if individual growth rates in the nursery areas were so variable that fast growing fish with high vertebral counts from the Downs spawnings recruited in strength to the Bank stock. It can only be concluded that the majority of the fish originating from the Bank and Downs spawnings maintain their identity'. (Burd, 1962, p. 25.) The majority of fish join the parent group because the growth pattern of the recruits is primarily dependent on the season in which they were born.

Zijlstra has approached the problem from another angle. There are differences between the two spawning groups in VS, the proportion of otoliths with narrow first 'winter' zones, and in the radius of the otolith nucleus. If length is the important factor in the recruitment mechanism, recruits to either group with the same l_1's should show no difference with regard to these three characters. But Zijlstra (1958, 1963) showed that there are differences in the proportion of the narrow type otoliths, in the size of the otolith nucleus, and in the mean VS, between Bank and Downs fish with identical l_1's. This suggests that there are other factors, apart from length, which determine the group to which a fish recruits. Furthermore, Zijlstra (1958) found no evidence to support Hodgson's suggestion that low l_1 fish were winter-spawned and high l_1 fish summer-spawned, there being no positive correlation between the size of the otolith nucleus and l_1 and no inverse relation between l_1 and VS. Zijlstra suggested that the polymodality in the l_1 distributions might reflect the effect of different growth rates on different nursery grounds up to the time of formation of the first 'winter' ring.

The position may be summarized as follows. It is apparently accepted, but has not been proved, that the majority of herring recruit to the parent spawning group. According to Hodgson there is some mixing between groups. Davis suggested that the numbers involved were relatively low, while Burd's hypothesis is that growth, and recruitment-by-length, form the essential part of the mechanism which determines the group to which a fish recruits. While growth and length may be of fundamental importance in determining the age at which a herring comes to maturity, Zijlstra believes that other factors are involved in the recruitment to a particular group. At present the matter cannot be resolved one way or the other. A more detailed study of the VS-l_1 and l_2 relationship might help, as would serological data, but work on the latter line is still in its early stages. Studies on fecundity (egg size and number) might prove conclusive. There are differences between the groups (Baxter, 1959) but it would be unreasonable to attach too much weight to them as so little is known about the factors controlling fecundity in the herring.

The return to the parent spawning ground and bed

The grounds on which herring spawn are remarkably consistent from year to year. For instance, it appears that herring spawn every year to the south and west of the Sandettié Bank, off Calais. A spawning ground could cover an area of several square miles within which there may be one or more beds on which the eggs are laid. The beds are small, and it is not known if spawners use a particular bed, or any one of a number of possible beds, each year. The problem of the return to the parent ground itself is difficult because, as Hodgson (1936, p. 19) writes 'it is impossible to produce even the slightest piece of direct evidence as to the place of origin of a shoal of herrings'. The young fish cannot be marked on the grounds where they were hatched, and evidence as to their return must of necessity be circumstantial.

There are several grounds within the spawning area of each group. The Bank group may comprise three sub-groups spawning on the Whitby-Scarborough, Dogger, and the Dowsing grounds respectively, but there are not enough data available to pursue this idea critically.

Better material is available for the Downs group. Le Gall recognized three sub-groups, the Dyck-Sandettié group, Group 1 (Cap Blanc to the Somme), and Group 2 (south of the Somme). It is convenient to refer to the first and last sub-groups as the Sandettié and Ailly spawners. There is a consistent difference in the VS data between these two groups. Ancellin (1957) has summarized the material with the following results:

Spawning ground	Mean VS during the season	
	1928–37	1945–55
Sandettié	56·56	56·55
Ailly	56·64	56·64

The differences are just as consistent when comparisons are made between year-classes. Zijlstra (1958) obtained a significant value of 't' between Sandettié and Ailly mean VS's of 56·55 and 56·62, but there is some doubt as to whether such a statistical test is valid as the number of frequency classes is so small. Inspection of Le Gall's (1935) figures 23 and 25 show that the Ailly samples have a high proportion of fish with vertebral counts of 57 and 58 and fewer with 56 and 55. During the spawning season the water temperatures at Ailly are 2 to 3°C lower than at Sandettié and Ailly-spawned fish would be expected to have a higher mean VS. Are the consistent differences between the mean VS of the two groups of fish due to the predominant return of fish to the parent ground? Critical evidence to support the hypothesis could be provided by comparing the vertebral count distributions among the larvae hatched on the two grounds with those of the two groups of recruit spawners from the same brood. This has not been done.

Sandettié and Ailly spawners also differ in the size of their otolith centres, the Ailly fish having a greater proportion with smaller radii. Postuma and Zijlstra (1958) and Zijlstra (1963) have shown that l_1 for l_1, there are differences between the two sub-groups in mean VS, the average size of the otolith radius and in the proportion of otoliths with narrow first 'winter' zones. These differences suggest that recruitment to either spawning ground is unlikely to be determined on a length basis. The data show that there is some order in the return and are consistent with a return to the parent ground. However, no tests of significance are given in respect of the differences in VS, otolith radius, and proportion of narrow-zoned otoliths with l_1 cm groups.

As an alternative hypothesis to account for the differences in mean VS betweeen the two sub-groups, it is possible that the Ailly spawners include a number of strays from the Channel group, which have a higher mean VS of about 56·74 (Le Gall, 1935). The Ailly VS of 56·64 could then be generated by a mixture of about equal numbers of Downs spawners (VS typical of Sandettié, 56·55) and Channel spawners. Hodgson (1926) suggested that North Sea and Channel herring were mixed on the French coast spawning grounds. After spawning some of the Channel fish may move back with the Downs herring into the North Sea. If this explanation is correct, the Ailly recruits with high vertebral counts should not be found in the East Anglian Fishery. Tesch (1934) has shown that samples with a VS distribution typical of Ailly spawners are taken at Smith's Knoll towards the end of the season (see Fig. 41), but the data are not restricted to recruits. It is of interest to note that Tesch (1939) showed the 3-year-old recruits in 1937 had a mean VS typical of the Sandettié group throughout the season, but that in 1938, as 4-year-olds, they showed an increase (56·49 to 56·61) in December and January.

To summarize: it is fair to say that the evidence does tend to support the hypothesis that the majority of recruits spawn on the parent ground. But the data are not conclusive and further analysis for the l_1-VS, l_1-otolith radius and l_1-narrow-zoned otoliths relationship is needed. Some means of identifying the recruits as survivors of a particular group of larvae would be conclusive if this ever became possible.

The identity of the fully recruited year-classes

After full recruitment to a spawning group, a year-class appears to maintain its identity until its extinction. Although Buchan, Bank and Downs herring mix together during the feeding season, there is no evidence of any significant interchange between the fully recruited spawning groups. But the difficulties of tagging preclude the possibility of using direct evidence such as would be provided by tagging Stage VI fish and their recapture from other areas as spawners in subsequent years.

Evidence for the stability of the fully recruited year-classes comes from the following sources:

1. Hodgson's (1929, Fig. 25) data on the l_1 composition of the 1921 year-class at East Anglia 1925–28. The agreement between the frequency curves from the annual samples makes it unlikely that there can have been many strays to the Downs group. Burd's (1962) more recent data tend to confirm this.

2. Cushing (1962) points out that the success of Hodgson's pre-war forecasts of the East Anglian age distributions could not have been achieved if there was any significant infiltration from another group.

3. Cushing (1958, Table 1) compared the vertebral counts of the East Anglian year-classes by age groups. He showed that the range between year-classes was 2 to 3 times that within them, and that there was no trend of mean VS with age within a year-class. This suggests that there are no significant numbers of strays from another group.

4. Raitt's (1961) analysis of the proportion of fish with narrow and wide first 'winter' otolith zones in Whitby spawners (Bank) and East Anglian (Downs) fish. His data for the 1948 and 1949 year-classes are given below, the proportion of doubtful otoliths being omitted.

The percentage of narrow or wide otoliths

| Year of sampling | Year-class 1948 | | | | Year-class 1949 | | | |
| | East Anglia | | Whitby | | East Anglia | | Whitby | |
	N.	W.	N.	W.	N.	W.	N.	W.
1951	11	84	90	4	—	—	—	—
1952	3	94	80	15	6	94	66	28
1953	23	77	100	—	16	79	65	30
1954	15	75	90	10	9	87	63	34

Inspection of the data will show that the differences between the year-classes are maintained and there is no trend with age such as would be expected if there were any significant degree of mixing between the two groups.

From the evidence available it is reasonable to conclude that the majority of herring return to spawn with the group to which they recruited.

CANADIAN DATA ON HOMING BY HERRING

Tagging experiments with Pacific herring

On the west coast of Canada, the population of *C. pallasi* is divided into a number of sub-groups which differ in meristic and morphometric characters. These anatomical differences, combined with evidence from age compositions, suggest that there is little intermingling between them (Tester, 1937).

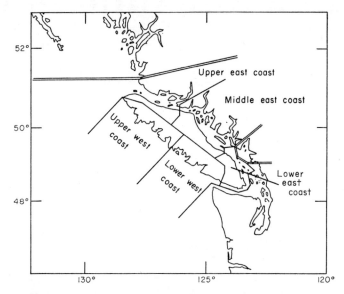

Fig. 42. Sub-districts at Vancouver Island, British Columbia, relevant to the tagging experiments with *Clupea pallasi* summarized in Table 18. (From a chart supplied by Dr. F. H. C. Taylor.)

Extensive tagging experiments with internal magnetic tags have been carried out since 1936, and about 90% of the tagged fish were spawning or spent fish. Stevenson (1955) has described the experiments, which involve over 500,000 fish. As the fish were tagged and recaptured during the spawning season, work on this scale provides a mass of data relating to the consistency with which herring return to spawn in the area in which they previously spawned. Dr. F. H. C. Taylor (Fisheries Research Board of Canada, Biological Station, Nanaimo, Vancouver Island) has very kindly allowed me to use the data relating to a number of tagging experiments carried out between 1936 and 1956 on different parts of Vancouver Island. The results are summarized in Table 18, and the tagging districts are shown in Fig. 42. Most fish are recovered in the district in which they were tagged, although in the Lower West and Lower East coast districts the proportion of strays increases in the fourth or fifth year after tagging. The Middle East coast districts showed the highest overall proportion of strays (31·3%), while the proportion in the other areas was about 20%.

Table 18. Canadian tagging experiments with *Clupea pallasi*, 1936–56. The tagging sub-districts are shown in Fig. 42. The returns are not adjusted for the efficiency of the magnets or for the proportion of the catch that entered plants without magnets. (Data from Dr. F. H. C. Taylor, personal communication.)

Tagging sub-district	Number tagged	Year after tagging	Number recovered	West Upper	West Lower	East Lower	East Middle	East Upper	Others	Total percentage of strays to other sub-districts	Overall percentage of strays to other sub-districts
Upper West	119,844	1	2,996	75.7	20.1	1.2	0.2	0.0	2.8	24.3	19.5
		2	1,118	82.7	10.5	1.6	0.8	0.3	4.1	17.3	
		3	259	80.3	11.2	1.2	1.2	0.0	6.1	19.7	
		4	96	82.3	7.3	2.1	1.0	0.0	7.3	18.0	
		5	31	87.1	9.7	0.0	3.2	0.0	0.0	12.9	
		6	17	94.1	5.9	0.0	0.0	0.0	0.0	5.9	
Lower West	141,784	1	3,946	13.7	81.0	4.6	0.4	0.1	0.2	19.0	23.1
		2	1,303	23.9	68.8	5.8	1.1	0.2	0.2	31.2	
		3	268	24.3	64.5	5.6	2.2	0.0	3.4	35.5	
		4	57	26.3	61.4	3.5	1.8	0.0	7.0	38.6	
		5	19	63.1	31.6	0.0	5.3	0.0	0.0	68.4	
		6	6	83.3	16.7	0.0	0.0	0.0	0.0	83.3	
Lower East	156,076	1	1,542	0.4	5.4	84.4	9.0	0.1	0.7	15.6	18.5
		2	323	0.3	7.5	74.6	16.4	0.3	0.9	25.4	
		3	110	2.7	6.4	68.2	22.7	0.0	0.0	31.8	
		4	25	0.0	4.0	60.0	32.0	4.0	0.0	40.0	
		5	10	0.0	20.0	50.0	30.0	0.0	0.0	50.0	
		6	2	0.0	0.0	100.0	0.0	0.0	0.0	0.0	
Middle East	125,803	1	1,361	0.7	1.7	22.2	68.8	3.4	3.2	31.2	31.3
		2	526	1.0	1.3	24.1	67.3	2.7	3.6	32.7	
		3	155	1.3	0.7	24.5	69.0	1.9	2.6	31.0	
		4	28	0.0	3.6	14.3	82.1	0.0	0.0	17.9	
		5	21	0.0	0.0	14.3	85.7	0.0	0.0	14.3	
		6	5	0.0	0.0	0.0	100.0	0.0	0.0	0.0	
Upper East	35,713	1	724	0.7	0.0	0.3	3.3	86.0	9.7	14.0	17.0
		2	218	1.8	0.9	0.0	11.0	75.7	10.6	24.3	
		3	37	0.0	2.7	2.7	10.8	73.0	10.8	27.0	
		4	58	0.0	0.0	0.0	5.2	75.8	19.0	24.2	
		5	6	0.0	0.0	0.0	0.0	83.3	16.7	16.7	
		6	9	0.0	0.0	0.0	0.0	100.0	0.0	0.0	
Total	579,220		15,276								

Using vertebral count data, Tester (1937) was unable to obtain evidence of heterogeneity in herring samples taken from localities within the tagging districts, although it now seems clear that each run probably contains up to 20% of strays. The runs to the different spawning localities appear to be able to maintain their identity, as judged by the analysis of meristic characters, against such a background of infiltration.

Chapter 7

The Cod

INTRODUCTION

The cod, *Gadus morhua* Linn., to give the fish its correct scientific name (Cohen, 1959), has been called 'the beef of the sea' (Innis, 1940, p. 6) and in 1965 its total catch of 2·7 million tons was exceeded only by that of the Atlantic herring (4·0 million tons) and the anchoveta (7·7 million tons). Over two-thirds of the cod is taken by the fishing fleets of European countries and about 10 to 20% of the catch is dried or salted and sold in Spain, Portugal, South America, and Africa. In England and Scotland the cod takes first place both for the size and the value of its landings, as can be seen in Table 19.[1] It is also quite cheap (see Table 20).

Table 19. Catch (in thousands cwt) and value (in thousands £ sterling) of some fish landed by British vessels in the United Kingdom in 1965. (Data from DAFS, 1966).

Fish	Landings in thousands of cwt	Value in thousands £ sterling
Cod	6,240	25,063
Haddock	3,318	10,851
Plaice	786	5,703
Herring	1,963	2,930
Whiting	973	1,768
Coalfish	939	1,660
Hake	131	1,567
Skate and rays	251	1,112
All wet fish		58,002
All shellfish		2,953
Total value		**60,955**

The cod is found all over the North Atlantic, or more specifically, the North Boreal Region in Rass' (1959) classification of the biogeographical fishery complexes. The larger cod are found in relatively cold water, from 1°C up to 12–14°C. The upper and lower lethal temperatures are about +20°C and −2°C respectively (Wise, 1958a). In general cod are most abundant in water of 1 to

---

[1] Table 19 shows that in 1965 the landings of fish by British vessels were valued at £58 million. In the same year, imports of fresh, frozen, cured and tinned fish were valued at £67 million, to which £40 million can be added for whale meat and marine animal oils. With exports, in 1965 valued at £11 million, it is clear that on balance the value of imported fish and fishery products exceeds the first sale value of home landings by British vessels (data from DAFS, 1966; MAFF, 1967).

Table 20. First sale price, per hundredweight and per pound weight of some fish landed in England and Wales in 1965. (Data from MAFF, 1967).

Fish	First sale price			
	per cwt		per lb	
	s.	d.	s.	d.
Hake	263	3	2	4·2
Plaice	149	3	1	3·9
Skate and rays	98	8		10·6
Haddock	88	5		9·5
Cod	79	9		8·5
Herring	41	3		4·4
Whiting	37	9		4·0
Coalfish	37	4		4·0

5°C, nearer the lower than the higher lethal. On the western side of the Atlantic their southernmost limit is along the coast of North Carolina, in the region of Cape Hatteras (Wise, 1958*b*). To the north they are found on the Nantucket shoals, off Cape Cod, on the Newfoundland Banks, along the Labrador coast, through the Davis Strait to their northern limit near Upernavik, on the west coast of Greenland, on the shore of Baffin Bay (Jensen, 1939, p. 5). On the eastern side of the Atlantic cod are taken at East Greenland, Iceland, Faroes, Jan Mayen, in the Bay of Biscay, the Irish and Celtic seas, the Channel, the North Sea, and into the Baltic to the Gulf of Bothnia and the Gulf of Finland. To the north there are cod along the Norwegian coastlines up to Bear Island and from Bear Island northwards to the top of West Spitsbergen, and eastwards into the Barents Sea to the edge of the polar water. In the summer they reach the shallow water near Novaya Zemlya, and the south-west part of the Kara Sea (Maslov, 1944).

The great cod fisheries of the world take place in relatively shallow waters, on banks or within the continental shelf. Important areas are the Newfoundland Banks, Greenland, and Iceland, Faroes, the North Sea, the Barents Sea, and Svalbard—the Bear Island, Hope Island and Spitsbergen region—and the Norwegian coast. The relative importance of these areas to the United Kingdom cod fisheries can be judged from Table 21.

The analysis of meristic characters, in particular the numbers of vertebrae and fin rays (Schmidt, 1930), and the results of tagging experiments have shown the extent to which cod from one area mix with those from another. Cod tagged on the spawning grounds to the south-west of Iceland have been recaptured at Newfoundland, Faroes, North Cape, and the North Sea. However, these movements are exceptional and evidence shows that there are several separate stocks of cod, between which there is only a very small degree of mixing. Thus the cod in the Newfoundland area can be considered as a stock on its own and there is little mixing between the fish from this area and those from West Greenland. Within the Newfoundland stock itself there is evidence of local sub-divisions, particularly of the young immature fish (Thompson, 1943). Similarly, the cod at the Faroes, in the North Sea, and in the Baltic, may be considered as separate stocks. On the other hand, there is a close relationship between the West and East Greenland cod and those of Iceland; and between the cod of the Barents Sea and those of the Norwegian coast. Some of the cod which grow up in Greenland waters migrate to Iceland to spawn, and most of the Barents Sea cod migrate many hundreds of miles to the south to spawn near the Norwegian coast, mainly at the Lofoten Islands. These two migrations, from Greenland to Iceland, and from the Barents Sea to Lofoten, have been

Table 21. Fishing areas for cod landed by British vessels in the United Kingdom during 1965. Catch is given in thousands cwt. (Data from MAFF, 1967).

Fishing area	Catch in thousands cwt
Iceland	2,212
North Sea	1,101
Bear Island and Spitsbergen	665
Newfoundland	474
Barents Sea	448
Norwegian coast	362
West Scotland	292
West Greenland	225
Faroe	219
Labrador	147
Irish Sea	57
East Greenland	15
Other areas	23
Total	**6,240**

studied in some detail. Russell's (1937) account, based on the data that were then available, is the most concise. But before going into the details more fully, something will be said about the life history of the cod.

LIFE HISTORY

Spawning season

Cod spawn in February, March, April, and May. In the Newfoundland area the period of maximum spawning may, however, be early in June (Thompson, 1943, p. 88). Sometimes there is a second spawning later in the year. Graham (1929b, p. 13) gives some evidence that this takes place in the North Sea during October and November. McKenzie (1940) records the autumn spawning of cod in Nova Scotian waters, and Hansen (1958, p. 34) records the capture of two female cod with large eggs off Angmagssalik, East Greenland, in September 1957, which would probably have spawned in October or November that year. But the autumn spawning is probably very small and of little significance compared with that of the spring and early summer.

Sex ratios

At Lofoten the bigger and older fish arrive on the spawning grounds first. As the males mature, on the average, a year younger and at a smaller length than the females, most of the fish that arrive at the beginning of the season are females. In 1937 the proportion of males and females at Lofoten was as follows (data from Rollefsen, 1938, p. 29):

	% Males	% Females
February	35	65
March	43	57
April	60	40

The proportion of males increased towards the end of the season as the younger and smaller 8-year-old males, most of them first-time spawners, came into the fishery. In 1937 the overall sex ratio of males:females was 1:1·35 (obtained by raising the total catch data given by Sund (1938*b*, p. 20, Table 1), by Rollefsen's (1938) figures for the proportion of males and females). This ratio may be significantly different from 1:1, and it is of interest to see what the sex ratio is in immature and mature fish at Bear Island. Some unpublished data are available from cod caught by trawl for otolith samples, on the research vessel 'Ernest Holt'. These samples were taken for several years during November, December, and January in the Bear Island area. There will have been some selection of these cod for length on deck, but within a length group there was no selection for sex. The data available are as follows:

	Length group cm	Males	Number of fish Females	Ratio	χ^2
Immature cod	40–50	80	93	1:1·16	0·832
Mature cod	over 80	103	174	1:1·68	9·100

There seems to be no significant departure from the 1:1 ratio in the immature fish. Similarly, on the north and east coasts of Iceland, males and females are almost equally represented among the immatures (Tåning, 1931*a*, p. 37). But this is clearly not the case with the mature Bear Island cod, and the difference in the proportion between the sexes is significant.

It is of interest to compare the sex ratio at Lofoten with that on one of the main spawning grounds of the Baltic cod in Gdansk Deep, off Gdansk, the present name for the old free port of Danzig. In the Deep many more 2- and 3-year-old males are taken than females, but the disparity disappears with age until in the older age groups, the 5-, 6-, and 7-year olds, there is an excess of females (Chrzan, 1950). The explanation given for this is that more males mature in their second year than females, and that the males arrive on the spawning grounds sooner and stay there longer. This explanation is similar to that given by Hefford (1916, p. 34) to account for the greater number of male plaice on their spawning grounds in the Southern Bight. It is worth noting that female salmon leave the beds soon after spawning but the males tend to stay on (J. W. Jones, 1959, p. 130). If the male cod do stay on the spawning grounds longer than the females, more of them will be caught during the season. In addition the males of a particular year-class will suffer an extra year's fishing mortality on the spawning ground as they come to their first maturity a year earlier than females. Both these factors could contribute to the greater number of females in the older age groups.

Spawning

Cod generally spawn in water with a temperature from 3 to 6°C. But in West Greenland fjords, cod many spawn in water of about 1 to 2°C (Hansen, 1949, p. 26). At Lofoten it is usual to find the fish towards the top of the warm water, just below the cold surface layer, at or near the depth of the thermocline. Spawning takes place in midwater or near the bottom, depending on the temperature conditions. Ewart and Brook (1885) and Rollefsen (1934*a*) have observed the spawning of cod in tanks. A summary of Rollefsen's and two earlier accounts, one by G. M. Dannevig and the other by Nielsen, has been given by Templeman (1958). More recent observations of the mating behaviour of cod have been made by Brawn (1961). The behaviour is quite complicated and is accompanied by grunting noises produced by the male. These noises come from the swim-bladder which has well-developed sound-producing muscles. Eventually the male and female fish come together and swim along belly to belly while the eggs and milt are released. Rollefsen (1934a) found that cod sperm, like that of plaice, rapidly loses its power to fertilize eggs when it is dispersed in sea-water, whereas 90% of the eggs are viable for two hours. In the cod the milt and eggs are probably not released all at once, and complete spawning may take several days. Earll (1880, p. 714) thought that spawning might take 2 months. Meek (1924) kept a female cod that spawned 6 times at intervals of 3 to 4 days over a period of 17 days. It seems unlikely that all the eggs would be ready for release at one time. In the last stages of maturation their density is reduced by the uptake of follicular fluid and their volume increases by about 3 times. Smith (1957, p. 331) argues that the female could not possibly hold all the swollen eggs at one time, and it is difficult to see how the amount of fluid required, which is about equal to the volume of the fish, could be made available in a short period.

The drift of eggs and larvae

A female cod produces from 0·5 to 15 million eggs, depending on her size. Healthy fertilized cod eggs just float in sea-water (Jacobsen and Johansen, 1908; Rollefsen, 1930) but they are unlikely to collect at the surface of the sea as the turbulence and movement due to wind action is probably sufficient to ensure that they are evenly distributed throughout the upper 100 m of the water column. The pelagic eggs are carried about by the water currents and at 5 to 6°C the larvae hatch out in about a fortnight. For the first few months of their life the larvae swim about in midwater, and so long as they are out of sight of the bottom they are probably carried along passively in the body of water in which they are living. Lee (1962) has summarized the data relating to the northward drift of cod eggs and larvae from the Lofoten spawning grounds. It is difficult to say exactly how long the little cod stay in midwater but it is between 3 and 6 months. In shallow water, as in the North Sea, they probably start to take to the bottom within 3 to 4 months after hatching (Graham and Carruthers, 1926). When over deeper water they may not get to the bottom until they are 4 or 5 months old (Corlett, 1958). Deep water does not seem to stop the cod going down to the bottom and they have been found there at depths of 200 to 400 m (Schmidt, 1909c, p. 153; Corlett, 1958). These early months are very important ones in the life of the cod and it is during this period that the young are dispersed from the spawning grounds. The distances that they could be carried during the time they are in midwater are surprisingly high. A current of 10 cm/sec (0·2 knot) will carry a young fish about 600 miles in 5 months, and some oceanic currents move 4 or 5 times as fast as this.

The movements of the immature cod

Very little is known about the movements of the young cod in their early years on the nursery grounds: O- and I-group fish are too small to be tagged satisfactorily. There is the possibility that they make a seasonal migration to shallow water during the summer and return to deeper water in the winter. But at the moment there is no evidence to support this. Graham (1934, p. 71) and Thompson (1943) believe that the young cod stay very much where they are until they are big enough to eat the smaller herring, shoals of which they might then follow. Early Danish and German tagging experiments, off Iceland and in the North Sea, summarized by Hjort (1914, p. 111) certainly support this view, as do Strubberg's (1916, 1933) results. Strubberg managed to tag a number of 2-year-old cod at the Faroes and found that they were more or less stationary for a year or so but that the older and still immature fish moved about much more. These movements are almost certainly related to feeding.

In the Barents Sea the immature cod appear to winter in much deeper water than that in which they are caught during the summer months. The evidence for this is Trout's (1957) analysis of the radio reports received by R.V. 'Ernest Holt' from trawlers: the best fishing is in deep water in the winter and shallow water in the summer. The 3- and 4-year-old immature cod move about in the Barents Sea, and the Norwegians know them as 'Loddetorsk' when they follow the capelin to the coast during the spawning season of these little salmonids in March and April. These immature cod form the basis for the early Finmark fishery (Hjort, 1914, p. 113) and in the summer they leave the coastal area and disperse, feeding on capelin and herring over the Barents Sea.

The movements of the mature cod

When they are older the young cod join the mature fish and make their first full spawning migration. There is some evidence that, even as immatures, the Bear Island cod make a partial migration, the so-called 'dummy run' (Trout, 1957) towards the spawning ground, and it is interesting to note that it has been suggested that immature cod from Greenland may accompany the matures on their spawning migration to Iceland (Hansen, Jensen, and Tåning, 1935, p. 72). The mature cod are believed to swim close to the bottom of the sea. At any rate the Arcto-Norwegian cod are trawled on the bottom at Malangsgrunden, Svensgrunden and Andenes, off the Norwegian coast, along the line of their migration route to Lofoten. However, Maslov (1944) has considered the possibility that some fish may be in midwater as large cod have been taken by surface trawl in the western Barents Sea during the winter. Furthermore, Iversen (1934) has tagged cod at Jan Mayen which have been recaptured on the spawning grounds at Iceland and to do this these fish must have been in water over 1,000 m deep to get there. It is rather unlikely that cod swim as deep as this, although they have been trawled in depths up to 460 m.

The age and size at which cod come to first maturity varies for different stocks and there is a considerable range of age within a single stock. For example, the Arcto-Norwegian cod first matures between 6 and 14 years old, but the majority do so at 8, 9, and 10 years. But there are significant differences in the mean age at first maturity between year-classes. Furthermore, males mature, on the average, a year earlier and at a smaller size than females.

After spawning the spent cod return to their feeding grounds. It is not known if the return journey is made close to the bottom or in midwater. As the summer advances they move into shallower water (Trout, 1957) and many of them may spend a good deal of time away from the bottom. Braarud and Ruud (1932) observed cod at the surface 200 miles to the north-east of Angmagssalik off East Greenland, in July and August 1929. Cod have been seen at or near the surface at West Greenland during this pelagic phase (Hansen, 1949; Rasmussen, 1953), and the Norwegians have developed, since 1951, a successful summer fishery for them with midwater lines which they shoot in the Holsteinborg Deep between the Store and Lille Hellefiske Banks (Rasmussen, 1954). Cod have also been caught by midwater lines during the summer in the central part of the Barents Sea (Iversen, 1934, p. 5). Tåning (1937, p. 30) gives other examples of pelagic fisheries for cod over deep water and this aspect of their life is one about which very little is really known, and the same can be said of their diurnal vertical movements, for which Ellis (1956) has provided the only evidence from echo-sounder records.

Once they have matured cod appear to spawn every year until they die. Evidence for this comes from Rollefsen's (1934b) work on the otolith structure. After the first spawning the annual opaque zones are very much thinner and the regular succession of these narrow opaque zones observed in older cod has been taken as showing that they do spawn every year.[1] Cod may live for 20 years or more, but fish as old as this are rarely caught as the fishing intensity is such that few live that long.

THE ICELAND-GREENLAND MIGRATION
(For place names see Fig. 43)

Bottom topography and water currents (for surface currents in the area see Fig. 44)

Accounts of the bottom topography and water currents in the Iceland-Greenland area are given by Kiilerich (1943, 1945), Hermann and Thomsen (1946), Dunbar (1951), Hackey, Hermann, and Bailey (1954) Stefánsson (1962), and Dietrich (1965). The north-west Atlantic is partly separated from the north-east Atlantic by the mid-Atlantic ridge which joins the continental shelf at south-west Iceland along the line of the Reykjanes Ridge. Iceland itself stands on the submarine ridge which runs from Scotland to Greenland and is separated from Greenland by the waters of the Denmark Strait. The extension of the submarine ridge between north-west Iceland and East

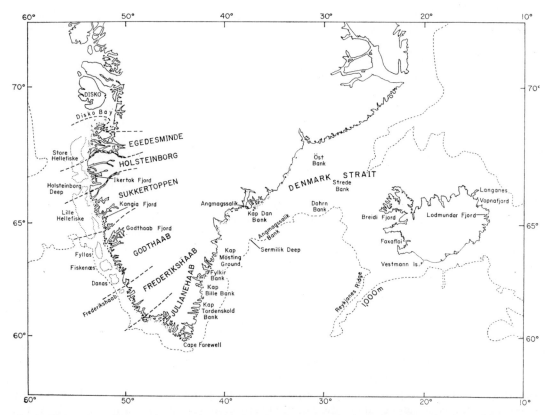

Fig. 43. Place names of interest in connexion with the migrations of cod in the Iceland-Greenland area. The 1,000 m contour is shown. (Some place names are taken from a German Consol chart, others from Rasmussen, 1959; and West Greenland districts from Hansen, Jensen and Tåning, 1935, Fig. 1. Outline based on an International Hydrographic Bureau (Monaco) chart.)

[1] Messiatzeva (1932, p. 151) states that cod do not spawn every year.

Greenland is broken by a narrow channel, 600 m deep, which runs south-west to north-east and effectively separates the continental shelf of Iceland from that of Greenland. At East and West Greenland the continental shelf is relatively wide but it is very narrow on either side of Cape Farewell at south-west and south-east Greenland. Between Labrador and West Greenland the bottom rises to form the north-western edges of the Labrador Basin, which is separated from the more northerly Baffin Bay Basin by a ridge joining West Greenland and Baffin Island beneath the waters of the Davis Strait. The water which occupies that part of the Labrador Basin bounded by the

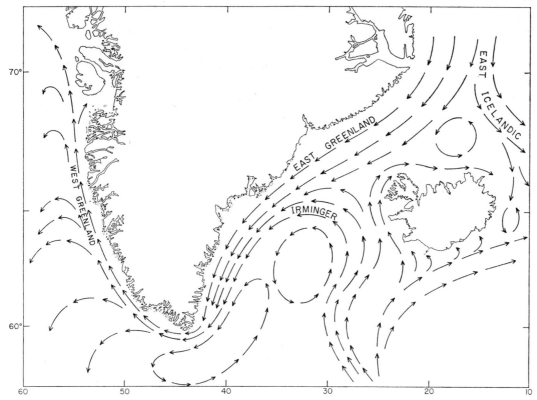

Fig. 44. Surface-water currents in the Iceland-Greenland area. (After Hermann and Thomsen, 1946; Hachey, Hermann, and Bailey, 1954; and Stefánsson, 1962. Outline based on an International Hydrographic Bureau (Monaco) chart.)

East Greenland continental slope and the mid-Atlantic ridge is generally known as the Irminger Sea. The Iceland-Greenland ridge separates the Irminger Sea from the Iceland Sea.

The main current systems of the area are shown in Fig. 44. The cold East Greenland current, of which the East Icelandic current is a branch, carries low salinity polar water through the Denmark Strait and down the coast of Greenland to Cape Farewell. The warm Irminger current, an offshoot of the North Atlantic drift, divides after crossing the Reykjanes Ridge. One branch continues clockwise around Iceland as the North Icelandic Irminger current but the main body of water is deflected west and south-west across the Denmark Strait and runs parallel to, and partly beneath, the East Greenland current down to Cape Farewell. Here the two water masses mix as they move northwards up the coast of south-west Greenland, and the cold polar water soon loses its identity. The north-going coastal water forms the West Greenland current which sends off western branches as it progresses towards Upernavik where it can still be detected. Some of the Irminger current water is deflected anti-clockwise back into the Irminger Sea near Cape Farewell. This water contributes to the cyclonic circulation of the Irminger Sea, and there may be two cyclonic (anti-clockwise) gyrals in this area.

The cod at Iceland

The Icelandic cod spawn off the south and south-west of the island in the warm water of the Irminger current, which carries many of the eggs and larvae from the spawning ground round to the north and east coasts. Schmidt's (1909c) beautiful series of charts clearly show the clockwise (anti-cyclonic) spread of the eggs and pelagic larvae in this area (see Fig. 45).Some of the eggs and larvae are carried towards Greenland by the branch of the Irminger that goes out across the Denmark Strait (Tåning, 1937). It has not been conclusively shown that the larvae actually reach East

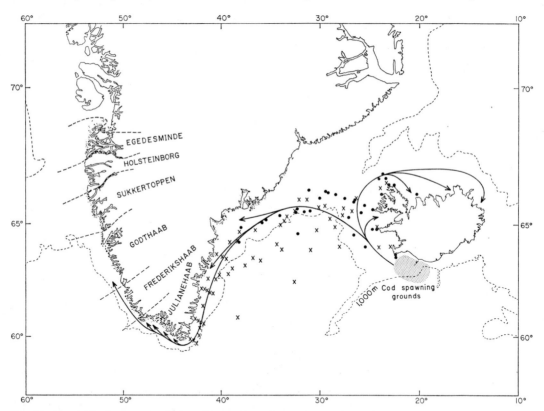

Fig. 45. The drift of eggs and pelagic cod larvae from the south-west Iceland spawning grounds (after Schmidt, 1909c). The drift of larvae across the Denmark Strait towards Greenland was followed by Tåning (1937). (Outline based on an International Hydrographic Bureau (Monaco) chart.)

KEY
● Stations where cod larvae were caught.
× Stations where no cod larvae were caught.

or West Greenland waters (Tåning, 1958), but it is certainly possible for them to get there. It is just over 1,000 miles from the Icelandic spawning grounds to Cape Farewell, and assuming the average velocity of the Irminger current to be about 20 cm/sec (0·4 knot), which is reasonable enough (Kiilerich, 1943, p. 9), the journey would take the larvae 3 to 4 months. The results of one of Tåning's (1931*b*) drift bottle experiments is of interest here. One bottle released on the spawning ground in February 1929 was recovered at Sydproven, Julianehaab District, south-west Greenland, 133 days later. These experiments were carried out in style: it is usual to use lemonade or ginger pop bottles in this sort of work, but Tåning used ordinary champagne bottles.

The Danish cod tagging experiments began at Iceland in 1904 and the results are given by Schmidt (1907, 1931*a*), Sæmundsson (1913) and Tåning (1937). The first experiments were with immature fish and the results showed that they stayed more or less where they were tagged. The north-east coast fish did not appear on the south coast spawning grounds for several years after tagging, when they were probably mature. Jónsson's (1953) later experiments have given a similar result. It seems as if the north coast cod get to the southern spawning grounds by going round the west coast of the island, but it is not clear what route the east coast fish (for example, the ones Schmidt tagged at Lodmundar Fjord) take. Do they go the long way round by the north and west coast against the Irminger current, or do they take the much shorter distance with the current and go along the south-east coast? Sæmundsson (1913), who records the only two south-east coast recoveries of Schmidt's Lodmundar experiments, infers in his Fig. 2 that the fish take the south-east route. There appears to be no reason at all for supposing this, and if one examines Schmidt's (1907) returns a case could be made out that the fish go along the north coast, as the last recaptures from this experiment were all taken along the north coast. But the evidence can be used either way, and this point, which is really a very important one, does not seem to have been cleared up.

The tagging of the mature fish on the spawning grounds began in 1909. Schmidt (1931*a*) and Tåning (1937) have summarized the results which show that the spent fish disperse round Iceland but may be taken on the spawning grounds again in the following years. A number of cod tagged on the spawning grounds have also been recaptured outside Icelandic waters, some on the Norwegian coast, others at Faroes and Newfoundland (Tåning, 1934*b*). One was recovered from, the stomach of a Greenland shark in the Denmark Strait but most of these distant recoveries 17 out of 23 between 1923 and 1935, have been taken at the West Greenland banks, most of them between July and September in the year they were tagged on the Icelandic spawning ground.

The cod at Greenland

Cod have been found off the west and east coasts of Greenland for many hundreds of years but it seems certain that their numbers have varied periodically. Jensen (1925), Schmidt (1931*b*), and Jensen and Hansen (1931) have brought together much of what is known about the early Greenland cod fisheries. There are probably two groups of cod in Greenland waters; the Fjord cod which spawn in Ikertok, Kangia, and Godthaab Fjords on the west coast, and Bank cod, which spawn on the off-shore banks on both the west coast (Store and Lille Hellefiske banks, Fylla, Fiskenæs and Danas banks) and the east coast (Anton Dohrn Bank and nearby banks) (Jónsson, 1959; Meyer, 1959). It is easiest to consider the west and east coasts separately.

THE WEST COAST

The coastal waters of West Greenland have been divided into different areas but unfortunately there are no less than three different schemes in use. The first, based on districts, was

6

used by Hansen, Jensen, Tåning (1935). A second system was used by Hansen (1949), who divided the area into nine zones, and a third is used by the International Commission for the North-West Atlantic Fisheries (ICNAF, 1954). For the present purposes the division into districts is the most useful and this is the system followed here. The details of the districts are shown in Fig. 43. Numerous tagging experiments have been carried out in West Greenland waters but it is not necessary to follow the results in close detail here. They are fully described by Hansen, Jensen, and Tåning (1935), and in other papers by Tåning (1937) and Hansen (1949) and, more recently, in the yearly reports in the *Annales Biologiques* published by ICES.

Fjord cod

The cod of certain of the west coast fjords, such as Ikertok, Kangia, and Godthaab, can be regarded as local stocks. There are differences in vertebral counts, numbers of rays in the second dorsal fin (D_2), and growth rates, between these fish and those of the coastal waters. Very few of the fish tagged in these fjords are recovered outside Greenland waters (Hansen, 1949), and the majority are returned from the fjords or the nearby coastal areas.

Bank cod

The movements and migrations of the west coast bank cod are not fully understood but it seems as if this group has two components, a northern stock made up from the cod of the Disko, Egedesminde, Holsteinborg, Sukkertoppen, and Godthaab districts, and a southern stock from the Frederikshaab and Julianehaab districts. There is some evidence for differences in meristic characters (number of vertebrae, number of rays in D_2), age at first maturity, and in the past at least, in growth rates, between the two stocks. Furthermore, quite a high proportion of the fish tagged in the Frederikshaab and Julianehaab districts have been recaptured on the spawning grounds at Iceland, but the proportion is very much less among the fish tagged in the more northern districts of West Greenland, as Table 22 shows. Cod tagged in the two southern districts have also been recaptured on the Anton Dohrn bank (Hansen, 1957, p. 135; 1958, p. 35).

Table 22. Returns from Greenland and Iceland of cod tagged at West Greenland. (Data from Tåning, 1937).

Tagging district at West Greenland	Number tagged	Returns of tagged cod					
		From Greenland			From Iceland		
		Number	% tagged	% returns	Number	% tagged	% returns
Northern districts	5,640	250	4·4	75·3	82	1·5	24·7
Southern districts	2,860	64	2·2	28·0	165	5·8	72·0

The northern stock of West Greenland bank cod. Norwegian tagging experiments, summarized by Rasmussen (1959), have shown that the mature fish of the northern stock make a seasonal migration along the West Greenland coast. During July 1956, the Norwegians tagged cod in the Holsteinborg Deep, between the Store and Lille Hellefiske banks, where they carry out their pelagic line fishery. The returns showed a winter migration of these fish to south-west Greenland where spents were taken on the Danas and Frederikshaab banks in May and June the following year. Later recoveries during the summer of 1957 showed a return of the spent fish to the Egedesminde district, and then the fish were probably accompanied by their eggs and larvae moving passively in the warm water of the north-going West Greenland current. Small cod are found in Disko Bay (Hansen, 1949), and the more northern districts are very probably the nursery grounds for this stock. The Norwegian tagging experiments have been carried out for a period of five years, from 1953 to 1957, and the results from other years show the same pattern as those of 1956, which Rasmussen gave as an illustration (see Fig. 46).

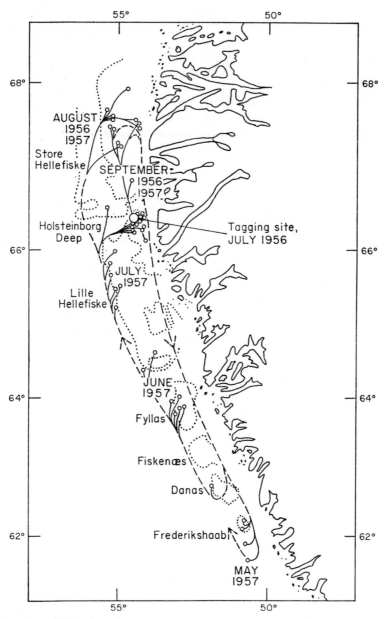

Fig. 46. The migrations of West Greenland bank cod. Cod were tagged in the Holsteinborg Deep in July 1956. Some fish were recovered to the north of the tagging site in August and September 1956. During 1957 the distribution of recoveries showed a progression from Frederikshaab Bank in the south (during May) to Store Hellefiske Bank in the north (during August). (After Rasmussen, 1959, p. 123, Fig. 13.)

The southern stock of West Greenland bank cod. In the 1930s there was little or no spawning in the Frederikshaab and Julianehaab districts, but young cod could be caught around the coast in considerable numbers. Unless there was a local spawning which passed undetected, it seems reasonable to suppose, as Hansen (1949, p. 48) has done, that these fish must have been the survivors of larvae carried round Cape Farewell by the Irminger current and that they originated from either the East Greenland or Iceland spawning grounds or from both. The vertebral counts of the south-west Greenland cod are closer to those of the Icelandic cod than are those of the northern stock and the Danish tagging experiments show, without any doubt, that many of these south-west Greenland cod migrate to Iceland to spawn. The route they take is not known, but Tåning (1934*b*, *c*) believes it to be along the line of banks on the edge of the East Greenland shelf and then to the south of the Greenland-Iceland ridge. Following this route some fish would probably pass close to the Dohrn Bank, where recapture of southwest Greenland fish have recently been made in the new trawl fisheries.

THE EAST COAST

Little is known about these cod. Most of the ground is too rough for trawling and it is only in the last few years that suitable banks have been discovered and exploited. Cod tagged off Angmagssalik have been shown to migrate to the spawning grounds at Iceland (Iversen, 1934; Hansen, Jensen, and Tåning, 1935; Tåning, 1937; Hansen, 1949, p. 61), and it was once thought that there was no east coast spawning ground. However, it has now been established that cod do spawn in East Greenland waters (Meyer, 1958, 1959) along the eastern and southern Greenland shelf. It seems certain that the eggs and larvae from this area probably round Cape Farewell into the Frederikshaab and Julianehaab districts. Similarly, it is likely that East Greenland receives eggs and larvae from the Icelandic spawning grounds.

The migration pattern

It is now time to bring the different parts of the Greenland-Iceland migration story together. Leaving, for the moment, the fjord cod, there are three main spawning areas in this part of the north-west Atlantic. The first is along the banks of West Greenland, the second on the banks and shelf of East Greenland and the third on the south-west coast of Iceland. All three areas come under the influence of the warm water of the Irminger current and the West and East Greenland banks must, at times, be marginal spawning grounds for the cod. Temperature conditions on these banks depend on the relative strength of the Irminger and the cold East Greenland current, and the survival of the young cod must, to a large extent, be related to water temperature.

The eggs and larvae liberated on the spawning grounds are carried downstream by the Irminger current. Thus the spawning products of south-west Iceland are carried round to the north and east coasts and to East, and possibly south-west, Greenland; those of East Greenland will be carried to south-east and south-west Greenland; and those of the West Greenland banks northwards towards Disko Bay. Thus the immature fish which grow up in Icelandic waters will have been spawned on the Icelandic grounds; those of East, south-east and south-west Greenland will have been spawned at East Greenland and Iceland; but the greater part of the northern stock of the West Greenland bank cod will be of West Greenland origin, although some degree of infiltration of East Greenland- and Iceland-spawned fish might be expected in years when the hydrographic conditions favour a high transport of the Irminger current.

At Iceland the cod which grow up on the north and east coasts migrate to the south-west coast to spawn. Now with the salmon the best evidence for the Parent Stream Theory comes from the recovery of mature adults, previously marked as smolts, in the parent stream. Cod fry are too small to be marked by fin clipping or any other of the techniques now in use, and it seems unlikely that direct evidence for their return can ever be obtained with cod or, for that matter, with plaice, eels or herring, all of which disperse from the spawning grounds when only a few days old. But in this case the lack of direct evidence seems unimportant, and the conclusion that the majority of the cod in the north and east coasts of Iceland return to their parent spawning area is reasonable enough from the evidence available. To what extent the spent cod disperse from the spawning area is less certain. Fish tagged on the spawning grounds at south-west Iceland have been recovered in the Denmark Strait, and at south-west Greenland 3 to 5 months later. The difficulty is that the history of these fish is not known. They may have been fish born and bred at Iceland which have dispersed from the spawning grounds, or they may have been fish born at Iceland but bred at Greenland which were returning to south-west Greenland waters after spawning at Iceland. So far no Greenland recoveries have been made of fish tagged on the north or east coasts of Iceland as

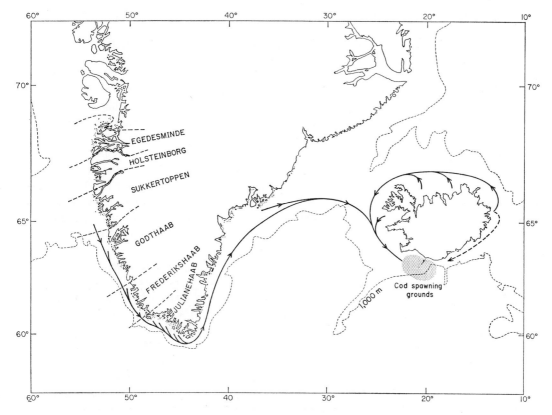

Fig. 47. The migrations of mature cod from south-west Greenland, East Greenland, and North and East Iceland to the spawning grounds at south-west Iceland. The broken line round the south-east coast from Lodmundar Fjord to the spawning grounds indicates the uncertainty concerning the route taken by the east coast fish. (Outline based on an International Hydrographic Bureau (Monaco) chart.)

immatures. But these fish do leave Icelandic waters as 3 have turned up on the Norwegian coast (Jónsson, 1953). Double recapture experiments with Greenland tagged fish may solve this problem. In such experiments cod would be tagged and released at West Greenland; fish recaptured at Iceland should be released again in the hope that some would be caught again at West Greenland.

Cod migrate from south-east and south-west Greenland to spawn at south-west Iceland. The journey takes place in the autumn or the winter (Tåning, 1937) and it is worth noting that the velocity of the Irminger current is at its maximum at West Greenland in September and October (Kiilerich, 1943, p. 20). It has not yet been established with certainty that these fish are of Icelandic origin, although the evidence points that way. It is not known if these fish return to Greenland after spawning. As cod tagged at Greenland have been taken at Iceland up to 5 months after the end of the spawning season (Hansen, Jensen, and Tåning, 1935, p. 77) at least some of these fish do not return to Greenland immediately, and it is possible that some may remain at Iceland.

It has been shown that some of the northern stock of West Greenland bank cod migrate to Iceland. Here again it is not known where these fish were born. They may be of Icelandic or Greenland origin. Figure 47 summarizes the spawning migrations of Greenland and Icelandic cod to the grounds at south-west Iceland.

Discussion

The Greenland-Iceland story is complicated and there is so much that is still not understood. The climatic and hydrographic conditions in the north-west Atlantic not only vary from year to year but there is also evidence of a succession of cold and warm periods throughout the whole North Atlantic area. A warm period started in the 1920s. The causes of these climatic changes are not known but they are almost certainly to be looked for among cosmic phenomena. While the cause of a warm period is not understood, its consequences, such as the increase in air temperatures, increase in volume transports of the great warm water currents, and the northward spread of boreal warm water species and a retreat of cold Arctic species, are fairly well documented. Some information about these changes is given in the papers presented at the special scientific meeting held by the International Council for the Exploration of the Sea on 'Climatic changes in the Arctic in relation to plants and animals' (Ahlmann, 1949). It is certain that there have been changes in the distribution and abundance of cod in the North Atlantic waters as a result of these changes although, as Bell and Pruter (1958) have pointed out, some of the data presented as evidence hardly bear critical examination.

At the beginning of this century it is probable that the hydrographic conditions were unsuitable for cod to spawn with any great success on the West Greenland banks, although cod did live and spawn in the fjords. Most of the cod in Greenland waters would then have been local fjord cod, but there may have been a cadre of north-west bank cod and, to the south-west, a few survivors grown up from the larvae carried from Iceland. A change in the relative volume transports of the cold East Greenland and warm Irminger currents could lead to more favourable conditions on the banks and thus to a greater survival of the young resulting from the spawning of the northern stock of West Greenland bank cod. There is evidence to show that the good year-classes of West Greenland cod are associated with the higher bottom temperatures on the banks (Hermann, 1953). Similar changes could favour a greater survival of the larval fish carried to south-west Greenland from the Icelandic spawning area.

There is no doubt that while some degree of mixing takes place between the northern and southern bank stocks, it would be possible for either stock to develop good year-classes independently of the other. If some degree of mixing does take place, and Iceland-spawned cod do return to Iceland to spawn, a year-class which is outstanding in south-west Greenland should give a higher proportion of Icelandic returns among tagged north-west Greenland bank cod.

There has been a great increase in the abundance of cod at West Greenland from 1917 onwards. No information about the hydrographic conditions at West Greenland is available for that year (Kiilerich, 1943) but cod were more plentiful in the Julianehaab and Frederikshaab districts. The majority of these fish seem to have been five-year-olds belonging to the 1912 year-class (Jensen and Hansen, 1931, p. 22). It seems very unlikely that these fish can have been of Greenland origin. The only local spawning in this area takes place in Amitsuarssuk Fjord, which is nearly cut off from the sea (Jensen and Hansen, 1931, p. 19). It seems as if the fish which were caught at south-west Greenland in 1917 were survivors of larvae carried from Iceland in 1912. No hydrographic data are available for 1912. It is not known if any of the 1912-year-class went to spawn at Iceland when they reached first maturity in 1918 or 1919; no tagging experiments were carried out in the Julianehaab and Frederikshaab districts until 1928, when three fish were tagged.

The warm period was well under way in the late 1920s and 1930s, when there was a spectacular rise in the number and weight of cod taken by the Greenlanders. Although statistics are not available to convert the total catch into catch-per-unit-of-effort, the increase is probably a fair measure of the abundance of cod on the west coast of Greenland.

Tagging experiments began in Greenland waters in 1924 and for the first five years work was, apart from the three fish tagged in Julianehaab district in 1928, restricted to the northern districts. Only a few of the fish tagged in the northern districts in 1924–28 were returned from Iceland. Large-scale tagging experiments began in the Frederikshaab and Julianehaab districts in 1929, and continued until 1939, when the war years interrupted the work. Many of the cod tagged in the southern districts were recaptured at Iceland, and these results have been interpreted by Hansen, Jensen, and Tåning (1935) as showing that the Greenland-Iceland migration began on a large scale in 1929. This may be true but it does not follow from the facts: there are no data before 1929 to compare with the later experiments in the southern districts. Schmidt (1931a, p. 11) made this very point and he went so far as to stress that it was in 1929 that tagging experiments started in the southern districts and that there was the possibility, which has since been confirmed by the Norwegian work, that the southern and northern populations differed in biological and migrational tendencies. But comparable data are available for the northern districts, and if corrections are made for the different numbers of fish tagged and for the increase in the Icelandic fishing effort at Iceland after 1928, it can be shown (Table 23) that the Icelandic returns of north-west Greenland tagged cod in 1929–33 were three times greater than might have been expected on the returns of 1924–28. There does seem to have been an increase in the migration from Greenland to Iceland due, no doubt, to the great year-classes of 1922 and 1924, larvae of which may have been carried from Iceland to south-west Greenland.

It would be interesting to correlate the hydrographic conditions of 1922 and 1924 with the outstanding year-classes they produced. Kiilerich (1943) says that 1924 was a very warm year and indicates that the volume transport of the Irminger current was probably high. There are no hydrographic data available for 1922. Information about the hydrography of the West Greenland banks from 1920–40 is fragmentary and it is difficult to make any dynamic computations of the volume transports in the area during this period.

However, on the fish tagging side, one fact stands out quite clearly, namely that the Icelandic returns of Greenland tagged fish are the greatest from those year-classes which are the most

Table 23. Icelandic returns, by Icelandic boats, of cod tagged in the Northern districts of West Greenland in two periods, 1924–28 and 1929–33. (Data from Hansen, Jensen, and Tåning (1935). The measure of Icelandic effort at Iceland has been obtained from their Table 73 which gives the Icelandic catch of large (=mature) cod, and the English statistics for catch per 100/hr fishing (=stock density) for the two periods.)

Period	Number of cod tagged in the Northern districts of West Greenland	Returns of tagged cod		Icelandic fishing effort at Iceland
		At Iceland by Icelandic boats	At Greenland	
1924–28	1,378	6	70	100
1929–33	2,806	45	75	130

Note. The number of cod expected to be returned from Iceland in 1929–33, taking into account the increased number tagged and the increased effort at Iceland, is 16 fish. The actual return, 45, is considerably greater than the number expected.

abundant at south-west Greenland (Hansen, 1949). On the other hand, a good year-class at north-west Greenland, such as that of 1926, which was poorly represented at south-west Greenland, gave few returns from Iceland. Although the evidence is not as good as one wants, and must be complicated by a number of factors, such as tagging techniques, area of tagging, reliability of returns and all the practical difficulties that come into work of this sort, the facts are not inconsistent with the hypothesis that the majority of the Greenland tagged fish caught at Iceland are Icelandic-born fish returning to their parent spawning area.

There are anomalies and difficulties in accepting the evidence outright but these might well be explained if one had all the hydrographic and biological data at one's finger tips. But it is only since the International Commission for the North-West Atlantic Fisheries was set up in 1949 that the research effort and cover in this area can be said to be adequate. There is really very little data on what was happening in Greenland waters in earlier years when the warm period was beginning. This is not to belittle in any way the work the Danes did thirty or more years ago. What does astonish one is the amount they managed to do with the very limited means at their disposal but obviously no amount of hard work can make up for the lack of ships, men, and money, in tackling problems of this sort.

THE BARENTS SEA–NORWEGIAN COAST MIGRATION

(For place names see Figs. 27, 30, 33, and 48. The surface currents of the area are shown in Fig. 28)

Cod spawn all along the coast of Norway and to the east of North Cape, in Motovski Gulf, on the Murman coast, but the great skrei, or mature cod fisheries, take place in the Norwegian districts of Romsdal and Nordland. Some of these fish, perhaps about a quarter, are local coastal or fjord cod, but the rest belong to the Arcto-Norwegian stock and have migrated to the spawning grounds from the Barents Sea. Rollefsen (1954, p. 45) has listed some of the features which can be used to distinguish between the two groups. These include differences in body shape, vertebral count, otolith structure, growth rate, and age at first maturity. Direct evidence for the migration of Barents Sea cod to and from the Norwegian coast comes from two sets of tagging experiments.

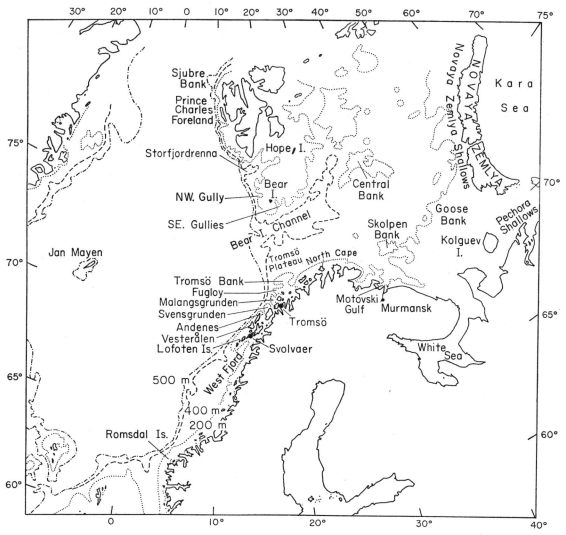

Fig. 48. Place names of interest in connexion with the movements and migrations of the Arcto-Norwegian cod. (Position of depth contours from Stocks, 1950. Outline from a Meteorological Office chart; place names from an Admiralty chart.)

The first is from the recapture on the spawning grounds of cod tagged in the Barents Sea, and the second is from the recapture, in the Barents Sea, of cod tagged on the spawning grounds.

Fish tagged in the Barents Sea (see Fig. 49)

Cod have been tagged in the summer months at Spitsbergen, Hope Island, and the south-east Barents Sea (Hjort, 1926; Idelson, 1931; Messiatzeva, 1932; Maslov, 1944; F. M. Davies (see Graham *et al.*, 1954, Appendix I); and Trout, 1957). Recaptures have been made off Bear Island, the Norwegian coast, and at the spawning grounds.

The Cod

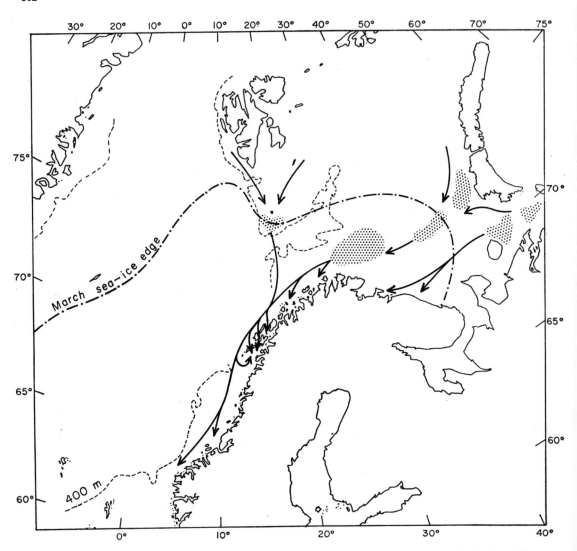

Fig. 49. Migrations of the Arcto-Norwegian cod. In the autumn there is a contraction in the distribution of the cod which concentrate in areas south-west of Bear Island, between Goose Bank and Novaya Zemlya, and to the north and east of Kolguev Island. The immature fish overwinter to the south of Bear Island, but in the south-eastern part of the Barents Sea there may be a movement westward towards the North Cape Bank area later in the season. The mature and ripening fish do not remain on the autumn and winter grounds and move to the spawning area which lies between Motovski Gulf and Romsdal. The diagram is based on the data given by Iversen (1934), Lee (1952), Trout (1957), and Maslov (1960). Autumn and winter areas are stippled. The heavy broken line indicates the approximate southern limit of sea ice in March (Deutsches Hydrographisches Institut, 1950). (Depth contour from Stocks, 1950. Outline from a Meteorological Office chart.)

The picture that builds up from the results of these experiments and the movements of the fisheries is as follows. In August and September the mature and immature fish are at the northern limit of their summer feeding migration at Spitsbergen and the north-easterly parts of the Barents

Sea. In October they turn south and west towards Bear Island and the Norwegian and Murman coasts.

The area over which the cod are found in winter is much smaller than that over which they are found in summer. In the Bear Island area dense concentrations of cod build up on the bottom along the line of the front between the warm Atlantic and cold polar waters (Lee, 1952). Other concentrations are found in the eastern part of the Barents Sea (Maslov, 1960) near the Goose Bank and the Pechora shallows. In cold winters these concentrations move towards the North Cape Bank area, but in mild years as in 1937 and 1938, the cod may over-winter on the Goose Bank (Maslov, 1960). The areas in which the winter concentrations are found may be called the winter grounds, and the movements which bring about the contraction in distribution can be regarded as a migration from the feeding area to the wintering grounds. Tagging returns (Maslov, 1960, p. 195, Table 2) suggest that the fish are averaging about 3 miles a day during the migration.

In December both immature and mature cod can be found in the deep water concentrations at the edge of the Bear Island Bank. But neither here, nor in the eastern Barents Sea, do the mature fish remain long on the winter grounds. The large cod move on to the spawning grounds. Trout's (1957) interpretation of this movement is that it is essentially a change of depth, a migration from shallow to deeper water, which brings the cod into the main streams of the Spitsbergen and North Cape currents. In January and February a trawl fishery, mainly for mature and ripening cod, develops off the Norwegian coast at Malangsgrunden, Svensgrunden, and Andenes. However, not all the cod which migrate down the Norwegian coastline are mature fish. They are accompanied by a number of the larger immatures which are believed to be making a 'dummy run' towards the spawning grounds (Trout, 1957, p. 2; Woodhead, 1959) where recaptures of ripe fish are made in February, March, and April. Maslov's (1960, p. 197, Table 4) tagging experiments carried out in 1937 give returns indicating an average speed of 7 miles a day from the south-eastern Barents Sea to the Norway coast spawning grounds.

Fish tagged on the spawning grounds (see Fig. 50)

The results of these experiments have been given by Hjort (1914, 1926), Iversen (1934), Dannevig (1953), and Maslov (1960). They show that mature cod tagged at the spawning grounds on the Norwegian coast, particularly at Lofoten, migrate northwards when the spawning season is over. The spent cod leave the coastal banks at the beginning of April. Dannevig (1949) has shown that they move quite quickly up the Norwegian coast and Lofoten tagged fish have been recovered at North Cape at the end of April. They appeared to be going north at about 18 miles a day. Some are recaptured on the Bear Island banks in May and June and later in the year to the north-west of the island, towards Spitsbergen. Others move round North Cape into the central and south-eastern parts of the Barents Sea. Some cod are recaptured on the Finmark coast in the summer fishery. Hjort's (1914) tagging experiments in this area showed that these fish move eastwards along the Murman coast towards the Kanin Peninsula, and Lofoten tagged fish are taken in the south-east Barents Sea in May, June, and July (Dannevig, 1953). The recaptures then fall off in this area and in August, September, and October returns come in from latitues to the north of 75°N., from Hope Island and the eastern banks, the limits of the feeding migration. In October the cod return to the south and west. In November and December tagged cod are again taken in the south-east Barents Sea and in February and March of the following year at the spawning grounds on the Norwegian coast.

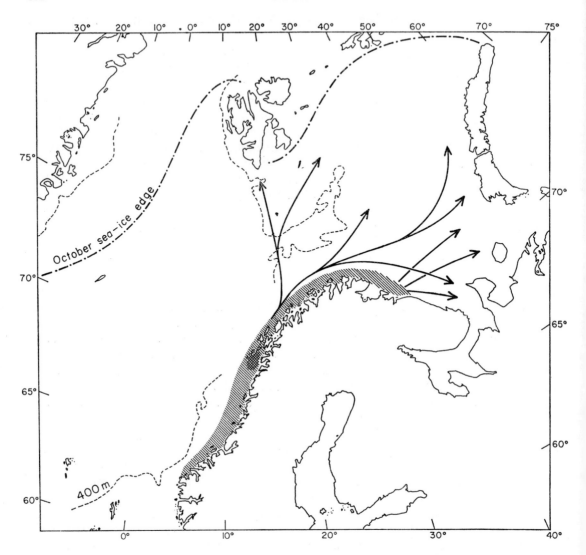

Fig. 50. Migrations of the Arcto-Norwegian cod. The spawning area (diagonal lines) extends from Motovski Gulf on the Murman coast to Romsdal at SW. Norway, but the most important ground is within the arm of the West Fjord, at the Lofoten Islands. The arrows indicate the return of spent fish from the spawning area to the feeding area. The diagram is based on data given by Iversen (1934), Dannevig (1953), and Maslov (1960). The heavy broken line indicates the approximate southern limit of sea ice in October (Deutsches Hydrographisches Institut, 1950). (Depth contour from Stocks (1950). Outline from a Meteorological Office chart.)

It appears that the cod may not always return to the part of the Barents Sea which they occupied the previous year. Trout (1957) showed that the opaque zones of the older cod are split by a thin hyaline zone and that the proportion of the split type otoliths is greater in the eastern part of the Barents Sea. These results are consistent with the hypothesis that cod which grew up to the west on the Spitsbergen shelf migrate to the south-eastern Barents Sea after spawning. Tagging returns support this hypothesis, and some of the cod tagged by Trout on the West Spitsbergen shelf have been recaptured several years later from the south-eastern Barents Sea.

The evidence from tagging is straightforward; cod tagged in the Barents Sea are recaptured on the spawning grounds on the Norwegian coast, and cod tagged on the Norwegian coast are recaptured in the Barents Sea. The spread and drift of eggs and larvae in the north-going Norwegian coastal current is also fairly well known (Hjort, 1914), and more data are becoming available as to the distribution of the O-group cod when they take to the bottom in the Barents Sea (Corlett, 1958).

Quantitative aspects of the migration

Some very interesting problems arise when more quantitative aspects of the migrations are considered. The greatest of the skrei fisheries takes place at Lofoten. Some of the fishing takes place over the banks outside the Lofoten Islands but the greater part of the catch is taken within the West Fjord and landed at Svolvaer. The season is short, lasting from the middle of February to the end of March but the fishery must be one of the most intensive in the world. In these 6 weeks 2,000 or more boats manned by about 10,000 fishermen take, by line, gill net and purse seine, from 7 to 40 million cod a season. From the point of view of migration, and homing, it would be interesting to know what proportion of the mature cod of the Arcto-Norwegian stock spawn at Lofoten, and whether a fish which spawns once at Lofoten returns there the following year.

The first step is to make an estimate of the number of mature cod in the Arcto-Norwegian stock. It is fairly safe to assume that over three-quarters of the cod of 75 cm and more in length are mature fish. The Fish Stock Record for 1958 (MAFF, 1959) shows that in 1957 about 25% of the cod caught by British trawlers in regions IIb and I (Bear Island and Eastern Barents Sea) were over 75 cm in length. Our total catch that year from the Barents Sea was 53 million fish. The Russian catch is about 3 times that of the British, and between them the two countries catch practically all the cod landed from these areas. So the total number of cod taken in 1957 was of the order of $53 + 159 = 212$ million. The overall fishing intensity in the Barents Sea is high, and it is estimated that half the exploited stock is caught each year. This gives an estimate for the total exploited stock as $212 \times 2 = 424$ million fish. The size distribution of the Russian catch is much the same as that of the British and one-quarter of the stock, 106 million fish, can be assumed to be of 75 cm or more in length. Three-quarters of these fish, say 80 million, will be mature. How many of these fish spawned, in 1958, at Lofoten?

The Lofoten catch in 1958 was 8·3 million fish (Hylen, Midttun, and Saetersdal, 1961, p. 102, Table 2). The next problem is to estimate the number of spawning cod at Lofoten and to do this one must know the fishing intensity. Now the Lofoten fishery is very concentrated and estimates of fishing mortality based on the recovery of Lofoten tagged fish recaptured in the same season as they are released are almost certainly too high (Dannevig, 1953). A better estimate can be made from recaptures in the season after tagging, when the results are expressed as a percentage of the number of tagged fish known to be at liberty (number tagged—number of tagged caught) at the end of season during which they were released. Making a times 2 correction for the 'away from Lofoten' mortality between spawning seasons, data for the 1958 returns of 1957 tagged fish suggest a fishing intensity of 20% at Lofoten (Hylen *et al.*, 1961, p. 106, Table 5). This gives an estimate for the number of spawning cod as $8·3 \times 5 = 41·5$ million, only about half that of the estimate for the total number of mature cod in the Arcto-Norwegian stock.

Errors can, of course, creep into calculations of this sort. An over-estimate of the fishing intensity in the Barents Sea could lead to an over-estimate of the number of mature fish. But as the chances are that the figure of 50% is an under-estimate, rather than an over-estimate for fish over 75 cm long, it does seem as if only half of the mature fish come to Lofoten to spawn. Where does the other half of the stock go? It seems very probable that they spawn right along the Norwegian coastline, from Romsdal to North Cape and Motovski Gulf on the Murman coast, and that the enormous length of the coastline over which they are distributed makes their density such that no great fishery develops for them.

The recoveries of cod tagged off the Norwegian coast, at Malangsgrunden, during cruise 1/1959 (January) of the 'Ernest Holt', are of some interest in this connexion. There can be little doubt that most of these fish were mature and were caught on their way to their spawning grounds to the south. Seventy-one of the tagged fish were recaptured within or near the Lofoten Islands during the spawning season the same year. Another 20 fish were taken further down the coast, below 66°N., and of these 20, no fewer than 9 were taken in the Romsdal area, between 62° and 63°N. These results suggest that about 25% of the fish found off the coast at Malangsgrunden in January were going to spawn well to the south of Lofoten in February and March, and this evidence could be used to support the view that the Arcto-Norwegian cod spread themselves over the Norwegian coastline. However, before this evidence can be accepted at its face value, it is important to identify the recaptured fish, by their otolith structure, as belonging to the Arcto-Norwegian stock and not to the coastal or fjord stock. It is quite possible that the Norwegian coastal cod, like the northwest Greenland bank cod, make an extensive spawning migration to the south. But there are little or no published data available which help to solve this problem.

If in fact the Arcto-Norwegian cod do spread out along the Norwegian coast when they spawn, it would be very interesting to know what proportion of Lofoten fish, identified as Arcto-Norwegian cod, are taken on spawning grounds other than Lofoten the following year. Hylen *et al.* 1961, (p. 106, Table 4) have shown that of the spawning cod tagged at Lofoten between 1953 and 1959, 2% of the 1960 recoveries were taken to the south of Lofoten. A Russian recovery is worth mentioning here. Maslov (1944) records that a cod tagged in April 1939, which had certainly previously spawned in Motovski Gulf, was recaptured the next year at the Lofoten Islands. So there is the possibility that some of the cod may spawn on different parts of the coast in different years.

More remains to be learnt about the migrations of the Arcto-Norwegian stock of cod. It is clear that they spawn near the Norwegian coast and that they make very long journeys between the spawning grounds and their feeding grounds in the Barents Sea. But there is no evidence to show that the mature fish return to spawn on that part of the coast on which they were born. Most of the fish that spawn at Lofoten probably spawn there again the following year, but some stray to other parts of the coast.

Chapter 8

The Plaice

INTRODUCTION

After cod and haddock, the plaice is the most important fish landed in the United Kingdom. The total value of the plaice landed far exceeds that of any other of the flatfish (Table 24). In 1964, the last year for which comparable figures have been published, the market value of the plaice landed by United Kingdom fishing boats was about £5,392,000 and in the same year the imports of plaice into the United Kingdom were valued at £1,813,000 (MAFF, 1965). The greater part of the imported plaice (£1,149,000) came, as usual, from Denmark.

Table 24. Catch (in thousands cwt) and value (in thousands £ sterling) of plaice and other flatfish landed by British vessels in the United Kingdom in 1965. (Data from MAFF, 1967).

Fish	Landing in thousands cwt	Value first sale in thousands £ sterling
Plaice	786	5,703
Lemon sole	117	1,161
Halibut	65	914
Dover sole	24	664
Turbot	34	542
Dabs	40	128
Megrims	23	104
Witch	23	101
Brill	5	67
Flounder	3	7

The plaice is of great economic importance to Belgium, Denmark, Holland, England, Germany, and Scotland. At the beginning of this century the biology of the plaice became the subject of international investigations directed by the newly formed International Council for the Exploration of the Sea. A committee was set up to investigate the biology of the flatfish and among its members were Garstang, Fulton, Heincke, and Petersen. Our knowledge of the biology of the plaice in the North Sea is very largely derived from work carried out between 1902 and 1911 under the direction of this Committee. Garstang was in charge of the United Kingdom's work. At that time the Marine Biological Association, which undertook the general responsibility for our share of the international investigations, was very short of funds and the research vessel used in the seagoing work, 'Huxley', was bought by Dr. G. P. Bidder, and chartered to the Association on favourable terms. Without Bidder's help the United Kingdom would not have been able to do any real work at sea.

As a result of the international investigations the scientific literature on the plaice is fairly extensive, and much of it has been brought together in Wimpenny's (1953) book, while various aspects of the biology of the plaice are dealt with in Graham's (1956) *Sea Fisheries*.

The plaice is found throughout the shallow coastal waters of Northern Europe. It ranges from the White Sea and Murman coast in the north, down the Scandinavian coastline and into the Baltic to the Gulf of Bothnia. It is abundant in the North Sea and is present in the Channel, the Irish Sea and off the west coast of Scotland. To the south it is taken off the Atlantic coasts of France, Spain, and Portugal and has been recorded in the Mediterranean. Plaice are found at the Shetlands, Faroes, and Iceland, but not at Jan Mayen, Greenland, or along the Atlantic coast of the American continent.

There are several more or less self-contained stocks of plaice between which there is little mixing. The Murman coast, Icelandic, Faroese, and Baltic stocks are examples. The position is more complex in the North Sea and other coastal waters surrounding Great Britain. The Irish Sea stock is fairly distinct but plaice certainly move between the Irish Sea, the Channel, and the North Sea. In the North Sea itself, there appear to be four spawning stocks between which there is a certain amount of mixing: the Scottish East Coast, Flamborough, Southern Bight, and German Bight stocks. The bulk of the United Kingdom catch of plaice comes from the North Sea.

As most is known about the movements and migrations of plaice in the North Sea, it is therefore convenient to consider these fish first and then to go on to see how the plaice in two other areas, Iceland and the Irish Sea, compare with those in the North Sea.

NORTH SEA PLAICE

(Place names are given in Figs. 34 and 35, and the surface currents in Fig. 36)

Distribution

Heincke (1913) has summarized our knowledge of the distribution of the plaice in the North Sea. The very young stages are found in the shallow coastal waters from where they disperse seawards towards the deeper water. A year-class is progressively reduced in numbers in successive years and the survivors spread from a relatively narrow coastal zone to a wider area as they grow older. Thus the coastal regions, from 0 to 20 m deep, are the nursery grounds for the young juvenile plaice up to their third year. Plaice from 3 to 5 years old are found in depths from 20 to 60 m, and the larger and older fish in still deeper water. Heincke (1913, p. 16) formulated a general rule for their distribution according to age. This is often known as Heincke's Law and states that 'the size and age of the plaice of any definite part of the North Sea are inversely proportional to the density of their occurrence, but on the other hand directly proportional to the distance of the locality from the coast and its depth'.

The majority of the North Sea plaice are found south of a line drawn from Flamborough Head round the northern edge of the Dogger to the Skaw. The spawning grounds north of this line are off the east coast of Scotland, in particular the Moray Firth. In the southern North Sea plaice eggs can be found over a wide area during the spawning season, but there are concentrations of eggs near Flamborough Head, in the central Southern Bight, and in the Heligoland or German Bight which suggests that there are definite spawning grounds in these three areas.

The spawning season

In the North Sea plaice spawn from November to May but the production of eggs reaches its peak at different months in different areas as shown in Table 25. Temperature is believed to be the most important single factor in determining the time of peak egg production.

Table 25. Spawning seasons of plaice in different areas. (Data from Simpson, 1959*a*.)

Spawning area	Spawning season	
	Range	Peak egg production
Scottish East coast	November–May	February–March
Flamborough	January–April	March
Southern Bight	December–March	January
German Bight	January–March	February

Sex ratios

There is a slightly greater number of males than females among juvenile plaice. In the southern North Sea males come to first maturity when two years old (as II-group fish, in their third year, and at about 22 cm in length), a year earlier than the females. The growth rates of both sexes are very similar among O-, I-, and II-group fish, but thereafter the growth of the males falls off and among the mature fish the females are larger than males of the same age, and they are more numerous, as the following figures show (taken from Hefford, 1916, p. 5, Table 2).

Number of plaice caught by various international research vessels, 1903-07

Length in cm	Under 15	15–19	20–24	25–29	30–34	35–39	40–44	45 over
Males	8,801	18,894	17,260	9,682	3,711	1,288	367	57
Females	7,099	17,060	17,586	10,501	4,160	1,979	1,091	1,046
% males	55	53	50	48	47	39	25	5

In the Southern Bight spawning area there are more older fish present at the start of the season and the younger fish, mostly males which are spawning for the first time, arrive later (Simpson, 1959*a*). More males than females are caught in the spawning area. Hefford's explanation of this is that the males stay on the grounds longer. Chrzan (1950) offered a similar explanation to the account for the greater catches of male cod on the spawning grounds off Gydnia. It seems probable that the higher fishing mortality that male plaice undergo during the spawning season, and the fact that they mature a year earlier and thus suffer a greater total fishing mortality than the females, must be part of the explanation of the greater number of females among the older fish. This may not, however, be the whole story. Beverton (personal communication) has followed the survival of certain year-classes of plaice through the 1939–45 war period when fishing mortality was virtually nil, and has been able to show that the males appear to have a greater natural mortality than females. This may play some part in accounting for the greater number of females among the older fish.

Spawning

Plaice spawn in relatively warm water, ranging from 4 to 10°C in the different spawning areas in the North Sea. In the Southern Bight the average sea temperature at spawning is 7·5°C (Simpson,

1959a). It is not known whether plaice spawn near the bottom or up in midwater. Forster (1953) observed two plaice spawning in a tank at the Plymouth Aquarium. 'The two plaice were swimming in mid-water about two and a half feet from the bottom, the female lying slightly diagonally across the back of the male, their vents being close together. The female, considerably larger than the male, was quivering violently and emitting a rapid stream of eggs.' The Plymouth spawnings took place in the evening. Plaice have also spawned in tanks at Port Erin and at Lowestoft, and the eggs are usually released some time between dusk and dawn. Fulton (1906) had the same experience with plaice at the Aberdeen hatchery, and found that a female took a month or more to spawn completely, eggs being released at intervals of a few days. There seems to be little doubt that females must take 2 to 3 weeks to complete their spawning. As Fulton observes, it is physically impossible for a female to hold all the eggs at the size they attain when they are mature, and they must therefore ripen gradually and in small batches. Furthermore, the eggs absorb a large quantity of water during the final stages of maturation, and Fulton calculated that a female must supply her eggs with an amount of water equal to nearly half her volume. It seems unlikely that this quantity of water could be supplied in a few days.

The drift of eggs and larvae

A female plaice produces from 16,000 to 350,000 eggs according to her size. The healthy fertilized eggs float in sea-water. Development of the embryo proceeds faster at higher temperatures. At 6°C the egg hatches in 20 days, at 8°C in 16 days. When the larvae hatch out they are about 6 to 7 mm long, and are quite symmetrical. Metamorphosis starts about 5 weeks after hatching and is completed by the 7th or 8th week, the exact time depending on the temperature and the availability of food. The baby plaice, about 10 to 14 mm long, then take to the bottom.

The dispersal of eggs and larvae from the spawning areas depends on the direction and strength of the residual surface currents. A chart showing the main residual currents of the North Sea is given in Fig. 36. It will be seen that there are clockwise eddies in the Moray Firth and the Firth of Forth and these tend to keep most of the eggs and larvae hatched on the Scottish East Coast grounds in the coastal waters until they take to the bottom after metamorphosis (Bowman, 1921). There is a similar eddy over the Flamborough Off ground and the young plaice spawned in this area are not carried out across the North Sea towards the German Bight, but stay more or less where they are and eventually come inshore to their nursery grounds on the Yorkshire coast. Most of the O-group plaice found along the English north-east coast, particularly in Bridlington Bay (Wimpenny, 1960), are probably spawned on the Flamborough Off ground.

In normal weather conditions eggs and larvae spawned in the Southern Bight and German Bight will be carried to the north-east by the residual current. Simpson (1959a) has shown that plaice eggs spawned in the Southern Bight drift to the north-east at a speed of about 2·4 miles a day and have an overall drift of 150 to 170 miles during the pelagic phase. Most of the fish from the Eastern Channel-Southern Bight area will take to the bottom off the continental coast between Ymuiden and Norderney and move inshore to the shallow water nursery grounds, Similarly the German Bight spawned fish should, in normal conditions, end up on the Jutland coast, between Sylt and Horns Reef.

Movements of juvenile plaice off the Dutch coast

Redeke (1905), Garstang (1909), Heincke (1913), and Wimpenny (1953) give accounts of the movements and distribution of the juvenile plaice on the Dutch coast nursery grounds. The fish spend their first summer as O-group fish in water less than 5 m deep. In the late summer and autumn they move off shore to slightly deeper water where they winter. The following April the plaice have their first anniversary. They are now I-group fish and about 9 to 10 cm long and it is at this time of the year that the first opaque (summer) zone is formed in the otolith. As the water temperature rises the plaice spread out to deeper water, down to about 20 m, the bigger fish going first. The formation of the clear (winter) zone in the otolith starts in July, at about the same time as the off shore movement gets under way. In the autumn the average length of the I-group is 15 cm. There is another winter pause and after their second anniversary, the II-group fish, now in their third year, carry on with the off shore movement. In the autumn the II-group fish are from 10 to 23 cm in length, the smaller fish being nearer the coast.

During the following winter the largest of the II-group males reach their first maturity and move southwards to the spawning area. The remainder of the juvenile II-group stay more or less where they are, moving perhaps a little inshore during the following summer. The tagging experiments described by Garstang (1905a, experiments 1, 2, and 3) show the difference in the migratory behaviour of the smaller juvenile and the larger and probably maturing fish.

Those members of the II-group which migrated southwards to the spawning area do not return to the Dutch coastal waters as spent III-group fish. After spawning they leave the Southern Bight to the west of the Brown Ridge for the feeding grounds to the north and north-east and are recaptured at Smith's Knoll and on the Leman ground. The following autumn some of these III-group males go south for their second spawning where they are joined by others of their year-class, most of which will now have reached first maturity. After spawning the spent fish return to the feeding grounds in the north. There are, then, two migration routes to the Southern Bight spawning area. The first-time spawners, the recruits from the coastal nursery area, come in from the north-east, from the Texel to the Egmond ground, and so across the Broad Fourteens to the Hinder ground. The older plaice, which have spawned before and live in the deeper water towards the centre of the North Sea, come in more to the west, across the Winterton Twenties to the Winterton Shoal, to the Knoll Flat, East Deep Water, and so to the Hinder ground. As spent fish they all return by the western route (see Garstang, 1912, p. 172, for his comments on the Dutch experiment No. 34).

Other nursery areas

The movements of juvenile plaice off the German and Danish coasts appear to be very similar to those observed off the Dutch coast. There is a spread towards the deeper water as the fish get older. The Scottish East Coast and Flamborough spawned fish probably disperse in a similar manner but in these areas the 40 m depth contour is near the coast and the ground over which the plaice can spread is very restricted compared with conditions in the southern North Sea. Moray Firth fish probably spread to the Firth of Forth and Firth of Forth fish to the Moray Firth, and fish from both areas may come down the Northumberland coast keeping within the 40 m contour. Similarly Flamborough plaice may go to the north-west or to the south-east across the Off ground and then towards the Wash or Well Bank Flat.

The return to the parent spawning area

The winter spawning migration of the older plaice from the Leman and more northern fishing grounds to the Hinder, and their return to the north in spring and summer, has been shown by the English tagging experiments (1902 and 1903 experiments, Garstang, 1905a; 1904 and 1905 experiments, Garstang, 1912; 1906–08 experiments, Atkinson, 1912; 1909–11 experiments, Borley, 1916). Other tagging experiments have shown similar spawning migrations for the Scottish East Coast (Fulton, 1919) and German Bight spawners (Garstang, 1905b; and Wimpenny's 1953 summary). A problem which is of interest here is whether the fish return to spawn in the same area as that in which they themselves were born and to what extent there is a return to the parent area in successive spawnings.

RECRUIT SPAWNERS

Sockeye, coho and Atlantic salmon born in a particular stream can be identified without any real difficulty as they stay in the parent stream until they are big enough to mark. But larval plaice may be carried miles away from their parent area and when they are big enough to tag they may have dispersed and intermingled with other fish so there must be some doubt as to where an individual fish was spawned. But one would probably be quite justified in assuming that the great majority of I-group fish found in the Firth of Forth, Bridlington Bay, off the Dutch coast, and near Sylt, were Scottish East Coast-, Flamborough-, Southern and German Bight-spawned fish respectively. So the distribution of the recoveries of spawning fish tagged as I- or even II-group in selected areas could throw some light on the problem of the return to the parent spawning area. But on going through the detailed tables of the English tagging experiments 1902–11 it is clear that on only a few occasions have really small fish been tagged (Garstang, 1912; Experiment 34 off Ymuiden; Experiment 35, Bridlington Bay). Such recoveries as were made during the spawning season are useless as Garstang does not give any details of the maturity of the fish on recapture. There do not appear to be any experiments that could be used to settle the point as to whether plaice generally spawn for the first time in the parent area. Nevertheless, on going through the tables and figures one cannot but help being struck by the fact that the smallest plaice are generally recaptured, within a year or two, close to the point of liberation. There is no evidence to show any movement of juvenile fish from one nursery to another. If it is reasonable to assume that fish spawn in the nearest area when they come to first maturity, it seems as if the majority will do so in the area in which they themselves were born.

MATURE FISH

The bigger and older plaice spread over a greater area of the North Sea than the smaller and younger ones. Hickling's (1938) analysis of the 1929–32 tagging experiments show this quite clearly. This means that there will be some mixing between adult plaice spawned in different areas. Where do these adult fish spawn when they come to their second, third, or fourth maturity? Do they go back to the parent area, or do they chop and change depending on where they happen to be at a critical stage in their maturation cycle? This question is best answered by the subsequent recovery of spawners that were tagged as spawning fish a year or two previously. Atkinson (1912, p. 254) notes the recovery of a fish which probably spawned in the Flamborough area one year and in the Southern Bight the next. But on going through Atkinson's (1912) and Borley's (1916) tables I have been unable to find any recaptures of spawning fish tagged when spawning, which is what one really wants.

De Veen and Boerema's (1959) work on the otoliths of spawning plaice in the Southern Bight and German Bight is of interest here. They found that German Bight spawners had a smaller mean width for the first and second otolith year rings (measured longitudinally to the inner margin of the opaque 'summer' zone) as compared with the Southern Bight spawners. Their results are shown in Fig. 51. The difference in the width of the first two year rings probably reflects a higher growth rate of the Southern Bight spawners on their nursery grounds. Just dealing with the first-year ring, de Veen and Boerema showed that the differences between year-classes on the two spawning grounds are maintained in successive years which suggests that there is little mixing between the two groups during the spawning season.

These results revived interest in the spawning area problem and a series of tagging experiments were initiated by the Netherlands Fishery Institute in a programme to which the Fisheries Laboratory at Lowestoft has contributed. De Veen (1961, 1962) has made preliminary reports on the

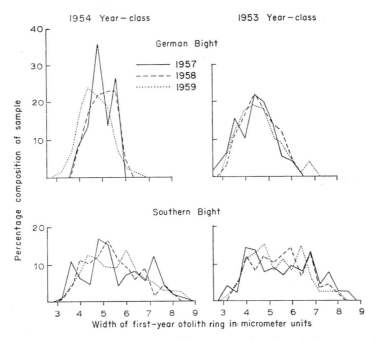

Fig. 51. First-year otolith ring width in German and Southern Bight plaice. There are consistent differences between the two groups, which are maintained when a year-class is sampled in successive years. (From de Veen and Boerema, 1959, Fig. 5a.)

work. Spawning fish have been tagged on the Flamborough Off ground (No. 55 in Fig. 35) and in the German and Southern Bight areas. The out-of-spawning-season recoveries have confirmed Hickling's earlier work that there is some overlap in the distribution of fish spawning in the three areas (Fig. 52). Recoveries of plaice in the spawning areas during the season following that in which they were tagged suggest that most of the fish return to the area where they had previously spawned (see Fig. 53). Dealing with the German Bight tagged fish, de Veen reported that of the 83 fish recovered in the 1961 spawning season, 81 were returned from the area in which they spawned the previous year. No 1960 Southern Bight spawners were recovered in the German Bight during the 1961 spawning season. These results suggest that most plaice return to spawn in the area where they previously spawned. A complete report on these experiments, which have now been carried on for a number of years, must be awaited with considerable interest.

The position with regard to the North Sea plaice may be summarized, somewhat tentatively, as follows: the juvenile fish do not move from one nursery to another and it seems very probable that the majority of the fish spawn in the parent area when they come to first maturity. The adult fish disperse over a wider area than the juveniles and many of them return to spawn in the same area in later years.

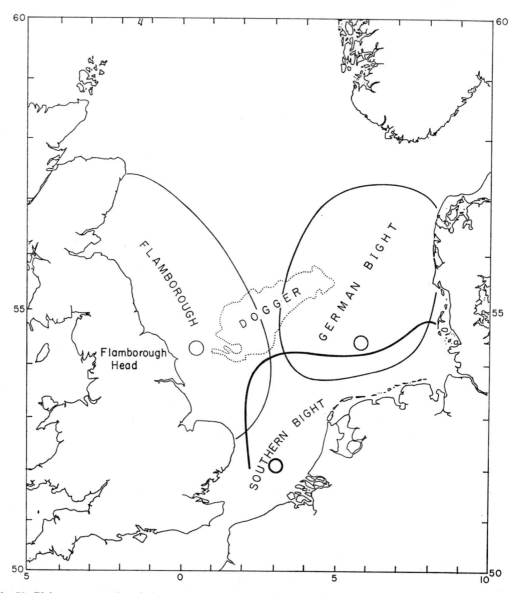

Fig. 52. Plaice were tagged on their spawning grounds in 1961 and 1962. The chart shows the areas within which fish tagged on the three grounds were subsequently recovered. There is relatively little overlap in the areas occupied by the three spawning groups. (After de Veen, 1962, Fig. 4. Outline from an Admiralty chart.)

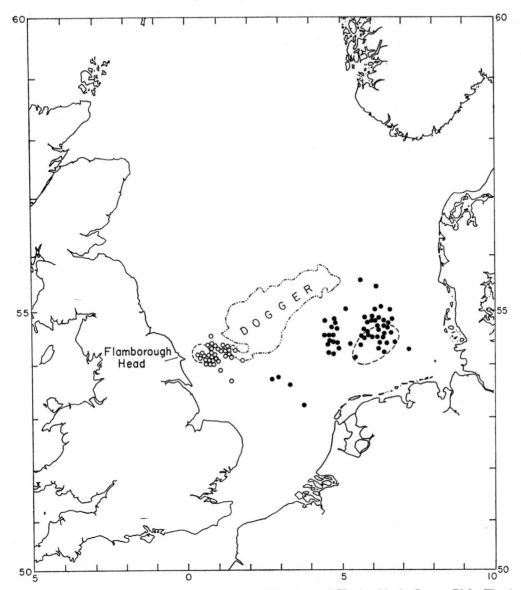

Fig. 53. Plaice were tagged on their spawning grounds off Flamborough Head and in the German Bight. The chart shows the position of recapture of tagged fish in the first spawning season after liberation. With the exception of four strays from the German Bight, the plaice were recovered on, or close to, the spawning ground where they were tagged the previous year. (After de Veen, 1962, Fig. 3. Outline from an Admiralty chart.)

THE MIGRATIONS OF PLAICE IN OTHER AREAS

Plaice migrations at Iceland

Plaice are found all round the coast of Iceland down to depths of about 80 m. The main spawning areas are in the relatively warm water off the west and south coasts where spawning reaches its peak in March and April. Some spawning also occurs on the north and east coasts, but later in the year, in May and June. Egg and larval surveys carried out in 1904 and 1924 (Tåning, 1929) showed that in these years the south and west spawnings were far more important than those on other parts of the coast. This is probably still true today.

The eggs and larvae are carried from the south and west coast spawning areas clockwise round the island in the warm water of the Irminger current. While some of the larvae metamorphose and take to the bottom on the south and west coasts, others are carried right round to the north and

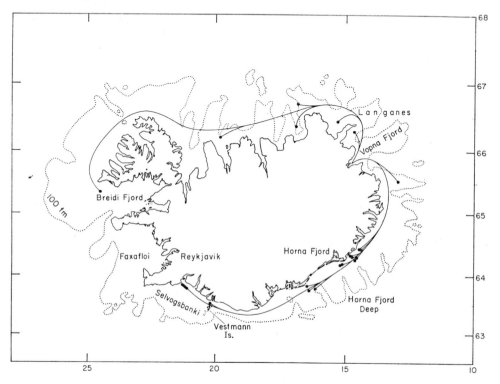

Fig. 54. Icelandic place names and recoveries from the 1931 plaice tagging experiment in Vopna Fjord. Twenty fish recovered within 10 miles of the tagging area are not shown. (After Tåning, 1934a. Outline from an Admiralty chart.)

east. There seems to be little doubt that most of the east coast fish are derived from larvae spawned on the southern and western areas (Tåning, 1934a, p. 9).

Many of the plaice that grow up on the north-west, north, east, and south-east coasts of Iceland migrate to the south and west coasts to spawn. This has been shown by the tagging experiments described by Schmidt (1907), Sæmundsson (1913) and Tåning (1934a). The movements of the east coast fish are of particular interest. The shortest route by which east coast plaice could reach the south and west coast spawning areas would be to go south and clockwise round the island. The 1905 tagging experiment in Vopna Fjord, described by Schmidt and Sæmundsson, suggested that this was indeed the route they took. Tåning repeated this experiment in 1931. The recaptures from this experiment, shown in Fig. 54, led Tåning (1934a, p. 7) to conclude that 'a somewhat haphazard scattering takes place from the place of marking on the east coast both to the north and to the south; but the more intensive fishery on the banks of south Iceland presents the greatest chances for recoveries from there.' In 1905 there was little fishing off the north and east coasts and the distribution of recoveries from Schmidt's experiment might well reflect the differences in fishing intensity that existed at that time.

More recently Einarsson (1956a) has described the results of a tagging experiment at another locality on the east coast, Hamarsfjord. In this experiment more fish were recovered to the north of the fjord than to the south.

These tagging experiments are of importance in connexion with the hypothesis that the prevailing or residual current provides a directional clue to the fish during the migration. Let us for a moment assume this to be true. As E. S. Russell (1937) points out, one might then expect the east coast Icelandic plaice to go against the current, that is northwards and anti-clockwise round the island, whereas Tåning's experiment shows that some plaice very probably take the southern route. This could be taken as suggesting that the direction of the residual current was of little importance or, as Tåning himself suggests, that there may be a north-going (anti-clockwise) bottom current coming from the south which has not yet been detected.

However, it is perhaps unwise to press the results of the Icelandic plaice experiments too far. The numbers involved are small, and the geographical distribution of the recoveries in the first twelve months after tagging do not really provide critical evidence as to the course of the migration. As Tåning says, it seems as if the east coast fish scatter north and south and eventually reach the south and west coast spawning areas. It is not known if they return to the east coast after spawning, or if they stay off the south-west part of the island where the environmental conditions are more suitable.

Plaice migrations in the Irish Sea

Bowden (1955) defines the Irish Sea as the area from the North Channel southwards to a line joining Land's End to Cape Clear. Place names within the area are given in Fig. 34.

SPAWNING GROUNDS AND NURSERY GROUNDS

The plaice spawning grounds in the Irish Sea have been delimited by noting the occurrence of eggs in early stages of development. Simpson (1959b) gives the main spawning grounds as being off the north coast of Cornwall, in Cardigan Bay, off Great Orme's Head and between the Isle of Man and the Cumberland coast. Some spawning also occurs along the Irish coast and in Caernarvon Bay. Spawning starts in January and probably goes on into April. Simpson's surveys showed that the eggs were not carried far from the main spawning grounds. From Lee's (1960) account of the hydrography of the Irish Sea it appears that there are eddy systems in the Bristol Channel, Cardigan Bay, and to the east of a line joining Anglesey to the Mull of Galloway, which would prevent the plaice eggs from becoming widely distributed and the baby plaice probably take to the bottom in the bays near the grounds on which they were spawned.

MOVEMENTS OF PLAICE

The Cumberland coast nursery ground is the only area in the Irish Sea where the movements of the juvenile plaice have been studied in any great detail. Johnstone, Birtwistle, and Smith (1922) give an account of earlier work, and more recently very large numbers of small plaice have been tagged in the area in connexion with problems relating to the discharge of radioactive effluent from Windscale. The details of these extensive experiments have not yet been published but from Hill's (1956) preliminary account it appears that the results confirm and extend those of the earlier tagging experiments. The juvenile plaice stay on the nursery grounds until they come to maturity. Within the nursery area there is a general off-shore movement in summer and a return in the winter, but the older fish stay further off shore so that the inshore catch is mainly made up of one-year-old plaice.

From the published results of tagging experiments it is difficult to get a clear picture of the spawning migrations. One might expect fish tagged on the north-east coast of Anglesey to spawn on the local grounds off Great Orme's Head, or in Morecambe Bay, but this is not what comes out of the tagging experiments described by Fleming (1931), and Daniel and Fleming (1933). The results of one of their experiments may be examined in detail. In December 1929–February 1930, 373 tagged plaice were released in Red Wharf Bay, on the north-east coast of Anglesey. Up till May 1932, 172 fish were recovered and examination of the data shows that the Red Wharf Bay fish spread southwards all over the Irish Sea and that some leave it even within a year of tagging. In the main spawning months (February and March) immediately following tagging, Red Wharf Bay fish were recaptured in Cardigan Bay, near Lundy, off Trevose Head and off the Coningbeg Light. One fish was retaken six miles south of the Eddystone within three months of tagging. Daniel and Fleming (1933) interpreted these movements as spawning migrations, although at that time the existence of spawning grounds off the north Cornish coast, Lundy and south-west Ireland had not been established. They believed that some of the plaice that went down St. George's Channel to spawn returned northwards to the Red Wharf Bay-Liverpool Bay area in October–December of the same year, as some recoveries were made in Red Wharf Bay during these months. But no tagged fish were recaptured in Red Wharf Bay in 1931, although further recoveries were made in the more southerly areas. Daniel and Fleming concluded that the fish had by this time left the Red Wharf Bay-Liverpool Bay area for ever.

Unfortunately, the majority of the plaice returned in their experiments were gutted and in only four fish was it possible to make an estimate of the maturation stage of the gonads. But the data suggest that many of the fish which went south, and those which were recovered in Red Wharf Bay the following October–December, were mature fish. Daniel and Fleming (1933, p. 44) draw attention to the point that some of the fish taken to the south during the first year after tagging were of such a size that it was unlikely that they were ready to spawn for the first time. However, it appears from Simpson's (1959*b*) data on the length composition of the mature male and female plaice in the main spawning areas that the smaller fish in Daniel and Fleming's experiments may well have been coming to their first maturity.

On their face value, and although the evidence is by no means as complete as one might wish, the results of the Red Wharf Bay experiment suggest that some of these fish go south for spawning, to Cardigan Bay, to Lundy, to north Cornwall and to south-west Ireland. At any rate there are no February or March recoveries off Great Orme's Head, the local spawning ground, although there were some returns in January. Was the absence of recoveries in these two months due to a low level of fishing, or did the fish really leave the area? In January 1931 a further batch of plaice was released in Red Wharf Bay with results that go some way towards confirming those of the previous year. The only experiment that can be compared with those at Red Wharf is the experiment made in Caernarvon Bay during December 1929–February 1930. During the spawning season following tagging only one recovery was made on the local grounds, but others were made in Cardigan Bay (2), near Lundy (1), off Trevose Head (1) and the Coningbeg Light (2). Here again, fish which were probably mature, and had, or were about to spawn, were recaptured to the south of the area where they were tagged.

The position in the Irish Sea may then be summarized as follows: the eggs do not seem to drift far from the spawning grounds and the young fish probably grow up in local nurseries. The tagging results suggest that plaice spawn for the first time to the south of the nursery area in which they themselves grew up. After spawning it seems likely that plaice disperse all over the Irish Sea and that many of them leave it. Some idea of the extent of the dispersion is given by the position of the recapture of plaice tagged on the north Cornwall spawning grounds in April 1957 (Fisheries Laboratory, Lowestoft; unpublished data). Adult plaice tagged off Trevose Head were later recaptured out to the south-west beyond the Scillies, off the Irish coast, South Wales, and to the north in Morecambe Bay. The latter recoveries are particularly interesting as they fit in with Daniel and Fleming's (1933) suggestion that some of the fish which leave Red Wharf Bay to spawn in the south return to the north later in the year. But it is clear that more work needs to be done in the Irish Sea.

Bowman's Shetland Islands experiments

An account of plaice migrations would be incomplete without some reference to the series of tagging experiments carried out off the Shetland Islands by Bowman (1933).

Between 1923 and 1931, 2,457 tagged plaice were released, most of the fish being juveniles taken from the east coast of Scotland and liberated in approximately the same depths in Shetland waters as those in which they were caught. Many of the fish were recaptured close to where they were released but 99 individuals were recaptured at considerable distances from the liberation centres. Referring to his text figure, Bowman (p. 226) says 'Consideration of the position of liberation and recapture of these migrants shows that the movement is a "directional" one. The fact that twelve of the migrants from centre A and eighteen from B were recaptured to the north of these liberation positions (at Balta and Flugga) definitely establishes the direction of migration on the east coast of Shetland as a northerly one. It is therefore not unreasonable to assume that the twenty-four individuals from these two liberation centres recaptured on the west coast (Foula grounds) traversed the same route as far as Flugga (the most northerly point of Shetland) and rounding the islands, turned southwards along the west coast.' Bowman's (p. 227) conclusion is that 'The main migratory path of adult fish is therefore northwards along the east coast and southwards along the west coast, fish coming to the west from the east coast via the north of Shetland. The movement is counter-clockwise round the islands or in the direction contrary to that of the prevailing movement of the water masses in the area. Migratory fish may or may not accomplish the encircling movement in one migratory season.'

Bowman's experiments would seem to establish the fact that plaice migrate against the direction of the prevailing or residual current. Bowman's work has indeed become something of a classic, and is quoted by E. S. Russell (1937), Tait (1952), Wimpenny (1953), Beverton and Holt (1957, p. 159), and Verwey (1958). It is therefore of some interest to look at Bowman's results in greater detail.

The best way of using tagging data to show a movement of fish is to plot the position of recapture on monthly or quarterly charts. If suitable corrections are made for differences in fishing intensity, the monthly or quarterly changes in the distribution of recaptures should give a reasonably good picture of the movement of the fish. In the case of the Shetland Islands experiments data relating to fishing intensity are not available, and Bowman does not give any information as to the time interval between the release and recapture of the 99 plaice shown in the chart accompanying his paper. Fortunately the latter data are still available, and Dr. C. E. Lucas, Director of Fisheries Research in Scotland, has allowed me to use the original material. The position of the recaptures of the long-distance migrants released at centres A and B are shown in Figs. 55 and 56. The time interval, in days, between tagging and recapture in the first year after tagging are also given. Inspection of the figures shows that only 2 fish released at A were recaptured within a year of liberation and that these fish were caught to the south-west of the liberation centre. Of the fish released at B, 16 were recaptured within the first year, and of these fish the first 3 returns came from the south-east

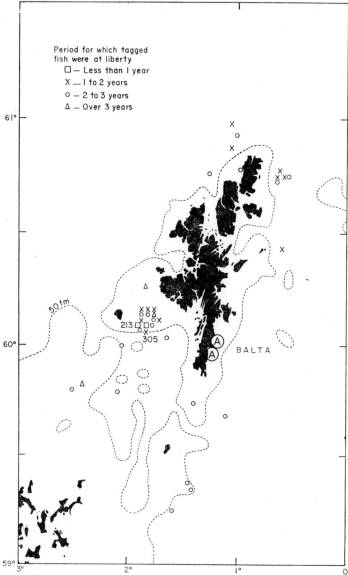

Fig. 55. Plaice tagging experiment carried out by Bowman (1933) at the Shetlands. Recoveries from the Balta releases at positions marked A. The 'days out' are given for the two fish recaptured within a year of liberation. (Outline from an Admiralty chart.)

and south-west. It is very difficult to see how Bowman's conclusion that the fish migrate north-wards round the islands follows from these results. If a verdict has to be given, the Scottish verdict of 'not proven' would seem more than equitable; for, if the experiments show anything at all, they show that the fish move to the south rather than to the north. The truth of the matter may very well be similar to that which appears to hold good for the east Icelandic plaice; they scatter north and south from the area of liberation.

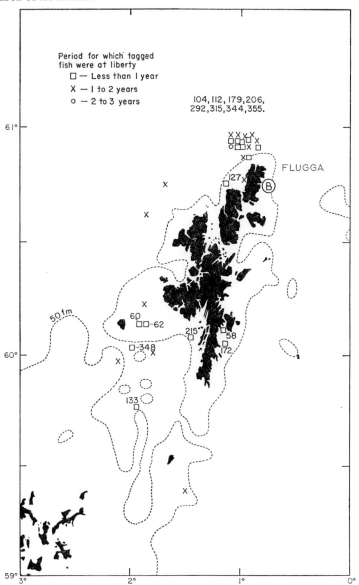

Fig. 56. Plaice tagging experiment carried out by Bowman (1933) at the Shetlands. Recoveries from the Flugga releases at position marked B. The 'days out' are given for the 16 fish recaptured within a year of liberation. (Outline from an Admiralty chart.)

Chapter 9

A Recapitulation

Migration has been defined as 'a class of movement which impels migrants to return to the region from which they have migrated' and homing as 'the return to a place formerly occupied instead of going to other equally probable places' (p. 2, 4). The evidence that has been reviewed in the previous chapters shows that there are well documented instances of homing and migration by salmon, cod, herring, plaice and, quite possibly, the European eel.

HOMING

A spawning area could include several spawning grounds, each with, in the case of a fish with demersal eggs, one or more spawning beds (p. 17). Thus a first-time spawner could return, with increasing precision, to the parent area, to the parent ground, or to the parent bed. When the fish spawns more than once during its life, there is the possibility of repeated annual returns to the parental or adopted home. Some examples are given below.

The return of first-time spawners

(a) *To the parent area*
   Cultus Lake sockeye to the Fraser river (p. 45).
   Norwegian herring to Norway coast (p. 111).
   Arcto-Norwegian cod to Norway coast (p. 160).
   Plaice to German and Southern Bights (p. 171).
(b) *To the parent ground*
   Cultus Lake sockeye to Cultus Lake (p. 45).
(c) *To the parent bed*
   No example (but see p. 260 for Harrison Rapid sockeye).

The return in subsequent years

(a) *To the previous spawning area*
   Atlantic salmon kelts (p. 54).
   Bank and Downs herring (p. 140).
   Pacific herring at Vancouver Island (p. 141).
   Arcto-Norwegian cod (p. 165).
   Plaice to German and Southern Bights (p. 172).
(b) *To the previous spawning ground*
   Pacific herring at Vancouver Island (p. 141).
   Cod to south-west Iceland (p. 153).
   Cod to Lofoten (p. 166).

(*c*) *To the previous spawning bed*
   No example.

Salmon, cod, herring, and plaice feed over a wide area in summer; their winter distribution is more restricted, and their spawning areas relatively small. Homing also occurs in connexion with feeding and wintering, but the area to which the fish return may not always be centred about the same geographical location. For example, each spring the spent Norwegian herring migrate from their spawning area towards the polar front in the western part of the Norwegian Sea (p. 107). This is their main feeding area, the location of which may shift from year to year depending on hydrographic factors. The home to which the fish returns may therefore be a particular set of environmental conditions rather than a specific locality. This might also be the case for the wintering area of the Norwegian herring (p. 104), the feeding and wintering areas of the Buchan and Bank herring (p. 128) and those of the immature cod of the Barents Sea (p. 163). The precision required in returning to the feeding and wintering areas is probably less than that required to reach the spawning areas, successful reproduction taking place only in a small proportion of the range occupied by the stock to which the fish belongs. In freshwater populations, particularly in streams, conditions are different, and feeding, wintering, and spawning areas may be equally restricted with comparable demands on the precision of homing. Examples are given later (p. 243).

MIGRATION

Salmon, eels, cod, herring, and plaice migrate over long distances during their lives. The complete pattern can be broken down into a number of legs as indicated in the examples given below.

Larval, juvenile and young fish

(*a*) *From spawning area to nursery area*
   Pink salmon fry leave freshwater for estuarine and coastal waters (p. 50).
   Eel leptocephali cross the Atlantic (p. 75).
   The movements of larval herring (p. 125).
   Cod larvae reach the Barents Sea (p. 148).
   Southern Bight-spawned plaice to the Dutch coast (p. 170).
(*b*) *Seasonal movements within the nursery areas*
   Norwegian herring in coastal waters (p. 105).
   Bank and Downs herring in southern North Sea (p. 125).
   Plaice off the Dutch coast (p. 170).
(*c*) *Leaving the nursery areas*
   Salmon smolts to the open sea (p. 43).
   Elvers enter freshwater and move up rivers (p. 76).
   Norwegian herring leave coastal areas for their oceanic stage (p. 106).
   Bank and Downs herring leave the Bløden to feed north of the Dogger (p. 126).
   Buchan herring from the Scottish Firths join the spawning shoals (p. 129).
   Some herring may join the Downs spawners direct (p. 135).
   Cod more mobile when 2 to 3 years old (p. 148).
   Plaice move from the Dutch nursery grounds to Southern Bight spawning area (p. 171).

The older fish

The migrations of the older fish can be represented diagrammatically as shown in Fig. 57 where the pattern has been broken down into 6 legs of which the following are examples.

(*a*) *Feeding area to winter area*
Immature oceanic and mature Norwegian herring (pp. 106, 107).
Immature and mature Arcto-Norwegian cod (pp. 149, 162).

(*b*) *Winter area to spawning area*
Norwegian herring (p. 110).
Arcto-Norwegian cod (p. 163).

(*c*) *Spawning area to feeding area*
Norwegian herring (p. 107).
Downs herring (p. 133).
Arcto-Norwegian cod (p. 163).
Plaice in southern North Sea (p. 171).

(*d*) *Feeding area to spawning area*
Salmon returning to freshwater (p. 43).
Icelandic summer spawning herring (p. 101).
Buchan, Dogger and Downs herring (pp. 128, 130, 133).

(*e*) *Spawning area to winter area*
Buchan and Dogger herring (pp. 128, 130).

(*f*) *Winter area to feeding area*
Buchan and Dogger herring (pp. 128, 130).
Immature Arcto-Norwegian cod (p. 149).

Reference to Fig. 57 shows that the clockwise sequence 1, 2, 3, is typical of winter and spring spawners, while the anti-clockwise sequence 4, 5, 6 is typical of summer-autumn spawners. The sequence for the Icelandic summer spawners is probably 4, 3, 1, 6.

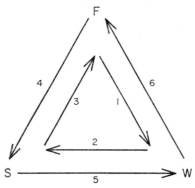

Fig. 57. The migrations of the older fish can be represented by a triangular diagram with spawning (S), wintering (W) and feeding (F) areas at the corners.

MIGRATION, HOMING, AND THE ENVIRONMENT

In Chapter 3 it was argued that migration could be regarded as an adaptation towards abundance and that a return to the parent spawning ground, or area, as a means by which particularly favourable sites could be exploited. For example, within the area over which it is distributed a species might have several spawning grounds, but during a given period the bulk of the population would be recruited from only one or two of these grounds. The progeny of each ground would grow up in different nursery areas and under different environmental conditions, and there could be differences between the survivors with regards to morphometric and meristic characters, growth rate and mortality. This is the biological origin of the stock, the Fishery Biologist's unit of management. A return of the survivors to the parent spawning ground allows a successful ground to be fully exploited, but the maintenance of a cadre of spawners on other grounds, and some straying, provides a measure of flexibility to meet changing conditions. Homing could be a disadvantage when fish persist in returning to spawn in an area or on a ground where conditions have become unfavourable to the survival of eggs but not necessarily to the act of spawning. Frost (1963) cites the disappearance of charr (*Salvelinus willughbii*) from Ullswater (English Lake District) as a case where this might have happened. The only biological insurance against this is a satisfactory level of straying and a multiplicity of spawning grounds, whose contribution to the population as a whole would change as environmental conditions varied.

In freshwater, and particularly with regards to salmon, freshets, landslides, and pollution are some of the environmental changes that could be detrimental to particular spawning areas or grounds. Such changes are almost cataclysmic, and in the sea one might expect to be dealing with changes spread over a relatively long period of time. The spawning grounds, or areas, appear to be strategically sited in relation to the nursery areas and in temperate and arctic waters spawning must be geared to the production cycle so that the larvae hatch when food is available. If the time of spawning at a particular ground is more or less fixed—endogenously—then a relatively small shift in the timing of the production cycle could leave the larvae without food. If the shift in the production cycle was maintained over a period of years, the survivors from a particular spawning ground could be so reduced in numbers that its contribution to the population as a whole could dwindle to an insignificant proportion.

Cushing (1966) has reviewed the biological and environmental changes that have taken place in British waters during the last thirty years and has suggested (p. 247) that the shift in balance between the German Bight and Southern Bight plaice spawning grounds may be related to some modification of the production cycle. For herring, Cushing (1967) suggests that autumn, winter, and spring spawning groups correspond to the central North Sea, coastal Atlantic, and oceanic Atlantic production cycles: the spread of spawning in space and time covers all the variation that might be expected in the production cycle. This could account for the herring's evident success as measured by the extent of its distribution and its abundance.

For temperate and arctic waters it might be concluded that the fully adapted and successful species should be migratory and should home to its parent spawning ground; that the population as a whole should be made up of a number of units whose migration circuits were contained within the same or different gyrals; and that each unit would spawn on a fixed and restricted ground, and in a fixed and restricted season. As the environmental conditions change on a long-term basis, so the dominance swings from one spawning group to another. Thus the capacity to meet change lies, not in the flexibility of each unit, but in the multiplicity of units: there are stocks for all seasons. If this hypothesis is correct, it could provide some explanation for the demersal eggs of the herring: being laid on the bottom, the eggs can be sited with reference to local landmarks, and it is this precision which puts the eggs into the position from which the larvae are able to take advantage of the seasonal timing of the production cycle within the spawning or nursery area.

7

In retrospect, it is surprising to find no cadres of summer or autumn spawning plaice. There is some evidence of cod spawning in the autumn (p. 146). In the event of prolonged climatic change, the future of the cod stocks and of the cod fisheries could depend on these fish.

DENATANT AND CONTRANATANT MIGRATIONS

The migration of larval and juvenile fish from the spawning area to the nursery area is usually denatant and with the current, and this is also true for salmon smolts when they leave freshwater for the sea. The spawning migrations of the mature fish appear to be contranatant in the sense that the fish are moving, over part or all of the journey, in the opposite direction to that in which they were dispersed during their young stages. But in detail the picture is not clear and we do not really know the relation between the movement of fish and that of the body of water in which they are living. No critical data are available for salmon during their marine life, and the same is true for herring, cod, and the European eel. So far as plaice are concerned, the migrations of the North Sea spawning groups are difficult, if not impossible, to reconcile with any simple swimming against the current (pp. 173, 234) and Bowman's Shetland Island experiments cannot be regarded as evidence for the classical contranatant view. On the contrary, the complete migration patterns (feeding, spawning, and wintering movements) of the Atlanto-Scandian, Buchan, and Dogger groups of herring appear to be in the same general direction as the residual water currents (pp. 107, 108, 129, 132). These observations are not in harmony with the view that water currents provide the directional clues to migrants, fish swimming contranatantly, against the stream, to spawn. There is little to be gained by pursuing the point further at this stage; it is enough to suggest that there must often be reasonable doubt as to whether the facts—so far as they are known—support the hypothesis that water currents provide the directional clues to migrants on passage. One can do no better than to approach this problem with an open mind.

The rest of this book is concerned with the behavioural mechanisms that could be used by fish in migration and homing. By way of introduction, the next chapter provides a short account of the reactions of fish to stimuli.

Chapter 10

The Reactions of Fish to Stimuli

INTRODUCTION

Tinbergen (1951, p. 2) defines behaviour as the 'total of movements made by the intact animal and later (p. 104) discusses the distinction between appetitive behaviour and the consummatory act. Whereas the latter is characteristically a relatively simple chain of more or less stereotyped motor responses, appetitive behaviour is more complex and embraces all the 'random', 'exploratory', and 'searching' movements into the environment or situation where the more specific consummatory patterns of behaviour are played out. In appetitive behaviour the locomotory activity of the fish is induced, altered, or orientated in response to external changes. The fish may start to move, or stop; swim slower or faster; turn more or less frequently; or swim in a particular direction. It is this aspect of the reactions of fish to stimuli—the response shown as changes in the locomotory activity characteristic of appetitive behaviour—that are of interest in connexion with homing and migration. What follows will be contained within the framework of Fraenkel and Gunn's (1940 and 1961) scheme of kineses, taxes, and transverse orientations.

The original edition of Fraenkel and Gunn's *The orientation of animals* contained only a handful of references to work on fish, but this reflected the need for further research rather than any omission by the authors. A number of reviews have since been published which cover much of the literature on fish behaviour and the reactions of fish to stimuli. (General accounts: Bull, 1952; Harden Jones, 1960. Chemical stimuli: Hasler, 1954; Teichmann, 1962; Wright, 1964. Temperature: Sullivan, 1954; Fisher, 1958. Mechanical stimuli: Dijkgraaf, 1963. Light: Verheijen, 1958; Woodhead, 1966.) Other accounts deal more specifically with fish behaviour, migration, and homing (Verwey, 1958; Hasler, 1956, 1960, 1966; Brett and Groot, 1963).

Kineses

'Variations in generalized, undirected, random locomotory activity due to variations in intensity of stimulation, are kineses' (Gunn, Kennedy, and Pielou, 1937). The variations in random locomotory activity can be expressed as changes in the speed of movement, the frequency of turning, and the magnitude of the angle of turn between one line of movement and the next. The distance between turns is the path or step-length, and the overall movement of an organism will be along the bearing in whose direction the step-length is a maximum.

Step-length can be increased by moving more quickly between turns (cm/sec) and/or (when speed is constant) turning less frequently (turns/sec). Step-length can be decreased by moving more slowly between turns and/or (when speed is constant) turning more frequently. If the direction in which the organism moves is as at random, the lines of movement, when referred to a fixed direction, will give a uniform distribution of angles between 0° and 360°. But a decrease in the mean angle of turn (for example, from an average turn of 30° to an average turn of 1°) will temporarily increase the step-length about a particular bearing, although the overall direction of movement is still random. Movement along a gradient of intensity can be facilitated by changing the step-length and the mean angle of turn; unfavourable areas can be avoided by increasing speed, and turning less frequently; aggregation in favourable areas can be achieved by decreasing speed, and turning more often.

In Fraenkel and Gunn's classification a change in the speed of locomotion (cm/sec) is an ortho-kinesis, while a change in the frequency of turning (turns/sec) and mean angle of turn (degrees/turn) are klinokineses. An orthokinesis is relatively simple and includes two responses: a change in speed, or a change in the frequency of movement for an organism whose range of speed is restricted. The light reactions of the freshwater planarian *Dendrocoelum lacteum*, originally described by Ullyott (1936) and discussed in detail by Fraenkel and Gunn (1940), are usually given to illustrate a klinokinesis. *Dendrocoelum* collects in the dim end of a trough which is illuminated from above so as to produce a relatively steep gradient of intensity from one end to the other.[1] The flatworms move at constant speed and their distribution in the gradient appears to be brought about by a klinokinesis. Ullyott expressed the klinokinesis quantitatively as a 'rate of change of direction', or r.c.d., measured as the sum of the angles turned through per minute. The r.c.d. increases if *Dendrocoelum* is exposed to an increase in light intensity, but soon falls to a basal level if the conditions are maintained. Ullyott suggested that the change in r.c.d., combined with adaptation, could account for the distribution of *Dendrocoelum* in the 'non-directional' light gradient, and this hypothesis is presented in detail in *The orientation of animals*. Patlak (1953, p. 455) examined one of the original *Dendrocoelum* tracks published by Ullyott (1936, p. 271, Fig. 6) and showed that the frequency of turning (turns/second) is constant after a sudden increase in light intensity. However, the degrees per turn fall away to a basal level as adaptation proceeds. Thus in *Dendrocoelum* the klinokinetic mechanism is not a change in the frequency of turning (as is usually stated) but a change in the angle of turn. On entering a brightly lit area *Dendrocoelum* starts to make larger turns, and overall movement back into dim light is facilitated.

Ullyott (1936) argued that the flatworms could only collect in the dim end of the gradient if a klinokinesis was combined with adaptation. Fraenkel and Gunn (1940, p. 53) carried the argument further and concluded that 'adaptation or some such complication is essential to klino-kinetic aggregation'. In their own words 'The point can be made clearer by a rather far-fetched analogy. Imagine that an animal must accumulate a certain quantity of light before it can turn, as if it were filling a jug. When it turns it empties the jug and then has to fill it again before it can turn once more. In the gradient the light is raining down, a downpour at the bright end and a drizzle at the dim end. All this is appropriate if the r.c.d. is dependent only on the light intensity at the moment, with no adaptation. In such a case, on going up the gradient the jug fills slowly at first and then more quickly, and on going down it fills quickly and then more slowly. If the animal crawls up a distance sufficient to fill it, on the return journey it will crawl exactly the same distance before turning, for the jug takes the same time to fill whichever way the animal traverses a particular stretch. Now if there were instantaneous adaptation, the jug would be expanded or contracted to suit the light, and it would always be filled in exactly the same time. The r.c.d. would be constant at all intensities, at the basal rate, and there would be no aggregation.' (Fraenkel and Gunn, 1940, p. 52). But as Patlak (1953, p. 458) notes, there is another way of looking at the problem. Suppose

---

[1] Ullyott (1936) assumed that there was no difference in the horizontal light intensity along the length of the trough, and described the gradient as 'non-directional'. The assumption is probably incorrect, because more light would be scattered horizontally in the bright end of the gradient than in the dim end.

that a chemical E is produced by the animal which turns when the between-turn production of E exceeds a threshold value. The concentration of E falls to zero when the animal turns, so paralleling the emptying of the jug. Fraenkel and Gunn would assume that the threshold is fixed, while the rate of production of the substance is determined by the intensity of the stimulus. Patlak suggests that the rate of production could be constant, while the threshold is determined by the stimulus, and under these circumstances the animal would behave as shown in Fig. 58. The animal leaves A and moves at constant speed up the gradient to turn at B when the production of E has reached the threshold. At B it turns to move down the gradient, past A, to turn again at C when the concentration of E has once more reached threshold. If this pattern of behaviour is repeated the overall

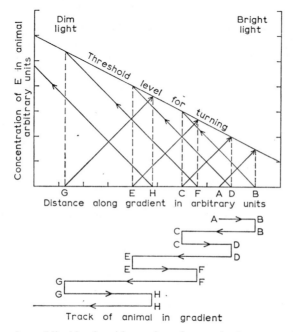

Fig. 58. A diagram to show how a klinokinesis, without adaptation, can lead to aggregation. For a full explanation of this diagram see text.

movement of the animal will be down the gradient into the dim light where the step-length is longer, although there is no adaptation.

Patlak (1953, p. 357) has also suggested that under certain conditions a klinokinesis, without adaptation, could result in animals collecting where the step-length was the shortest. Suppose that the animal moved down a chemical gradient from A to B and that it turned after a time interval inversely proportional to the stronger stimulus received at A. Similarly, when it moves up the gradient, it turns after a time interval inversely proportional to the weaker stimulus received at B. There will then be an overall movement up the gradient in the direction of the maximum step-length, but the animals will collect in the area where the chemical is more concentrated and where the step-length is shortest. This could take place if the environment were tested only after the animal had turned. Intermittent sniffing would provide a suitable sampling mechanism, the delay between a sniff and the next turn being inversely proportional to the strength of the stimulus. This could provide a behavioural mechanism for the aggregation of pelagic fish on to zooplankton patches detected at a distance by chemical clues.

Taxes

There are three classes of taxes: a klinotaxis, in which the direction of movement is determined by a sequential comparison of intensities; a tropotaxis, in which there is a simultaneous comparison of the intensity of stimulation of bilateral receptors, and a telotaxis, in which no comparison is involved. A telotaxis depends on the animal being able to localize the source, even with a single sense organ, and movement is either directly towards or away from the source. The light compass reaction is a special case of the telotaxis, and movement is at a fixed or varying (azimuth compensated) angle to the horizontal projection of the line between the animal and the light source.

Taxes are often loosely referred to as directed movements or reactions. Tinbergen (1951) follows Lorenz in recognizing that a taxis can be split into two separate components: the pure taxis, which ensures that the animal is heading in the right direction; and the fixed locomotory pattern, the means by which the animal travels in the right direction. Once direction is determined, swimming speed may depend on a number of internal or external factors so that there may be a combination between a taxis and an orthokinesis.

Stimulus and response

Fraenkel and Gunn (1940, p. 270) make a distinction between stimuli such as light, gravity, water currents, mechanical displacements, and electric fields, all of which have directional properties, and chemical stimuli, which vary only in intensity. In water, temperature stimuli must be similar to chemical stimuli in this respect: while it is not physically impossible that heat can be transferred underwater by radiation, it is unlikely to be of significance under natural conditions. When the transfer is by conduction through contact, as it nearly always must be, the stimulus field will be a temperature gradient of intensity without direction. However, when convection is involved, and the movement of energy is by diffusion or flow with the ultimate transfer by conduction, the source may be located if the animal can detect the direction of flow. While a fish might be expected to make directed reactions, taxes, in responses to stimuli which have directional properties, only undirected reactions, kineses, and a klinotaxis (sequential comparison of intensity) would be expected in response to chemical and temperature stimuli, although a tropotaxis (simultaneous comparison of intensity) would be possible if the gradient was steep enough to be detected across the width, or length, of the body.

THE MINIMUM STIMULUS

A distinction can be made between: (a) the absolute physiological sensitivity as determined by electrophysiological techniques; (b) the minimum stimulus to which the fish can be trained to respond as determined by conditioned reflex experiments; and (c) the minimum stimulus to which fish can be observed to react under natural conditions. The physiological threshold is often lower than the biological threshold: the potential is better than performance. Furthermore, the minimum stimulus as determined by conditioned reflex experiments may be lower than that determined by an unconditioned response, and both levels may vary with the physiological condition of the fish. Studies on sensitivity logically start with the limits of quality and intensity, pass on to discrimination, again of quality and intensity and the change of both in time, and finally, when applicable, to the localization of the source of a stimulus. The threshold levels, as determined by the conditioned reflex technique, are known for a number of stimuli (for example, Bull, 1952, gives a temperature threshold of 0·03°C, and a salinity threshold of 0.05°S‰), but the minimum stimulus to which the fish responds has usually been determined as an instantaneous, or very rapid, change at one background level. The relation between ΔI, the minimum instantaneous change to which the fish responds, and I, the stimulus level to which it is initially adapted or conditioned, is not known. Under natural conditions the change to which the fish is subjected will depend on the steepness of the gradient and the speed with which the isolines (lines of equal stimulus intensity) and fish move relative to one another. The threshold stimulus of most interest is therefore $(\Delta I/I)$/unit of time.

SIGN STIMULI

In the aquatic environment horizontal temperature and chemical gradients are usually very gentle and those that can be detected by fish will usually be found across fronts between water masses, or in association with more local features (estuaries, warm shallow bays, cold fjords). It seems unlikely that migrations involving movements of several hundred kilometres could be brought about by kineses made in response to temperature or chemical gradients found in the open sea although an ortho- or klinokinesis could restrict a fish to the boundary zones where the gradients are relatively steep.

Temperature and chemical clues could act as sign stimuli by releasing a directed response to other stimuli, for example, orientation to a water current. The response could be released at a particular temperature, or in the presence of a specific chemical, and be of an all-or-nothing character.

REACTIONS TO CHEMICAL STIMULI

In vertebrates the olfactory receptors are innervated by the olfactory nerve but the gustatory organs, the taste buds, may be innervated by one or more dorsal roots of the cranial nerves, the profundus, trigeminal (V), facial (VII), glossopharyngeal (IX), and vagus (X). In fish the nerves principally involved are the VIIth, and Xth. The VIIth innervates the taste buds in the mouth, the IXth and Xth those in the gill region. All three may contribute to the innervation of taste buds when they are present over the general body surface. The skin of the catfish *Ameiurus* is still sensitive when the relevant branches of the cranial nerves are cut: some chemical receptors may therefore be innervated by spinal nerves.

Parker (1922) gives a classical account of the relation between the olfactory, gustatory and common chemical senses, the receptors being innervated by the olfactory, cranial, and spinal nerves respectively. Of the three chemical receptors, the nose is by far the most sensitive. Ethyl alcohol has both smell and taste, and stimulates the common chemical sense. In man the detection thresholds for alcohol are, for the three sensory systems, 0·000125 M, 3 M, and 5–10 M respectively (Parker, 1922, p. 171). Similar experiments do not appear to have been carried out for fish, but it looks as if the threshold of smell (for eels, β-phenylethyl alcohol, 10^{-18} M) is very much lower than that of taste (for minnows, NaCl 10^{-5} M, saccharose 10^{-5} M). More recent work, particularly that by Teichmann (1959), has extended our knowledge of the sensitivity of the sense of smell in fish. Teichmann found that the eel could detect β-phenylethyl alcohol at concentrations as low as 1,700 molecules per cm^3 water, a performance comparable to that of a dog. The olfactory organ deals with such minute quantities that it has been rightly classed by Parker (1922, p. 172) as a distance receptor.

This raises the question of the role that olfaction might play in finding food and locating areas which could be characterized by chemical clues. Steven (1959) discusses the problem. Relatively few studies have been made on the means by which fish locate objects by chemical clues. Teichmann (1959) found that eels follow a convoluted track when travelling up an olfactory gradient or along an olfactory trail. The appearance of the tracks suggests that the response would be classified as a klinotaxis.

REACTIONS TO TEMPERATURE STIMULI

Temperature may act on a fish through two channels; the first is through sensory receptors and thus the central nervous system, the second by a more direct action on the metabolism. The behavioural response of the fish to a temperature change thus depends both on its thermal history and immediate thermal environment. In teleosts the thermal receptors, which have not yet been identified, are scattered over the body surface. They are probably innervated by spinal nerves. Teleosts can be trained to respond to temperature changes down to $0.03°C$ (Bull, 1936), and can distinguish between an increase and decrease in temperature when the change is about $\pm 1°C$ (Dijkgraaf, 1940). Bardach (1956), working with goldfish found that the threshold of response to a local heating of a 2 mm^2 area of skin was an increase of $2°C$, but the fish could be trained to respond to changes of $+0.1°C$. Thus the thermal receptors appear to function according to the principle of area summation.

Sullivan (1954) refers to the means by which fish collect in a particular region of a temperature gradient and both ortho- and klinokineses appear to be involved. Ivlev (1960) has shown that the aggregation of young salmon (*S. salar*) and carp in a temperature gradient can be accounted for by an orthokinesis, the fish collecting within the temperature range over which their velocity was minimal.

It is of interest to speculate on the minimal temperature gradients that a fish could detect. Bull (1936) showed that fish could detect temperature increases of about $0.03°C$, and under the conditions of his experiments the effective stimulus will have been given by a cloud of warm water travelling down the experimental tank. The leading edge of the cloud would tend to be broken up by turbulence so the fish in the far end might receive a gradual increase in temperature rather than a sharp wave or front. Let us suppose that the temperature around the fish increased by $0.03°C$ over a period of 1 to 10 sec (an increase of $0.03–0.003°C/\text{sec}$). A 50 cm fish with the same threshold cruising at 100 cm/sec (2L) would then be expected to detect gradients of the order of $0.03–0.003°C/\text{m}$. Lumby and Ellett (1965) measured the sub-surface temperature with a thermistor across a front between polar and Atlantic water at East Greenland. The water temperature fell $4.5°C$ in a distance of about 400 m, the gradient being of the order of $0.01°C/\text{m}$. It is reasonable to suppose that this change could be detected by a fish swimming across the front. More recent work by Bardach and Bjorklund (1957) confirms these guesses. They found that some freshwater species (goldfish, trout, etc.) responded to temperature changes of $0.01–0.05°C$ when the rate of change of temperature was over $0.05°C/\text{min}$, or about $0.001°C/\text{sec}$.

So far as the detection of spatial gradients are concerned, the response of the fish appears to depend partly on the speed at which the fish crosses the isotherms, and therefore the faster fish might do better. Other things being equal, this could lead to the larger (and older) fish having a different distribution in relation to temperature to that shown by the smaller (and younger) fish.

REACTIONS TO WATER CURRENTS: RHEOTROPISM

So far as migration is concerned, the reaction of fish to water currents is one of the most interesting aspects of their behaviour, largely because of the widely held, but unproven, hypothesis that water currents play a considerable part in orientating and directing the course of their movements. The term rheotropism, which is itself something of a misnomer, is generally used to describe the reaction of fish to currents and, strictly speaking, it only covers their reactions to water flow. But the meaning may be extended to cover all the reactions that a fish might make directly or indirectly as a response to a water current, thus including the so-called pseudo-rheotropic responses such as locomotory reactions to visual stimuli arising from the displacement of the background, and responses to angular and linear accelerations produced by movements of the fish in space.

Detection of water currents

The conditions under which a fish could detect a water current can be considered under six headings.

1. WATER FLOW LINEAR, AT CONSTANT VELOCITY

A fish will respond to visual clues if it can see the bottom or some external reference point. In a smooth flowing stream, a blind fish, in midwater and clear of the bottom. does not head upstream but is carried passively with the flow (Lyon, 1904, 1909; Dijkgraaf, 1933). Fish have never been shown to orientate with or against the current unless they are close to or in touch with the bottom. But a blind fish, swimming in midwater, will orientate to a jet of water. Dijkgraaf showed that this reaction was abolished if the lateral line was cut.

When a fish rests on the bottom, it could be directly stimulated by the flow of water over the body. The receptors could be displacement receivers scattered over the body or in the acoustico-lateralis system. The plaice is an example. However, Harden Jones (unpublished) found that plaice failed to respond to strong jets played over the upper (right) or lower (left) surface, or on to the lateral line system. Water currents were also without any effect until they were strong enough to move the fish along the bottom. A jet played under the margins of the median unpaired fins, lifting them off the bottom, also produced a response. Here, as with other fish, tactile clues indicating a relative movement between the fish and bottom appear to be the important stimuli in the rheotropic response.

2. WATER FLOW LINEAR, WITH ACCELERATIONS

Theoretically, it would be expected that a fish out of sight and out of contact with the bottom should be able to orientate to such a flow as the otolith organs are sensitive to linear accelerations. However, Löwenstein (1932) and Gray (1937) failed to detect a response to linear accelerations. Harden Jones (1956) described an apparent response of a blind goldfish to a linear acceleration with a threshold of the order of 200 cm/sec^2. The reaction was very clear, but the stimulus to which the fish was responding was uncertain, as the accelerations and decelerations were accompanied by sudden pressure changes in the tank. The apparent threshold of response is high when compared with the minimum perceptible linear acceleration of 6 to 13 cm/sec^2 in man (Jongkees and Groen, 1946).

Fish will be subjected to accelerations when they move across horizontal or vertical velocity gradients. It is not known if the gradients and the speed of the fish are ever great enough to produce accelerations of the order to which the fish appear to respond.

3. WATER FLOW CURVILINEAR, AT CONSTANT VELOCITY

Even in the absence of visual and tactile stimuli, some fish will orientate to and swim against the direction of rotation if placed in a body of water moving at constant angular velocity. Dijkgraaf (1933), Gray (1937), and Harden Jones (1957c) have described this response. Howland and Howland (1962) have suggested that the fish compensates for the rotation at a rate approximately equal to the precession of a Foucault pendulum, but the sensory basis of the response is not yet fully understood.

The threshold for the response in blind goldfish appears to be a rotation of about 3°/sec (1 rev in 120 sec, 0·5 rev/min). A fish with a similar threshold should be able to orientate in small swirls, and with a flow of 1 knot (50 cm/sec), the diameter of such a swirl would be 20 m.

4. WATER FLOW CURVILINEAR, WITH ANGULAR ACCELERATIONS

The semicircular canals are the receptors for angular accelerations. In man the minimum perceptible angular acceleration is about 0·5°/sec^2 (Groen and Jongkees, 1948) and it is reasonable to suppose that the canals of fish have a similar sensitivity. Fish might therefore be expected to orientate in swirls where there are angular accelerations of sufficient magnitude to stimulate the semicircular canals.

5. ORIENTATION TO VELOCITY GRADIENTS

(a) *By mechanical clues.* In very steep horizontal or vertical velocity gradients (such as at a discontinuity, or on the edge of a jet), orientation could be achieved by the simultaneous comparison of the intensity of stimulation of displacement receivers on the left and right, or dorsal and ventral, surfaces of the body. This possibility was originally discussed by Lyon (1904, p. 157). Such a mechanism, a tropotaxis, could account for the orientation of fish in water currents close to the walls of tanks in the apparent absence of visual or tactile clues (Höglund, 1961, p. 72). But the problem still awaits experimental investigation.

Deelder (1958) claims that elvers are able to locate a freshwater outlet whose flow is strong enough to cause turbulent eddies, and concludes 'contrary to the common opinion, that elvers are able to orientate themselves towards freshwater not only at the surface, but also in deeper water, provided that in both cases the freshwater flowing in causes sufficient turbulence' (his p. 144). In Deelder's experiment a freshwater jet streamed into a tank of sea-water, and his observations are consistent with the hypothesis that a jet strong enough to cause turbulence also produced velocity gradients steep enough for the elvers to orientate tropotactically. In any case the stimulus to which the elvers respond must have been a water displacement and not a pressure change as suggested by Deelder (1958, p. 142). Stuart (1962) has shown that salmon will leap when stimulated by falling water, and the leaps are not orientated unless the fish can see the position of the weir, or obstacle, over which the water falls. There is no evidence to support the hypothesis that mechanical disturbances likely to be associated with turbulence (water displacement, pressure, or water noise) provide clues which would enable fish to orientate to currents.

(b) *By visual clues.* In open water velocity changes take place across thermal or salinity discontinuities, and I propose the use of the term rheocline (analogous to thermocline and halocline) to describe this phenomena. Reference to Fig. 59 shows that a fish lying below a rheocline will look up into faster moving water, and a fish lying above a rheocline will look down into slow moving water. If there are particles (debris, zooplankton, etc.) being carried along with the current, the fish may be able to receive visual clues from which it could orientate to the direction of flow. A more detailed discussion of the conditions under which orientation could take place are given later (p. 220). Here it is only necessary to make the point that a rheocline may provide the stimulus situation where a pelagic fish, both out of sight and out of touch of the bottom, could orientate to the current. It is of interest to note that a diver has reported that the direction of the current can be determined under these conditions (report of observations by Lt.-Cdr. H. J. Hodges, in Cushing, Lee, and Richardson, 1956, Appendix, p. 12).

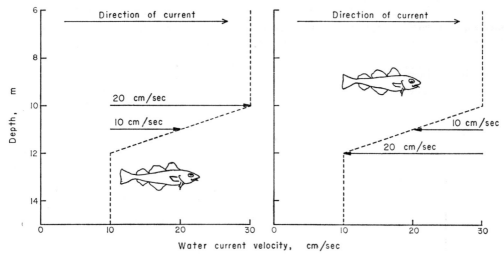

Fig. 59. Orientation at the rheocline. A fish lying below or above the rheocline could see particles moving with the relative velocities indicated alongside the arrows.

6. ORIENTATION USING ELECTRICAL CLUES

When water moves horizontally across the vertical component of the earth's magnetic field, an e.m.f. is induced transverse to the direction of flow according to the equation $E = VZL \times 10^{-8}$ volts, where E is the induced e.m.f., V the velocity of flow in cm/sec, Z the vertical component of the earth's magnetic field in gauss, and L the length of the water filament. Although the possibility of detecting the movement of sea-water by electromagnetic induction was foreseen by Faraday in 1832, it was not until the 1950s, following von Arx's work, that the method became a practical oceanographic technique. Accounts of the theory and practice of towed electrode work and the use of geomagnetic electrokinetograph recorders (GEK) are given by Bowden (1953), von Arx (1962), and Vaux (1965).

For a flow of 1 knot (50 cm/sec), and $Z = 0.4$ gauss, and $L = 1$ cm, the potential gradient is of the order of $0.2\ \mu V$ cm. In the northern magnetic hemisphere the electrical current flows from right (positive) to left (negative) when facing downstream, that is, in the direction in which the water is moving. The e.m.f. corresponding to a water current of 1 knot is of the same order of magnitude as the threshold of *Gymnarchus* ($0.15\ \mu V$ cm; Machin and Lissmann, 1960), and within the range of detection of the elasmobranch's ampullae of Lorenzini ($0.1\ \mu V$ cm; Dijkgraaf, 1963). For comparison, the threshold for an ordinary lateral line organ is about $10\ mV$ cm. A fish with very sensitive bilateral receptors would detect the maximum e.m.f. when lying along the axis of the water current, the right receptor being positive with respect to the left when heading downstream, the polarity being reversed when heading upstream.

Regnart (1932) must have been one of the first to suggest that the e.m.f. generated by moving water could have some biological significance, and Thornton (1932) argued that attention should be given to the possibility that deep-sea fish could detect one another by means of the electric currents produced by their own motion through the earth's magnetic field. Deelder (1952, p. 215) suggested that electrical clues might be used by elvers to orientate in the line of the tidal streams during their migration through the English Channel. As a variant of this hypothesis Murray (1962) has considered the possibility that some fish might be able to discriminate between easterly and westerly movements by reference to the potential gradient between the dorsal and ventral surfaces induced by the fish's movements through the *horizontal* component of the earth's magnetic field.

There is no evidence to show that fish make use of the phenomenon of electromagnetic induction in the ways suggested by Thornton, Deelder, and Murray.

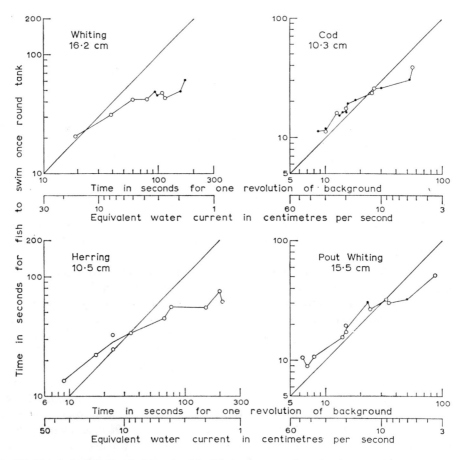

Fig. 60. Rheokinesis in fish. A rotating striped background was used to simulate the visual clues produced by displacement in a water current. Details of the experiments are given by Harden Jones (1963).

Response to water currents

RHEOTAXIS

A fish usually turns to head into a water current, and thresholds for visual and tactile orientation have been determined. Höglund (1961) found that roach, *Rutilus rutilus,* orientated to a water flow as low as 0·25 to 0·5 cm/sec, and that there was no significant difference between the threshold of fish tested in the dark and the light. Gregory and Fields (1962) found comparable thresholds of 0·4 to 0·5 cm/sec for juvenile coho salmon. There was no significant reduction in the threshold when visual clues were eliminated.

Brawn (1960a) gives a flow of 3 to 9 cm/sec as the threshold for a rheotactic response in herring and Harden Jones (1963) found that cod, whiting, pout whiting, and herring would orientate to background displacements equivalent to flows of 2 to 5 cm/sec.

All these results suggest that the visual and tactile thresholds required to elicit a rheotactic response correspond to relatively low current velocities. On the continental shelf, where the tidal currents are rarely below 5 cm/sec even at 'slack' water, a fish with access to visual or tactile clues should always be able to orientate to the current.

RHEOKINESIS

Water currents affect the swimming speeds of fish. Elson (1939), Davidson (1949), Lowe (1952), and Mackinnon and Hoar (1953) have shown this for trout, salmon, and eels. Harden Jones (1963) studied the response of several marine species to a moving background, simulating the visual stimuli which would be produced by displacement in a water current. Fish will follow a moving background in a circular tank and swim faster when the background is speeded up. As shown in Fig. 60, they gain ground when the background is rotated at speeds equivalent to slow water currents, but lose ground at higher background speeds.

REACTIONS TO LIGHT

The eye is the principal but not the only receptor for light. In some fish (for literature, see Healey, 1957) the pineal area and other parts of the diencephalon are light-sensitive. Dermal photoreception also occurs in fish (Steven, 1963). The significance of extra-ocular light perception in fishes is not fully understood and more work is needed in this field.

Fish react photokinetically and phototactically to light. Under natural conditions the most striking feature of their response to a change in light intensity is often a vertical migration from deep water by day to shallow water by night. This might be important during migration as fish rising off the bottom will lose their visual or tactile reference points and could enter a body of water moving at a different speed, and in a different direction, to that in which they were swimming during the day.

The phototactic reactions of fish to light are of particular interest in connexion with the possibility that celestial clues are used by fish on migration. A fish resting in a tank or light gradient will often face towards the direction of maximum intensity and this response is probably a simple telotaxis. A fish can be trained to swim to a particular compartment of a tank under the open sky. When taken indoors and tested with a fixed artificial sun, the fish will go to a different compartment at different times of the day. The angle between the chosen compartment and the fixed artificial sun is the same as that between the compartment which it was originally trained to enter at that time of day. The fish behaves as if it was orientated with reference to the sun and was correcting for the movement of the sun in azimuth during the day. This is the starting point for the hypothesis that a light-compass reaction to the sun could be the means by which fish maintain a steady course in open water. This possibility has attracted a lot of attention in North America, where much of the work has been carried out by A. D. Hasler and his co-workers. The use of celestial clues by migrants is discussed in Chapter 11 (p. 235).

Chapter 11

Movement without Reference to Local Landmarks

INTRODUCTION

Gerking (1959, p. 241) defines homing as 'the return to a place formerly occupied instead of going to equally probable places' and homing is implicit in Heape's (1931, p. 16) definition of migration as a 'class of movement which impels migrants to return to the region from which they have migrated'. Reference has already been made (p. 6) to the biological significance of migration and homing. Migration can be regarded as an adaptation towards abundance by making the most of a varied environment; and homing as a means to ensure the repeated exploitation of those parts of the environment which are particularly favourable. Migration and homing are, then, biologically interwoven: the one complements the other. But a distinction can be made here on behavioural grounds. Recognition of the home may depend on a response to local physical or chemical landmarks, while different clues may be used by a fish on passage. There are two problems. Firstly, how does a returning migrant get home? Secondly, how does the migrant recognize the home when it has reached it? The two problems overlap when clues characteristic of the home, which may be used for its recognition, also serve to guide a migrant back from a distance. The use of local landmarks in homing is akin to pilotage and this will be considered in the following chapter. What follows here concerns the means by which a fish goes from one area to another without reference to the local landmarks characteristic of the home. It is assumed, as Griffin (1952) did for birds, that there is a well defined area which a fish can recognize as home. The home could be reached by one or other, or any combination of the following methods:

1. Passive drift.
2. Search, the direction of the locomotory movements being at random or conforming to some systematic pattern. The locomotory movements are not influenced by the environment and the search proceeds until the home is reached or movement ceases.
3. Undirected movements or kineses; the direction of the locomotory movements is at random, but the speed of movement or frequency of turning (and thus step-length), or angle of turn (and thus the persistence of direction about a particular bearing) are dependent on the intensity of the stimulus. Here the fish does respond to changes in the environmental field before the home is reached, and this is the basis of the distinction between search and kineses.
4. Directed movements, which include the taxes and the transverse orientations.

PASSIVE DRIFT

Many aquatic animals drift with the currents because they are poor swimmers. Powerful swimmers will drift if they cannot direct the course of their movements.

The pelagic larvae of marine fish are thought to drift with the currents and this is very probably true for the early stages of the eel, cod, herring, and plaice. Evidence that the larvae move downstream has been referred to in earlier chapters and evidence relating to other species can be found in the literature cited by Walford (1938), Bishai (1960), and Colton and Temple (1961). The larvae and water move in the same direction and there is no evidence to suggest that the larval movements are significantly different from those expected by passive drift alone.

Young herring and plaice larvae can only cruise at 2 to 3 cm/sec (Bishai, 1960; Ryland, 1963) but this allows them to cover distances of 1,700 to 2,600 m a day, which would be significant if they were able to maintain a steady course. The later stages, which are bigger, could do better if the cruising speed of three fish lengths per second found by Ryland (1963) for plaice larvae applies to other species. In freshwater the fry of pink salmon emerge from the gravel when they are 32 to 38 mm long and soon go downstream to the sea. The migration takes place at night in the surface water and some of the fry actively swim downstream with the current. Neave (1955) suggests that directional clues may be provided by mechanical stimuli produced by the flow of water past the banks and bottom features. Conditions in the open sea are different and here there are no obvious clues which could be used for orientation. In the absence of evidence to the contrary, it does not seem unreasonable to assume, as the simplest hypothesis, that both the early and late pelagic larval stages of marine fish drift passively with the current.

Drift is also thought to provide the means for transport of spent fish from the spawning to their feeding grounds. As with the larvae, the movement of the spent fish is downstream in the direction of the current. Examples are the northward movement of cod from Lofoten, and the return of Channel spawning herring into the Southern Bight of the North Sea. By and large, the movements of the spent fish, as judged from the recovery of tagged cod or change in the pattern of the fishery for spent herring, are what would be expected from drift. Hodgson (1934, p. 49) implies that the herring drift with the currents because they are in a weakened condition after spawning, but there is no evidence for this hypothesis. In the summer months cod shoals often swim pelagically in the Barents Sea. Trout (1957, p. 41) suggests that the north and north-eastward movement of immature and recovering spent fish could be accounted for by drift alone and he argues that the currents are strong enough to carry the fish to the known limits of their distribution by the end of the summer.

An argument in favour of the drift hypothesis is the apparent absence of any reference point which could be used by pelagic fish for orientation. Experiments in the laboratory and observations at sea suggest that fish which are both out of sight and out of touch of the bottom drift with the current (p. 193). Let us assume that this does indeed happen in the open sea. The movements of a pelagic fish must then be largely determined by the oceanic circulatory system as suggested in Fig. 5, p. 14, where some aspects of the theoretical relationships between migration and gyrals are shown. Some measure of independence from the drift of the surface layers could be achieved by vertical movement from shallow to deep water, and back again, on a circadian or seasonal basis. As the deep water moves slower than the surface layers, or, when there is a counter-current, in the opposite direction, a combination of drift and vertical movement would allow for considerable variation in horizontal displacement. The suggestion that fish might use a current and counter-current system for migration was first clearly stated by the Swedish oceanographer Otto Pettersson. 'Hydrographers consider that the migrations of fish are governed by the oceanic circulation which is ruled by the law of continuity. Every current finds its compensation in another. The under-current of the Kattegat is an integral part of the circulation and has its counterpart in the outflowing, so-called, Baltic current. The fish follow the water in which they live so long as it suits their physiological wants, i.e. until it becomes too cold or too diluted or void of oxygen or plankton etc., in which case they seek refuge in the waters of the compensatory current or find a temporary rest in the intermediary layers where the motion is nil.' (Pettersson, 1926, p. 325.) On the following page Pettersson describes the use of a current and its counter-current by fish as being similar to the way in which 'mariners use the tradewinds for the transit to America and the anti-trades for the return journey'.

In the shallower waters of the continental shelf vertical movements could bring the fish close enough to the bottom to obtain the visual or tactile clues essential for orientation. If the fish were close to the bottom by day and in midwater during the night, horizontal displacements could result from an interaction between orientated movement by day and passive drift by night. The inter-action would be complicated by the relation between the tidal cycle and the times of sunrise and sunset. But this aspect of the hypothesis will be considered later and the present discussion limited to drift.

If drift is accepted as a possible means of transport the problem of migration is then no longer of how a fish moves from one area to another—it is carried passively—but why it should spawn, feed, and winter in one part of the gyral rather than another. The fish must be reacting to local environ-mental conditions and the stimuli to which it responds could act as releasers for certain behaviour patterns. For example, a fish might drift into an area where a combination of visual stimuli (features of bottom topography) and chemical stimuli (derived from bottom flora or fauna) release the first acts of spawning behaviour. The bottom features might be recognized innately, while the chemical stimuli could have been imprinted during the early larval stages. Furthermore, the behaviour of the fish must be subject to some controlling mechanism so that it leaves or joins a gyral at a time that will allow its arrival or departure from a spawning, feeding, or wintering ground to be geared, not only to seasonal environmental conditions, but also to its own maturation cycle. It is almost certain that the endocrine organs must play some part in the controlling mechanism. The field has been reviewed by Hoar (1953), Fontaine (1954), and more recently by Woodhead and Woodhead (1965).

The following points are relevant when considering the extent to which fish migrations could be accounted for by drift.

1. Norwegian spring spawning herring

The migrations of the mature fish are generally downstream in the direction of the current, and the stock appears to be contained within the Norwegian Sea gyral. Some of the spents leave the Norwegian coast spawning grounds on a limb of the North Atlantic drift to reach their main feeding grounds in the Jan Mayen area. They return in the East Icelandic current. North and east of the Faroes this current may dive under the North Atlantic drift and carry the herring towards the Norwegian coastal water.

2. Herring in the North Sea

The migrations of the mature herring of the Buchan and Dogger spawning groups are essentially downstream in the direction of the residual currents. Spawning takes place in the western part of the North Sea, and the spent fish winter to the east on the edge of the Norwegian Rinne and in the Skagerrak. The evidence for their counter-clockwise migrations has already been reviewed (p. 128). The relation between the migration of the Downs spawning herring and the residual current is not so clear. The mature herring move down the Southern Bight in the autumn. On the western side of the East Deep Water (Fig. 35, No. 24) there is a south-going residual current (Fig. 36). The inshore water clearly has a south-going residual, as evidenced by beach erosion, and this band of water may extend for several miles off the coast. Extensive drops of Woodhead sea-bed drifters were made in the Southern Bight in the autumns of 1960 and 1961, and some drifters were re-covered well to the south of their release points (unpublished data held at the Fisheries Laboratory, Lowestoft). One notable recovery came from a drop made at a position 52° 43′N., 2° 19′E. (Smith's Knoll, Fig. 35, No. 34) on 10 October 1961. One of these sea-bed drifters was subsequently recovered by a French trawler on 15 February 1962 (128 days later) at a position 50° 30′N., 1° 15′E. (between the Bassure de Baas and the Vergoyer, Fig. 35, Nos. 4 and 5). This drifter must have been carried in a south-going current at a speed of about 1 to 1·5 nautical miles per day, which raises the question as to whether herring could be similarly transported. Echo patches, believed to be due to herring, appear to move down the Southern Bight at a speed of 1·5 to 2·0 miles per day (Tungate, 1958). However, herring migrate down both the western and eastern sides of the Southern Bight, and in the eastern half the residual currents run to the north-east. Here the spawning migration must be against the residual current.

3. Salmon in the Western Pacific

In their marine life these stocks are probably contained within the Western subarctic domain, which may extend, in the summer, to embrace the Okhotsk Sea gyral, the Western subarctic gyral, and the Bering Sea gyral. Japanese fishermen believe that the migration routes of salmon moving towards the coastal waters from the high seas are determined by the currents. These ideas have been investigated by Taguchi. In 1940–41 water current observations were made using drift bottles that could be recovered by salmon gill-nets (Taguchi, 1956). Further observations on water movements between the Aleutian Islands, the Komandorski Islands, and the east coast of Kam-chatka have been made, using data on water temperature, colour, transparency, current meters, and drift bottles (Taguchi, 1955, 1957a, 1959; Taguchi and Hirose, 1954; Taguchi and Shoji, 1955). Catch statistics of the Japanese gill-net fleet in the western Pacific show changes in the abundance of red, chum, and pink salmon as measured in terms of catch-per-effort per statistical rectangle (Taguchi, 1957b). During the season, from May to August, the direction and speed of movement of the fishery appears to be consistent with the hypothesis that the salmon are drifting with the current: 'salmon travel their long migration tour by riding just on the *very superficial flow of the ocean waters*' (Taguchi, 1956, p. 399).

4. Salmon in other parts of the Pacific

Data comparable to those collected by the Japanese are not available for other parts of the Pacific where salmon fishing is limited to the coastal waters. Dodimead, Favorite, and Hirano (1963) have described the oceanography of the subarctic region of the Pacific and their report provides a background against which the results of tagging experiments can be set. The surface currents in the area are shown in Fig. 61 and, more diagrammatically, in Fig. 62. Canadian experiments show that salmon tagged in the Gulf of Alaska are recovered on their spawning grounds from the Colum-bia River to Bristol Bay. American tagging experiments reported by Hartt (1962) have been con-centrated in the waters south of the Aleutian chain. Most of the recoveries from these have been returned from the western Pacific and the Bristol Bay area. The distribution of the recoveries from all these tagging experiments is consistent with the hypothesis that the salmon migrate down-stream in the direction of the oceanic currents revealed by the drift bottle experiments described by Dodimead and Hollister (1962) and Dodimead *et al.* (1963, p. 182, Fig. 2). The currents could take fish from the central subarctic waters into the Canadian coastal waters, and so on to the Alaskan stream waters, through the Aleutian passes and into the Bering Sea gyral and the coastal waters of Bristol Bay (Dodimead *et al.*, 1963, p. 111, Fig. 109; p. 124, Fig. 135; p. 167, Fig. 216.) To complete the homing migration it would be necessary for the salmon to leave the gyral on coming into a coastal domain recognized as containing home coast or home river water, as shown diagrammatically in Fig. 63. Such a mechanism would allow salmon destined for different watersheds to leave the gyral in turn as they came under the influence of local landmarks and the

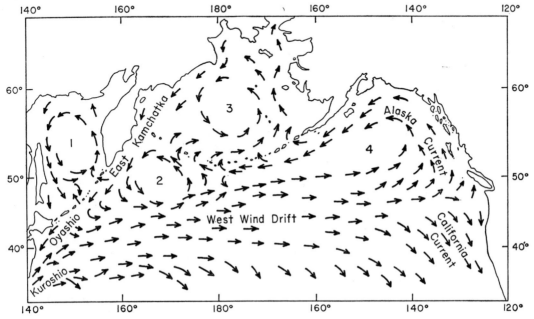

Fig. 61. Main features of the circulation of the surface waters in the North Pacific. (After Neave, 1964, p. 1238 Fig. 7. Outline from an Admiralty chart.)

KEY

1 Okhotsk Sea gyral; 2 Western subarctic gyral; 3 Bering Sea gyral; 4 Alaskan gyral. Some place names in the North Pacific are given in Fig. 18 (p. 66) and a more generalized chart of the oceanographic regions and gyrals in the sea area is given in Fig. 62.

hypothesis is therefore consistent with the fact that salmon tagged at one station have been recovered in widely separated coastal areas and rivers.

If the spawning migration is a drift migration there must be a controlling mechanism to ensure that a biologically sufficient number of fish arrive at the right place and at the right time: this is fundamental to any hypothesis of migration and the fact that such a requirement exists in no way invalidates the possibility that transportation is achieved by drift. The behaviour of the ripening fish must be modified so that it joins the gyral at an appropriate stage of its maturation cycle. For a salmon a change of depth from relatively deep (200 m) to shallow water (0 to 60 m) would take it into the faster surface layer: the fish effectively joins the gyral. Sockeye salmon appear to make this seasonal change in depth, the change-over taking place in early June (Manzer, 1964).

According to the drift hypothesis, salmon destined for widely different coastal areas may be found together on the high seas in late spring and early summer. For example, Neave's (1964) Fig. 2 (shown here as Fig. 64) shows that sockeye tagged at the position 53° 30'N., 146°W. on 27 April 1962 were recovered at Bristol Bay, Kodiak Island, Cook Inlet, the Skeena and Fraser Rivers. The different stocks probably spawn at about the same time, in December. If the fish reach their home coastal waters by drift there is a problem of timing: the transport system is common to all, but some salmon (Bristol Bay) have further to go in the sea than others (Skeena and Fraser Rivers). The Bristol Bay fish might therefore be expected to join the gyral first, one or even two

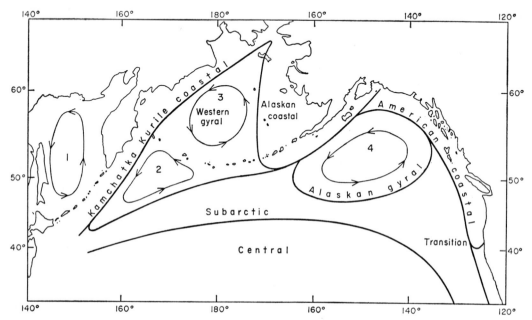

Fig. 62. Oceanographic regions in the North Pacific (after Fleming, 1955) with surface gyrals (after Dodimead *et al.*, 1963).

KEY

1 Okhotsk Sea gyral; 2 Western subarctic gyral; 3 Bering Sea gyral; 4 Alaskan gyral. Some place names in the North Pacific are given in Fig. 18 (p. 66), and a more detailed chart of the surface circulation is given in Fig. 61. (Outline from an Admiralty chart.)

months earlier than the Skeena and Fraser River fish. Although the times at which the fish join the gyral may be partly controlled by genetically determined endocrine cycles differing between stocks, the salmon may be distributed over such a wide area of the gyral that the arrival of the spawners in their home coastal water could be spread over a number of weeks, or months. The first arrivals must wait for the latecomers, and I suggest that they do so in assembly areas, within their home coastal water and under the influence of the parent river but beyond the reaches of the inshore commercial fisheries. So far as I know, there is no evidence to show that Pacific salmon assemble in the coastal waters before moving inshore, as a body, to the parent river. But aggregations of pre-spawning fish are known in other species, and these aggregations could have similar functions to the assemblies suggested for salmon. Lake trout collect around streams before going

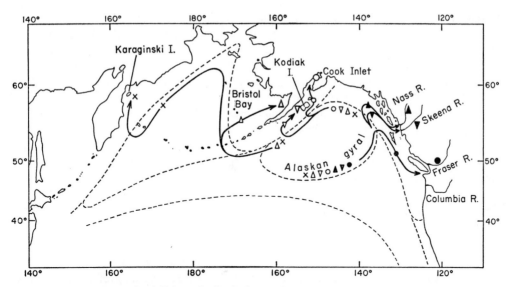

Fig. 63. Diagram to illustrate the drift hypothesis of salmon migration outlined on pp. 202–3. Salmon destined for different rivers mix together on the high seas and drift with the surface currents. Salmon leave the gyrals when entering coastal water containing chemical clues recognized as being characteristic of the parent river system. (Oceanographic regions after Fleming, 1955. Outline from an Admiralty chart.)

ORIGIN OF SALMON

● Fraser R.　　▼ Skeena R.　　▲ Nass R.　　○ Cook Inlet.　　▽ Kodiak I.　　△ Bristol Bay.　　× Karaginski.

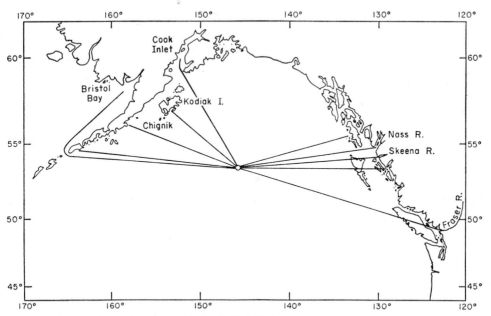

Fig. 64. Recoveries of sockeye salmon tagged in the Gulf of Alaska on 27 April 1962. It is clear that salmon recovered in widely separated coastal areas may be found together on the high seas. (After Neave, 1964, p. 1231, Fig. 2. Outline from an Admiralty chart.

up to spawn (Stuart, 1953); dwarf suckers behave in a similar manner (Dence, 1948, pp. 88, 94). Maslov (1960, p. 194, Fig. 7) figures pre-spawning concentrations of adult cod in the south-east Barents Sea. Norwegian herring enter the coastal waters 5 to 6 weeks before they spawn. These full fish form the basis of the Large herring fishery which usually takes place off Stadt (Aasen, 1962). After a delay these fish move off to the spawning grounds, which now lie mainly between Kristiansund and Egersund, where the Spring fishery for spawning herring develops. Dr. D. H. Cushing (personal communication) has drawn my attention to the fact that in the middle North Sea pre-spawning herring collect on well-known fishing grounds, such as Bayman's Hole and Brucey's Garden, before spawning on nearby grounds. These observations, although they are not rigorously documented, are consistent with the hypothesis that herring aggregate on assembly grounds before moving off in a body to spawn elsewhere.

5. The Arcto-Norwegian cod

The migration of the spent and feeding fish is essentially downstream. Trout's (1957) views as to the role of drift in these movements have already been mentioned. Sund (1932, 1938a, 1939) has suggested that drift might also account for at least a part of the spawning migration. While the currents along the Norwegian coast are predominantly north-going, Sund refers to a south-going bottom current at a depth of 300 to 700 m lying just outside the north-going Atlantic current. Sund gives the speed of the south-going current as 10 cm/sec, equivalent to a displacement of about 9 km a day. Sund suggested that the cod are carried south in this current and noted that the time taken by fish tagged and released at Andenes to reach Lofoten is consistent with this hypothesis. Very few details are available concerning the south-going current. Pettersson (1904, p. 10), commenting on a suggestion made by Hjort, considered the possibility of a current flowing south from the Barents Sea along the line of the Norwegian coast. The water would be cold but saline, being formed from a mixture of Atlantic water and Arctic melt water in the eastern Barents Sea. This outflow probably does exist, as the south-going current was detected during the Norwegian hydrographical investigations during the IGY (Eggvin, 1961). Eggvin (1964) has given some further details of this current, which is colder and slightly less saline than the north-going water. Could the Sund-Eggvin counter-current correspond to the Pettersson-Hjort outflow, and could this current carry the cod south from the Barents Sea to their spawning grounds?

6. The West Greenland cod

It is tempting to suggest that there should be a deep north-going current running along the edge of the shelf from Cape Farewell to the Greenland-Iceland ridge, thus providing a passive transport system for those fish which leave Greenland to spawn at Iceland. There is no evidence to show that such a current exists. But a north-going counter-current could be present to replace the water lost by entrainment to the cold, low-salinity, East Greenland polar current as it crosses the Greenland-Iceland ridge.

7. The European eel

The leptocephali are carried from the spawning grounds to Europe by the Atlantic current. The larvae almost certainly drift but there are problems here (see p. 77) relating to the speed of drift and the age of the larvae at the Azores, western Channel, and the Nile. Very little is known about the return journey. Swedish tagging experiments in the Baltic (for example, Trybom, 1904, 1907;

Trybom and Schneider, 1907; Hessle, 1929) with silver eels give a distribution of recoveries south and west of the release points, those going over 200 km averaging 10 to 20 km/day. The movements of the eels in the Swedish coastal waters are certainly in the direction of the Baltic outflow. Määr (1947) has tagged silver eels along the southern shore of the Gulf of Finland, and of those recovered a high proportion were recaptured to the south and west along the Swedish coast. The relation between the movements of these fish and that of the water currents during the autumn is not clear. Witting's (1912) charts suggest that water leaving the Gulf of Finland is then moving north and north-west rather than south-west. But the currents in the Baltic are sensitive to weather conditions and some caution should be exercised in the interpretation of Määr's tagging experiments which were unaccompanied by hydrographic or meteorological observations. Lühmann and Mann (1958) tagged migrating eels in the Elbe and two of their fish were recovered in the North Sea off the Danish coast, a movement downstream in the direction of the current. But none of these tagging experiments gives any information as to how the European eels get back to the Sargasso. They could drift back, in a deep counter-current (Harden Jones, 1965), or in the Canary-Antilles current.

The circumstantial evidence suggests that the drift hypothesis is worth some consideration, but in no case are there any data which could be regarded as critical or conclusive. Although salmon and herring appear to migrate with the current rather than against it, the movement may be more than drift. Marty (1959, p. 34) says that Atlanto-Scandian herring, on their feeding migration, travel downstream faster than the current's mean velocity: fish and water move in the same direction but not at the same speed, but no evidence is given to show that this takes place. The relative movement between fish and water could be determined by measuring their velocities simultaneously, but one of the elegant sonar techniques which could be used for such work at sea has only recently become available (Voglis and Cook, 1966). Over a longer time scale, that is weeks and months rather than minutes or hours, tagging returns could give useful information. Thus the minimum travelling speed of the fish between release and recapture may be so high as to be obviously inconsistent with drift. I have not been able to find any body of published data which can be used to show this. However, some unpublished data relating to the Pacific sockeye salmon have been made available to me by the Director of the International North Pacific Fisheries Commission, Vancouver. Biologists from the Nanaimo Biological Station have tagged salmon on the high seas in the Alaskan gyral, the tagging and recapture data relating to the 1962 and 1963 experiments being relevant. Fish tagged within the rectangle bounded by 48°–52°N. and 140°–150°W., centred about Ocean Weather Station Papa (50°N., 145°W.) are particularly interesting, as the dates of the recapture of tagged fish in the coastal waters can be compared with the returns of drift bottles released at OWS 'P' in 1957, 1958, and 1959, which are summarized by Dodimead and Hollister (1962). For both fish and drift bottles the recovery areas used for the comparison are limited to the coastal regions south-east Alaska, Charlottes, West Coast, Washington, and Oregon. Inspection of the drift bottle data shows that bottles released at OWS 'P' in April, May, and July (there were no June releases) indicate an average drift current towards the coast of about 5 miles a day. The coastal region where the effects of freshwater discharge are marked can be considered as a belt extending 100 to 200 miles westward from the mainland. As the Weather Station lies approximately 500 miles seaward from the edge of the coastal belt (see Fig. 65), it should take about 100 days to cover the ground by drift. Only the returns of sockeye salmon have been used, there being 49 fish in 1962 and 20 in 1963 recaptured in the selected coastal regions during the year in which they were tagged. The data are summarized in Fig. 66 where the month and day of recapture are given for fish tagged and released on different dates. The diagonal lines give the day and month the fish would be expected to arrive in the coastal regions if they drifted landwards at the reasonable speed of 5 miles a day, and the rather unlikely, but not impossible, speed of 10 miles a day. It is quite clear from this figure that some of the sockeye reach the coastal regions very much sooner than can be accounted for by the drift as estimated by the return of bottles. Nevertheless, it is possible that there may be 'jet streams' present in the area whose velocity might be several times that of the average drift: in 1959 a bottle released at OWS 'P' on 17 April was recovered 81 days later on the Oregon coast. The drift of this bottle (Dodimead and Hollister, 1962, Fig. 40) has been estimated at 12 miles a day. The drift hypothesis, although suspect, should not be abandoned unless it can be shown that the proportion of tagged fish recovered which move faster than the mean drift is greater than that which would be expected if 'jet stream' transport took place.

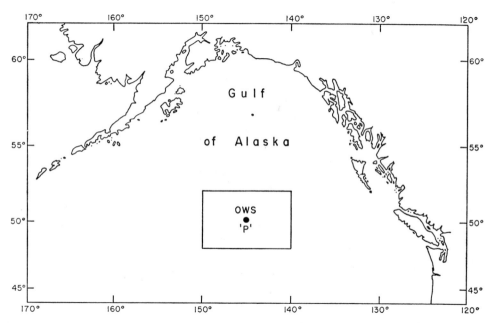

Fig. 65. The position of Ocean Weather Station 'Papa'. The rectangle encloses the sea area from which the returns of tagged salmon have been compared with those of drift bottles released from the Weather Ship. (Outline from an Admiralty chart.)

The downstream migratory movements of fish invite comparison with those of the desert locust, whose movements are essentially down-wind and at a ground speed approximating to that of the wind (Rainey, 1951, 1960). Here there seems to be little doubt that the migration is accomplished by drift. Rainey argues that the down-wind displacement of the locust swarms will, in general, carry them to areas where the winds converge and it is in these areas that rainfall is appreciable and conditions suitable for breeding. It is tempting to suggest a parallel in fish which could ride the ocean gyrals to their feeding grounds at the productive polar fronts and return to their spawning grounds on the other limb of the gyral or in a deeper counter-current.

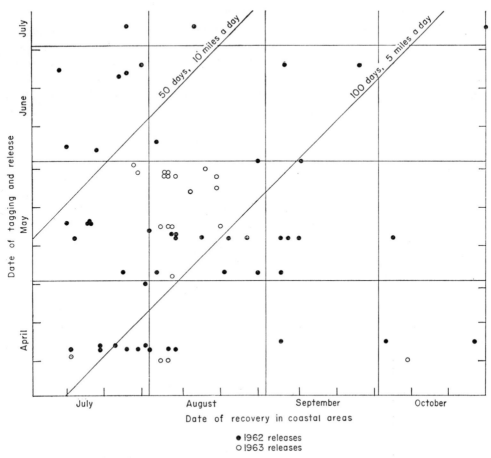

Fig. 66. Release and recovery dates of maturing sockeye salmon tagged near OWS 'P' (see Fig. 65) and subsequently recovered in the coastal waters. The diagonal lines indicate the dates at which fish drifting with a 5 or 10 miles a day current should be expected to reach the coastal waters. Some fish appear to do better than could be reasonably accounted for by drift. (Based on unpublished data held at the Biological Laboratory, Nanaimo, British Columbia.)

SEARCH

The search for the home area could proceed randomly or according to a systematic pattern. Both methods of search have been considered for birds. Wilkinson (1952) has shown that a hypothesis of random search could account for many of the phenomena associated with the homing of wild birds, and Griffin (1952) has examined the results of certain homing experiments in terms of specific exploratory patterns. It is only very recently that fish migrations have been treated along similar lines.

Random search

Saila (1961) and Saila and Shappy (1963) have examined fish migrations from this point of view, with particular reference to the winter flounder and the Pacific salmon.

THE WINTER FLOUNDER (*Pseudopleuronectes americanus*)

From December to March winter flounders spawn in shallow brackish ponds on the coast of Rhode Island, USA. Saila (1961) selected Green Hill Pond, Charlestown, as a site for a series of tagging experiments during the 1956–57 and 1957–58 spawning seasons. A chart of the area is given in Fig. 67. The returns of tagged fish from these experiments were consistent with an off shore movement from June to November, followed by a return to the spawning ground between

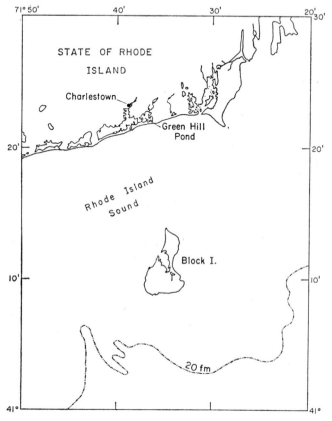

Fig. 67. Coastal area of Rhode Island State, USA, where Saila (1961) carried out tagging experiments with flounders. Fish were tagged in Green Hill Pond during the winter and from June to November were recovered in off shore areas out to Block Island and the 20 fathom depth contour. (Outline from an Admiralty chart.)

November and June. During the summer and autumn the Green Hill flounders were recovered between the coast and the 20 fathom depth contour, some 15 miles seaward. Saila used the June to November tagging returns to obtain quantitative estimates of the directional and random components of the flounders' movements. The method used was that suggested by Jones (1959), who derived the following formulae for V, the directional component of the fish's velocity, and a^2, the dispersion coefficient.

$$V = \frac{\sum r \cos \theta}{\sum t} \tag{1}$$

$$a^2 = \frac{1}{n}\left[\sum\frac{r^2}{t} - \frac{(\sum r\cos\theta)^2}{\sum t}\right] \tag{2}$$

where for each tagged fish recaptured

r = straight line distance travelled

t = number of days free

θ = direction of travel in degrees measured from the axis of the coastline

n = number of fish returned.

R. Jones gives worked examples in connexion with the returns of haddock tagged off the north-east coast of Scotland and those interested in this method of analysis should refer to his original paper. Applying the method to the winter flounder data, Saila obtained very low values for V, approximately 0·03 mile/day, indicating very little directed movement. The values of a^2 were 1·1 and 0·67 mile²/day. The higher value for a^2 was then used to calculate the proportion of flounders that would return to the coast by random search. The fish were assumed to be initially uniformly dispersed, and at all times contained, between the coast and the 20 fathom depth contour. Calculation showed that 75% of the population would have reached the coast after 90 days of searching, a period shorter than that during which flounders entered and spawned in Green Hill Pond. The fish reaching the coast were assumed to get home relatively quickly by a combination of random search and pilotage, their movements being restricted to a narrow coastal belt within which the home pond water could be recognized by a chemical clue. Saila's analysis shows that a combination of random searching movements and pilotage near home could account for the spawning migration without the fish having to refer to environmental clues on passage. But the success of the model does not prove that the flounders find the coast by searching randomly and direct evidence for or against the hypothesis could only be provided by plotting the tracks of individual fish.

PACIFIC SALMON

The mathematical approach to migration problems is possibly more fruitful if it can be shown that random search alone cannot account for the facts so far as they are known. Saila and Shappy's (1963) analysis of Pacific salmon migration provides an example. They devised a numerical probability model in which a salmon is assumed to swim along a straight path whose length, the step- or swim-length, varies within certain limits. When the fish turns, all angles of turn are assumed to be equally probable.

The pattern of step- or swim-lengths was described by a heart-shaped curve, or cardioid, where the radius of curvature, R, at any angle θ is given by the equation

$$R = P + Q\cos\theta$$

The parameters P and Q are constant for any given cardioid and R is direction-sensitive as its value depends on the randomly chosen value of θ. If $A = Q/P$, then

$$R = P(1 + A\cos\theta)$$

When $A = 0$, R is equal for all values of θ and the search pattern is a circle. When $A = 1$, the search pattern is a typical cardioid, but when $A = 0·25$, the form of the cardioid departs only very slightly from a circle. So A is a measure of the directed movement and in the Saila and Shappy model is called 'the coefficient of directed versus undirected movement'.

A computer programme was designed to simulate the movements of a fish at a point 1,200 naut. mile (2,224 km) west of the coast. Certain parameters were used for swimming speed, step-length, days allotted for migration and radius of the home area and calculations were made of the return probability with different values of A. Of the parameters chosen, those for distance from the coast, time allotted for migration and swimming speed are consistent with the facts of salmon biology. But the radius of the home area (74 km) may be an under-estimate and the range of step-length (0–37 km) probably an over-estimate. To cover the mean step-length of 18·5 km between turns, the model requires that a salmon swimming at 125 cm/sec (2·5 naut. mile/hr) maintains course for 4 to 5 hr before turning to swim along the new course. Step-length appears to raise some problems on its own account. However, using these parameters the Saila and Shappy model shows that with random search and step-length equal in all directions, fish 2,224 km away from home fail to return within the allotted 175 days. But when $A = 0·3$, the return probability corresponds to the 10% recovery rate actually obtained in the coastal regions from fish tagged on the high seas, some allowance having been made for tagging mortality and a failure to report tags. The homeward bias that has to be imposed on the search pattern to bring 10% of the salmon home is relatively small, the step-length directly towards home $(+1·3)$ being a little less than twice that $(-0·7)$ directly away from home. Saila and Shappy (1963, p. 159) suggest that the homeward bias may result from a form of sun-compass mechanism, with the implication that the step-length is greater when the randomly selected direction in which the fish swims falls within a rather wide sector, whose mean bearing relative to the sun changes throughout the day to compensate for the sun's movement in azimuth. But there is no evidence to show that salmon use a sun-compass mechanism during their spawning migrations. Furthermore, there is really no need to suggest, as Saila and Shappy (1963, p. 153) have done, that the model requires even a 'low degree of orientation to an outside stimulus'. The model only requires that the step-length varies as $\cos \theta$ and that the bias is in the direction of home. This could be achieved by an orthokinesis (increasing the homeward step-length) or a klinokinesis (decreasing the frequency of turning, or angle of turn, and so increasing the step-length about a particular bearing) or by a combination of the two. A suitable environmental field would produce a homeward bias without orientation to an environmental stimulus. This possibility is discussed further below.

It is also possible that the homeward bias could be provided by drift. The Alaskan gyral moves anti-clockwise and salmon on its fringes will be carried into the coastal (home) waters. Drift will not change the step-length between turns through the water, but it will affect the step-length over the ground: with an onshore current, the step-length over the ground between turns will be greater towards than away from the shore. A 50 cm salmon cruising at 50 cm/sec (1 L sec) in a quarter knot current (12·5 cm/sec, 6 naut. mile/day) will have over the ground step-lengths in the ratio $(50 - 12·5)$ to $(50 + 12·5)$, that is 37·5 to 62·5, or 1:1·67. This compares favourably with the step-length ratio of 0·7 to 1·3, or 1:1·85 in the Saila and Shappy cardioid where $A = 0·3$.

Other migrations, such as those of the Arcto-Norwegian cod, the Atlanto-Scandian herring, and the North Sea plaice, have not yet been subjected to analysis in a manner similar to that carried out on the Rhode Island flounders and the Pacific salmon. It would be worth while doing this work if only to show that random search alone can, or cannot, account for the facts. While simple hypotheses are not necessarily correct, they should be shown to be inadequate before accepting the need for more complicated ones.

Orientated search

Griffin (1952) has considered the extent to which the homing flights of wild birds might be accounted for by one or other of a number of search patterns, and made some quantitative estimates of the results to be expected from linear radial scattering, expanding zigzag and expanding spiral patterns.

EXPLORATION BY LINEAR RADIAL SCATTERING

This type of orientated search pattern, in which animals spread out in straight lines from a point of release, provides an example which can be applied to fish and in particular to salmon in the north-western Pacific. Griffin (1952, p. 374) has shown that the probability that an animal released at a point will reach home after searching by linear radial scattering can be calculated from the formula

$$P = \frac{g + 2r}{2\pi D}$$

where g = length of the home area normal to the direct line between home and the release point
r = average distance at which the home area can be recognized
D = the shortest distance between home and the release point.

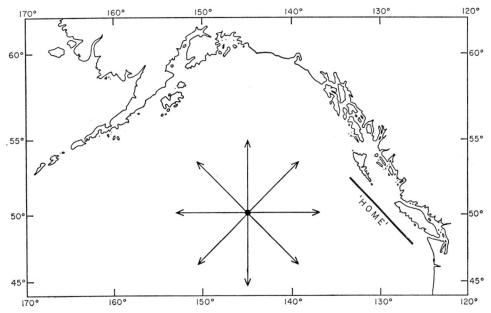

Fig. 68. Exploration by linear radial scattering from OWS 'P'. The 'home' coastline is shown by the black line. (Outline from an Admiralty chart.)

With a bird the value of r corresponds to the range at which local landmarks can be recognized visually. Here it is assumed that there is no recognition of the coastal region at a distance, so $r = 0$, and the fish must swim all the way to qualify as a successful migrant.

For an example, consider salmon in the Alaskan gyral released at various distances off shore along the line of the 50°N. parallel. Their home area will be assumed to be a 300 naut. mile length of coast between 47° 30′N. and 52° 30′N., as indicated in Fig. 68. The probability of a fish returning home on a basis of linear radial scattering can be calculated and at a distance of 900 miles

$$P = \frac{300}{2\pi \times 900} = \frac{1}{18}$$

indicating a 1 in 18 chance of success and that 5·5% of the fish would get home. The fastest time in which a fish could cover the distance, assuming a cruising speed of 2·5 L/sec maintained for 24 hr/day, is easily calculated. For a 50 cm salmon the cruising speed would be 2·5 naut. mile/hr (125 cm/sec), and the fish would cover the distance in 360 hr, or 15 days. Fig. 69 shows the percentage returns expected and minimum times that the fish would take over the journey for a number of release points. The percentage returns expected from distances of 500 to 1,200 miles off shore range from 4 to 10%, and are similar to the percentage of returns from all areas in the high seas tagging experiments. Those fish that returned home from distances 400 to 600 miles off shore could do

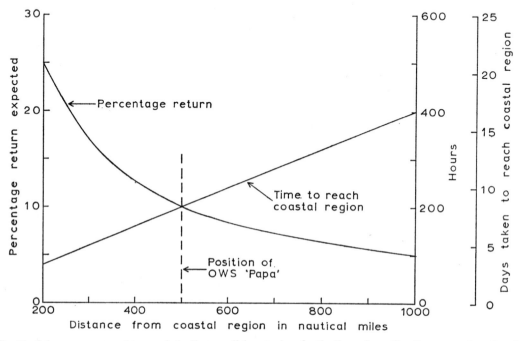

Fig. 69. Salmon are assumed to search, by linear radial scattering, for the 'home' coastline from a number of positions along the line of the 50°N. parallel. The figure shows the proportion of expected returns when the fish start at different distances from the coast, and the minimum times in which a successful fish could cover the ground, assuming a cruising speed of 125 cm/sec maintained for 24 hr/day.

so in 7 to 10 days, somewhat faster than the quickest returns recorded in Fig. 66. The point is that the tagging results are not inconsistent with homing by linear radial scattering, and on the available data the hypothesis cannot be dismissed out of hand.

But, as with other search patterns, linear radial scattering does raise the question as to the accuracy with which a fish can keep on course for any length of time. A similar problem arose with step-length in the Saila and Shappy model. Griffin (1952, p. 379) made the same point in connexion with spiral flight paths. Hoar (1956) has shown that pink and chum salmon fry establish and maintain a definite direction of swimming (clockwise or anti-clockwise) in a circular channel or basin, and that the established direction was stable for periods up to 48 hr. While these results are of considerable interest on their own account, it is not quite true to say, as Hoar (1956, p. 324) does, that the fry were 'maintaining their directions in a surprisingly precise manner'. When fish swim in a circle they are constantly changing their direction, and it is the pattern of directional changes which is constant, and not the direction of movement. Maintenance of the pattern might depend on the diameter of the circular path and the speed at which the fish swims. My own observations (Harden Jones, 1957c) have shown that blinded goldfish consistently swim in a clockwise or anti-clockwise direction, which suggests that the labyrinth might be involved in the response. But we do not know if a fish can maintain a straight course in the absence of clues from external reference points. Under these conditions men go round in circles. This is documented by air crews who have survived desert crashes (Howard, 1953); skaters caught in a fog (de Wit, 1953, p. 11); and by Schaeffer (1928), who carried out a remarkable series of experiments with blindfolded men who were set free to walk or to drive motor cars in snow-covered fields where their tracks were clearly marked. Breder and Nigrelli (1938) maintain that fish behave in the same way, but the work was done with snails and not with fish, which proved to be awkward subjects, and their argument is not convincing. Barlow (1964) has suggested that the labyrinth could be used as a sensor for inertial navigation, and the hypothesis is attractive until it is remembered that the apparent threshold accelerations to which vertebrates respond ($0.5°/sec^2$, and 6 cm/sec^2) are 3 to 4 orders of magnitude greater than that which would be tolerated in a precision system. Kalmus (1964) considers the existence of an inertial guidance system in animals as 'rather dubious'. This is a fair comment in the light of available data.

KINESES

(See also p. 187)

Aggregation at boundaries

Kineses can bring about changes in distribution if the step-length between turns is varied in response to environmental factors. Step-length can be varied by a change in the speed of loco-motion or a change in the frequency of turning. Step-length about an average bearing can be varied by changes in the mean angle of turn. A suitable environmental field for these reactions is a spatial or temporal gradient of intensity. The response could be determined by the absolute value of the stimulus to which the animal is immediately subjected, or to the rate of change of stimulus. In the case of the spatial gradient, the rate of change of stimulus will partly depend on the speed at which the animal swims. Animals usually, but not invariably (see p. 189), collect where the step-length is at a minimum, a decrease in step-length being brought about by a decrease in swimming speed or an increase in the frequency of turning.

Fish respond kinetically to light and temperature, and to other physical and chemical clues. Difficulties arise when attempts are made to account for fish migrations in terms of kineses because the horizontal gradients found in the open sea are usually very gentle and there must be some doubt as to whether fish can detect them. Verwey (1958, p. 439) makes the same point. But horizontal gradients may be relatively steep at the boundaries between water masses and a decrease in step-length would enable fish to collect in a narrow band of water once they had arrived in the front. The fish could be brought to the front by drift or random movement.

Vertical gradients of temperature and salinity (thermoclines or haloclines) are other boundaries or corridors where fish might collect by kinetic reactions. Horizontal displacement within the band might take place by passive drift or as a result of a rheotropic response. However, the circum-stances in which aggregations take place are rather special. While fish are known to concentrate near the boundaries between water masses (for example, herring in the East Icelandic current; cod at Bear Island) it is difficult to envisage how kineses could account for changes in distribution over long distances if intensity gradients are the only effective environmental field.

In general, conditions in the open sea suggest that the role of kineses in migration is that of aggregating fish into narrow boundary zones (10^1 to 10^3 times the length of the fish) rather than acting as the behavioural mechanisms directly involved in movements over long distances (10^5 to 10^6 times the length of the fish).

A special case

However, under certain conditions an orthokinesis could bring about changes in distribution in a uniform horizontal field. The reaction of fish to water currents provides an example. A current can be detected by visual clues and in the laboratory a moving background can be used to simulate the optical stimuli produced by displacement in a current. Using this technique I have shown (Harden Jones, 1963) that the response to a moving background has an orientating and a kinetic component. A fish turns to swim in the same direction as the background (the orientating component) and swims faster when the background is speeded up (the kinetic component). But the swimming speed of the fish also depends on whether it swims with or against the moving background. This was first observed in a series of preliminary experiments made with roach, *Rutilus rutilus*. From time to time a fish gave up swimming with the background and turned about to swim against it. The swimming speed against the background was always less than that which the fish maintained when swimming with the background. In some experiments the decrease in speed was clearly due to fatigue, but in others it was apparent that the difference was due to the direction in which the stripes were approaching the fish, from tail-to-head when swimming with the background, and from head-to-tail when swimming against it. The difference in swimming speed was observed during the experiments in which the fish showed a strong orientated response to the background and during the experiments in which there was no orientation. In the latter experiments the fish swam for more or less equal periods with and against the background. These observations showed that there was a kinetic response which was independent of the orientated response.

Marine species were found to behave similarly to roach. Some quantitative and hitherto unpublished data for whiting, *Gadus merlangus*, are shown in Fig. 70. The speed of the fish swimming round the tank with the background was divided by the speed when swimming against the background, and the quotient has been plotted against the background speed. Each point represents the quotient obtained from a mean of 15 to 25 circuits with the background and 5 to 15 circuits against it. The figure shows that the fish usually swims faster when travelling with the background, and that there is a trend for the quotient to increase with the background speed. As the fish were always swimming below their cruising speed (estimated at 3 fish lengths/sec), the effect was not due to fatigue.

These results are of interest when considering the horizontal movements of a fish lying close enough to the bottom to pick up visual clues and whose swimming movements are nevertheless random in direction. If the fish is displaced by a current so that there is a visual stimulus to which it reacts kinetically, the step-length between turns will be longer upstream than downstream. The overall movement could be against the current although there is no orientated response. Similarly, a fish lying below a thermocline across which there was a relatively sharp reduction in velocity, so that the movement of the upper water could be detected visually (see p. 194), could move downstream in the direction of the current. In the case of the salmon this would produce the homeward, that is downstream, bias required in the Saila and Shappy model. Although there is no evidence to show that salmon do behave in this way, there is evidence to show that they are at the level of the thermocline during the day (a recent paper by Manzer, 1964, confirms the earlier Japanese observations) and therefore could be positioned to detect the movement of the upper water should a velocity gradient exist.

If displacements are brought about in this way, the behavioural mechanism might be classified as a kinesis. The speed of swimming, and thus the step-length between turns, is varied according to the relative bearing between the direction of swimming and the direction of the current. But the field of stimulation in the horizontal plane is uniform and there is no spatial or temporal gradient of intensity.

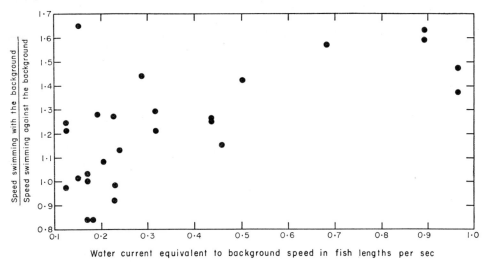

Fig. 70. The kinetic response of a whiting to a moving background. The response of this fish to a moving background was tested in the apparatus described by Harden Jones (1963). The speed of the fish swimming round the tank with the background was divided by the speed when swimming round the tank against the background. The quotient is plotted against a measure of the background speed. At slow background speeds the quotient is about unity, and a fish whose movements are random in direction will neither gain or lose ground relative to the water. The quotient rises as the background speed is increased. Although the movements of the fish are still random in direction, it will gain ground relative to the water, as the step-length between turns will be longer upstream than downstream.

DIRECTED MOVEMENTS
(See also p. 190)

Orientated movements include taxes and transverse orientations. In a taxis orientation can be indirect (klinotaxis) or direct (tropo- or telotaxis). Among the transverse orientations, the light-compass reaction is the one of most interest for studies in fish migration.

TAXES

Chemical and temperature stimuli

Chemical and temperature stimuli can vary in intensity but do not have directional properties. So only undirected reactions (kineses) and a klinotaxis (sequential comparison of intensities)

8

would be expected in response to chemical or temperature stimuli, although a tropotaxis (simultaneous comparison of intensities) could take place if the gradient were steep enough for two parts of the body to be stimulated simultaneously by different intensities. But the chemical and temperature gradients found in the open sea are probably only steep enough for a tropotaxis along fronts between water masses or across vertical discontinuities (thermo- and haloclines). Steele (1961, p. 17) has suggested that a shoal might act as a 'detection unit' and so wheel away from, or towards, a particular area as a result of differential stimulation, and thus differential swimming, across the shoal. This aspect of shoal behaviour is one to which little attention has been given. McInerney 1964, p. 1015) makes a similar suggestion.

Very little is known about the behaviour of fish in or around chemical or temperature corridors in the sea. Direct observations of the response of sharks to olfactory stimuli have been described by Hobson (1963). Observations were made from an underwater chamber, cage, or glass-bottomed boat moored in the lagoon at Eniwetok Atoll, Marshall Islands. One of the most remarkable incidents recorded concerns the response of a whitetip shark (*Triaenodon obesus*) to an olfactory corridor or trail produced by a parrot fish (Scaridae). The parrot fish was wounded by a spear and sheltered in a large coral head where it attracted the attentions of the shark. After a chase among the coral, the parrot fish slipped the shark, swam away from the coral head on a straight course for about 30 m, made a 90° turn and continued straight along the new course till it was lost from sight. When the shark came out of the coral head a few seconds later, the parrot fish was already lost to view. The shark circled briefly, then swam along the same path taken by the parrot fish. The shark overshot the position of the 90° change of course, slowed, turned, and after a brief period of circling picked up the new corridor and followed it out of sight. There was no tide running at the time these observations were made. Although the behavioural mechanism by which the shark kept within the corridor is not clear from Hobson's account, it is almost certainly a klino- or tropotaxis. But it is more difficult to decide how the shark knew which way to swim. The fish might be expected to swim along the corridor and up the gradient but it seems unlikely that diffusion or turbulence can have been sufficient to set up an appreciable intensity gradient along the length of the trail in the few seconds separating pursuer and pursued. Hobson (personal communication) suggests that the directional clue might have been obtained by the shark during the two brief periods of circling, firstly when leaving the coral head, and secondly at the position of the 90° turn. Circling would have allowed the fish to sample two widely separated segments of the corridor between which there may have been a detectable difference in olfactory stimulus. The behavioural mechanism would be a klinotaxis and, from the point of view of the pursuer, orientation would be facilitated if the chemical attractant decayed quite rapidly so as to make differences more pronounced.

In the presence of a current the olfactory corridor will be carried downstream. The source could be located if the fish kept within the olfactory corridor by a klinotaxis or a tropotaxis, and swam upstream as the result of a positive rheotaxis. Hobson (1963) describes a number of experiments which show that an olfactory source can be located efficiently by sharks in this way. The olfactory stimulus not only initiates the response to swim against the current but is used by the fish to locate the source, which in this instance was a clear plastic pipe acting as a siphon for colourless fish extracts. The use of an olfactory and anemo- or rheotactic response to air and water currents is a common and effective combination for locating food by animals (see Fraenkel and Gunn, 1961) and the same mechanism could be important in fish migrations, combining a very sensitive detector (the olfactory organ), with an unambiguous directional clue (the water current). The appropriate olfactory stimulus could initiate or release a rheotropic response and contain the fish within a relatively narrow corridor along which it swims. This may prove to be the significant role of olfaction in migration. The same may be true for temperature. Rheotropic responses can be initiated by temperature changes (Northcote, 1962) and fish are known to collect along temperature corridors between water masses and at thermoclines. Velocity gradients across fronts or thermoclines could provide visual stimuli which would enable the fish to orientate to the current (p. 194), the response to temperature containing the fish within the critical boundary zone.

Water currents

Water currents are thought to provide directional clues during migration, fish usually swimming upstream and against the current to reach their spawning grounds. The historical background to the hypothesis has already been reviewed (p. 15) and it has been noted that the results of Bowman's (1933) plaice tagging experiments at the Shetlands (p. 179), often cited as the classical supporting evidence, show exactly the opposite, if indeed they show anything at all. Nevertheless, the relation between water currents and migration is clearly important (p. 186) and their role in providing directional clues must be considered.

There are a number of ways in which a fish could detect a water current (p. 193). Fish lying on the bottom could be stimulated directly by water flowing over them, and flatfish provide a group whose reactions to water currents might be determined by direct mechanical stimulation. But apart from a few preliminary observations of my own (Harden Jones, 1963) nothing appears to be known about the reactions of flatfish to water currents. For other fish visual and tactile clues are probably the most important, unless there are velocity gradients steep enough to be detected across the width or dorsal-ventral dimension of the body. Orientation appears to be direct so a klinotaxis is not involved. In the case of tactile and mechanical clues the response is probably a tropotaxis depending on the stimulation of bilaterally arranged receptors. Lyon (1909) showed that a fish blinded in one eye responded normally to a moving background so a tropotaxis cannot be the mechanism of orientation to visual clues. The essential feature of the taxis is that the fish turns and swims to keep the visual field more or less constant, as in a simple light-compass reaction. But a kinetic response is usually superimposed on the compensatory swimming movement so that within a certain range of velocity the fish gains ground against the current. Reference has already been made to this aspect of the rheotropic response (p. 197). To receive tactile clues the fish must remain near the bottom with which it will have to make regular contact. It is usually assumed (e. g. Harden Jones, 1965) that a fish will have to remain in sight of the bottom to receive visual clues and that a pelagic fish, both out of sight and out of touch of the bottom, would be unable to detect or respond to a current. But if the suggestion that a fish can receive visual clues across a rheocline is accepted as a working hypothesis (p. 194), a conceptual barrier is removed which opens up new lines for thought, observation, and experiment. As visual orientation to a current must normally fail at night or whenever the fish leave the bottom or the rheocline, their overall movement will be the outcome of an interaction between orientated swimming and passive drift, which could be complicated when a tidal cycle is superimposed on the daily changes in light intensity. Some aspects of this problem will be examined in more detail (p. 230), but the discussion will be limited, for the moment, to visual orientation.

THE THRESHOLD CURRENT

Using visual clues, a fish will swim against simulated water currents as slow as 1 to 5 cm/sec (p. 197). The threshold for orientation may be lower, but the fact that fish will respond to a 5 cm/sec current (0·1 knots, 2·4 naut. mile/day) is the important point, as migratory fish are generally in faster moving water. So far as visual clues from the bottom are concerned, the current will be above threshold.

THE LIMITS OF VISUAL DETECTION

Near the bottom

In practice the detection of a water current will probably depend on the range at which the fish can receive visual clues. When bottom features are used their size, reflectivity and contrast, light intensity, scattering, and height of the fish above the bottom must all be important factors. The visual range is probably small, and even under good conditions may not exceed a few metres. Visual contact with the bottom is almost certainly lost during the night and may be impossible during the day at low light intensities in deep water.

At the rheocline

Similar limitations must apply when orientation depends on the visual detection of movement across the rheocline. In addition the velocity gradient must be steep enough to elicit a response within the range at which the fish can see targets drifting past. Visual detection of a current across a rheocline must be impossible at night unless the targets are phosphorescent.

Boulet (1958) gives data on the response of fish to small moving targets which have a bearing on orientation at the rheocline. A perch (*Perca fluviatilis*) took little notice of a ball, 2 mm in diameter, moving horizontally through its visual field. The target was presented at a range of 10 cm, and therefore subtended an angle of about 1°. Perch reacted to larger targets, 4 to 7 mm diameter (subtended angle 2 to 4°), at rotations corresponding to velocities as low as 2 cm/sec, and the fish followed these targets at velocities of over 3·4 cm/sec (Boulet, 1958, pp. 44–45). But there seems to be little doubt that perch could see a 2 mm target as they responded when the horizontal movement was replaced by a 'hop-and sink' motion characteristic of *Daphnia*. Boulet's results suggest that perch can detect targets 2 to 4 mm in size moving at velocities of about 3 cm/sec. Observations in aquaria suggest that marine teleosts make attacks on small copepods up to ranges of 1 m. Divers' observations are relevant to this problem. Bainbridge (1952) records that *Calanus finmarchicus* was visible at ranges of 1·3 to 1·6 m in clear water off Millport Marine Station, Scotland, and says that 'the clearest views could be seen by looking about 10° either to the left or right of the bright patch formed by the sun on the surface of the water. In this manner a sort of dark ground illumination is obtained and even the most transparent forms stand out very clearly' (Bainbridge, 1952, p. 108). The total length of adult *Calanus* varies from 2·7 to 5·4 mm (Marshall and Orr, 1955, p. 81). It seems reasonable to conclude that under good conditions a fish could see and follow an individual *Calanus* drifting above it at a relative velocity of 5 cm/sec and at a range of 1 m. This gives an estimate of the velocity gradient across the rheocline that would probably be steep enough to provide a satisfactory visual clue for orientation.

The flow across the shear zone would probably have to be laminar if the visual stimulus were to elicit a clear response. Dr. C. H. Mortimer has pointed out to me that this condition will prevail so long as R_i, the Richardson number, does not fall below 0·25, in the equation

$$R_i = g(dq/dz)/(dv/dz)^2$$

where g = acceleration of gravity, q = density, v = velocity and z = depth (Mortimer, 1961). Substituting values of 0·25 for R_i, 981 for g and letting the velocity gradient (dv/dz) be 5 cm per 100 cm the density difference (dq/dz), required to stabilize the flow across the shear zone is 0.637×10^{-4}. Reference to *Tables for sea water density* (Anon, 1952a) shows that at 10°C this density difference would be well covered by a temperature difference of 0.5°C/m (sea-water 1·026971 at 10°C, 1·026884 at 10.5°C, difference 0.87×10^{-4}). Over a wider spread of temperature the difference per metre ranges from 0.5° at 6°C to 0.25° at 20°C. The critical values should be approximately doubled in freshwater. As these temperature differences are normally found in well-developed summer thermoclines, a shear of 5 cm/sec/m should not lead to instability.[1]

Visual-chain response

Fish nearest the bottom, or to the rheocline, could act as markers for the rest of a shoal extending into midwater. Dr. C. C. Hemmings (Marine Laboratory, Aberdeen), an experienced diver, has observed such a visual-chain response in a shoal of *Chromis chromis* (Pomacentridae) near a group of isolated rocks on the south side of the Bay of Naples, Italy. The shoal was strung out into midwater and only a part of the shoal could have seen the vertical rock face. As the shoal was maintaining its position against a 1 to 1·5 knot current it is probable that the fish strung out in midwater were ultimately keeping station relative to those close enough to see the rocks (Hemmings, personal communication). A similar situation could take place in midwater, fish well above or below the rheocline keeping station relative to others orientating to visual stimuli across the boundary zone.

GAINING OR LOSING GROUND

Fish usually orientate to a moving visual field so that the image passes over the retina in an antero-posterior direction, the background passing from tail to head (Lyon, 1909). A fish receiving visual clues from the bottom will then orientate to head upstream. But the fish lying below the rheocline and orientating to targets drifting past above will head downstream, and those lying above the rheocline and orientating to targets drifting past below will head upstream (Fig. 59). So the position of the fish in the rheocline would be critical for orientation up or downstream. As rheoclines will often be associated with temperature or salinity discontinuities, the position of the fish in relation to the thermocline or halocline may be the deciding factor in determining whether the fish faces with or against the current. Aggregations in temperature or salinity gradients must be brought about by ortho- or klinokinesis, or klino- or tropotaxes. It has already been suggested (pp. 216, 219) that when temperature and chemical stimuli are involved, the role of these behavioural mechanisms in migration is to aggregate the fish into critical boundary zones or corridors, rather than to give *direct* effect to large scale movements from one place to another.

When orientated the fish swims with the background and, up to a certain velocity, gains ground. The critical velocity at which the fish must always lose ground will be just above its cruising speed. Fig. 60, p. 196, shows the speed of certain fish in relation to that of a moving background and the water current equivalent to the visual stimulus. This figure has already been referred to in Chapter 9. A measure of the gain or loss that a fish makes relative to a particular background movement is given by the quotient obtained by dividing the time in seconds for the background to complete one revolution by the time in seconds for the fish to swim once round the experimental tank. Data relating to the pout whiting are set out in Table 26 and Fig. 71. In general terms, the fish gained on background speeds equivalent to water currents less than 1 fish length per second (Table 26 column 7, quotient, greater than unity) and lost ground at faster background speeds (quotient less

[1] Woods and Fosberry (1967) have described velocity profiles across the thermocline.

Table 26. Reaction of fish to a moving background simulating the optical stimuli equivalent to displacement by a water current.

Pout whiting *(Gadus luscus)* L = 15·5 cm

Background movement			Fish movement			Quotient background fish	Speed of fish cm/sec	Gain or loss in cm/sec
Seconds for one revolution	Equivalent current cm/sec	Equivalent current L/sec	Seconds to swim once round tank	n	sd			
1	2	3	4	5	6	7	8	9
	B					D	B × D	
6·4	49·1	3·165	10·5	12	0·97	0·610	30·0	− 19·1
7·0	44·9	2·895	8·8	10	1·09	0·795	35·7	− 9·2
8·0	39·25	2·532	10·7	10	0·39	0·747	29·3	− 9·9
14·0	22·44	1·448	15·5	44	2·22	0·903	20·3	− 2·1
15·0	20·94	1·351	17·1	46	1·98	0·877	18·4	− 2·5
15·0	20·94	1·351	19·5	54	2·88	0·769	16·1	− 4·8
23·0	13·66	0·881	30·5	7	4·00	0·754	10·3	− 3·4
24·0	13·09	0·845	26·5	23	4·57	0·906	11·9	− 1·2
33·0	9·52	0·614	32·2	31	4·36	1·025	9·8	+ 0·3
35·0	8·98	0·580	30·0	9	8·90	1·167	10·5	+ 1·5
50·0	6·28	0·405	32·7	6	5·39	1·529	9·6	+ 3·3
87·0	3·61	0·233	51·7	12	6·39	1·683	6·2	+ 2·6

than unity). Inspection of the data in column 8 of Table 26 shows that the pout whiting swam very slowly, 6 to 10 cm/sec, with the slower background speeds. Although the fish swam 1·5 to 1·6 times as fast as the background (column 7), the actual gain was small, and only amounted to 2 to 3 cm/sec (column 9), that is 0·04 to 0·06 knot, or about 1 naut. mile/day. The other fish used in these laboratory experiments gave similar results, with the exception of herring, which swam somewhat faster at equivalent speeds expressed in fish lengths per second. In the case of the pout whiting, and the other gadoids, the ground gained on the background was rather small. But at slow background movements all the fish, including herring, swam at speeds well below that at which they should have been able to cruise for long periods without fatigue. Fish should be able to cruise at a speed

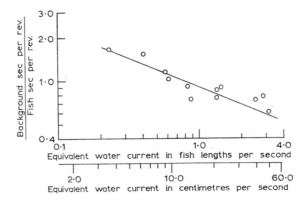

Fig. 71. The kinetic response of a pout whiting to a moving background. The fish gains ground at background speeds equivalent to water currents of less than 1 fish length per second and loses ground at faster background speeds. Data from Table 26.

equivalent to 2 to 3 times their own length per second (p. 16). But the pout whiting, length 15·5 cm, was only swimming at 6 to 10 cm/sec as compared with a possible 31 to 47 cm/sec. If migrating fish swam at their cruising speed when orientated by visual displacements just above threshold (say 5 cm/sec), they would gain ground rapidly, the larger fish making the most headway. This could be a difference between the behaviour of the immature fish observed in the laboratory experiments and the mature fish on migration. An 'all or nothing' response would appear to be the most effective way of using a water current as a directional clue on migration: the visual stimulus provides the orientation, and the fish swims at full cruising speed. But the distance that the fish covers over the ground must also depend on the speed of the water in which it is swimming. If the fish is migrating upstream and against the current, it should be in the slowest water consistent with receiving an adequate visual stimulus, and vice versa. The following examples should help to clarify this point.

1. Orientating clue received from the bottom. *Migration upstream.* The current should be slowest at the bottom where it will be retarded by frictional forces. The fish should hug the bottom as it swims upstream. *Migration downstream.* The fish should stay as far above the bottom as is consistent with receiving an adequate visual stimulus for orientation.

2. Orientating clue received across the rheocline. *Migration upstream.* The fish can use visual clues provided by slower moving targets which *appear* to be drifting upstream below it. So the fish should avoid the faster moving water and be as low down in the rheocline as is consistent with receiving adequate visual clues. *Migration downstream.* The fish can use visual clues provided by faster moving targets drifting downstream above it. The fish should get into the fast moving water, and be as high up in the rheocline as is consistent with receiving adequate visual clues.

Fish moving downstream may therefore lie above fish moving upstream, the reverse of the arrangement portrayed in Fig. 59.

LOSS OF VISUAL ORIENTATION

Loss of visual orientation could follow directly from a fall in light intensity at dusk, or if the fish left the sea bottom, or the rheocline, as a consequence of a vertical migration. In either case the effect is the same: the fish drifts with the current. A fish which has been orientating from bottom clues and heading upstream will now drift in the opposite direction, and the same will be true for a fish orientating against the current at the rheocline. But fish which were originally swimming downstream at the rheocline will continue in the same direction.

OTHER WAYS OF DETECTING WATER CURRENTS

If velocity gradients are very steep, orientation could be achieved by the simultaneous comparison of the intensity of stimulation of bilaterally arranged mechanoreceptors. This possibility was originally discussed by Lyon (1904, p. 157). Such a mechanism, a tropotaxis, could account for the orientation of fish in water currents close to the walls of tanks in the apparent absence of visual or tactile clues (Höglund, 1961, p. 72).

THE INTERACTION BETWEEN DRIFT AND ORIENTATED MOVEMENT

Reference has already been made to the possibility of an interaction between passive drift and orientated movement (p. 219). Visual orientation will usually be impossible at night and must fail if a vertical migration takes the fish away from the bottom or the rheocline. The occurrence of diurnal vertical migrations is well documented among migratory species (flatfish and gadoids,

Woodhead, 1965; herring, Blaxter and Holliday, 1963; salmon, Manzer, 1964; for a general review, see Woodhead, 1966) so there is a possibility of orientated movement during the day being followed by passive drift at night, the course and distance covered by the fish being an interaction of the two. Complications could also arise if the rheotactic response were modified, or reversed, by environmental factors, such as the temperature or chemical properties of the water.

The possibility of migration being achieved by transport in tidal currents provides an example. Creutzberg (1958, 1961) and Verwey (1958) credit G. P. H. van Heusden as being the first to develop the hypothesis that elvers could discriminate between ebb and flow, holding ground near the bottom against the ebb tide and drifting passively with the flood tide. Van Heusden thought that elvers used salinity differences to tell ebb from flood, but Creutzberg (1961) has now shown that an olfactory stimulus provides the clue.

WATER CURRENTS AS DIRECTIONAL CLUES TO MIGRANTS

The evidence that water currents provide directional clues to migrants must be examined critically. To determine the relation between the movements of the fish and those of the water, the speed and direction of both must be measured. It is important that the velocity of the current should be measured at the depth at which the fish are swimming. The measurement of current speed and direction raises problems of instrumentation. The depth of the fish can be determined by a suitable narrow beam echo-sounder, but this method may have to be supplemented by special traps or nets when the fish are very close to the surface. It is a more difficult problem to determine the speed and direction of movement of a fish in its natural environment. Under certain conditions critical information could be obtained from their capture in nets. Attempts have been made to follow individuals trailing a surface float (Hasler *et al.*, 1958; Winn *et al.*, 1964) or fitted with a sonic tag (Bass and Rascovich, 1965). Shoals have been tracked with conventional echo-sounding techniques (Harden Jones, 1962) or followed with sector scanning sonar (Harden Jones and McCartney, 1962; Cushing and Harden Jones, 1966). The results of all these experiments must be interpreted with care, as the observations may not be accurate enough to resolve the points at issue.

Salmon

Downstream migration. Among the Pacific salmon, pink and chum go down to the sea as fry, sockeye and coho as smolts. So far as sockeye smolts are concerned, a reasonable lake outflow is thought to be essential for successful migration, and the failure to rehabilitate certain barren lakes, for example the Horsefly on the Upper Fraser (Anon, 1960*b*, p. 17), has been attributed to a combination of factors (poor outflow, wind direction across or up-lake, and a sill across the outlet) adding up to a 'poor outlet attraction'. On the basis of certain laboratory experiments Hoar (1951, 1954) suggested that the downstream migration is essentially a passive displacement, the movement being accelerated at night when both visual and tactile clues were less efficient for orientation. Hoar's hypothesis seems very reasonable but has been criticized by Neave (1955) and Mackinnon and Brett (1955) as being inconsistent with field observation and experiment. Neave suggested that the downstream movement of pink salmon fry in Deltamen Creek (Queen Charlotte Islands) is an active migration and that a variety of unknown mechanical stimuli provide the fish with directional clues. But there is agreement on two points: firstly, that at night most of the migrants are very close to, and probably within 15 cm of, the surface; and secondly, in shallow water at least, the downstream movement is restricted to the hours between sunset and sunrise.

Hoar's hypothesis is the more economical of the two and should stand until it can be shown that the downstream movement of the migrants cannot be accounted for by passive displacement. For example, his hypothesis would be suspect, but not necessarily disproved, if the downstream movement of fry was faster than could be accounted for by passive displacement in the water in which they were swimming. Neave (1955) offers no evidence on this point. He did not measure the speed of the current or the speed of the fry. He reported (p. 372) that the fry which produced a bow-wave at the surface were swimming downstream faster than the current and noted that 'while these observations are insufficient to prove that all or even most of the fry were travelling downstream in this manner, no random or upstream swimming was observed'. Neave also quotes Pritchard's (1944a) earlier observations on pink fry at McClinton Creek. Pritchard (1944a, p. 223) wrote that 'the fry are not passively carried by the current out to sea but actually make a swift and vigorous migration. They may move downstream as quickly as 15 to 20 ft (4·6 to 6·1 m) per sec, the only indication of their presence being given by the wake behind them'. It is not clear from Pritchard's account whether the downstream movements of 4·6 to 6·1 m/sec are relative to the ground or to the water. The fry were 3·2 to 3·8 cm long (Pritchard, 1944a, p. 222) and if the speeds were relative to the water the fish were swimming 12 to 19 times their own length per second. The fry could not maintain this performance for more than a few seconds, and Pritchard's estimates may well have been ground speeds, fast currents being common in McClinton Creek.

Although the fact that some fry have been seen to move actively downstream does not disprove Hoar's hypothesis that the migration is essentially a passive displacement, both Pritchard's and Neave's observations suggest that some of the migrants might be orientated to head downstream.

However, it is possible that the downstream orientation is taken up passively. Northcote's (1962) careful observations on rainbow trout fry migrating downstream in the Loon Lake system are relevant. Downstream movement of fry at Inlet and Hihium Creeks takes place at night. Using an infrared viewing apparatus, Northcote watched fry crossing an aluminium strip placed across the bed of the stream. Fry were counted as heading downstream if they crossed the strip head first, however acute the angle of approach. More than 70% of the migrants came downstream head first. Prior to the evening downstream movement the fry gathered in narrow bands along the edges of the stream where they held their ground. Disturbance of these groups by other fry coming downstream was followed by an explosive reaction, fry scattering wildly out into midstream, 'whereupon they themselves headed downstream' (Northcote, 1962, p. 238). Northcote goes on to suggest (p. 265) that the majority of the disturbed fry may initially have headed downstream to avoid the intruders. This could account for part of the downstream orientation. But there must be a velocity gradient across the width of the stream and a fry striking out from the bank will be turned passively to face downstream so long as the head is in water moving faster than the tail. Dead spermatozoa behave in a very similar way in a parabolic velocity gradient (Bretherton and Rothschild, 1961). Northcote (p. 223) records that migrants which passed close to stones or wood in midstream which provided fixed reference points turned and swam against the current for a short time before continuing the movement downstream. This observation supports the hypothesis that the fish are not actively orientated with respect to the current when swimming with the current. If downstream migration is brought about by fry alternately holding-by-the-bank and 'swimming wildly into midstream', which is the picture that emerges from Northcote's account, the majority of the migrants should be heading, and swimming, downstream. Furthermore, if the ground gained per second in midstream was greater than that lost per second while holding station by the bank, the overall downstream movement would be greater than that which could be achieved by passive drift. But the mechanism of downstream migration would be essentially that of a passive displacement, as Hoar originally suggested.

There are two other papers to consider in connexion with the downstream migration of fry and smolts.

1. Mackinnon and Brett (1955). Salmon fry and floats were released late one evening in an impounded water basin on Vancouver Island, and the times of their arrival at the outlet recorded. The first fry reached the outlet 1·5 hr after release, and 10 hr before the first float. Commenting on the fact that the fry arrived earlier than the floats, Mackinnon and Brett (1955, p. 367) state that 'some bias must be operating to produce a net movement in the direction of the outlet. Fry must therefore be swimming during darkness at a greater rate than the current drift in a direction predominantly towards the outlet. It would appear that random movement enhanced by passive drifting does not satisfy the characteristics of migration through the impoundment.' But the conclusion that random movement fails to account for the facts does not seem to be justified. The distance between the release point and the outlet was approximately 300 m. The fastest float covered the ground in 11 hr, indicating a mean current of 0·075 cm/sec. The mean length of the pink fry released was 3·45 cm, and of those recovered on the first night, the fastest could have covered the 300 m in 90 min at an average speed of 5 cm/sec (1·5L/sec), the slowest in about 8 hr, at an average speed of about 1 cm/sec (0·3 L/sec). The point is that the speed to reach the outlet is well below their cruising speed of 2 to 3 L sec, so most of them could have reached the outlet by an indirect path. As only 14% of the pinks released reached the outlet on the first night, the results appear to be consistent with the hypothesis that the trap only caught those fish which arrived, by chance, in the immediate vicinity of the outlet before dawn.

2. Johnson and Groot (1963). Babine Lake is the main sockeye rearing area on the Skeena River, British Columbia. Johnson and Groot have studied the downstream migration of the smolts from the lake to Babine River. They maintain that the migration is a well-orientated, non-random movement, and that the possibility of current as a guiding mechanism can be eliminated. They suggest that migration to the outlet is facilitated by a form of celestial navigation. The evidence relating to the downstream migration of the smolts will be considered in detail, for it is clear that the case for celestial navigation partly depends on being able to show that there are no other means by which the fish could be guided, or carried, to the outlet.

Babine Lake and Morrison Lake, which empties into it, have been described by McMahon (1948) and Withler, McConnell, and McMahon (1949). Important place names are shown in Fig. 72. The lake is 93 miles long, and lies in a north-westerly direction parallel to the Babine mountains on its western shore. There is a water discharge gauge at Fort Babine and a water height gauge at Topley Landing (Anon, 1963). The nearest weather station is at Smithers, 50 miles away beyond the Babine mountains. The winds tend to blow along the long axis of the lake.

Downstream movement of the smolts. Smolts leave the lake in May and June. Migrants (their length is not given) were tagged at Sandpit, Morrison River, and Halifax Narrows. Those tagged at Sandpit were recovered at Halifax Narrows and Nilkitkwa Outlet; those tagged at Morrison River were recovered at Halifax Narrows and Nilkitkwa Outlet; and those tagged at the Narrows were recovered only at Nilkitkwa Outlet. The speeds of travel calculated from the recapture of smolts at Nilkitkwa Outlet are given in Johnson and Groot's (1963) Fig. 4. In 1961 they increased from 3 miles a day in May to 6 miles a day in June.

Water currents. No measurements are given of the speed and direction of the water currents at the depths at which the migrants were swimming. Only two references are made to water currents in the body of the paper. The first, on p. 924, claims that the increase in migration speed observed in June cannot be fully accounted for by an increase in water discharge rate. The data and calculations on which this claim is based are not given. The second reference, on p. 928, summarizes the reasons why water currents appear to be eliminated as a guiding mechanism. The passage will be quoted in full. '(1). We have made numerous simultaneous observations on the direction of the near-surface migration activity and near-surface currents and no relationship is shown; active migration on

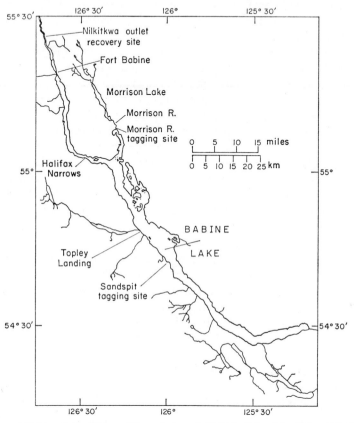

Fig. 72. Place names at Babine Lake (Skeena River drainage), British Columbia. (After Withler *et al.*, 1949, and Johnson and Groot, 1963.)

the route leading to the outlet persists irrespective of current direction (Fig. 7), (2) there simply is no direct current throughout the lake oriented with respect to the outlet, (3) as pointed out by Hasler (1960) and Verwey (1958), current as a guiding mechanism can likely be eliminated *a priori* for pelagic, near surface fish.' Johnson and Groot may be right in concluding that water currents cannot guide, or carry, migrants to the outlet, but they provide no data to substantiate their second point, while Fig. 7, the only evidence for (1), has several shortcomings. For example, no indication is given as to how the direction of the near-surface currents were measured, or of their direction and velocity in relation to depth and bottom topography. As there is no scale it is difficult to know what significance should be attached to differences between the direction of the current and that of the near-surface schools of sockeye.

The case for passive displacement. The account given of the water currents in the lake is not satisfactory. It is implied that there is no appreciable or consistent flow between Halifax Narrows and Fort Babine, where the discharge rises from 2,500 cubic feet per second in early May to between 5,000 and 6,000 cubic feet per second in June (Anon, 1963). Johnson and Groot (1963) have not shown that the fish tagged at Halifax Narrows and recaptured at Nilkitkwa Outlet cover the 27 miles at a speed inconsistent with passive displacement in the fastest water available. Similar criticisms can be made with regard to the Morrison River and Sandpit smolts recovered at the Narrows. The discharge current between Sandpit and the Narrows may be slow, but no measurements are given. Although reference is made to Johnson's (1961) earlier observations on the passive displacement of sockeye in the lake by wind-driven currents, the same mechanism is not considered for the migration of the downstream smolts.

The Sandpit release site is 36 miles up-lake from the Narrows. Forty smolts tagged at Sandpit were recovered at the Narrows, but their average speed of travel is not recorded. A figure of 4 to 4·5 miles a day seems a reasonable estimate. Let us consider a smolt which drifts with the water and lies close to the surface for 8 hr during the night and lies at an average depth of 5 m for the rest of the day. Stevenson (1958) has summarized the data on the relation between water current velocity and wind speed. The surface 15 cm moves downwind at a velocity equal to 2·5% of the wind speed. The deeper water moves slower, and at 5 m the water will move at 1·25% of the wind speed. Our smolt would therefore drift downstream at a mean velocity equal to $(8 \times 2·5) + (16 \times 1·25)/24 = 1·66\%$ of the wind speed. To cover 4 to 5 miles a day by passive drift from Sandpit to the Narrows would require a downlake wind of 10 to 11 mph.

No wind data have been published which refer to conditions over Babine during the period when the smolts are leaving the lake. The nearest weather station is at Smithers, to the west of the Babine range, and the conditions here are no real guide to those on the lake. However, some unpublished data are available from a site near the lake outlet and Dr. P. A. Larkin (Director, Biological Laboratory, Nanaimo) has allowed me to see the data for 1962 and 1963. The wind speed and direction as measured at Nilkitkwa Outlet give no support to my hypothesis: on the contrary, the measurements suggest that the winds blow up, rather than down, the axis of the lake. Measurements at stations on the lake itself would settle the matter.

Migration on the high seas. It has been suggested that the movements of salmon from the high seas to the coastal areas could be accounted for by passive drift (p. 202). A weakness of the drift hypothesis brought out in Fig. 66, p. 209, and stressed by Neave (1964, p. 1239), is that the velocity of the currents may be inadequate to account for the rate of travel. The migration could be accounted for if the fish were swimming in the direction of the current. Neave (1964, p. 1240) is not prepared to accept that the current would provide a directional clue in the absence of fixed reference points, but this argument is no longer valid if orientation takes place at the rheocline. If 50 to 75 cm salmon cruise with the current at only twice their own length per second for 14 hr/day they would cover 28 to 42 naut. mile/day, to which up to 1 to 10 naut. mile/day would be added by the current. This would give a ground speed of more than the 25 to 30 naut. mile/day commonly observed (Neave, 1964, p. 1241), and would account for the fastest fish in Fig. 66. As a cruising speed of 2 fish lengths per second is an under-estimate rather than an over-estimate, the migrants would have some time in hand for feeding.

Neave (1964, p. 1240) has a further objection. 'If orientation *could* be effected it would still be necessary to explain how the fish could determine the places or times at which changes in orientation would be needed to maintain an appropriate direction of travel.' A possible explanation is that migrants swim in the same direction as the gyral but at a faster speed, and only leave the system when they reach coastal water which contains an olfactory clue to which they have been previously conditioned, or which they recognize innately. The salmon then proceed by the use of local land-marks. Fish which do not reach a known or recognizable coastal water are lost at sea. But the problem of timing is a real one for which an explanation has already been suggested in connexion with passive drift (p. 204): the fish which have furthest to travel start first, and the first arrivals in the coastal waters wait for latecomers in assembly areas before moving towards the parent river in a body.

These arguments would appear to meet Neave's objections to the suggestion that currents could provide directional clues to migrating salmon on the high seas. But there is no direct evidence to show that the hypothesis is true. Critical evidence, one way or the other, must await observations on the movements of salmon in relation to those of the water currents at the depths at which they are swimming.

Spawning migration of Arcto-Norwegian cod

Cod tagged in summer near Bear Island are recovered on their spawning grounds at Lofoten in the following year. Trout (1957) suggested that water currents provide the directional clue to the migrating fish. According to his hypothesis, the cod move into the deeper water to the west of the Bear Island Bank during November–December and swim southwards against the north-going West Spitsbergen current. To reach the Norwegian coastal grounds (Tromsö Plateau, Tromsö Bank, Fuglöy Grounds) the cod must move at least 180 miles from 74°N. to 71°N., and cross the deep water of the Bear Island Channel. It is not known when the cod start to move south of 74°N., but inspection of the data filed at the Fisheries Laboratory, Lowestoft shows that the first Norway coast returns of Bear Island tagged fish are made in early January, so the cod probably cross the Bear Island Channel in December. In these high latitudes the sun is always below the horizon at this time of the year (see Table 27). During the latter part of November and throughout December the noon surface illumination between 74° and 68°N. never exceeds 10 mc and the surface illumination throughout most the day is more than 5 orders of magnitude lower (Anon, 1952b, Plate 38). It is unlikely that there can be sufficient light for visual orientation to currents near the bottom at depths down to 460 m in the Bear Island Channel. Trout (1957) suggests that orientation is maintained by tactile clues, the fish hugging the bottom as they move south.

Table 27. Dates of last sunset and first sunrise at different latitudes. (Data from a Nautical Almanac.)

Latitude	Date of last sunset	Date of next sunrise
74°	11 November	1 February
72°	18 November	25 January
70°	27 November	16 January
68°	9 December	4 January

Inshore migration of elvers

The leptocephali larvae of the European eel appear to reach the continental shelf by passive drift in the surface layers of the Atlantic and the drift continues in the direction of the residual current during the period of metamorphosis. When the elvers are close inshore they move into freshwater by a combination of passive drift and orientated movement. The elvers are carried in on the flood tide, but on the ebb they burrow into the bottom or swim against the tide, so that they are not borne back towards the sea. Creutzberg (1961) has shown that the elvers are able to discriminate between ebb and flood tide because they can detect a chemical substance in the ebb water which appears to be characteristic of inland water. Creutzberg (1961, p. 333) suggests that this chemical substance may be of a widespread occurrence in inland waters, from Hammerfest to Casablanca, and that elvers may be attracted to rivers and streams wherever they strike the coast. It seems unlikely that the chemical substance can be one to which the eels have been conditioned, and the recognition of the chemical is therefore probably innate. So the young eel appears to reach its feeding area, freshwater, by a behavioural mechanism dependent on the innate recognition of a chemical clue.

The mechanism invites comparison with that suggested by Kleerekoper and Mogensen (1963) for the sea lamprey, which appears to use a chemical clue to locate its prey. Newly metamorphosed ammocoetes appear to show an innate response, increased locomotory activity, when stimulated with water in which trout have been living. The chemical clue has been provisionally identified as an amino acid which appears to act as an attractant to a number of predators (Kleerekoper, 1963).

Herring in the Southern Bight of the North Sea

Pacific herring are caught in purse seines in Swanson Channel on the south-east coast of Vancouver Island, British Columbia. The fishing season lasts for about two months, from the middle of October through to the middle of December. The herring are full mature fish on their way to the spawning grounds further round the coast. The catch-per-effort in the Swanson Channel fishery is greatest when the tidal range is low (neap tides, moon in first and third quarters) and lowest when the tidal range is high (spring tides, new and full moon). Tester (1938b) suggested that the changes in catch-per-effort reflect changes in the abundance of herring in the Channel, fish coming in from the open sea through the Juan de Fuca Strait. Herring have been tagged at Sooke, outside the Strait, and in 1937 relatively more of these fish were taken in Swanson Channel when the catch-per-effort was high. Tester (1938b, p. 13) put forward the following hypothesis to account for the facts: 'In moving from the Strait of Juan de Fuca to Swanson channel, even though the fish may be travelling under their own power at a certain speed, they will be carried forward and backward with the tide. In following their migration route they pass from an area where one type of tidal fluctuation occurs to an area where an entirely different type is present. It may be that in some way the change induces a bunching of the fish so that more arrive at Swanson channel during one tidal cycle than during another. Or perhaps, for some reason, the fish move towards Swanson channel only during particular tidal series.'

It is possible that the spawning migrations of other herring stocks might be related to tidal movements, and, prompted by Tester's suggestions, I have considered the migration of herring in the Southern Bight of the North Sea from this aspect (Harden Jones, 1965). During October and November Downs herring move through the Southern Bight to their spawning grounds in the Channel. I have suggested that the herring stem the tide, and gain ground against it during the day, but drift at night, the overall movement to the south being the resultant of the interaction between orientated movement and passive drift. If the migration was carried out in this way, its success must depend on a seasonal relationship between the lunar cycle and day length, as it is not suggested that the herring can discriminate between the north-going ebb and the south-going flood tide. The mechanism has been analysed with the help of a simple model (Harden Jones, 1965) in the following way.

1. A 25 cm herring starts at a position 53°N. 27·5′N., 2° 46·0′E. (Admiralty Tidal Station B 12) to the east of the Indefatigable Banks at sunset on 1 October 1961 (see Fig. 73).

2. The times of sunset and sunrise are those given in a nautical almanac for the appropriate day.

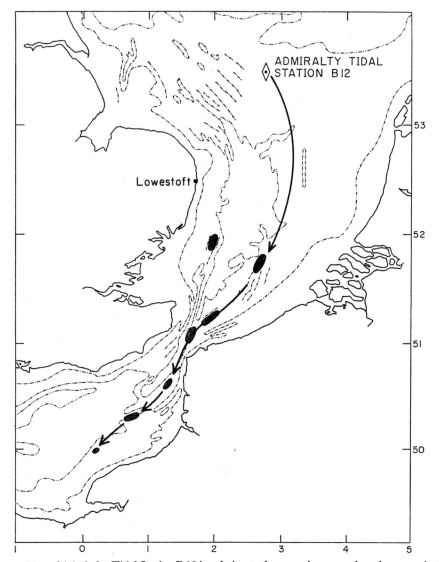

Fig. 73. The position of Admiralty Tidal Station B 12 in relation to the spawning grounds and supposed migration route of the Downs herring. (Outline and details from an Admiralty chart.)

3. Between sunset and sunrise it is assumed that the herring loses tactile and visual contact with the bottom and drifts passively with the tidal stream.

4. Between sunrise and sunset the herring regains tactile or visual contact with the bottom, orientates to face upstream and swims against the tide at a speed 1·4 times that of the current. The

multiplier 1·4 is based on laboratory experiments (Harden Jones, 1963) relating the swimming speed of small herring to that of a moving background simulating the optical stimuli produced by a water current. The average tidal current in the surface waters at Station B 12 is about 1·5 knots (75 cm/sec). Profiles in the Southern Bight have shown that the water current 5 m from the bottom is approximately two-thirds of the surface speed, giving, at B 12, a speed of 1 knot (50 cm/sec),

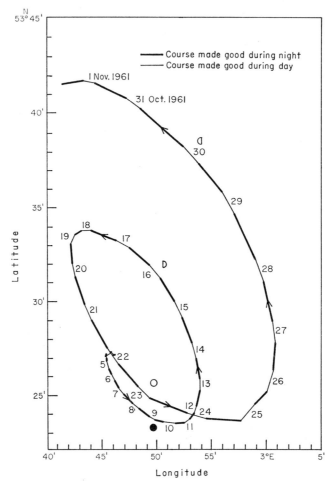

Fig. 74. Herring migration model. The noon positions (alongside date numerals) of a fish leaving Station B 12 at sunset on 1 October 1961. Phases of the moon are indicated.

equivalent to 2 fish lengths per second for the 25 cm fish in the model. The laboratory experiments showed that herring gained ground by a factor of 1·4 at background speeds equivalent to a water current of 2 fish lengths per second.

The results of the model are shown in Fig. 74, where the noon positions of the fish are shown from 2 October to 1 November 1961. Inspection of this figure shows that there are two periods when the fish makes ground to the south, between 4 and 10 October and 19 and 24 October, the periods of the new and full moon and the spring tides.

The semi-lunar periodicity in the south-going movement suggests that if a fish arrives at Station B 12 on certain days it might get into a 'tidal-fishway' and make rapid progress southwards. Figure 75 shows the noon position on 25 October of fish that left Station B 12 at sunset each day from 1 to 24 October inclusive. This figure was derived from Fig. 75 in the following way. The course and distance made good between any day from 1 to 24 October and 25 October was given by the line joining the sunset position on the first day to the noon position on the 25 October. The course and distance run were then transferred to B 12. It is clear that fish that arrive at B 12 between 15 and 21 October move rapidly southwards if they drift passively with the tide by night

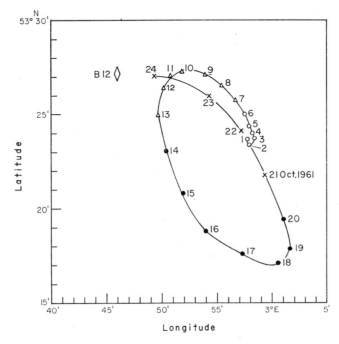

Fig. 75. Herring migration model. Fig. 74 showed that the fish made ground to the south between 4–10 October and 19–24 October. This figure shows the noon position on 25 October of fish that left Station B 12 at sunset each day from 1–24 October inclusive.

and swim against it by day. The model does provide a mechanism for a south-going migration based on assumptions that are consistent with our knowledge of the behaviour of the fish.

There is no direct evidence to substantiate the hypothesis that herring move down the Southern Bight in this way. So far as indirect evidence goes, a preliminary attempt has been made to simulate the behaviour of a herring shoal with a parachute drogue. The drogue is rigged as shown in Fig.76, and its movement is determined by the water current at the depth of the parachute, the effect of wind on the surface pole and radar reflector being almost negligible. The experiment was carried out in the following way. The drogue was released at sunrise and allowed to drift, its position being noted at regular intervals by the attendant research vessel. Half an hour before sunset the drogue was recovered and released as soon as possible at a new position on the opposite course to its overall drift between sunrise and sunset, and at a distance 1·4 times that covered by the drogue during the day. Thus the drogue was made to simulate the movement of a herring shoal swimming against the tide, at a speed 1·4 times its velocity, between sunrise and sunset. The drogue drifted during the night, its position at sunrise being noted so that it could be recovered and released again in the appropriate position the following sunset. My colleague, Mr. A. C. Burd, released the drogue near Admiralty Station B 12 at sunrise on 17 October 1964 and followed this procedure until sunrise on 20 October. During the 72-hour period the artificial shoal had moved 5 miles south. Further studies with parachute drogues are to be made over longer periods.

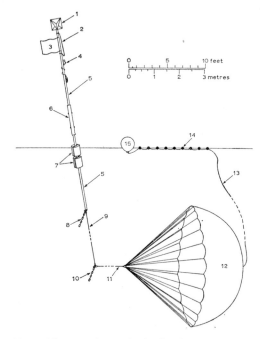

Fig. 76. Parachute drogue used in tracking experiments in the Southern Bight. The parachute is not drawn to scale and the type used has a diameter of 3·7 m.

KEY

1 radar reflector; 2 lifting strop; 3 flag; 4 photocell-actuated flashing-light; 5 alloy poles; 6 junction between the two poles; 7 floats; 8 chain; 9 wire; 10 chain; 11 wire to parachute; 12 parachute; 13 buoyant recovery line; 14 small floats; 15 buff.

Plaice in the southern North Sea

The Dutch tagging experiments (p. 173) have shown that plaice probably return to spawn on the ground where they previously spawned. Recoveries of fish tagged on the three main spawnng grounds—at Flamborough, and in the German and Southern Bights—show that the spawning ground itself is in the southern part of the area over which the returns from each ground are distributed (de Veen, 1962), and that there is relatively little mixing between the groups during the summer feeding seasons. The spawning migrations are essentially movements from north to south. While the migration is upstream and against the residual current for some of the German Bight and many of the Southern Bight spawners, it would appear to be downstream for most of the Flamborough spawners. de Veen (1961) has analysed the summer and autumn recoveries of spawners tagged in German and Southern Bights and has shown that the older and younger fish feed in different areas of the southern North Sea. For the German Bight fish, small males dispersed in all directions, the medium-sized males had a preference towards the Danish coast, and the large males went towards the Dogger Bank. From the Southern Bight the larger fish went to the Silver Pit-Leman Bank area, and to the Oyster Ground, while the smaller fish tagged later in the season went to the Oyster Ground only. So even within each of these two groups there appears to be a difference in the direction of the spawning migrations, the younger fish moving S. to SW., the older fish moving SE. to E. It is difficult to reconcile these differences with any simple contranatant hypothesis of migration. If the currents do provide directional clues to the migrants, it is very likely that there is an interaction between drift and orientated movement similar to that suggested for the Downs herring. Plaice are known to leave the bottom at night (Woodhead, 1966) when they probably drift passively with the tide. If they are on the bottom during the day, orientation to the tidal current could be facilitated through contact or the flow of water over the skin. Large plaice could be suitable fish to track with sonic tags, and useful information could be obtained if the tag could relay, by a change in repetition rate, the depth of the fish. Accurate information as to the depth of the fish would not be needed: it would probably be sufficient to know if it was on or off the bottom.

TRANSVERSE ORIENTATIONS

Orientation by day: the sun-compass reaction

Laboratory work

Tåning (1934*a*, p. 7) suggested that migrating plaice might use the sun as a directional clue, but considered that the results of the East Icelandic tagging experiments gave no support to the hypothesis. Interest in the possible use of the sun as a directional clue by migrants has been revived by the results of laboratory experiments carried out by Hasler and his colleagues. The type experiment carried out on a 70 mm bluegill, *Lepomis gibbosus*, is described by Hasler *et al.* (1958), Braemer (1960), and Hasler (1960). Tests with this single fish showed that it could be trained, under the open sky, to take refuge in the northerly compartments of a radially divided tank. Correct choices were not made under overcast conditions. When the fish was taken indoors and tested with a fixed artificial sun, it selected different hiding boxes in the morning and afternoon, the angle between the chosen compartment and the artificial sun being similar to that between the northerly compartment and the real sun at that time of day. The more extensive laboratory experiments reported by Braemer (1959) involved training at different times of the day, and alterations in the light/dark regime to upset the fish's chronometer which produced predictable changes in the azimuth bearing of the selected compartment. All these experiments lead to the conclusion that certain fish can use the sun as a reference point and are able to correct for its change in azimuth during the day. Further work has shown the correction for the change in azimuth of the sun is dependent on the day length or photoperiod (Schwassmann and Braemer, 1961) and sun altitude itself (Schwassmann and Hasler, 1964). Hasler (1966) summarizes the results to date.

If the sun-compass reaction is used by migrants to keep on course, a fish must be able to determine the bearing of the sun in azimuth at the depth at which it is swimming. Furthermore, it may have to determine the altitude of the sun if this parameter plays an important role in the compensatory mechanism.

The sun underwater

REFLECTION, REFRACTION, AND THE SNELL CIRCLE

When a ray from the sun strikes a smooth water surface part is reflected and the remainder refracted. Sunlight passing through the surface is refracted downwards towards the normal, in accordance with Snell's Law, so that the angle of the refracted ray to the vertical is always less than that of the incident ray, except when the sun is at the zenith. With this exception, the sun will always appear at a higher elevation under water than above water. The percentage of incident light from the sun that is reflected, the angle of refraction, and apparent altitude of the sun under water, are set out in Table 28 for different angles of incidence.

Table 28. Percentage of sunlight reflected at the surface (from Ångström, 1925, p. 337, Fig. 5), angle of refraction and apparent altitude of the sun underwater at different angles of incidence to the surface.

Angle of incidence	Altitude of the sun	Percentage of sunlight reflected at the surface	Angle of refraction	Apparent altitude of the sun underwater
0	90	2·0	0·0	90·0
10	80	2·0	7·0	83·0
20	70	2·1	15·0	75·0
30	60	2·1	22·0	68·0
40	50	2·5	29·0	61·0
50	40	3·5	35·0	55·0
60	30	6·0	40·5	49·5
70	20	13·4	44·5	45·5
80	10	35·0	47·5	42·5
85	5	62·0	48·0	42·0
90	0	100·0	48·5	41·5

Surface refraction restricts the fish's view of the sky to a manhole subtended by an angle of 48·5° from the vertical, and on underwater lines of sight outside the critical angle with the surface the fish cannot obtain a direct view of the sun. The surface of the sea acts as a wide-angle lens so that the whole vault of the sky is contained within the manhole, which is sometimes called the Snell Circle. At the edge of the manhole there is considerable compression and distortion of objects near the horizon, as can be seen in the photographs taken by Wood (1906, 1934) with a special camera designed to simulate the fish's view of the world above the water.

THE SUN'S DISC UNDERWATER

At low sun altitudes the sun's disc will appear as a glitter patch close to the periphery of the manhole, lying about a particular bearing in azimuth. At higher altitudes the glitter patch will move towards the centre of the manhole. But the actual disc of the sun will only be visible within a few metres of the surface, say 5 to 10 m, and then only under the best conditions.

The accuracy with which fish can position the disc of the sun is not known, but Leibowitz, Myers, and Grant (1955) have shown that man can localize the position of a luminescent disc subtending an arc of 35′, similar to the sun, to within 4 to 6°, over a wide range of intensity, provided the disc is bright enough to be seen. A fish can probably do just as well and, when within a few metres of the surface, should be able to position the sun to 6° in azimuth and 6° in apparent altitude.

But a fish would not be able to resolve real altitudes within the range of 0 to 25°, which will be seen as apparent altitudes of 41·5° to 47·5° under water.

RADIANCE DISTRIBUTION AND POLARIZATION PATTERNS

When the fish is more than 5 to 10 m below the surface, the position of the sun must usually be determined from the radiance distribution, the bearing of the bright patch giving the position in azimuth, and the elevation of the bright patch giving the apparent altitude. The position of the sun could also be determined from the underwater polarization patterns. Submarine illumination is partially polarized, one component originating in the sky and being restricted to the Snell Circle. This component is only visible close to the surface (Waterman, 1954), while the second and major component originates in the water itself and is visible in all directions at depths greater than a few metres. Waterman found that both the proportion and plane of polarization of submarine light varied with the position of the sun and the line of sight. The position of the sun could therefore be determined by a fish in two ways: by the radiance distribution or by the polarization pattern.

The radiance distribution

Sun altitude and azimuth bearing. At a fixed depth the distribution of the light with azimuth angle in the horizontal plane varies with the altitude of the sun. Tyler (1961) gives a clear account of the phenomena. The underwater horizontal light vector diagrams should approach symmetry about the vertical axis when the sun is just below the horizon, or at its zenith at local noon. Between these two extremes the vector diagram stretches into a pseudo-ellipse, with a maximum distortion at an intermediate sun altitude. These changes can be followed in the series of light measurements made by Sasaki *et al.* (1958, p. 51, Fig. 8), and suggest that the bearing of the sun in azimuth could be most easily determined by a fish during the mid morning and mid-afternoon, and that the most difficult periods would be at dawn, noon, and dusk.

Azimuth bearing, sun altitude and depth. The direction of the 'bright' spot in the underwater light field moves towards the zenith with an increase in depth, and the radiance distribution approaches a characteristic shape which is symmetrical about the vertical and horizontal axes. The subject is fully discussed by Tyler (1960) and Tyler and Preisendorfer (1964), and it has been shown that the final shape of the radiance distribution depends only on the optical properties of the hydrosol, that is the volume scattering function and absorption coefficient. Inspection of Tyler's (1960) Tables 4 to 10 shows that the maximum of the vertical light vector diagram in line with the sun approaches the zenith with an increase in depth. So the apparent altitude of the sun will increase as the fish swims deeper and there will be a corresponding decrease in the information that the radiance distribution can give about the sun's bearing in azimuth. A fish which uses the sun as a reference for a light-compass reaction must swim at a depth where the sun's bearing in azimuth can be determined; and if the sun's apparent altitude is important to the compensatory mechanism, the fish must stay at the same depth, or be able to correct for the change in the apparent altitude with depth.

Bearing discrimination. The use that a fish can make of the sun as a reference point must be partly determined by its ability to detect and locate the bright patch within the radiance distribution, and it would be of interest to know to what depth this can be done. The sensory problem is one of intensity discrimination but suitable data relating to fish do not appear to be available. For the human eye, a plot of $\Delta i/i$ against i, where Δi is the just noticeable intensity difference observed at different values of the intensity i, gives thresholds of 5% at 1 mc, 10% at 0·1 mc, 20% at 0·01 mc and 45% at 0·001 mc (Wright, 1938, p. 14, Fig. 8). If it is assumed that the fish eye has an equal performance and that the bearing of the sun in azimuth must be located to within $\pm 20°$, estimates can be made of the depth at which a fish could use the sun as a reference point, in Lake Pend Oreille (on the Columbia River, numbered 8 in Fig. 9, p. 46), where Tyler (1960) made his radiance distribution measurements. On a clear spring day the vertical light intensity on the water surface will be about 10^4 mc. Inspection of Tyler's Tables 4 to 10 suggests that the numerical values given for the radiance distributions are, to an order of magnitude, equivalent to 10 times the light intensity in mc (Table 4 gives a zenith radiance of 204,000 at 4 m). So for the purposes of intensity discrimination, the intensity to which the fish is adapted can be taken as equal to the radiance $\times 10^{-1}$ in metre candles. From Tyler's Table 8, depth 41·3 m, it can be seen that the fish would be unable to locate the sun to within $\pm 20°$ in the horizontal line of sight, as the difference between the 0 and 20° azimuth readings, 51·3 and 50·4, amounts to only 1·8%, below the threshold of 5% required at 5 mc. But the fish could locate the sun within the required limits by looking upwards along lines of sight corresponding to angles of tilt less than 70° and more than about 10°. Inspection of Tyler's Table 9, 53·7 m, shows that the differences between the radiance values at 0 and 20° azimuth angles are always less than those that could be discriminated by the fish at equivalent levels of intensity. So for this lake 54 m would appear to be the limiting depth for the use of the sun as an azimuth reference.

In Lake Pend Oreille the zenith radiance decreased by 3 log units from 204,000 at 4·3 m to 202 at 53·7 m. As the decrease in light intensity is affected by the same physical properties of the water as those which even out the radiance distribution, the limiting depth at which a fish can locate the sun to within $\pm 20°$ of its azimuth bearing corresponds to the depth at which the light is reduced by 3 to 4 log units to 0·01–0·1% of the sub-surface intensity. This is below the photic zone whose bottom level is at a depth where the light is reduced by 2 log units to 1% of the sub-surface intensity. Clarke (1936) lists the thickness of the layer causing a reduction in light intensity of one log unit for several types of water. In the Sargasso Sea, where a reduction of 1 log unit takes place over 43 m, the limiting depth for using the sun as a reference point would appear to lie between 129 and 172 m. This water is exceptionally clear. Other limiting depths would be 23 to 30 m off Woods Hole, 33 to 44 m in Crystal Lake, Wisconsin, 2 to 12 m in L. Mendota (Birge and Juday, 1929), and, using Pearsall and Ullyott's (1934) data, 10 to 13 m in Windermere, English Lake District.

Altitude discrimination. The apparent altitude of the sun will correspond to the elevation of the line of sight coinciding with the bright patch in the radiance distribution. A horizontal reference seems essential but this need not take the form of a real or artificial horizon: it may be sufficient for the head to be kept level and that there should be provision for interaction between labyrinth and visual stimuli within the central nervous system. The apparent altitude of the sun underwater will vary from 41·5° at dawn and dusk to nearly 90° at noon. For the fish the problem is one of intensity discrimination, as was the case in determining the bearing of the sun in azimuth. Tyler's radiance distributions were measured with a Gershun tube with an angular field of 6·6°, measurements in the vertical plane being taken at 10° intervals of tilt. The vertical radiance distributions are therefore somewhat smoothed, and the distribution seen by the fish may be more clearly defined than that given by the photometer. Inspection of Tyler's data suggests that a fish in Lake Pend Oreille should be able to position the apparent altitude of the sun to within 10° at a depth of 53·7 to 66·1 m, this depth being a little below that at which it could determine the sun's bearing in azimuth. As it is unlikely that the fish will be able to determine the apparent altitude of the sun from the bright patch of the radiance distribution with an accuracy greater than the nearest 10°, true altitudes between 0° and 30° will not be resolved underwater.

Polarization patterns

It is not known if fish can detect and orientate to naturally occurring polarized light. But if they could, Waterman and Westell's (1956) work has shown that both the azimuth bearing and apparent altitude of the sun could be determined from the underwater polarization planes and, though with less reliability, from the proportion of polarized light present. However, the linear polarization of submarine light appears to be largely dependent on the scattering of directional radiant energy, and when the radiance distribution is symmetrical about the vertical axis the polarization pattern is similarly uniform. As Waterman (1961, p. 107) points out, it is possible that the polarization pattern could provide a better indicator of the sun's azimuth and altitude than the direct use of the radiance distribution. The point can only be resolved by experimental work.

To summarize: when the surface is smooth and the water clear fish within 5 to 10 m of the surface should be able to see and position the disc of the sun to within 6° in azimuth and 6° in apparent altitude. In deeper water the position of the sun must be determined from the radiance distribution. It is unlikely that a fish could use the sun as a reference point for a light-compass reaction at depths where the radiance is reduced by more than 3 to 4 log units (to $0 \cdot 1$–$0 \cdot 01 \%$) of the sub-surface intensity.

Field evidence for the sun-compass reaction

HOMING OF WHITE BASS (*Roccus chrysops*) IN LAKE MENDOTA

The white bass has two major spawning grounds in Lake Mendota, Maple Bluff and Governor's Island (see Fig. 80, p. 250). Fish captured on the spawning grounds and tagged and released in the middle of the lake are recaptured on the home ground. Hasler *et al.* (1958) tried to follow their tracks by attaching a small float to the fish with a nylon line, and plotting the range and bearing of the floats an hour after release. Fifty-five fish were tracked from a mid-lake release station on clear days. For comparison 3 fish were released on overcast days and a further 12 fish were fitted with plastic opaque eye caps. The results (Hasler *et al.*, 1958, p. 356, Figs. 3–6) are said to show that the fish released in mid-lake on clear days 'moved generally north, towards the spawning grounds'. A polar plot of the original data shows that this is not really true. As can be seen from Fig. 77, only 21 out of the 55 fish (38%) moved off in the quadrant embracing the home sector. Correcting the movements for drift in the currents improved the proportion to 49% (23 out of 47 fish). However, the basis on which the correction for drift was made is not stated, and no reason is given for excluding 7 fish in the drift-corrected data. Haslet *et al.* (1958, p. 358) state that the result of these experiments 'suggests that the white bass possess a sun-compass mechanism which is used for orientation in the open water'. But in the absence of details for the drift correction, and the inadequacy of the controls (transparent eye caps must be tested against opaque eye caps before the results with the latter can be accepted), the results are not convincing.

MOVEMENTS OF SALMON SMOLTS IN BABINE LAKE

Johnson and Groot (1963) have suggested that sockeye salmon smolts make use of celestial clues for orientation when they leave Babine Lake, British Columbia. Celestial orientation was considered because other means (drift, response to water currents, use of topographic clues) were thought to be inadequate to enable the migrants to reach the outlet. Groot (1965) observed the orientation of individual migrants in small (usually 30 cm diameter) circular tanks, and noted the frequency with which a smolt headed into any one of the eight 45° sectors into which the tank was divided for recording purposes. The method was similar to that used in studies on birds, the Kramer orientation cage having been modified into a Groot orientation tank. No precautions appear to have been taken to guard against experimenter bias (see Rosenthal, 1963; Rosenthal and Fode, 1963).

Groot's experiments with the Morrison Lake smolts are particularly interesting, the preferred direction taken up in the orientation tank shifting from SE. to NW. over the period of down lake

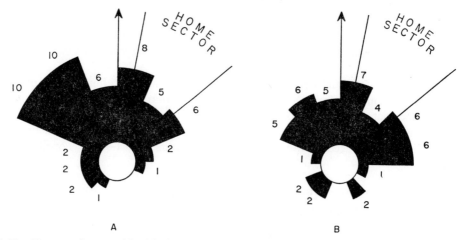

Fig. 77. Tracking experiments with white bass (*Roccus chrysops*) in Lake Mendota. Hasler *et al.* (1958) took fish from their spawning grounds at Maple Bluff and Governor's Island and released them at a position near the middle of the lake (see Fig. 80). The data relating to take-off direction (derived from range and bearing one hour after release) has been replotted from Figs. 3 and 4 in Hasler *et al.* (1958). A, without correction for drift; B, with correction for drift. The numbers refer to the fish within each 22·5° sector. The 'home sector' is also indicated.

migration. This is the very change in direction that the Morrison arm smolts would have to make to reach Halifax Narrows and the Babine outlet at Nilkitkwa (see Fig. 72, p. 227). Groot argues that these and other results support the hypothesis that celestial clues are used by migrants on their way to the lake outlet.

The next stage in this work must be to relate the tank observations to the movements of the smolts observed in the lake itself. A first step in this direction has been taken by Groot and Wiley (1965), who have carried out trials with a mechanically scanned sonar to track migrants in Babine Lake. The results of this work must be awaited with interest.

ORIENTATION EXPERIMENTS WITH PARROT FISH IN BERMUDA

In Bermuda parrot fish (*Scarus guacamaia* and *S. coelestinus*) feed during the day along the shore and in bays, and return at night to off shore caves. They are said to keep to the same caves and feeding areas for several months and Winn, Salmon, and Roberts (1964) have tried to determine what clues the fish use when moving between the two sites. Adult fish were caught on their feeding grounds along the south shore of the eastern half of Main Island and released elsewhere off the north or south shore. The adult fish were 48 to 71 cm long. No fish were released where they were caught. They could be followed from the surface by tracking small balloons attached near the dorsal fin by a nylon line. A battery and small bulb were attached to the float to facilitate tracking at night. In some experiments the fish were followed for distances up to 240 m, but ranges of 120 m were more usual. The depth of water is not explicity stated in the paper, but probably varied between

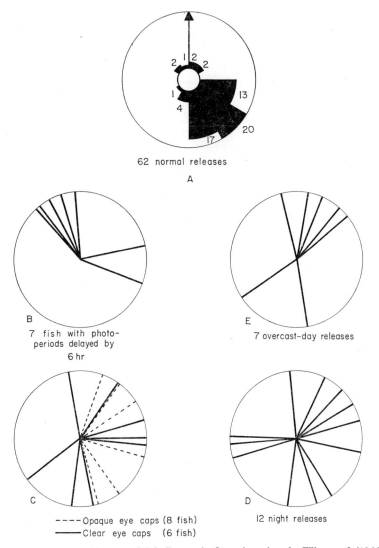

Fig. 78. Orientation experiments with parrot fish in Bermuda, from data given by Winn *et al.* (1964). The diagrams show the mean direction in which fish swam after being caught on their feeding grounds and released elsewhere.

3 and 7·5 m. Releases with adult fish were carried out during the day in sunny and overcast conditions, and at night. Some fish were fitted with open or opaque eye caps. One group was kept under artificial light for 9 to 10 days before release with a light/dark regime delaying the fish's photoperiod by 6 hr with respect to local time.

The results are summarized in Fig. 78. Of the 62 adult fish released when the sun was visible, the majority swam away towards the south-east, 135° (Fig. 78A). Five of the 7 fish whose photoperiods were delayed by 6 hr swam NNW., 336° (Fig. 78B). The difference (336° − 135° = 201°) is more than the angle of 165° through which the sun moved in azimuth during the 6 hr between 0900 and the fish's release at 1500 hr. The experiments with opaque and open eye caps (Fig. 78C) were few in number and give no clear picture. Fish released at night (Fig. 78D) spread out on release, while 5 out of the 7 released during the day, when cloud cover was complete, moved about the bearing NNE., 23°, (Fig. 78E).

The results with the fish whose photoperiods were delayed by six hours suggest that some compensatory mechanism was disturbed and leads to the conclusion that both these and the normal fish were orientating to the sun. These results are, to date, the most convincing evidence that fish make use of a sun-compass mechanism in their natural environment. But of no less interest are the results obtained with the fish released under complete cloud cover, most of which moved NNE. The tracks of 3 of these fish are given by Winn *et al.* (1964) in their Fig. 5, and are characterized by clockwise circling (of 9 circles, 8 are clockwise), alternating with relatively long straight stretches during which the fish maintained a more or less steady course. Here again the fish may have been orientating to some environmental clue, the nature of which is not clear.

The sun-compass reaction and migration

The sun compass reaction has been demonstrated in a number of non-migratory freshwater fish under laboratory conditions, and although Braemer (1960) refers to some work with salmon, full details of these experiments have never been published. So far as field work goes, only that carried out by Winn *et al.* (1964) on parrot fish in shallow water off Bermuda is convincing. The successful experiments have in common the fact that the fish were probably able to see the disc of the sun, which is only visible underwater within a few metres of the surface. There is no evidence to show that a fish can make use of the sun-compass reaction if the disc cannot be seen, when the sun's position would have to be determined by reference to the radiance distribution.

If migrants use the sun as a reference point, it is reasonable to expect that they should swim near the surface during the day. While cod and herring (p. 35) have been seen at the surface, such observations are outstanding exceptions to the general rule that fish swim deep by day and come up towards the surface at night. There can be little doubt that this is generally the case with salmon, herring, plaice and cod, and the adult eel is believed to be bathypelagic during its return to the Sargasso. Nevertheless, salmon in the Pacific at depths of 40 to 60 m should be able to determine the position of the sun during the day, but it is unlikely that herring moving from Iceland to the Norwegian coast at depths of 200 to 600 m can do so. The problem of cloud cover could also be a disturbing feature; in the months during which salmon leave the high seas of the western Pacific for the coastal areas, the sky is 7 to 8 tenths obscured by cloud (Dodimead *et al.*, 1963, p. 45, Fig. 11). During the months when the Arctic cod are moving from Bear Island towards their spawning grounds at Lofoten, the sun is below the horizon (Table 27): in this instance the sun cannot be used as a reference.

Orientation at night

Migration of sole (*Solea vulgaris*) in the southern North Sea

Opportunities to observe the orientation of fish at sea during the night do not often arise, and one of the two reports known to me is that cited by Hasler (1960, p. 112), who refers to an unpublished observation made by Dr. C. A. Barnes (University of Washington). Barnes 'observed salmon migrating at right angles to his oceanographic research vessel which was on course at night in the north-eastern Pacific. Because of a luminescent sea, this school of large salmon could be clearly seen. The fish swam on a fairly straight course until out of sight.' This observation, although anecdotal, is of considerable interest, particularly in view of the recent observations on sole in the southern North Sea reported by de Veen (1967).

Sole have been seen at the surface during the night. The sightings are most common in March, April, and May when the spawning migration is under way. de Veen (1967) gives an account of the phenomenon largely based on the analysis of reports from fishermen in the years 1963, 1964, and 1965. Sole are most frequently seen at the surface when the tidal streams are flowing NE., E., SE. or S. and would, in the southern North Sea, carry the fish towards their spawning grounds which are in the coastal waters of Holland, Germany and Denmark. Many of the results are presented in the form of spoke diagrams and most of these are convincing, and must fall into types II and III according to the Matthews Test for significance.[1] de Veen suggests that the sole seen at the surface are those at the upper ceiling of the main body of the migrants which have left the bottom for midwater to use the tidal stream as a passive transport system. It is not known how the diurnal vertical movements of the sole are synchronized with the tidal cycle so that they leave the bottom, at night, on an easterly tide.

Sole seen at the surface are nearly always still, and drift with the tide. Fishermen report that these sole are generally orientated to head E. or NE., even on those relatively few occasions when they are seen at the surface on N.-, NW.-, W.-, SW.- and S.-going tides. Although the number of observations is rather small, the reports suggest that sole head E. or NE. on moonless nights and when there is complete cloud cover. There is at the moment no satisfactory explanation for these observations.

[1] The Matthews Test for significance: 'this is based on visual inspection and classifies circular "distributions" into three categories, those whose orientation is type I, "not obvious", type II, "obvious" or type III, "bloody obvious"' (Matthews, 1966).

Chapter 12

Homing and the Use of Local Landmarks: Pilotage

INTRODUCTION

In this chapter the evidence for homing in several freshwater species will be reviewed before passing on to consider the sensory channels involved. The salmon will then be dealt with in some detail and the chapter concludes with an extension of the discussion to marine species.

HOME RANGE, TERRITORY, AND STATION

The problem of recognition will partly depend on the extent of the area to which the fish returns. The area is often relatively small as many species have a very restricted range of movement. Gerking (1959) lists 34 species whose movements are said to be restricted to a home range over which they normally travel. The limited extent of the home range has been demonstrated by marking or tagging fish and observing the distribution of the recoveries over a period of weeks, months, or years. In freshwater the home range is generally limited to a particular pool, a 50 to 100 m stretch of a stream, or one area of a lake, within which the majority of the recaptures are made. The few marine species that have been studied live in habitats that are reasonably accessible to the biologist, such as tide pools on rocky shores, or reefs.

Many of the freshwater studies reviewed by Gerking (1959) and the more recent work of Gunning (1959, 1963) and Gunning and Shoop (1962, 1963) conform to the same general plan. A stretch of water selected as a study area was divided into a number of sections. Fish taken by net, or an electric shocking device, were marked or tagged and then released where they were caught, the distribution of the recaptures throughout the study area being recorded on subsequent occasions. The results usually show that of those fish that are recaptured, the majority are taken in the section of the study area in which they were originally caught.

An experiment by Gunning and Shoop (1963) will serve as an example. The study area was a 135 m stretch of Talisheek Creek, near Talisheek, St. Tammany Parish, Louisiana, USA. The stretch was divided into three sections, A, B, and C, A being the upstream section. On 21 July 1960, 35 longear sunfish (*Lepomis megalotis*) were caught in section B, fin-clipped, and returned to the stream. The whole study area was fished on 28 July 1960 and 27 marked fish were caught in section B to which they were returned. There were no strays in the other two sections. On 9 August 1960 the study area was fished again; 18 marked fish were recaptured in section B. Again there were no strays. Although there was no evidence of straying over the 13 days for which the fish were at liberty, only half of those originally marked were recovered at the end of the period. In long-term experiments the reduction in the number of recoveries is even more striking, 80% or more of the marked fish being unaccounted for a year later (Gerking, 1953, p. 353, Fig. 4, for rock bass, *Ambloplites rupestris*; Gunning, 1959, p. 119, Table 2, for longear sunfish). For the long-term experiments, Gunning and Shoop (1963, p. 329) argue that natural mortality is the main cause of the small proportion of marked fish recovered and that the numbers of stray fish recaptured should be higher than they usually are if emigration was occurring to any significant extent. But natural mortality can hardly account for the low proportion of the marked fish taken in many of the short-term experiments. The low proportion of recoveries may reflect the inefficiency of the sampling technique (Gunning, 1959, p. 117, gives the efficiency of an electric shocking equipment as 25 to 50%) rather than an emigration of marked fish. The relative and absolute numbers of marked and unmarked fish caught could throw some light on this problem but the data are not given.

One limitation of fin clipping experiments is that individual fish can rarely be identified. But Gerking (1953, p. 357) records the case of a longear sunfish caught in the same section of the stream for three consecutive years, while two of Gunning and Shoop's (1962) eels were repeatedly caught within a limited stretch of water over a period of 10 to 13 months. Numbered tags allow individuals to be identified and with this technique it has been shown that brown trout, *S. trutta*, are restricted in their movements (for example, Allen, 1951, in the Horokiwi Stream, North Island, New Zealand). Clipping and tagging experiments carried out by Saunders and Gee (1964) have shown that Atlantic salmon fry and parr also occupy restricted areas in a stream.

The degree to which marking and tagging experiments can delimit the boundaries of the home range depends, in part, on the size of the sampling sections into which the study area is divided. For finer detail field observations are needed (as from a submerged chamber, Newman, 1956, or by diving, Bardach, 1958). In this connexion Kalleberg's (1958) stream-tank observations on territoriality in juvenile salmon and trout are relevant. Kalleberg found that young salmonids defend a territory from a strictly localized position which he called the station. Salmon parr are recorded as keeping to the same station for at least 59 days (Kalleberg, 1958, p. 68). The territory appears to have particular significance for feeding, the tenant waiting there to take the food carried downstream. As a fish makes quite extensive excursions outside the territory, to which it returns, it must have local knowledge of an area considerably greater than that defended. This known and familiar area over which the fish travels probably corresponds to the home range revealed by marking and tagging experiments.

THE EVIDENCE FOR HOMING

Migrant or displaced fish often return to their home range. Gerking (1959) has reviewed some of the evidence and a number of examples are given below to supplement those given in previous chapters.

The return of migrants

1. *Wild brown trout in Crystal Creek, New York State, USA*

Schuck (1943) tagged the brown trout (*S. fario*) in 13 sections (average length 60 to 70 m) of the stream. The trout were tagged after the fishing season, during the first two weeks of September from 1939 through to 1942. A weir check in October–November showed that many of the tagged fish moved upstream to spawn. Of the recoveries made during the following fishing season, 64% were caught where the fish were tagged the previous September. During the course of the annual sampling Schuck recaptured 46 trout which had been tagged the year before, and 42 of them were taken in the original sections. The picture that follows from these results is of trout migrating upstream to spawn and then returning to the home section.

Table 29. Recoveries of dwarf suckers marked in the north and south inlet streams of Wolf Lake, Huntington Forest, Newcomb, New York. (Data from Dence, 1940, 1948. Data for the numbers of suckers released in 1939 and 1940 are not available.)

Year of marking	Inlet of marking	Number marked	1939 N.	1939 S.	1940 N.	1940 S.	1941 N.	1941 S.
1938	N.	1,043	526	13	329	3	88	1
	S.	593	5	103	10	73	0	26
1939	N.		—	—	617	2	42	0
	S.		—	—	27	34	14	37
1940	N.		—	—	—	—	533	0
	S.		—	—	—	—	0	52

2. Dence's (1948) experiments with the dwarf sucker at Wolf Lake, Huntington Forest, New York State, USA

There are north and south inlet streams to Wolf Lake which are used by dwarf suckers *Catostomus commersonnii utawana*, for spawning. From 1938 to 1942 suckers taken in each inlet were marked by fin clipping and recoveries of marked spawners in the two inlet streams were recorded from 1939 to 1946. In all 12,817 fish were marked so these experiments should have been able to give valuable information concerning homing and straying, in a manner similar to the Canadian experiments on herring (p. 141), although on a much smaller scale. Unfortunately, the data for the Wolf Lake experiments were never published in detail and Professor Dence (personal communication) has told me that all the original unpublished material has now been lost, through no fault of his own. Such data as can be extracted from Dence's (1948) Tables 10, 11, and 12 are summarized in Table 29. Dence (1948, p. 127) himself draws attention to the spawner's habit of returning to the stream in which they had previously spawned, a fact which clearly emerges from the results of the three years for which the relevant details are available.

Table 30. Recapture of spring and autumn spawning charr caught, tagged, and released on their spawning grounds in Windermere. (Data from Frost, 1963, p. 76, Table 1.)

Spawning group	Site of capture and tagging	Number released 1950–52	Holbeck	Brathay	Red Nab	Low Wray Bay
Spring	Holbeck Point	946	373	0	0	0
Autumn	River Brathay	394	0	103	1	0
Autumn	Red Nab	612	0	0	96	2
Autumn	Low Wray Bay	114	0	0	3	6

3. *Frost's (1963) experiments with charr in Windermere*

There are two stocks of charr (*Salvelinus willughbii*) in Windermere, English Lake District, one spawning in the autumn (October–December), the other in the spring (January–April). The autumn spawners breed in the River Brathay and in shallow water around the shore of the lake, while the spring spawners breed in deeper water in the lake. Spring and autumn spawners have been tagged on the spawning grounds shown in Fig. 79. Two points emerge from the results,

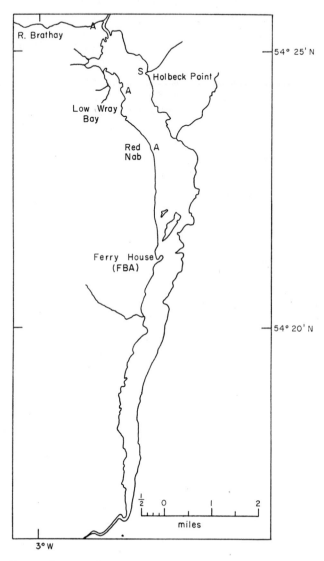

Fig. 79. Place names of interest in connexion with Frost's (1963) homing experiments with charr in Windermere, English Lake District. Fish were tagged on the autumn grounds (A) at Purdom's Dub in the R. Brathay, in Low Wray Bay and off Red Nab, and on the spring ground (S) at Holbeck Point (near Low Wood). The results are set out in Table 30. (Based on an Ordnance Survey map.)

which are summarized in Table 30. Firstly, there is no evidence to show that the charr change their spawning season. Secondly, among the autumn spawners there is apparently very little interchange between the river and the lake fish, the charr returning to spawn on the ground where they were tagged.

4. *The woolly sculpin in Californian rock pools*

Williams (1957) studied the homing behaviour of these fish on the rocky shores of Los Angeles County, California, in the Palos Verdes Region, 33° 44·5′–33° 48·0′N. In Southern California there are two daily tides of unequal amplitudes and the sculpins (*Clinocottus analis*) and opaleyes (*Girella nigricans*) are abundant in stranded pools at the lower low-water level. These pools do not get very hot in summer as the low tides then occur during the night or close to sunrise or sunset, a remarkable fact to which Williams draws attention.

The sculpins and opaleyes leave the pools on the incoming tide and move inshore, retreating again on the falling tide. The fish do not appear to collect in pools which subsequently dry out through sub-surface drainage. In four experiments carried out at low tide (3, 4, 5, and 6) Williams tagged 138 sculpins and 67 opaleyes, and returned them to their original pools. Collections and observations were continued for several weeks, and 80% of the recaptures or sightings of tagged fish were made in the home pools. Williams considers the homing behaviour of these fish to be an adaptation to avoid being stranded by the falling tide in unsuitable pools.

5. *Homing of rainbow trout to the inlet and outlet streams of Loon Lake, British Columbia*

Rainbow trout (*S. gairdneri*) spawn in the inlet and outlet streams of Loon Lake, near Clinton, on the southern interior plateau, British Columbia. Lindsey, Northcote, and Hartman (1959) fin-clipped fry and fingerlings in their parent streams and later recorded the streams in which the marked fish were subsequently recovered during their first spawning season. In 1953 and 1954, 27,964 fry or fingerlings were marked in the spawning streams before they moved into the lake. In 1954, 1955, and 1956 a total of 922 marked fish were recovered in the inlet and outlet streams as first-time spawners. When allowances were made for sampling errors, the results showed that 93·8% of the trout returned to spawn in the parent stream. In 1953–55, 3,044 first-time spawners were marked or tagged in the inlet and outlet streams. The subsequent recovery of 163 of these fish in 1954–56 showed that 99·6% returned to spawn in streams where they had previously spawned.

The return of displaced fish

1. *Gerking's experiments in Richland Creek*

Gerking (1953) showed that longear sunfish occupied home ranges in Richland Creek, Greene County, Indiana. The study area was divided into four sections A, B, E, and F, the latter being the upstream section. The longears taken in each section were identified by removing the left (A) and right (B) pectorals, or the left (E) and right (F) pelvic fins. Fish were marked in 1948 and 1949, and recaptures made in the four years from 1948 through to 1951. The results, summarized in Table 31, show that the majority of the fish that were recaptured were taken in the section of the stream in which they were originally caught and released.

Following this convincing demonstration of home range, a homing experiment was carried out in 1951. Longears captured in the four sections were marked as before, and those from section B

Table 31. Marking experiment with longear sunfish (*Lepomis megalotis*) in Richland Creek. (Data from Gerking, 1953, p. 352, Tables 2 and 3.)

Section in which fish were caught	Number marked and released	Section of recapture			
		A	B	E	F
A	139	27	10	1	0
B	165	11	41	1	1
E	143	1	1	73	6
F	75	0	0	3	15

Table 32. Displacement experiments with longear sunfish in Richland Creek. Fish caught in sections A, E, and F were released where they were caught. Sixty-one fish caught in Section B were carried upstream across a riffle and were released in section E. The displaced fish included 6 marked in a previous year. (Data from Gerking, 1953, pp. 358–9, Tables 10 and 11.)

Section in which fish were caught	Number marked and released	Section of recapture two weeks after release			
		A	B	E	F
A	53	15	4	0	0
B	55	0	26	6	3
E	63	0	0	37	2
F	36	0	0	5	11

displaced to section E. A survey made 2 weeks later showed that the majority of the section B fish that were recaptured had returned to their home range. The results are summarized in Table 32.

2. *Beebe's (1931) experiments with the goby Bathygobius soporator*

Bathygobius is a small fish which lives in tide-pools of the western Atlantic. Beebe made some observations on the homing behaviour of *Bathygobius* in Bermuda. 'From three to seven fish are usually found in a tide-pool of good size, seldom more than one large one. Several times (six to be exact) I have changed marked individuals from one tide-pool to another, many yards away, and five out of six times the transferred fish were found next day in their original pools' (Beebe, 1931, p. 56).

3. *Hasler and Wisby's (1958) experiments with green sunfish and largemouth bass*

These experiments were carried out in relatively small ponds (25×90 m) or lakes (approx. 200 to 300 m diameter) near Wisconsin. Sunfish (*Lepomis cyanellus*) or bass (*Micropterus salmoides*) were caught and fin-clipped. The sunfish caught at the northern or southern ends of the pond were released at the other, and the bass caught in different sections of a lake were released at its centre. The majority of the recaptures (90 to 97% in sunfish, 68 to 73% in bass) were made at the end of the pond or section of the lake from which the fish were originally taken. Hasler *et al.* (1958, p. 354) cite this paper as evidence that largemouth bass and green sunfish 'use local sign posts as points of visual reference in locating food, nest, or home territory'. But in fact Hasler and Wisby (1958) did not give any critical evidence as to the clues used.

9

Fig. 80. Lake Mendota, Wisconsin, showing the two main spawning grounds of the white bass at Maple Bluff and Governor's Island. Hasler *et al.* (1958) took fish from these spawning grounds and released them near the middle of the lake. Their results are summarized in Table 33. (Outline from a U.S. Department of the Interior Geological Survey map.)

4. *Hasler et al.'s (1958) experiments with the white bass in Lake Mendota, Wisconsin*

The white bass (*Roccus chrysops*) has two major spawning grounds in Lake Mendota, at Maple Bluff and Governor's Island (Fig. 80). During the 1955, 1956, and 1957 spawning seasons, bass caught by fyke nets on the spawning grounds were tagged with Petersen tags and released during the day at a position near the middle of the lake. Male fish gave the best returns and of those that were recovered on the spawning grounds a high proportion were recaptured on the ground where they were originally captured. The results are summarized in Table 33.

Table 33. Recaptures of male white bass (*Roccus chrysops*) displaced from their spawning grounds in Lake Mendota. (Data from Hasler *et al.*, 1958.)

Spawning ground where fish were caught	Number tagged	Recoveries		Proportion of recoveries taken on the home ground
		Governor's Island	Maple Bluff	
Governor's Island	343	48	2	96%
Maple Bluff	849	14	112	89%

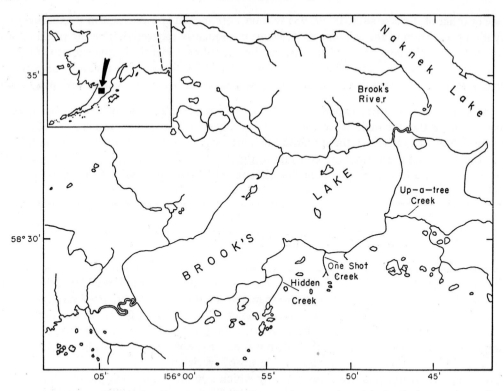

Fig. 81. Brook's Lake, Alaska, showing place names of interest in connexion with the displacement experiments carried out by Hartman and Raleigh (1964) with sockeye salmon. The details of one of their experiments are given in Table 34.

5. *Sockeye salmon in Brook's Lake, Alaska*

Brook's Lake lies on the shoulder of the Aleutian peninsula and joins Bristol Bay through Naknek Lake. Sockeye spawn in streams entering Brook's Lake and in its outlet, Brook's River. Some relevant place names are shown on Fig. 81. Hartman and Raleigh (1964) have carried out displacement experiments with pre-spawning adult sockeye seined at the mouth of three tributaries, Up-a-tree, One Shot, and Hidden Creeks, and the outlet, Brook's River. The fish were tagged and divided into two or more batches, one batch being released where the fish were caught, the remainder

Table 34. Recoveries of sockeye salmon caught at Up-a-tree Creek, and released at various sites in Brook's Lake. (Data from Hartman and Raleigh, 1964, Table 2, Exp. 3.)

Release site	Number released	Recoveries					Total Recoveries	
		Brook's River	Up-a-tree Creek	One Shot Creek	Hidden Creek	Headwater Creek	Number	%
Hidden Creek	49	1	34	0	1	0	36	74
Up-a-tree Creek	50	0	42	1	0	1	44	88
Brook's River	25	0	24	0	1	0	25	100
One Shot Creek	50	0	35	1	0	1	37	74

at one or other of the lake sites. In all, 985 salmon were tagged and released in 8 experiments. A very high proportion of the salmon, 83%, were subsequently recovered. The distribution of the recovered fish in the control and displaced batches was almost identical. One experiment, No. 3, will serve as an example. The details are given in Table 34, from which it can be seen that the majority of the recaptured fish returned to Up-a-tree Creek, where they were originally caught

A weakness in most of these experiments, with the notable exception of those carried out in Brook's Lake, is that the majority of the marked or tagged fish are not recaptured and there must be some doubt as to whether these missing fish are dead, are at home, or have strayed. But so far as those that are recaptured are concerned, the evidence for homing is good, the proportion of strays is low, and the geographical location to which the successful fish return relatively small.

THE RECOGNITION OF THE HOME

The possibility should be considered that a fish recognizes the location of its home range by reference to celestial or geophysical clues. In the examples that have been considered the extent of the home range is small, certainly no more than 100 to 200 m. An experienced navigator with a sextant (accurate to ± 10 seconds of arc), a chronometer (accurate to ± 0.5 seconds of time), and an almanac, can do little better than to fix his ship to within ± 800 m. It is unreasonable to expect a fish to improve on this performance, and there do not appear to be any geophysical clues which could be used to define a location within the required limits of precision.

Topographical features are obvious clues by which a home range could be recognized. They appear to be used by salmonids in Kalleberg's (1958) stream-tank. Williams (1957) came to a similar conclusion for the opaleye and woolly sculpin. The eyes are probably the most important sensory channel for the appreciation of topographical features. Thorpe (1956, p. 367) writes that 'the evidence that territorial recognition is normally based on vision is so overwhelming that it need hardly be discussed'. But there may be exceptions, particularly in turbid water. Here bottom features could be detected by their effect on electric fields (Lissmann, 1958). *Protopterus* can be cited as a case where tactile stimuli may be important, to which the blind cave fish *Caecobarbus* could be added (Thines, 1955, p. 117). Finally, the possible role of the lateral line should not be overlooked, in view of Löwenstein's (1957, p. 164) suggestion that it could give 'a fairly accurate three-dimensional sensory representation of the topographic features of the immediate environment'.

Direct evidence for the role of the various sensory channels in recognizing the home could be given by experiments in which changes in behaviour or distribution follow interference or removal of the sense organs or their nerves. But I have not found a published account of an experiment in which fish have been released in their home range, *without displacement*, after sensory impairment. Experiments dealing with homing following sensory impairment *and displacement* have been described by Wisby and Hasler (1954), Stuart (1957), Bardach (1958), and Gunning (1959). It is important to note that these experiments were not designed to make a distinction between the sensory channels used in recognizing the home and those that might be used in returning to the home from a distance. So a failure to return should not be necessarily interpreted as a failure to recognize the home as the fish may never have reached it. Fish that do return show that the sensory channel put out of action was not used in recognizing the home.

Wisby and Hasler's (1954) *experiments with coho salmon*

These experiments were carried out at Issaquah Creek, Seattle, State of Washington, USA, in November 1952. Issaquah Creek enters Lake Sammamish and its outflow reaches Puget Sound through Sammamish River, Lake Washington and Lake Washington Canal. There is a run of coho

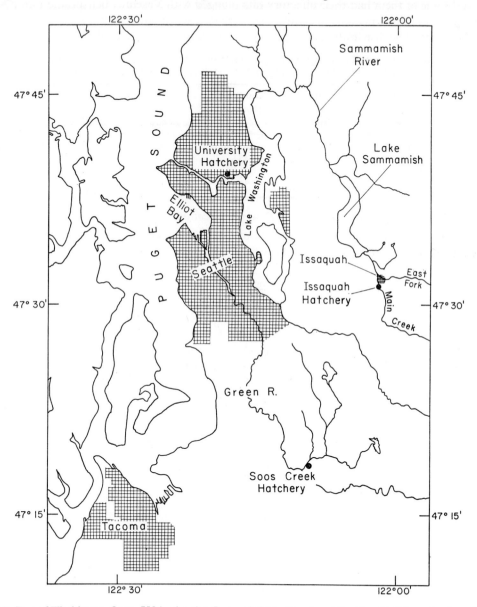

Fig. 82. Part of Washington State, USA, showing Issaquah Main Creek and the East Fork branch where Wisby and Hasler (1954) carried out an olfactory occlusion experiment with coho salmon. Soos Creek hatchery, on the Green River, and the University hatchery, are referred to on p. 266 when describing transplantation experiments carried out by Donaldson and Allen (1958). (Outline from a U.S. Department of the Interior Survey map.)

salmon (*O. kisutch*) to the creek which divides below Issaquah village into the main creek and the smaller East Fork (Fig. 82). Fish traps are worked on both streams, 1600 m and 2400 m above the fork respectively. Coho salmon migrating upstream were caught in these traps. The stream in which the fish were caught was assumed to be the home stream. The fish were tagged with Petersen discs, and some of them had their olfactory pits plugged with Vaseline, benzocaine ointment or cotton wadding. Experimental and control fish were released about 1200 m below the junction of the two streams. The distribution of the recoveries is summarized in Table 35.

Table 35. Recaptures of control and experimental coho salmon in the Issaquah Creek experiments. (Recapture data from Wisby and Hasler, 1954. Release data from A. D. Hasler, personal communication.)

Stream of origin	Treatment of fish	Number released	Number recaptured	
			Issaquah	East Fork
Issaquah	Controls	121	46	0
	Nose plugged	145	39	12
East Fork	Controls	38	8	19
	Nose plugged	38	16	3

Stuart's (1957) experiments in Dunalastair Reservoir, Scotland

Brown trout spawn in the 5 main streams of Dunalastair Reservoir (Fig. 83). Stuart (1957) marked the immature fish in what must have been their natal streams and over a number of years

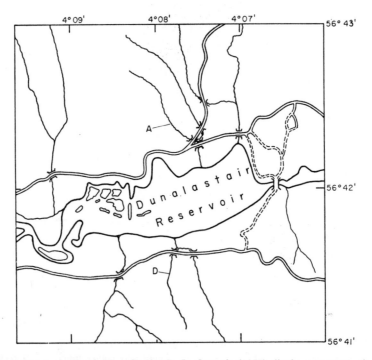

Fig. 83. Dunalastair Reservoir (Perthshire, Scotland). In Stuart's (1957) displacement experiments with trout, fish were taken from stream A to stream D. The olfactory pits of some of the displaced fish were plugged. (Based on an Ordnance Survey map.)

these fish have been recaptured as spawners in the parent stream with no evidence of straying. A special experiment was carried out in 1955, involving fish from the spawning run in stream A. A total of 113 trout were displaced from A to D, and of these 58 had their olfactory pits plugged with cotton wool alone, or impregnated with Vaseline or chloroxylenol. The results are summarized in Table 36. Unfortunately, the run failed 2 days after the experiment had started and the returns were disappointing. Nevertheless, 10 trout crossed the reservoir with plugs in position and entered the stream from which they had been displaced. These results suggest that olfactory clues may not have been used to identify the home stream, but the limited number of returns makes it difficult to come to any firm conclusions. However, Stuart's results are of considerable interest.

Table 36. The return of spawning trout displaced from stream A to stream D in Dunalastair Reservoir. (Data from Stuart, 1957.)

Treatment of displaced fish	Number released in stream D	Recaptures in stream A		
		Total	Plugs intact	Plugs lost
Noses plugged	58	14	10	4
Controls	55	18		

Heard and Hartman (personal communication) have been following up the displacement experiments with sockeye in Brook's Lake referred to earlier (p. 251) and have found that salmon still return to the stream from which they were moved after destruction of the olfactory organ. Further comment must await full publication of these results: Heard and Hartman (personal communication) have suggested that some other chemoreceptors may be involved.

Bardach's (1958) experiments with reef fish

Bardach carried out some homing experiments with several species on coral reefs near Bermuda. Only 2 species, *Epinephelus guttatus*, the red hind, and *E. striatus*, the Nassau grouper, gave evidence of homing after displacement from one reef to another. In an impairment and displacement experiment, 7 individuals of each species were released after cutting the optic nerve, and a further 7 of each species were released after plugging the internal and external nares. None of the blinded fish were recovered, and one red hind with plugged nares returned home.

Gunning's (1959) experiments with sunfish

Gerking's (1953) original homing experiments with longear sunfish in Richland Creek have already been mentioned (p. 248). Gunning followed up this work, and corroborated the home range concept. Six lengths of the stream were selected as study areas and each was divided into two or more sections designated A, B, and C, etc., A being the upstream section. Experiments were then made in which fish were blinded (removal of lenses, use of eye caps, or removal of eyes) or their olfaction impaired (heat cautery of olfactory epithelium or blocking the olfactory pits with liquid latex). The fish were fin-clipped so they could be identified and were released outside their home range. Gunning claims that the returns showed that blinded fish homed as quickly and as accurately as the controls, while the fish whose olfactory mechanism was impaired were less precise.

These results are summarized in Table 37. Inspection of the data shows that Gunning's claims are well founded. Blinded fish did return home, and there was no significant difference between the pooled returns of experiments 1, 2 and 3 and the controls 10, 13, and 14 where the time intervals between release and recapture were similar ($\chi^2 = 0\cdot047$, d.f. $= 1$, $p = 0\cdot81$). Gunning records in detail (1959, p. 122) the behaviour of one fish which became blind following the loss of its eye caps. This was one of the 12 marked fish fitted with eye caps and displaced from IIB to IIC on 10 July 1958. On 11 August one fish was recovered near a distinctive rock in IIB. The eye caps had been lost but the fish appeared to have been blinded by a fungal disease. The fish was re-marked and displaced again to IIC, to be recaptured on 16 August, 3 m from where it was found on 11 August. Displaced to IIC for the third time, this fish was recaptured on 8 September 1 m from the rock. Each homing trip involved a distance of about 116 m, and a laboratory test and examination confirmed that this fish was blind. Gunning makes the point that the repeated recapture of this individual suggests that vision was not important in homing and that the fish was returning to a very restricted part of the stream.

Fish whose olfactory organs were impaired were also recovered in the home range. But the results of the heat cautery experiments 15a and 15b (55% of recaptures homed) are significantly worse than those of the control experiments 8 and 13 (91% homed) $\chi^2 = 8\cdot38$, d.f. $= 1$, $p = <0\cdot005$. There is a similar difference between the returns of fish with olfactory pits plugged with latex (experiments 16 and 17, 38% homed) and the controls 10 and 13 (80% homed), $\chi^2 = 5\cdot79$, d.f. $= 1$, $p = 0\cdot018$. Gunning concluded that the heat cauterized or latex-treated fish moved randomly after being released and that the presence of the recaptured fish in the home section was a consequence of random movement.

A criticism that can be made of Gunning's work concerns the controls. On no occasion were controls carried out in the same section and in the same year as the experiments with which they are compared for statistical purposes (experiments 1, 2, and 3 against controls 10, 13, and 14; experiments 4, 5, 6, and 7, no controls; experiments 15a and 15b against controls 8 and 13; experiments 16 and 17 against controls 10 and 13). It could be argued that the experiments were inadequately controlled and this is certainly a fair criticism. Nevertheless, the overall picture given by the Richland Creek experiments is that blinding makes little or no difference to the proportion of fish that is recaptured, and of those that are recaptured a high proportion homed. These results suggest that vision plays little part in homing. The multiple recaptures of the blind fish in study area II could be taken to support this conclusion. If the three recaptures within a restricted area are not fortuitous the fish must have been able to recognize its immediate environment by some sensory channel other than that of the eye.

The experiments dealing with olfactory impairment cannot be considered as conclusive evidence that the olfactory sense mediates homing. The results show that compared with the control experiments, a lower proportion of the fish was recaptured after olfactory impairment, and of those recaptured, a lower proportion was taken in the home section. No experiments were made to show that this was not a traumatic effect. Gunning points out that among his control experiments the fish displaced downstream (experiments 8, 9, and 10) gave a higher proportion of homers than those displaced upstream (experiments 12, 13, and 14), a result consistent with the hypothesis that the fish were homing with the aid of an odoriferous substance carried downstream with the current. The difference between the upstream and downstream controls is statistically significant. The difficulty in accepting Gunning's argument is that the difference could equally well be attributed to a difference in study areas.

Gunning also carried out an experiment with 40 longear sunfish from whose eyes the lenses had been removed and whose olfactory pits were occluded with latex. These fish were displaced from IIB to IID. Four days later all of study area II, 30 m of stream separating areas II and III, and

Table 37. The return of displaced sunfish to their home range after sensory impairment. (Data from Gunning, 1959, Tables 3, 4 and 5.)

A After impairment of vision

	Lenses removed			With eye caps			Eyes removed
Experiment	1	2	3	4	5	6	7
Year	1957	1956	1958	1958	1958	1958	1957
Study area	II	I	V	II	III	III	III
Displacement	B to C	B to A	B to A	C to D	A to B	B to A	A to B
Fish released	43	40	31	11	23	13	47
Fish recaptured	15	20	6	6	6	5	6
Days at liberty	5	4	11	3	7	3	5
Fish that homed	11	14	6	4	4	4	6
Fish that did not home	4	6	0	2	2	1	0
Recaptured: released, %	41:114, 36%			17:47, 36%			6:47, 13%
Homed: recaptured, %	31: 41, 76%			12:17, 70%			6: 6, 100%

B After impairment of the olfactory organ

	Heat cautery		Latex occlusion	
Experiment	15a	15b	16	17
Year	1956	1956	1958	1958
Study area	IV	IV	II	IV
Displacement	A to B	B to A	B to C	B to A
Fish released	76	60	38	40
Fish recaptured	15	16	5	8
Days at liberty	7	7	4	1
Fish that homed	9	8	3	2
Fish that did not home	6	8	2	6
Recaptured: released, %	31:136, 23%		13:78, 17%	
Homed: recaptured, %	17: 31, 55%		5:13, 38%	

C Control experiments

	Displaced downstream			Displaced upstream		
Experiment	8	9	10	12	13	14
	1956	1957	1958	1951	1957	1957
Study area	III	III	II	IV	IV	V
Displacement	A to B	A to B	B to C	upstream	B to A	B to A
Fish released	66	36	37	61	46	26
Fish recaptured	19	19	12	35	13	10
Days at liberty	14	1	7	14	1	14
Fish that homed	19	19	10	26	10	7
Fish that did not home	0	0	2	9	3	3
Recaptured: released, %	50:139, 36%			58:133, 44%		
Homed: recaptured, %	48: 50, 96%			43: 58, 74%		
Test of independence	$\chi^2 = 8.47$, d.f. $= 1$, $p = <0.005$					

section A of area III were sampled. One fish was recovered in IIIA. Gunning (p. 125) concluded that 'the ability of the fish to orient with respect to their home range was lost following the impairment of both smell and sight'. But in this case negative evidence is no proof, whereas positive evidence of a series of recoveries distributed throughout the sampled areas would have been convincing.

No conclusions can be drawn from Stuart's (1957) or Bardach's (1958) results. Wisby and Hasler (1954) and Gunning (1959) showed that olfactory impairment is detrimental to homing. Gunning found that blinding had no effect on the homing of longear sunfish, and he concluded that his displaced fish recognized their home range by a characteristic odour, or combination of odours. The implication is that the blind fish recaptured three times within a few metres stretch of the stream was homing to a very restricted area recognized by an olfactory clue. This part of the stream (IIB) is about 0·75 m deep and 10 m wide (Gunning, 1959, p. 112). While it is possible that different streams, and different stretches of one stream, leach characteristic substances into the water flowing through them, Gunning's hypothesis implies a small-scale odoriferous mosaic which would enable a fish to home to a 10 m stretch of the stream. This is not impossible. But it is surely just as likely that this particular fish recognized its home by reference to topographical features, detected through a sensory channel other than its eyes, while olfactory clues may have been used at a coarser level to delimit the topographical search to a particular part of the stream.

Summary

Aquarium, stream-tank, and some homing experiments suggest that topographical clues are used by fish to recognize their home range, territory, or station. In some cases the eyes are undoubtedly the sensory channel involved. Gunning's (1959) results with blinded fish are open to the interpretation that another sensory channel may be used and this could be the acoustic-lateralis system. In the examples that have been considered here the fish were returning to, and must therefore have been recognizing, a particular geographical location. But neither salmon nor herring, both of which spawn in relatively restricted areas, have been shown to spawn on their parent bed. They may do so but the point has not been proved. So it is not clear whether a bed is selected because it is recognized as the parent bed, or because it happens to be the first available one that the fish comes to when it is physiologically set for spawning. Learning must be involved if the fish selects the parent bed when there are other sites to choose from. Learning may still be involved if the bed spawned on is the first available, as selection could depend on the recognition of a character common to both the chosen and the parent bed. On the other hand, the choice of a bed may be controlled by an innate releasing mechanism, any suitable bed sufficing so long as the fish is in an appropriate physiological condition. Salmon, plaice, and eels almost certainly spawn on their parent area or ground; cod and herring may do so. Here again homing may depend, not on the recognition of the parent area or ground as a place where they had been before, but on its recognition, innately, as a place suitable for spawning. The problem of homing could therefore lie not so much in the recognition of the parent area, ground, or bed, as in the means by which fish born there are brought back home ready to spawn. Chemical substances in the home water could provide clues which could be detected at a distance and the olfactory organs, as the most sensitive and versatile of the chemoreceptors, would be the most appropriate sensory channel to be involved. The olfactory hypothesis will now be discussed in detail with particular reference, in the first instance, to salmon.

THE OLFACTORY HYPOTHESIS AND SALMON

Buckland (1880, p. 302) suggested that 'when the salmon is coming in from the sea he smells about till he scents the water of his own river. This guides him in the right direction, and he has only to follow up the scent, in other words, to "follow his nose", to get up into fresh water, i.e., if he is in a travelling humour. Thus a salmon coming up from the sea into the Bristol Channel would get a smell of water meeting him. "I am a Wye salmon," he would say to himself. "This is not the Wye water: it's the wrong tap, its the Usk. I must go a few miles further on," and he gets up steam again.' These are the very bones of the hypothesis that North American workers, encouraged by Professor A. D. Hasler, have been trying to substantiate since the early 1950s. Hasler (1954, 1956, 1960, 1966) has summarized the arguments and data in support of the olfactory hypothesis. The sense of smell in fish is well developed; bluntnose minnows (*Hyborhynchus notatus*) can be conditioned to discriminate between plant rinses (Walker and Hasler, 1949) and between the waters from different streams (Hasler and Wisby, 1951); there is also evidence of memory. Hasler and Wisby (1951, p. 237) reported that salmon could also discriminate between stream odours but details of these experiments do not appear to have been published.

More recently Idler *et al.* (1961) have shown that migrating adult sockeye salmon respond to the waters of the lake or stream in which they were probably going to spawn. Fish were caught near the outlet of Great Central Lake, Vancouver Island, and in Sweltzer Creek, Cultus Lake, on the Fraser River, British Columbia. Laboratory tests showed that the addition of homestream water to the experimental tanks was followed by a dispersal of the shoal and an increase in the swimming speed of the fish. Equal quantities of water from other streams produced no response.

Idler *et al.* (1961) did not show that the sense of smell was involved in the response of sockeye salmon to what was assumed to be their homestream water. But their results do support the hypothesis that chemical clues play some part in homing. Creutzberg's (1961) work with elvers is relevant to this problem. Creutzberg showed that elvers have a preference for natural inland water. The presence of an attractive substance in the water determines their rheotropic response, elvers swimming upstream in sea-water diluted with inland water. In the case of the elvers it is unlikely that they can have had previous experience of inland water and the response to the substance is probably innate, whereas in the case of salmon, and possibly other fish, the rheotropic response would be released by a chemical substance or substances, previously experienced by the migrant. So far as I know, it has not been shown that the rheotropic responses of mature salmon are modified by homestream water in a manner similar to that demonstrated by Creutzberg for elvers.

The olfactory hypothesis raises a number of other problems.

1. The nature of the chemical clue

Idler *et al.* (1961) found that the active component in the homestream water was volatile, dialysable, neutral, and heat-labile. In Hasler and Wisby's (1951) experiments with bluntnose minnows the active component also proved to be volatile and heat-labile. Creutzberg (1961) found that the elver attractant in inland water could be removed by active charcoal and that its potency was lost during storage.

2. The learning mechanism

How do young fish learn the characteristics of their homestream water? Hasler (1960) and Brett and Groot (1963) have used the term 'imprinting' in this connexion. Imprinting is a distinct type of learning, being rapid and unrewarded. The process is restricted to a brief period of life often at an early stage in development. It is very stable and 'it is often completed long before the various specific reactions to which the imprinted pattern will ultimately become linked are established' (Thorpe, 1956, p. 116). Thorpe (1956, p. 117) repeats his earlier suggestion that the concept of imprinting could be extended 'to cover the possibility of attachment, not to a fellow-member of the species but to the type of immediate environment first perceived by a newly emerged organism so that this becomes the future breeding quarters of the individual'. But nothing is known in fish concerning the times of the sensitive periods, or the duration of the imprinting process. In salmon, the time spent in freshwater does not appear to have a marked effect on homing ability. Pink and sockeye salmon may be taken as an example. The eggs of both species take 2 to $3\frac{1}{2}$ months to hatch and the yolk sac stage remains for a further period of 1 to 3 months in the gravel. So the early stages of both species are exposed to the water bathing the spawning beds for about 5 months. Pink salmon fry go out to sea soon after emerging from the gravel but the sockeye stay for a further period of 1 to 3 years in lake residence. Do the sockeye home more successfully than the pink salmon? There does not seem to be a significant difference between the two, Foerster's uncorrected returns of sockeye to Cultus Lake being 1·8%, as compared with Pritchard's best result of 2·7% for pinks at McClinton Creek (pp. 48, 51). Furthermore, one stock of sockeye, namely that spawning on the Harrison Rapids gravel beds, below Harrison River on the Lower Fraser, does not remain long in freshwater. The scales of these fish lack the nuclear area corresponding to the period of freshwater residence in other sockeye, and the fry go down to the sea soon after emerging from the gravel (Gilbert, 1918). Nevertheless, sockeye with these 'sea-type' scales return only to the Harrison Rapids gravel beds. So a long period of freshwater residence does not appear to be essential for homing. A similar conclusion appears to hold for the white fish *Coregonus lavaretus* in the River Indalsälven, Sundsvall Bay, Sweden (Lindroth, 1957).

The young salmon may undergo a series of imprinting processes corresponding to each major change of environment made in freshwater; gravel bed, lake outlet, tributary river, main river. It could be important that the sequence in which these imprints are made should correspond exactly to the reverse sequence of stimuli that the upstream migrant receives on the way home. In the case of Cultus Lake sockeye a sequence of imprints would have to be made over a period of about 20 days, which is Dr. R. E. Foerster's (personal communication) estimate of the time taken by a smolt to move from the lake to the mouth of the Fraser.

3. The distance at which the chemical landmark can be detected

This is one of the most interesting problems arising from the olfactory hypothesis. Information is required on both the threshold of perception as determined by electrophysiological and conditioned reflex techniques, and the unconditioned response: on the dilution of the homestream waters in the parent river, and that of the parent river in the sea.

THRESHOLD CONCENTRATIONS

Hasler and Wisby (1951) did not determine a threshold concentration for the conditioned response in their experiments with bluntnose minnows. Idler *et al.* (1961) found that sockeye salmon made a consistent unconditioned response when 9 gallons of homestream water were added to the 400 gallons in the experimental tank, a dilution of approximately 1:40, and a concentration of 25 parts per thousand. There must be some doubts as to whether this relatively high concentration should be taken as a threshold level for the response to homestream water. The homestream water was stored at 5°C for an unspecified period before use, and Creutzberg (1961) found that inland water lost its attractiveness to elvers after being kept for a few days. For comparison with the results for the sockeye, the threshold concentration for the unconditioned response of elvers was found to lie between 1 and 3 parts per thousand.

CONCENTRATIONS OF HOMESTREAM WATER

Estimates of the concentrations of homestream and parent river water likely to be encountered by a returning fish can be made from flow-rate data at the time of their spawning migration. Cultus Lake sockeye will be used as an example.

Migration dates

Data on the times at which Cultus Lake sockeye pass through different areas are given by the recovery of Foerster's marked fish in the commercial fishery and the tagging of sockeye subsequently caught in Cultus Lake. Verhoeven and Davidoff (1962) summarize the data. Cultus Lake sockeye are in the coastal waters off the West Coast of Vancouver Island, in July and August; between Sooke and the mouth of the Fraser in August and September; and between the mouth of the Fraser and Sweltzer Creek during September, October, and November.

Stream discharge data

Cultus Lake joins the Fraser River through Sweltzer Creek, the Chilliwack, Vedder and Sumas rivers, as shown in Fig. 84. Dr. R. E. Foerster kindly helped me to obtain the stream discharge data.

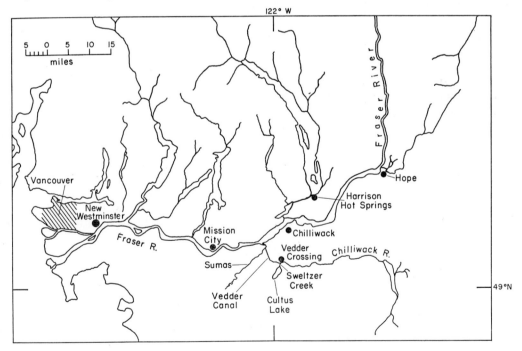

Fig. 84. Place names on the Lower Fraser River, British Columbia, mentioned in connexion with stream discharge data. (Based on an International North Pacific Salmon Fisheries Commission map.)

Some are given in a Water Resources Paper (Anon, 1963), and others in the unpublished data sheets R 79B supplied by the Canadian Department of Northern Affairs and National Resources, Engineering and Water Resources Branch, Water Resources Division, through the courtesy of Mr. H. T. Ramsden, the District Engineer at Vanvouver. Stream discharge data are available for Sweltzer Creek at Cultus Lake; for the Chilliwack River at Vedder Crossing; for the Fraser River at Hope, and for the Harrison River at Harrison Hot Springs. Discharge data are not available for the Sumas where it is joined by the Vedder Canal, or for the Fraser where it is joined by the Sumas. For the present estimates, which are only concerned with orders of magnitude, this is not serious. The discharge of the Sumas where it joins the Vedder Canal has been taken as equal to one-tenth of the discharge of the Chilliwack at Vedder Crossing (Ramsden, personal communication), and the Fraser where it is joined by the Sumas as equal to that of the Fraser at Mission City. The

Table 38. The concentration, in parts per thousand, of Sweltzer Creek and other stream waters in different parts of the Fraser River. Calculations based on flow data on the appropriate forms R 79B for 1961–62. Concentrations over 10 parts per thousand are assumed to be above threshold for detection by salmon and are printed in italic.

A Sweltzer Creek water

Month	In Chilliwack R. at Vedder Crossing	In Sumas R. below its confluence with the Vedder Canal	In Fraser R. at Mission City	In Fraser R. at New Westminster
September	*90·9*	*76·9*	0·76	0·72
October	*45·5*	*40·0*	0·71	0·68
November	*52·6*	*47·6*	1·17	1·11
December	*83·3*	*71·4*	3·04	2·86
January	*66·7*	*55·6*	4·08	3·79
February	*55·6*	*47·6*	2·17	2·06
March	*90·9*	*76·9*	2·15	2·06
April	*52·6*	*45·5*	1·13	1·10
May	*40·0*	*34·5*	0·62	0·60

B Sweltzer Creek and Chilliwack water

Month	In Fraser R. at Mission City	In Fraser R. at New Westminster	At the mouth of Juan de Fuca Strait, assuming a concentration of Fraser R. water of between 10 and 50 parts per thousand
September	9·3	8·9	0·089 – 0·445
October	*16·1*	*15·6*	0·156 – 0·780
November	*22·7*	*21·7*	0·217 – 1·085
December	*40·0*	*37·0*	0·370 – 1·850
January	*66·7*	*62·5*	0·625 – 3·125
February	*41·7*	*38·5*	0·385 – 1·925
March	*26·3*	*25·0*	0·250 – 1·250
April	*22·2*	*21·7*	0·217 – 1·085
May	*16·1*	*15·6*	0·156 – 0·780

C Sumas River (Sumas + Vedder Canal)

Month	In Fraser R. at Mission City	In Fraser R. at New Westminster	At the mouth of Juan de Fuca Strait, assuming a concentration of Fraser R. water of between 10 and 50 parts per thousand
September	*10·2*	9·7	0·097 – 0·485
October	*17·9*	*17·0*	0·170 – 0·850
November	*25·0*	23·8	0·238 – 1·190
December	*43·5*	41·7	0·417 – 2·085
January	*71·4*	66·7	0·667 – 3·335
February	*45·5*	43·5	0·435 – 2·175
March	*28·6*	27·0	0·270 – 1·350
April	*24·4*	23·8	0·238 – 1·190
May	*17·9*	*17·2*	0·172 – 0·860

discharge of the Fraser at Mission City was estimated as being equal to that of the Fraser at Hope plus 1·5 times the discharge of the Harrison River. Mr. Ramsden suggested the use of this coefficient. Having obtained figures for the monthly discharges from the different streams, estimates were made of the concentration of one stream water in another, and the results of the calculations for 1961–62 are set out in Table 38. Discharge data for Sweltzer Creek are not available for the period May–August inclusive, so that the calculations do not cover all the months of the year.

Fraser River water

The Fraser River discharge at New Westminster can be calculated by adding 1·9 times the Harrison River discharge to that of the Fraser at Hope (Ramsden, personal communication). The Fraser water leaves Georgia Strait through the turbulent passages of the San Juan archipelago, where it is mixed with sea-water so that there is little vertical stratification within the inner part of the Juan de Fuca Strait. The inner and outer parts of this Strait are divided by a sill lying between Victoria and Port Angeles. On the ebb tide mixed water moves seaward over the sill into the outer Strait. Here vertical stratification is re-established, the mixed water running over the denser sea-water in the deeper water of the outer Strait, and receiving additional freshwater from the local land drainage. Tully (1952, 1958) has described the structure of the typical estuarine system which consists of an upper and lower zone separated by a halocline. Within the upper zone the surface layer of freshwater moves seawards and entrains sea-water from below to form the halocline. The entrained water is carried out to sea. Below the halocline the water is of uniform salinity indicating that freshwater is not transferred into the lower zone where there is an overall movement of sea-water into the embayment to replace that lost by entrainment. Herlinveaux and Tully (1961) have described the water movement in the Juan de Fuca Strait in terms of an interaction between estuarine, tidal, and other factors. The residual current is seaward in the upper zone and landward in the lower zone, the depth of no-net-motion between the two zones lying deeper on the northern side of the Strait. The concentration of freshwater within the upper zone in the Strait was found to vary seasonally from 2 to 6%, the higher concentrations coinciding with the maximum discharge of the Fraser in May and June. At this time of the year the Fraser discharge makes up 70 to 80% of the run-off so that it seems clear that Fraser River water is present at concentrations between

10 and 50 parts per thousand in the surface water where the Juan de Fuca outflow reaches the open sea. Table 38 includes estimates of the concentration of tributary waters in the mouth of the Strait based on these figures.

Fraser River water in the open sea

Tully (1942) has discussed the circulation in the approaches to Juan de Fuca Strait and considered the various conditions which could have an effect on the course taken by the outflow. Theoretical considerations show that the stream should veer to the right on leaving the Strait but the final course results from an interaction between the wind-induced drift current in the sea and

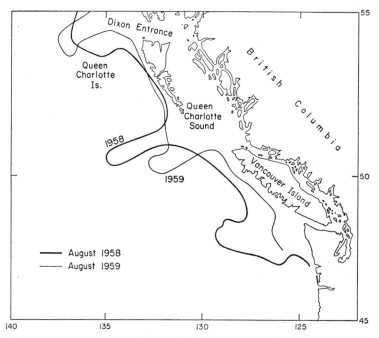

Fig. 85. The seaward spread of dilute surface water identified by the 32‰ S isohaline. (From Favorite, 1961. Outline from an Admiralty chart.)

the magnitude of the land drainage. With a north-westerly wind the drift current and land drainage flow are in opposition and the stream proceeds on its theoretical course so long as the latter is greater than the former. During south-easterly winds the stream flows north-westwards along the coast of Vancouver Island, with an eddy and counter-current developing on the seaward side. When the land drainage is at its maximum the Juan de Fuca stream goes farther out to sea before veering to the right. Under exceptional conditions, as in August 1958 (Favorite, 1961), the local run-off can be detected as a tongue of low salinity water ($<32 \cdot 0‰$) extending about 180 miles off shore. This is shown in Fig. 85. Favorite (1961, p. 319) makes the point that 'the extrusions of dilute surface water off the British Columbia coast provide an indication of the location in the ocean where the shoreward-migrating salmon first detect this dilution and may determine the point at which they enter the coastal waters.' But I have not been able to find an estimate of the concentration of Fraser River water likely to be present in the tongue that extended seawards from Juan de

Fuca Strait in 1958. Further mixing will have taken place and the concentrations at the 32‰ salinity contour may have fallen to less than 10 parts per thousand. By comparison with Barnes and Paquette's (1957) estimates for the Columbia River plume, the run-off water could take 2 months to travel from the Fraser mouth to the 32‰ contour 180 miles off shore. The effectiveness of the water as a stimulus to migrating salmon may depend as much on its age as its dilution. Fraser River water is certainly present in the coastal belt and, together with the run-off from Queen Charlotte Sound and Dixon Entrance, will be carried northwards along the shelf in the coastal waters of the Alaskan gyral. Most of this water will pass Kodiak Island, and move along the Aleutian chain as it is dissipated into the Bering Sea (Tully and Barber, 1960).

4. A sequential hypothesis for homestream detection

Estimates of the concentration of the homestream waters likely to be encountered by a sockeye returning to Cultus Lake are summarized in Table 38. To make use of this Table some figure must be assumed for the threshold concentration to which the fish responds. Idler *et al.*'s (1961) results suggest a figure of 25 parts per thousand for the lake water. But their experiments were not designed to determine thresholds and this concentration was the minimum to which the fish made a consistent and apparently unconditioned response under laboratory conditions. The real threshold may be lower, and in the discussion that follows it will be assumed to be of the order of 10 parts per thousand of parent stream or home river water. If this concentration is used as a working figure, reference to Table 38 shows that a sockeye would not react to Cultus Lake water in the Fraser River. Taking into account the concentration of Fraser River water at the mouth of Juan de Fuca Strait (10 to 50 parts per thousand), Sumas River water will be present at concentrations up to 3·3 parts per thousand. If the concentrations and thresholds are of the correct order of magnitude, the fish must depend on a succession of clues as it moves in from the sea to the spawning area. Thus a sockeye might detect the Fraser water within 100 to 200 miles of the Juan de Fuca Strait and certainly would do so at the mouth of the Strait. The Sumas discharge (made up of Sumas, Vedder, Chilliwack, and Cultus Lake water) could be detected within the Fraser. Having entered the Sumas River there should be no difficulty in locating the Vedder River and so on back to Sweltzer Creek and Cultus Lake. There are three main spawning beds within the lake itself, but it is not known if the fish return to spawn on the same one as that in which they were born, or what factors are involved in selecting one spawning bed in preference to another.

If the olfactory clues are used in this way, part of the homing mechanism may depend on the adult receiving the stimuli in a sequence which is the reverse of that imprinted in the young fish. I have found it helpful to imagine the olfactory imprints experienced by a downstream migrant as being stored sequentially in a manner analogous to coloured fruit pastilles lying one above another in a cylindrical pack. Let us suppose that a particular behavioural response is released when the olfactory stimulus matches the olfactory imprint at the top of the pack. The behaviour pattern could be a rheotropic response on which effect of the olfactory stimulus might be twofold; firstly, a kinetic component, the fish swimming faster; and secondly an orientating component, the fish swimming upstream. The rheotropic response would continue so long as stimulus and imprint matched and under normal conditions this would bring the fish under the influence of another set of olfactory stimuli to match the imprint next in the sequence. It is implicit in such a hypothesis that a matched imprint facilitates, but an unmatched imprint blocks access to the next in the series: you cannot have a blackcurrant pastille until the lime and strawberry ones have been eaten. A fish could pass a home tributary whose outflow was reduced below a threshold level during a drought, or whose passage was blocked by landslip or some other obstruction. If the salmon went on up the main river, the releasing stimulus and imprint would not match, the fish would swim slower and random exploratory movements replace those of the orientated rheotropic response. The fish would tend to collect in the main stream some distance above the junction with the home tributary. Ricker and Robertson (1935) have observed this behaviour in sockeye returning to Cultus Lake when Sweltzer Creek was blocked by a counting fence several hundred metres above its confluence with the Chilliwack at Vedder Crossing. Sockeye caught and marked at the fence and released below it in the creek were later observed in the Chilliwack both above and below the Sweltzer Creek junction. Of the 100 sockeye marked at the fence, all but one were later recovered in Sweltzer Creek.

The sequential hypothesis could be put to the test by carrying downstream migrants over part of their natural route to the sea and so destroying the sequence of imprints. Few of these fish would be expected to home. Similarly, adults known to be destined for a particular lake or stream could be caught and released at different positions in the main river so that the normal sequence of stimuli was disrupted. Evidence for the sequential hypothesis could come from returns to a lake which had routes to the sea through two different river systems, adults normally returning by the route through which they migrated downstream. If the proposed Skeena-Fraser diversion (Lindsey, 1957) were carried out, sockeye could leave and enter Babine and Stuart Lakes through either rivers, so providing the setting for such an experiment. Another possibility would be provided by the proposed diversion of the Upper Columbia River between Mica Creek and Revelstoke to join the Fraser at Shuswap Lake (see Fig. 9).

There are three lines of evidence in the literature to support a sequential hypothesis of homing.

1. Salmon transplanted as fingerlings usually return as adults to the point of release and not to the stream in which they were reared, although access to the rearing steam is readily available. Unpublished transplantation experiments which show this are referred to in the International Pacific Salmon Fisheries Commission's Annual Report for 1953 (pp. 27–8). For published work, that of Donaldson and Allen (1958) on silver or coho salmon, *O. kisutch*, may be referred to. Donaldson and Allen carried out an experiment with coho salmon reared at Soos Creek hatchery on the Green River, Washington State (see Fig. 82). The salmon were hatched early in 1951 and were kept at Soos Creek until 19 January 1952. A group of 72,000 fingerlings was divided into two lots. One group was taken to Issaquah hatchery, the other to the University of Washington School of Fisheries hatchery. In January and February the fingerlings were marked, the Issaquah fish by removal of the right pelvic fin, and those at the School of Fisheries by the removal of the left pelvic fin. The fingerlings were released on 18 March 1952. The fish from Issaquah Creek went down to the sea through Lake Sammamish, Sammamish River, Lake Washington and so into Lake Union where the other group of fingerlings was released. Both groups reached Puget Sound through the locks of the ship canal. These coho salmon returned to freshwater in the autumn and winter of 1953–54. None of the marked fish released into the Lake Washington drainage basin returned to Soos Creek where they were reared for the first year of their lives. Of 71 marked fish returning to Issaquah Creek, only 1 had a left pelvic fin missing. All of the 124 marked fish returning to the University hatchery had left ventral fins missing (Allen (1959, Table 1) gives the number of returns as 116).) These results show that the surviving adults returned to the stream in which they were released and not to the stream in whose water they were reared, although water from Soos Creek hatchery enters Puget Sound in Elliot Bay only some 5 miles to the south of the Ship Canal.

2. Another experiment which throws light on the mechanism of homing is reported in the International Pacific Salmon Fisheries Commission Annual Report for 1953 (IPSFC, 1954). This concerns a transplantation experiment carried out with sockeye in the Horsefly River, on the Upper Fraser. A map of the area is given in Fig. 86. It is important to note that neither the Little Horsefly River nor Horsefly Lake support a run of sockeye. The details of the experiment are summarized chronologically as follows.

1949: Artificially spawned eggs from Horsefly River sockeye were incubated, hatched, and the fingerlings raised at Quesnel Field Station hatchery.

1950: In November 94,000 fingerlings, of which 64,500 were marked by fin clipping, were taken by air to Quesnel Lake at the mouth of the Horsefly River. Scale studies showed that the finger-lings stayed in this area until they migrated downstream in the spring of 1951.

1952: Thirteen 3-year-old sockeye returned to the hatchery outlet; 9 of these fish were marked. Sockeye had never been taken there before, and no marked fish were taken elsewhere.

1953: One marked 4-year-old sockeye returned to the Upper Horsefly River, and 203 marked and 66 unmarked fish returned to the hatchery outlet. Fourteen dead marked fish were recovered near the Horsefly-Little Horsefly confluence. No other marked fish were recovered.

In this experiment, the fingerlings were released in the same watershed as that in which they were reared and the adults returned to the rearing area. Furthermore, to do so they travelled from

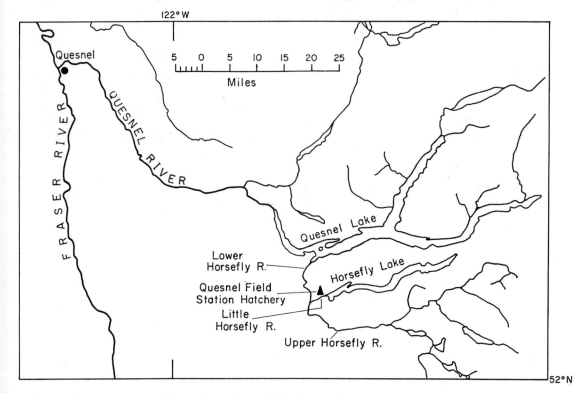

Fig. 86. Place names on the Upper Fraser River, British Columbia, relevant to the Horsefly River transplantation experiment. (Based on an International North Pacific Salmon Fisheries Commission map.)

Quesnel Lake via the Lower and Little Horsefly Rivers, over which they had been carried downstream by aeroplane. It is reasonable to suppose that a chemical substance carried downstream from the hatchery to Quesnel Lake, occurring in the correct sequence and at a concentration above threshold, was the important factor for the successful homing. If, in the Horsefly River experiments, rearing and release areas had been in different watersheds the fish might have returned to the release area, as Donaldson and Allen found. The fish might also have returned to the release area if this had been upstream, rather than downstream, from the rearing area.

3. There is a hatchery at Laholm, about 10 km from the mouth of the River Lagan, in Sweden. The Lagan runs into the sea at Laholm Bay, in the Kattegat. The Bay and river are shown in Fig. 34. Carlin (1955) compared the returns of Atlantic salmon smolts released into the river at the hatchery with those of smolts released into the sea from the shore some 8 km south of the river mouth. The results were as follows:

Two-year-old smolts tagged and released in 1952		Tagged fish recaptured as salmon in the summer of 1953	
	No.	Near river mouth	In the river
Released in river	1,461	30	47
Released in sea	623	14	6

Carlin points out that the numbers of recoveries in the sea near the river mouth are close to those expected (31 and 13) considering the numbers released, but there is a statistically significant difference (47 and 6 found as against 37 and 16 expected, $p < 0.01$) between the numbers recovered in the river itself. Carlin (1955, p. 68) concludes 'that it is not entirely the same mechanism which controls the orientation of the salmon towards the coast in the vicinity of the home river and which lead them into the river' (p. 68). This experiment was similar in design to that carried out at Horsefly River where the transplanted fish returned to the hatchery. A possible explanation of the failure of the Swedish experiment is that the fish released in the sea did not receive the set of imprints normally associated with the downstream movement between the hatchery and the river mouth which would enable them to home successfully.

Although the three sets of observations in no way prove the validity of the sequential hypothesis, they are consistent with a homing mechanism of this type and suggest that it would be worth while to carry out special experiments to put the matter to the test. It may be noted that Patten (1964) introduces a similar hypothesis into his mathematical approach to salmon migration.

5. The behavioural mechanism

Chemical substances characteristic of the home stream or parent river may be detected at a distance but the stimulus received by the fish can give no information as to the direction of the home unless the chemical gradient is steep enough to elicit a klino- or tropotaxis. Steep gradients may occur close to the source or on the boundaries between water masses. In the latter instance a fish may be able to move quickly into the water mass containing the home stream substance but having moved in will not obtain any further information as to which way to swim. The fish would get home if it responded kinetically to the home stream substance but the behavioural mechanism would be time consuming and probably inefficient over long distances. A chemical substance would be more effective as a simple sign stimulus which would release a pattern of behaviour, for example a positive rheotropic response, which would take the fish upstream towards the home. This would be efficient when the water flow is in one direction, as in a river or ocean current, and when the fish has the necessary clues to orientate to the flow. When tidal currents predominate, as in coastal or estuarine areas, movement upstream would be facilitated if, as Verwey (1958) suggests, the fish could discriminate between ebb and flood tide.

Creutzberg (1961) has shown that elvers probably migrate from the sea to freshwater by such a mechanism. He studied the rheotropic responses of elvers in a circular flume, and simulated ebb and flood tides by increasing and decreasing the content of inland water in the experimental chamber. On ebb tides the elvers swam against the current, and burrowed into the bottom at high velocities. On flood tides they rose from the bottom and either swam with or were carried passively by the current. Creutzberg showed that the change in the behaviour of the elvers to the current was made in response to an unidentified chemical characteristic of inland water. The results of these experiments were consistent with observations made at sea, which suggested an inshore movement of elvers in the top half of the water column on the flood tide and their presence nearer the bottom during the ebb. Creutzberg (1961, p. 334) draws attention to one difficulty in his hypothesis: 'when during the flood tide elvers rise to higher water levels they stay in the same water mass all the time. It is hard to see how under such conditions they can perceive the end of the flood tide'. This would be a problem if the water column were completely homogeneous but this will only occur under conditions of extreme turbulence. Many estuarine systems have the stratified structure described by Tully, to which reference has already been made in connexion with the Fraser outflow in the Juan de Fuca Strait. In such a system elvers would be carried passively towards the embayment in the lower sea-water zone where the residual motion is inshore. Creutzberg has not extended his hypothesis to a water body with a typical estuarine structure and it would be interesting to know what would happen to an elver which was carried, by entrainment, into the upper brackish zone. Without a reference point orientation to the current would be impossible and the elver would be carried out to sea unless it responded to the inland water substance by swimming down through the halocline into the lower zone.

It is not known if salmon travel from the coastal waters to the river mouth by a behavioural mechanism similar to that used by elvers. Tagging experiments with sockeye (Verhoeven and Davidoff, 1962) have given information regarding the migration route from the sea through Juan de Fuca Strait to the Fraser River, and certain aspects of the migration can be correlated with the river discharge (Gilhousen, 1960). But no attempts appear to have been made to relate the movements of the salmon or their depth of swimming—in short, their availability to the commercial fishery—to the oceanographic and tidal structure of the area. Babcock (1931, p. 57) gives the following account of their migratory behaviour: 'They travel forward in salt water always on the flood tide and close to the surface, commonly displaying their presence by leaping and breaking the surface of the water. On the ebbing of the tide they disappear, are not in evidence, and their movements are unknown. On the return of the flood they reappear on the surface close to the place where they disappeared, and continue their way to the Fraser. They enter the Fraser on the flood, going up as far as the tide goes, but when the tide ebbs they do not turn with it or disappear from the surface; they continue on up-stream.' While further observations may confirm or deny the truth of this account, what Babcock wrote would almost suffice as a description of the upstream migration of young eels. The behavioural mechanism of the two species might well be similar. But orientation to the current requires an external reference point and it is not clear where a salmon could get one over the deep water in Juan de Fuca Strait. The same problem arises if an olfactory stimulus is to release a rheotropic response when the fish are swimming pelagically in the coastal waters. If a reference point can be obtained at a discontinuity layer as suggested earlier (p. 194), the vertical distribution of the salmon should be closely related to the structure of the water column. But no data are available on this point.

THE OLFACTORY HYPOTHESIS AND MARINE SPECIES

Some herring return to spawn in the area in which they were born (Norwegian spring spawners). It has not been proved that herring spawn on the parent ground (Sandettié or Ailly grounds within the Downs spawning area) or on one of a number of spawning beds within a particular ground. Herring eggs are demersal and hatch in 10 to 14 days. The pro-larvae, with yolk sac attached, may spend a further 4 to 5 days close to the bottom but it is not known if they burrow into the gravel. As many herring spawning grounds are in areas where there are fast tidal streams the very young stages are unlikely to be able to maintain their stations over the spawning grounds for any length of time, so that the experience that a herring has of its parent spawning bed and ground must be restricted to a very limited period. The larval stages of the herring, like those of the cod, plaice and eel, which have pelagic eggs, are carried away from the immediate vicinity of the spawning ground, but the young fish drift for several weeks in the same body of water as that in which they were spawned and hatched. So the period over which they could receive imprints of the parent spawning ground water is comparable with, although usually less than, that available to pink salmon or the sockeye of Harrison Rapids.

But if olfactory clues are used as local landmarks by cod, plaice, herring, and eels, their role may differ from that suggested when describing homing behaviour of salmon. Salmon migrate upstream in estuaries and rivers, but it is by no means certain that the first spawning migrations of the other species conform to this pattern. Such a pattern may hold for plaice whose nursery grounds in the Southern and German Bights of the North Sea lie downstream from the main spawning grounds. Although the nursery grounds of the Arcto-Norwegian, Icelandic, and south-west Greenland cod stocks are also downstream from their spawning grounds, it has not been shown that the fish migrate upstream to spawn. Even if the migrations were shown to be upstream it would be unlikely that the maturing fish, which are believed to be near the bottom in depths of 200 to 500 m, would be swimming in the same type of water as that in which they drifted near the surface as larvae. A similar doubt exists in the case of the eel, whose leptocephali drift in the surface 60 m, while the adults return (if one accepts Schmidt's hypothesis and the evidence of anatomical changes in the maturing fish) at much greater depths, possibly from 500 to 1,000 m. There is no evidence of a spawning migration against the current by Icelandic, Buchan or Dogger herring. The Downs herring may be an exception in that they probably move south against the residual north-east current during part of their spawning migration down the Southern Bight of the North Sea. But unless the spawning migration is upstream it is difficult to see how a chemical stimulus could act at a distance and its role must be restricted to the immediate vicinity of the spawning grounds. Furthermore, if the adult fish are returning in a body of water which is of a different origin from that in which they left their parent spawning area or ground, they could not make use of a sequential imprinting and matching mechanism similar to that suggested for salmon.

Transplantation experiments have shown that salmon return not to where they were hatched or reared but to where they were released. They may only return to the hatching or rearing area if this is within a limited distance upstream of the release area. In these transplantation experiments the release area is equivalent to the freshwater nursery ground which normally lies on the route by which the adults return from the sea to the spawning grounds.

Some marine fish may recruit to the spawning grounds direct from the nursery and in so doing retrace the track over which they travelled in the larval and juvenile stages. Southern Bight plaice provide one example (p. 171). Two further examples are the recruitment of herring from the Scottish Firths to the Buchan grounds (p. 129), and the possibility that some Downs herring recruit to the Southern Bight grounds direct from the Bløden (p. 135). So far as the herring are concerned, the proportion of first-time spawners that migrate direct from the nursery grounds may be small. For example, Downs herring spawned on the Hinder and Sandettié grounds grow up on the Bløden south and east of the Dogger Bank. But many of the adolescent fish later move north-west and enter the English north-east coast summer fishery. When these recruits leave the north-east coast for their spawning grounds they do not return to the Bløden, but round the Norfolk Banks and run down towards the Hinder and Sandettié.

Some of the differences between the spawning migrations of salmon and those of cod, plaice, herring, and eels can now be summarized. During part of their migration salmon move upstream in the same type of water as that in which they went down to the sea. Odours, to which the fish may have been conditioned by imprinting, are believed to provide the sensory clues during this stage of the migration. In contrast to salmon, the spawning migrations of cod, plaice, herring, and eels may not be upstream and against the current and the fish may not be in the same type of water as that in which they were carried from the spawning ground to the nursery ground.[1] In these circumstances the use of olfactory clues by cod, plaice, herring, and eels during their spawning migrations seems unlikely and any role that they might have as local landmarks is probably restricted to the immediate vicinity of the spawning grounds.

[1] Not all salmonids swim upstream to spawn, the trout spawning in the outlet of Loon Lake, British Columbia, being an exception (Lindsey *et al.*, 1959).

Chapter 13

Epilogue

This enquiry set out to determine whether or not enough is known about fish migrations to account for the facts, and should the facts themselves prove inadequate, to suggest what further observations and experiments are required.

For salmon, eels, cod, herring, and plaice the general picture of homing and migration is clear. But there are several instances where there is reasonable doubt concerning important matters of fact, and until these problems are resolved, progress in the interpretation and the understanding of the mechanism of homing and migration will be slow. For example, we do not know what proportion of mature salmon successfully return from the high seas to the coastal waters; it has not been shown that European eels return to the Sargasso Sea to spawn; and it is not clear whether Buchan-, Bank-, and Downs-spawned herring return to their parent area, or their parent ground, as recruit spawners.

While there are inadequacies in matters of fact, there are none in the number of hypotheses to account for those facts that are known. Here the difficulty is to decide between them. For example, the return of mature salmon from the North Pacific to the coastal waters can be accounted for by drift, by random or systematic search, by orientation to water currents at a rheocline, or by orientation to celestial clues: all appear to fit the facts so far as they are known. The spawning migration of the Arcto-Norwegian cod would be explained by a drift with a south-going current, or an active movement against a north-going current.

The method of multiple working hypotheses has much to commend it, and the merits of this approach have been persuasively argued by T. C. Chamberlain in an old essay recently reprinted in *Science* (Chamberlain, 1965). Much of the fundamental work on the study of fish migration must necessarily be carried out at sea, from an expensive platform, the research ship.[1] A possible danger in applying the method of multiple working hypotheses to sea-going work is that the limited research effort will be spread so that no single aspect receives the concentrated attack that may be required to make observations and measurements conclusive.

The danger inherent in diversity could be reduced if there was one set of observations which was relevant to all hypotheses of migration: the available research effort could then be directed to obtaining the critical data. I believe that one of the fundamental questions to be asked, and answered, is simply this: what are the movements of migrants relative to those of the water at the depth at which they are swimming? No critical data are available for any species on migration in the open sea.

How can this problem be tackled? Fish must be located, identified, and followed singly or in groups, and at the same time the water currents must be measured at the depth at which the fish are swimming. This is really a problem of instrumentation and, so far as the fish are concerned,

---

[1] At today's prices (1967) a 60 to 70 m distant water research ship would cost not less than £750,000 to build and £400 a day to run.

sector-scanning sonar, to which reference has already been made (p. 40), would seem to be the appropriate technique. With this equipment it should be possible to track large single fish (70 cm and over) or groups of smaller fish at ranges up to, and possibly over, 200 m, for a period limited only by the weather and the will of the operator. Water current measurements are probably best made from a sister ship, which could track drogues and take spot profiles with a recording bathy-rheograph. The movements of salmon (in the North Pacific) and herring (in the Norwegian Sea) could be studied in this way. Fish close to the bottom in deep water (cod in the Barents Sea), or fish of relatively poor target strength (plaice), present a more difficult problem which may be solved with the use of transponding sonic tags, tracking being carried out with a scanning system.

A sector-scanner should give the track of the fish and, with the relevant information on water movement, it should be possible to decide how the fish was moving relative to the current. Furthermore, a high resolution scanning system may be able to position the fish with sufficient accuracy to measure the step-length between turns, the turning frequency, and the angle of turn. Detailed observations of this sort would be carried out over a relatively short time scale (minutes rather than hours), and it might be necessary to make corrections for linear motion of the ship relative to the target.

Tracking fish with a sector-scanning sonar should give relatively detailed information on the movements of single fish or shoals for periods up to several hours, or even one or two days, during which the target may have moved several kilometres. This is essentially a small-scale attack and it would be useful if the distance and time scale over which shoals were tracked could be substantially increased. Fixed-site surveillance sonar is used to give warning of the approach of submarines and while the operational range of modern equipment has not been disclosed, it is clear from Leary's (1965) account that detection is possible at ranges up to tens of kilometres. A large shoal of herring (200 m long, 50 m wide, 20 m deep, packing density 1 to 10 fish m^3, number of fish 10^5 to 10^6) is probably as good a target as a submarine, which raises the possibility of tracking shoals at long range, and over long distances, from selected sites. The sea-going platform is then replaced by one, or several, shore stations. The use of these sophisticated sonar techniques might give the fishery biologist a detection range comparable to that enjoyed by bird watchers working with radar (Eastwood, 1967). This is something for which we would all be grateful.

References/Author Index

AASEN, O. (1952). The Lusterfjord herring and its environment. *FiskDir. Skr.*, Serie Havundersøkelser, **10**: (2) 63 pp. [89]

AASEN, O. (1958). Norwegian herring investigations in the Norwegian Sea 1956. *Annls biol., Copenh.*, **13**: 176–8. [108, 110]

AASEN, O. (1959). Norwegian investigations in the Norwegian Sea, 1957. *Annls biol. Copenh.*, **14**: 148–9. [109, 110]

AASEN, O. (1962). On the correlation between the arrival and spawning of the Norwegian winter herring. *J. Cons. perm. int. Explor. Mer*, **27**: 162–6. [104, 111, 206]

AASEN, O., ANDERSEN, K. P., GULLAND, J., POPP MADSEN, K., and SAHRHAGE, D. (1961). ICES herring tagging experiments in 1957 and 1958. *Rapp. P.-v. Réun. Cons. perm. int. Explor. Mer*, **152**: 50 pp. [20, 125]

ADLER, H. E. (1963). Sensory factors in migration. *Anim. Behav.*, **11**: 566–77. [4,]

AHLMANN, H. W. (1949). Climatic changes in the arctic in relation to plants and animals. *Rapp. P.-v. Réun. Cons. perm. int. Explor. Mer*, **125**: 1–52. [158]

ALBERT, PRINCE OF MONACO (1932). A new chart of the currents of the North Atlantic (Read at meeting of British Association, 1892). *Résult. Camp. Scient. Prince Albert 1*, (84) 132–5. [77, 79]

ALEKSEEV, A. P. and ISTOSHIN, B. V. (1959). Chart of constant currents in the Norwegian and Greenland Seas. *Spec. scient. Rep. U.S. Fish Wildl. Serv. Fisheries*, (327) 69–76. [10, 99, 100, 101]

ALLEN, G. H. (1959). Behavior of chinook and silver salmon. *Ecology*, **40**: 108–13. [266]

ALLEN, K. R. (1951). The Horokiwi Stream, a study of a trout population. *Fish. Bull. N.Z.*, (10) 238 pp. [245]

ALM, G. (1934). Salmon in the Baltic precincts. *Rapp. P.-v. Réun. Cons. perm. int. Explor. Mer*, **92**: 1–63. [63]

ALM, G. (1958). Seasonal fluctuations in the catches of salmon in the Baltic. *J. Cons. perm. int. Explor. Mer*, **23**: 399–433. [63]

ALM, G. (1959). Connection between maturity, size, and age in fishes. *Rep. Inst. Freshwat. Res. Drottningholm*, (40) 5–145. [92]

ALVERSON, D. L. (1960). A study of annual and seasonal bathymetric catch patterns for commercially important groundfishes of the Pacific northwest coast of North America. *Bull. Pacif. mar. Fish. Commn*, (4) 66 pp. [33]

ALVERSON, D. L. and CHATWIN, B. M. (1957). Results from tagging experiments on a spawning stock of petrale sole, *Eopsetta jordani* (Lockington). *J. Fish. Res. Bd Can.*, **14**: 953–74. [24]

ANCELLIN, J. (1951). La pêche française en Sud de la Mer du Nord et de la Manche Orientale. *Annls biol., Copenh.*, **7**: 141–3. [90]

ANCELLIN, J. (1957). Considerations sur les harengs du Sud de la Mer du Nord et de la Manche Orientale. *Sci. Pêche*, (43) 10 pp. [139]

ANCELLIN, J. and NEDELEC, C. (1959). Marquage de harengs en Mer du Nord et en Manche Orientale (Campagne du 'Président-Théodore-Tissier,' novembre 1957). *Revue Trav. Inst. (scient. tech.) Pêch. marit.*, **23**: 177–201. [127, 133, 135]

ANDERSSON, K. A. (1946). Some remarks on the fluctuations in the herring fishing on the West Coast of Sweden. *Rapp. P.-v. Réun. Cons. perm. int. Explor. Mer*, **118**: 31–9. [98]

ANDERSSON, K. A. (1950). The herring fishery and the stock of herring in the northern North Sea and the Skagerak during the season 1949–50. *J. Cons. perm. int. Explor. Mer*, **17**: 40–3. [130]

ÅNGSTRÖM, A. (1925). The albedo of various surfaces of ground. *Geogr. Annlr*, **7**: 323–42. [236]

ANON. (1921). Use of aeroplanes in the fisheries. *Rep. U.S. Commnr Fish.* 1920, 10–11. [35]

ANON. (1932). A guide to fish marks. *J. cons. perm. int. Explor. Mer*, **7**: 133–65. [18]

ANON. (1952a). Tables for sea water density. H.O. Publ. (615). 265 pp. U.S. Navy Hydrographic Office, Washington, D.C. (no pagination). [221]

ANON. (1952*b*). Natural illumination charts. Report 374–1. Department of the Navy. Bureau of Ships. Washington 25 D.C. (no pagination). [229]

ANON. (1953). A guide to fish marks. *J. Cons. perm. int. Explor. Mer*, **19**: 241–89. [18]

ANON. (1955*a*). Night spotting of Sardine schools by airplane successful. *Comml Fish. Rev.*, **17**: (12) 19. [35]

ANON. (1955*b*). On the salmon in waters adjacent to Japan. *Bull. int. N. Pacif. Fish. Commn*, (1) 57–92. [65]

ANON. (1957). Helicopter's tests may prove revolutionary. *Fishg News, Aberd.*, (2292) 1. [35]

ANON. (1960*a*). Proc. Joint scient. meeting of ICNAF, ICES, and FAO on fishing effort, the effect of fishing on resources and the selectivity of fishing gear. Volume 1—reports. *Spec. Publs int. Commn NW. Atlant. Fish.*, (2) 45 pp. [87]

ANON. (1960*b*). *Rep. int. Pacif. Salm. Fish. Commn* 1959. 40 pp. [224]

ANON. (1963). Surface water supply of Canada. Pacific drainage, British Columbia and Yukon territory water year 1959–60. *Wat. Resour. Pap., Ottawa*, (131) 402 pp. [226, 228, 262]

ANON. (1966). A guide to fish marks (third edition). *J. Cons. perm. int. Explor. Mer*, **30**: 87–160. [18]

VON ARX, W. S. (1962). *Introduction to physical oceanography*. Addison-Wesley, Reading (Mass.) and London. 422 pp. [195]

ATKINSON, G. T. (1912). Report on the English plaice experiments, 1906–1908. *Rep. N. Sea Fish. Invest. Comm.*, (4) 1909. 225–90. [172]

BABCOCK, J. (1931). The Pacific salmon. *Rep. Commnr Fish. Br. Columb.* 1930, 56–61. [269]

BAINBRIDGE, R. (1952). Underwater observations on the swimming of marine zooplankton. *J. mar. biol. Ass. U.K.*, **31**: 107–12. [220]

BAINBRIDGE, R. (1958). The speed of swimming of fish as related to size and to the frequency and amplitude of the tail beat. *J. exp. Biol.*, **35**: 109–33. [16]

BAINBRIDGE, R. (1960). Speed and stamina in three fish. *J. exp. Biol.* **37**: 129–53. [16]

BALLS, R. (1951). Environmental changes in herring behaviour: a theory of light avoidance, as suggested by echo-sounding observations in the North Sea. *J. Cons. perm. int. Explor. Mer*, **17**: 274–98. [93]

BALMAIN, K. H. and SHEARER, W. M. (1956). Records of salmon and sea trout caught at sea. *Freshwat. Salm. Fish. Res.*, (11) 12 pp. [63]

BARDACH, J. E. (1956). The sensitivity of the goldfish (*Carassius auratus* L.) to point heat stimulation. *Am. Nat.*, **90**: 309–17. [192]

BARDACH, J. E. (1958). On the movements of certain Bermuda reef fishes. *Ecology*, **39**: 139–46. [245, 252, 255, 258]

BARDACH, J. E. and BJORKLUND, R. G. (1957). The temperature sensitivity of some American freshwater fishes. *Am. Nat.*, **91**: 233–51. [192]

BARLOW, J. S. (1964). Inertial navigation as a basis for animal navigation. *J. theor. Biol.*, **6**: 76–117. [215]

BARNABY, J. T. (1952). Offshore fishing in Bristol Bay and Bering Sea. *Spec. scient. Rep. U.S. Fish. Wildl. Serv. Fisheries*, (89) 30 pp. [36]

BARNES, C. A. and PAQUETTE, R. G. (1957). Circulation near the Washington coast. *Proc. 8th. Pacif. Sci. Congr.*, **3**: 585–608. [265]

BASS, G. A. and RASCOVICH, M. (1965). A device for the sonic tracking of large fishes. *Zoologica N.Y.*, **50**: 75–82. [40, 224]

BATTLE, H. I., HUNTSMAN, A. G., JEFFERS, A. M., JEFFERS, G. W., JOHNSON, W. H., and MCNAIRN, N. A. (1936). Fatness, digestion and food of Passamaquoddy young herring. *J. Fish. Res. Bd Can.*, **2**: 401–29. [93]

BATTLE, H. I. and SPRALES, W. M. (1960). A description of the semi-buoyant eggs and early developmental stages of the goldeye, *Hiodon alosoides* (Rafinesque). *J. Fish. Res. Bd Can.*, **17**: 245–65. [12]

BAXTER, I. G. (1958). The composition of the Minch herring stocks. *Rapp. P.-v. Réun. Cons. perm. int. Explor. Mer*, **143**: (2) 81–94. [103, 116]

BAXTER, I. G. (1959). Fecundities of winter-spring and summer-autumn herring spawners. *J. Cons. perm. int. Explor. Mer*, **25**: 73–80. [138]

BEAUGÉ, L. (1931). Rapport de mission a Terre-neuve et au Groenland (Campagne 1930). *Revue Trav. Off. (Scient tech.) Pêch. marit.*, **4**: 87–129. [64]

BEEBE, W. (1931). Notes on the gill-finned goby *Bathygobius soporator* (Cuvier and Valenciennes) *Zoologica N.Y.*, **12**: 55–66. [249]

BELL, F. H. and PRUTER, A. T. (1958). Climatic temperature changes and commercial yields of some marine fisheries. *J. Fish. Res. Bd Can.*, **15**: 625–83. [33, 158]

BERGERON, J. (1962). Bibliographie du saumon de L'Atlantique. *Contr. Dép. Pêch., Québ.*, (88) 64 pp. [43]

BERTELSEN, E. (1955). Danish herring tagging in the North Sea, 1949–1951. *Rapp. P.-v. Réun. Cons. perm. int. Explor. Mer*, **140**: (2) 9–10. [132]

BERTELSEN, E. and POPP MADSEN, K. (1954). Young herring from the Bløden Ground area. *Annls biol., Copenh.*, **10**: 155–6. [126]

BERTELSEN, E. and POPP MADSEN, K. (1957). Young herring from the Bløden Ground area. *Annls biol., Copenh.*, **12**: 197–8. [126]

BERTIN, L. (1956). *Eels, a biological study*. Cleaver-Hume, Lond., 192 pp. [26, 77, 80]

BEST, E. A. (1957). Tagged Dover sole (*Microstomus pacificus*) at liberty six years. *Calif. Fish Game*, **43**: 167. [22]

BEVERTON, R. J. H., GULLAND, J. A. and MARGETTS, A. R. (1959). Whiting tagging: how the tag return rate is affected by the condition of fish when tagged. *J. Cons. perm. int. Explor. Mer*, **25**: 53–7. [21, 22]

BEVERTON, R. J. H. and HOLT, S. J. (1957). On the dynamics of exploited fish populations. *Fishery Invest., Lond.*, Ser. 2, **19**: 533 pp. [15, 19, 22, 179]

BHATIA, D. (1931a). On the production of annual zones in the scales of the rainbow trout (*Salmo irideus*). 1. *J. exp. Zool.*, **59**: 45–59. [28]

BHATIA, D. (1931b). A critical study of the scales of two specimens of starved and excessively fed trout—*Salmo irideus*. *J. Cons. perm. int. Explor. Mer*, **6**: 266–72. [28]

BHATIA, D. (1932). Factors involved in the production of annual zones on the scales of the rainbow trout (*Salmo irideus*). II. *J. exp. Biol.*, **9**: 6–11. [28]

BHATTACHARYYA, R. N. (1957). The food and feeding habits of larval and post-larval herring in the northern North Sea. *Mar. Res.*, (3) 15 pp. [92]

BIDDER, G. P. (1906). Principal results of the experiments with bottom-trailers. *Rapp. P.-v. Réun. Cons. perm. int. Explor. Mer*, **6**: XXXV–XLII. [15]

BIRGE, E. A. and JUDAY, C. (1929). Transmission of solar radiation by the waters of inland lakes. *Trans. Wis. Acad. Sci. Arts Lett.*, **24**: 509–80. [238]

BIGELOW, H. B. and WELSH, W. W. (1925). Fishes of the Gulf of Maine. *Bull. Bur. Fish., Wash.*, **40**: (1) 567 pp. [77]

BISHAI, H. M. (1960). The effect of water currents on the survival and distribution of fish larvae. *J. Cons. perm. int. Explor. Mer*, **25**: 134–46. [16, 200]

BJERKAN, P. (1918). The young herring of the North Sea. *Rep. Norw. Fishery mar. Invest.*, **3**: (2) 21 pp. [125]

BLACKBURN, M. and TUBB, J. A. (1950). Measures of abundance of certain pelagic fish in some south-eastern Australian waters. *Bull. Commonw. scient. ind. Res. Org.*, (251) 74 pp. [36]

BLAXTER, J. H. S. (1958). The racial problem in herring from the viewpoint of recent physiological, evolutionary and genetical theory. *Rapp. P.-v. Réun. Cons. perm. int. Explor. Mer*, **143**: (2) 10–19. [24]

BLAXTER, J. H. S. and DICKSON, W. (1959). Observations on the swimming speeds of fish. *J. Cons. perm. int. Explor. Mer*, **24**: 472–9. [16]

BLAXTER, J. H. S. and HOLLIDAY, F. G. T. (1958). Herring (*Clupea harengus* L.) in aquaria. II. Feeding. *Mar. Res.*, (6) 22 pp. [93]

BLAXTER, J. H. S. and HOLLIDAY, F. G. T. (1963). The behaviour and physiology of herring and other clupeids. *Adv. mar. Biol.*, **1**: 262–393. [87, 224]

BÖHNECKE, G. (1922). Salzgehalt und Strömungen der Nordsee. *Veroff. Inst. Meeresk. Univ. Berl.*, NF A, (10) 34 pp. [120, 121]

BOLSTER, G. C. (1955). English tagging experiments. *Rapp. P.-v. Réun. Cons. perm. int. Explor. Mer*, **140**: (2) 11–4. [133]

BOLSTER, G. C. and BRIDGER, J. P. (1957). Nature of the spawning area of herrings. *Nature, Lond.*, **179**: 638. [91]

BORLEY, J. O. (1916). An analysis and review of the English plaice marking experiments in the North Sea. *Fishery Invest., Lond.*, Ser. 2, **3**: (3) 126 pp. [15, 172]

BOULET, P. C. (1958). La perception visuelle du mouvement chez la perche et la seiche. *Mém. Mus. natn. Hist. nat., Paris*, Serie A. Zool., **17**: 131 pp. [220]

BOWDEN, K. F. (1953). Measurements of wind currents in the sea by the method of towed electrodes. *Nature, Lond.*, **171**: 735–7. [195]

BOWDEN, K. F. (1955). Physical oceanography of the Irish Sea. *Fishery Invest., Lond.*, Ser. 2, **18**: (8) 67 pp. [177]

BOWERS, A. B. and HOLLIDAY, F. G. T. (1961). Histological changes in the gonad associated with the reproductive cycle of the herring (*Clupea harengus* L.) *Mar. Res.*, (5) 16 pp. [89, 90, 91]

BOWMAN, A. (1921). The distribution of plaice eggs in the Northern North Sea. *Scient. Invest. Fishery Bd Scotl.*, (1) 33 pp.   [170]

BOWMAN, A. (1933). Plaice marking experiments in Shetland waters 1923–1931 (inclusive). *J. Cons. perm. int. Explor. Mer*, 8: 223–9.   [8, 15, 179, 180, 181, 219]

BOWMAN, A. (1935). Lemon soles. Marking experiments in Scottish waters during the period 1919–31. *Scient. Invest. Fishery Bd Scotl.*, (1) 42 pp.   [15]

BRAARUD, T. and RUVD, J. T. (1932). The 'Øst' expedition to the Denmark Strait in 1929. 1. Hydrography. *Hvalråd. Skr.*, (4) 44 pp.   [149]

BRAEMER, W. (1959). Versuche zu der im Richtungsgehen der Fische erhaltenen Zeitschätzung. *Verh. dt. zool. Ges. Zool. Anz.*, suppl., 23: 276–88.   [235]

BRAEMER, W. (1960). A critical review of the sun-azimuth hypothesis. *Cold Spring Harb. Symp. quant. Biol.*, 25: 413–27.   [235, 242]

BRAWN, V. M. (1960a). Underwater television observations of the swimming speed and behaviour of captive herring. *J. Fish. Res. Bd Can.*, 17: 689–98.   [197]

BRAWN, V. M. (1960b). Seasonal and diurnal vertical distribution of herring (*Clupea harengus* L.) in Passamaquoddy Bay, N.B. *J. Fish. Res. Bd Can.*, 17: 699–711.   [93]

BRAWN, V. M. (1961). Reproductive behaviour of the cod (*Gadus callarias* L.). *Behaviour*, 18: 177–98.   [147]

BREDER, C. M. and NIGRELLI, R. F. (1938). The significance of differential locomotor activity as an index to the mass physiology of fishes. *Zoologica N.Y.*, 23: 1–29.   [215]

BRETHERTON, F. P. and LORD ROTHSCHILD. (1961). Rheotaxis of spermatozoa. *Proc. R. Soc.*, B, 153: 490–502.   [225]

BRETT, J. R. and GROOT, C. (1963). Some aspects of olfactory and visual responses in Pacific salmon. *J. Fish. Res. Bd Can.*, 20: 287–303.   [187, 259]

BROADBENT, V. W. (1947). The Japanese salmon industry. *Fishery Leafl. Fish Wildl. Serv. U.S.*, (230) 12 pp. (mimeo).   [65]

BROWN, M. E. (1946). The growth of brown trout (*Salmo trutta* Linn.). II. The growth of two-year-old trout at a constant temperature of 11.5°C. *J. exp. Biol.*, 22: 130–44.   [28]

BRUUN, A. F. (1937). Contributions to the life histories of the Deep Sea Eeels: Synaphobranchidae. *Dana Rep.*, 2: (9) 31 pp.   [70, 75]

BRUUN, A. F. (1963). The breeding of the North Atlantic freshwater eels. *Adv. mar. Biol.*, 1: 137–69.   [70, 72]

BUCKLAND, F. (1880). *Natural history of British fishes*. Unwin, Lond. 420 pp.   [259]

BÜCKMANN, A. (1942). Die Untersuchungen der Biologischen Anstalt über die Ökologie der Herinsbrut in der südlichen Nordsee. *Helgoländer wiss. Meeresunters.*, 3: 1–57.   [123, 124]

BÜCKMANN, A. (1950). Die Untersuchungen der Biologischen Anstalt über die Ökologie der Heringsbrut in der südlichen Nordsee. *Helgoländer wiss. Meeresunters.*, 3: 171–205.   [91, 95]

BÜCKMANN, A. and HEMPEL, G. (1957). Untersuchungen an der Heringslarven-bevölkerung der Innenjade. *Helgoländer wiss. Meeresunters.*, 6: 52–70.   [123, 124]

BULL, H. O. (1936). Studies on conditioned responses in fishes. Part VII. Temperature perception in teleosts. *J. mar. biol. Ass. U.K.*, 21: 1–27.   [192]

BULL, H. O. (1952). An evaluation of our knowledge of fish behaviour in relation to hydrography. *Rapp. P.-v. Réun. Cons. perm. int. Explor. Mer*, 131: 8–23.   [187, 191]

BURD, A. C. (1962). Growth and recruitment of the herring of the southern North Sea. *Fishery Invest.*, *Lond.*, Ser. 2, 23: (5) 1–42.   [92, 96, 133, 135, 137, 138, 140]

BUTLER, R. L. (1957). The development of a vinyl plastic subcutaneous tag for trout. *Calif. Fish. Game*, 43: 201–12.   [19]

CALDERWOOD, W. L. (1927). Atlantic salmon in New Zealand. *Salm. Trout Mag.*, (48) 241–62.   [42]

CALDERWOOD, W. L. (1937). Homing instinct in salmon. *Salm. Trout Mag.*, (88) 207–313.   [62]

CARLIN, B. (1955). Tagging of salmon smolts in the river Lagan. *Rep. Inst. Freshwat. Res. Drottningholm*, (36) 57–74.   [268]

CARLISLE, D. B. and DENTON, E. J. (1959). On the metamorphosis of the visual pigments of *Anguilla anguilla* (L.). *J. mar. biol. Ass. U.K.*, 38: 97–102.   [80]

CARLSTRÖM, D. (1963). A crystallographic study of vertebrate otoliths. *Biol. Bull. mar. biol. Lab., Woods Hole*, 125: 441–63.   [30]

CARRUTHERS, J. N. (1925). The water movements in the southern North Sea. Part I—The surface drift. *Fishery Invest., Lond.*, Ser. 2, 8: (2) 119 pp.   [120, 121]

CARRUTHERS, J. N. (1936). Continuous current measuring in the Southern Bight. *Rapp. P.-v. Réun. Cons. perm. int. Explor. Mer*, **100**: (3) 3–6. [120]

CCOFI. (1956). *Prog. Rep. Calif. coop. ocean. Fish. Invest.* 1955–1956. 44 pp. [36]

CHAMBERLIN, T. C. (1965). The method of multiple working hypotheses. *Science N. Y.*, **148**: 754–9. [272]

CHAPMAN, D. W. (1957). Use of latex injections to mark juvenile steelhead. *Progve Fish Cult.*, **19**: (2) 95–6. [18]

CHRZAN, F. (1950). Investigations on the Baltic cod. *J. Cons. perm. int. Explor. Mer*, **16**: 192–207. [147, 169]

CLARK, R. S. (1933). Herring larvae. The mixing of the broods in Scottish waters. *Rapp. P.-v. Réun. Cons. perm. int. Explor. Mer*, **85**: (3) 11–8. [91, 96, 123]

CLARK, R. S. (1936). North-western area 1935. Scotland. *Rapp. P.-v. Réun. Cons. perm. int. Explor. Mer*, **100**: (2) 43. [103]

CLARKE, G. L. (1936). On the depth at which fish can see. *Ecology*, **17**: 452–56. [238]

CLEMENS, W. A., FOERSTER, R. E., and PRITCHARD, A. L. (1939). The migration of pacific salmon in British Columbia waters. *Publs. Am. Ass. Advmt Sci.*, (8) 51–9. [64]

CLUTTER, R. I. and WHITESEL, L. E. (1956). Collection and interpretation of sockeye salmon scales. *Bull. int. Pacif. Salm. Fish. Commn*, (9) 159 pp. [26, 27, 60, 61]

COHEN, D. M. (1959). The scientific name of the common cod. *J. Cons. perm. int. Explor. Mer*, **25**: 50–52. [144]

COLEFAX, A. N. (1952). Variations on a theme, some aspects of scale structure in fishes. *Proc. Linn. Soc. N.S.W.*, **77**: (1–2) VIII–XLVI. [28]

COLTON, J. B. and TEMPLE, R. F. (1961). The enigma of Georges Bank spawning. *Limnol. Oceanogr.*, **6**: 280–91. [200]

CORLETT, J. (1958). Distribution of larval cod in the Western Barents Sea. *Spec. Publs int. Commn NW. Atlant. Fish.*, (1) 281–8. [148, 165]

CREUTZBERG, F. (1958). Use of tidal streams by migrating elvers (*Anguilla vulgaris* Turt.) *Nature, Lond.*, **181**: 857–8. [224]

CREUTZBERG, F. (1961). On the orientation of migrating elvers (*Anguilla vulgaris* Turt.) in a tidal area. *Neth. J. sea Res.*, **1**: 257–338. [37, 224, 230, 259, 261, 269]

CUSHING, D. H. (1951). The vertical migrations of planktonic crustacea. *Biol. Rev.*, **26**: 158–92. [93]

CUSHING, D. H. (1952). Echo-surveys of fish. *J. Cons. perm. int. Explor. Mer*, **18**: 45–60. [41]

CUSHING, D. H. (1955a). Production and a pelagic fishery. *Fishery Invest., Lond.*, Ser. 2, **18**: (7) 104 pp. [41, 92]

CUSHING, D. H. (1955b). On the autumn spawned herring races in the North Sea. *J. Cons. perm. int. Explor. Mer*, **21**: 44–60. [130, 132]

CUSHING, D. H. (1957a). The interpretation of echo traces. *Fishery Invest., Lond.*, Ser. 2, **21**: (3) 16 pp. [39]

CUSHING, D. H. (1957b). The number of pilchards in the channel. *Fishery Invest., Lond.*, Ser. 2, **21**: (5) 27 pp. [41]

CUSHING, D. H. (1958). Some changes in vertebral counts of herrings. *Rapp. P.-v. Réun. Cons. perm. int. Explor. Mer*, **143**: (2) 126–9. [140]

CUSHING, D. H. (1959a). The seasonal variation in oceanic production as a problem in population dynamics. *J. Cons. perm. int. Explor. Mer*, **24**: 455–64. [13]

CUSHING, D. H. (1959b). The Bloden ground fishery and its relation to the East Anglian Fishery. *Fishg News, Aberd.*, (2385) 6. [19]

CUSHING, D. H. (1959c). A new method of echo-survey at full speed. *Fishery Invest., Lond.*, Ser. 2, **22**: (9) 48–55. [41]

CUSHING, D. H. (1962). Recruitment to the North Sea herring stocks. *Fishery Invest., Lond.*, Ser. 2, **23**: (5) 43–71. [125, 126, 138, 140]

CUSHING, D. H. (1963). *The uses of echo sounding for fishermen.* HMSO Lond., 28 + 41 pp. [39]

CUSHING, D. H. (1966). Biological and hydrographic changes in British seas during the last thirty years. *Biol. Rev.*, **41**: 221–58. [185]

CUSHING, D. H. (1967). The grouping of herring populations. *J. mar. biol. Ass. U.K.*, **47**: 193–208. [185]

CUSHING, D. H. and BURD, A. C. (1957). On the herring of the southern North Sea. *Fishery Invest., Lond.*, Ser. 2, **20**: (11) 31 pp. [133]

CUSHING, D. H., DEVOLD, F., MARR, J. C., and KRISTJONSSON, H. (1952). Some modern methods of fish detection. Echo sounding, echo ranging and aerial scouting. *Fish. Bull. F.A.O.*, **5**: (3–4) 27 pp. [35, 39]

CUSHING, D. H., HARDEN JONES, F. R., MITSON, R. B., ELLIS, G. H., and PEARCE, G. (1963). Measurements of the target strength of fish. *J. Br. Instn Radio Engrs*, **25**: 299–303. [39]

CUSHING, D. H. and HARDEN JONES, F. R. (1966). Sea trials with modulation sector scanning sonar, with an appendix by J. A. Gulland. *J. Cons. perm. int. Explor. Mer*, **30**: 324–45. [40, 224]

CUSHING, D. H., LEE, A. J., and RICHARDSON, I. D. (1956). Echo traces associated with thermoclines. *J. mar. Res.*, **15**: 1–13.   [195]

CUSHING, J. E. (1956). Observations on the serology of tuna. *Spec. scient. Rep. U.S. Fish. Wildl. Serv. Fisheries,* (183) 14 pp.   [34]

CUSHING, J. E. (1964). The blood groups of marine animals. *Adv. mar. Biol.*, **2**: 85–131.   [34]

CUTLER, D. W. (1918). A preliminary account of the production of annual rings in the scales of plaice and flounders. *J. mar. biol. Ass. U.K.*, **11**: 470–96.   [28]

DAFS. (1966). *Scott. Sea Fish. statist. Tabl.* 1965. 52 pp.   [144]

DAHL, K. (1907). The scales of the herring as a means of determining age, growth, and migration. *Rep. Norw. Fishery mar. Invest.*, **2**: part 2 (6) 36 pp.   [98]

DAHL, K. (1928). The dwarf salmon of Lake Byglands fiord. *Salm. Trout Mag.*, (51) 108–12.   [42]

DAHL, K. (1937). Salmon migrations off Norway. *Salm. Trout Mag.*, (88) 229–34.   [63]

DAHL, K. (1939). Homing instinct in salmon. *Salm. Trout Mag.*, (94) 19–26.   [59, 62]

D'ANCONA, U. and TUCKER, D. W. (1959). Old and new solution to the eel problem. *Nature, Lond.*, **183**: 1405–6.
                                                                                                             [72, 74]

DANIEL, R. J. and FLEMING, R. A. (1933). Plaice-marking experiments in the Irish Sea, 1929–1931. *Rep. Lancs. Sea-Fish Labs*, 1932, (41) 17–70.   [178, 179]

DANNEVIG, A. (1925). On the growth of the cod and the formation of annual zones. *Rep. Norw. Fishery mar. Invest.*, **3**: (6) 23 pp.   [28]

DANNEVIG, A. (1956). The influence of temperature on the formation of zones in scales and otoliths of young cod. *FiskDir. Skr.*, Serie Havundersøkelser, **11**: (7) 16 pp.   [28]

DANNEVIG, E. H. (1956a). Chemical composition of the zones in cod otoliths. *J. Cons. perm. int. Explor. Mer*, **21**: 156–9.   [29, 31]

DANNEVIG, E. H. (1956b). Cod populations identified by a chemical method. *FiskDir. Skr.*, Serie Havundersøkelser, **11**: (6) 13 pp.   [34]

DANNEVIG, G. (1949). Merking ar tørsk i Lofoten 1947–49. *FiskDir. Småskr.*, (1) 22 pp.   [163]

DANNEVIG, G. (1953). Tagging experiments on cod, Lofoten 1947–1952: some preliminary results. *J. Cons. perm. int. Explor. Mer*, **19**: 195–203.   [163, 164, 165]

DAVIDSON, F. A. (1934). The homing instinct and age at maturity of pink salmon (*Oncorhynchus gorbuscha*). *Bull. Bur. Fish., Wash.*, **48**: 27–39.   [52, 53]

DAVIDSON, F. A. and HUTCHINSON, S. J. (1938). The geographical distribution and environmental limitations of the Pacific Salmon (genus *Oncorhynchus*). *Bull. Bur. Fish., Wash.*, **48**: 667–92.   [59]

DAVIDSON, V. M. (1949). Salmon and eel movement in constant circular current. *J. Fish. Res. Bd Can.*, **7**: 432–48.
                                                                                                             [197]

DAVIS, F. M. (1936). A contribution to the 'race question'. *Rapp. P.-v. Réun. Cons. perm. int. Explor. Mer*, **100**: (2) 12–3.   [137]

DEELDER, C. L. (1952). On the migration of the elver (*Anguilla vulgaris* Turt.) at sea. *J. Cons. perm. int. Explor. Mer*, **18**: 187–218.   [196]

DEELDER, C. L. (1958). On the behaviour of elvers (*Anguilla vulgaris* Turt.) migrating from the sea into fresh water. *J. Cons. perm. int. Explor. Mer*, **24**: 135–46.   [194]

DEELDER, C. L. and TUCKER, D. W. (1960). The Atlantic eel problem. *Nature, Lond.*, **185**: 589–92.   [72]

DEFANT, A. (1961). *Physical Oceanography.* **2**: Pergamon Press, Lond., 598 pp.   [9, 10, 118]

DENCE, W. A. (1940). Progress report on a study of the dwarf sucker (*Catostomus commersonnii utawana*). *Roosevelt wild Life Bull.*, **7**: 221–33.   [246]

DENCE, W. A. (1948). Life history, ecology and habits of the dwarf sucker, *Catostomus commersonnii utawana* Mather, at the Huntington Wildlife Station. *Roosevelt wild Life Bull.*, **8**: 81–150.   [206, 246]

DEUTSCHES HYDROGRAPHISCHES INSTITUT. (1950). *Atlas der Eisverhältnisse des Nordatlantischen Ozeans und Übersichkarten der Eisverhältnisse des Nord-und Südpolargebietes.* Hamburg. 24 pp. + 27 charts.   [162, 164]

DEVOLD, F. (1951a). Norwegian Investigations. *Annls biol. Copenh.*, **7**: 125–7.   [92, 105, 109, 110]

DEVOLD, F. (1951b). På jakt etter storsilden i Norskehavet. *Fiskets Gang*, (20) 217–22.   [110]

DEVOLD, F. (1952a). A contribution to the study of the migrations of the Atlantic-Scandian herring. *Rapp. P.-v. Réun. Cons. perm. int. Explor. Mer*, **131**: 103–7.   [108, 109]

DEVOLD, F. (1952b). 'G. O. Sars' tokt under sidens innsig vinteren 1951–52. *Fiskets Gang*, (11) 130–4.   [110]

DEVOLD, F. (1953a). Norwegian Sea. *Annls biol., Copenh.*, **9**: 167–71.   [109, 110]

DEVOLD, F. (1953*b*). Tokter Med 'G. O. Sars' i Norskehavet vinteren 1952–53. *Fiskets Gang*, (19) 235–9.   [111]

DEVOLD, F. (1954*a*). Rapport over tokter for sildeundersøkelser Med 'G. O. Sars' vinteren 1953–54. *Fiskets Gang*, (21) 261–4.   [111]

DEVOLD, F. (1954*b*). Rapport over tokter for sildeundersøkelser med 'G. O. Sars' vinteren 1953–1954. *Fiskets Gang*, (22) 275–8.   [111]

DEVOLD, F. (1955). 'G. O. Sars' sildetokt i Norskehavet sommeren 1955. *Fiskets Gang*, (51) 680–2.   [109]

DEVOLD, F. (1956*a*). Norwegian Sea. *Annls biol., Copenh.*, **11**: 118–20.   [111]

DEVOLD, F. (1956*b*). Rapport over sildetokter vinteren 1955–56 med 'G. O. Sars'. *Fiskets Gang*, (30) 413–6.   [111]

DEVOLD, F. (1957). Norwegian Sea. *Annls biol., Copenh.*, **12**: 169–70.   [111]

DEVOLD, F. (1959). Rapport over tokt med F/F 'G. O. SARS' 6/12–17/12 1958. *Fiskets Gang*, (5) 60–1.   [111]

DEVOLD, F. (1960). Rapport over sildeinnsiget 1960. *Fiskets Gang*, (16) 232–6.   [111]

DEVOLD, F. (1962). Sildeinniget 1962. *Fiskets Gang*, (17) 255–7.   [111]

DEVOLD, F. (1963). The life history of the Atlanto-Scandian herring. *Rapp. P.-v. Réun. Cons. perm. int. Explor. Mer*, **154**: 98–108.   [111]

DEVOLD, F., EINARSSON, H., JOENSEN, J., and YUDANOV, I. G. (1961). International herring investigations in the Norwegian Sea, June 1959. *Annls biol. Copenh.*, **16**: 175–6.   [109]

DIETRICH, G. (1950). Die Natürlichen Regionen von Nord-und Ostsee auf hydrographischer Grundlage. *Kieler Meeresforsch.*, **7**: (2) 35–69.   [121]

DIETRICH, G. (1965). New hydrographical aspects of the Northwest Atlantic. *Spec. Publs. int. Commn NW. Atlant. Fish.*, (6) 29–51.   [150]

DIETRICH, G., SAHRHAGE, D., and SCHUBERT, K. (1959). Locating fish concentrations by thermometric methods. In *Modern fishing gear of the world*, 453–61. ed. by H. Kristjonsson. Fishing News (Books) Ltd. 607 pp.   [122]

DIJKGRAAF, S. (1933). Untersuchungen über die Funktion der Seitenorgane an Fischen. *Z. vergl. Physiol.*, **20**: 162–214.   [193, 194]

DIJKGRAAF, S. (1940). Untersuchungen über den Temperatursinn der Fische. *Z. vergl. Physiol.*, **27**: 587–605.   [192]

DIJKGRAAF, S. (1963). The functioning and significance of the lateral-line organs. *Biol. Rev.*, **38**: 51–105.   [187, 195]

DODIMEAD, A. J. and HOLLISTER, H. J. (1958). Progress report on drift bottle releases in the northeast Pacific Ocean. *J. Fish. Res. Bd Can.*, **15**: 851–65.   [9,   ]

DODIMEAD, A. J. and HOLLISTER, H. J. (1962). Canadian drift bottle releases and recoveries in the North Pacific ocean. *Rep. Fish. Res. Bd Can. Oceanogr. Limnol.*, (141) 64 pp. + 44 Figs.   [203, 207, 208]

DODIMEAD, A. J., FAVORITE, F., and HIRANO, T. (1963). Salmon of the North Pacific Ocean Part II. Review of oceanography of the subarctic Pacific region. *Bull. int. N. Pacif. Fish. Commn*, (13) 195 pp.   [202, 203, 204, 242]

DONALDSON, L. R. and ALLEN, G. H. (1958). Return of silver salmon *Oncorhynchus kisutch* (Walbaum) to point of release. *Trans. Am. Fish, Soc.*, **87**: 13–22.   [253, 266]

DRAGESUND, O. (1956). Tagging experiments. *Annls biol., Copenh.*, **11**: 120–2.   [106]

DRAGESUND, O. (1958*a*). Reactions of fish to artificial light, with special reference to large herring and spring herring in Norway. *J. Cons. perm. int. Explor. Mer*, **23**: 213–27.   [93]

DRAGESUND, O. (1958*b*). Norwegian tagging experiments in 1956. *Annls biol., Copenh.*, **13**: 181–2.   [106]

DRAGESUND, O. (1959*a*). Norwegian fat herring tagging in 1957. *Annls biol., Copenh.*, **14**: 149.   [106]

DRAGESUND, O. (1959*b*). Norwegian herring tagging experiments in 1957. *Annls biol., Copenh.*, **14**: 158.   [108]

DRAGESUND, O. (1961). Norwegian immature herring investigations in 1959. *Annls biol., Copenh.*, **16**: 170–1.   [105]

DRAGESUND, O. (1962*a*). Norwegian fat and small herring investigations in 1960. *Annls biol., Copenh.*, **17**: 160–1.   [105]

DRAGESUND, O. (1962*b*). Norwegian tagging experiments in 1960. *Annls biol., Copenh.*, **17**: 168–70.   [108]

DRAGESUND, O. (1964). Norwegian tagging experiments. *Annls biol., Copenh.*, **19**: 129–30.   [108]

DUNBAR, M. J. (1951). Eastern arctic waters. *Bull. Fish. Res. Bd Can.*, (88) 131 pp.   [150]

EARLL, R. E. (1880). A report on the history and present condition of the shore cod-fisheries of Cape Ann, Mass., together with notes on the Natural History and artificial propagation of the species. *Rep. U.S. Commnr Fish.*, (6) 685–740.   [148]

EASTWOOD, E. (1967). *Radar ornithology*. Methuen, Lond., 278 pp.   [273]

EGE, V. (1939). A revision of the genus *Anguilla* Shaw, a systematic, phylogenetic and geographical study. *Dana Rep.*, **3**: (16) 256 pp.   [69, 70]

EGGVIN, J. (1940). The movements of a cold water front. *FiskDir. Skr.*, Serie Havundersøkelser, **6**: (5) 151 pp. [11, 103]

EGGVIN, J. (1961). Some results of the Norwegian hydrographical investigations in the Norwegian Sea during the IGY. *Rapp. P.-v. Réun. Cons. perm. int. Explor. Mer*, **149**: 212–8.   [206]

10

EGGVIN, J. (1964). Water movement in the central part of the Norwegian Sea based on recent material. *ICES CM* 1964. (138) 12 pp. (mimeo).   [206]

EHRENBAUM, E. (1931). Report on Meeting of Herring experts at Fisheries Laboratory, Lowestoft, 4–7 November 1930. *Rapp. P.-v. Réun. Cons. perm. int. Explor. Mer*, **74**: 116–20.   [89]

EHRENBAUM, E. and MARUKAWA, H. (1913). Über altersbestimmung und Wachstum bein Aal. *Z. Fisch.*, **14**: 89–127.   [75]

EINARSSON, H. (1951). Racial analyses of Icelandic herrings by means of the otoliths. *Rapp. P.-v. Réun. Cons. perm. int. Explor. Mer*, **128**: (1) (appendix) 55–74.   [32, 95, 96, 98, 112]

EINARSSON, H. (1952a). On parallelism in the year-class strength of seasonal races of Icelandic herring and its significance. *Rapp. P.-v. Réun. Cons. perm. int. Explor. Mer*, **131**: 63–70.   [97, 98]

EINARSSON, H. (1952b). Analysis of the Icelandic herring during the year 1950. *J. Cons. perm. int. Explor. Mer*, **18**: 172–86.   [96, 113]

EINARSSON, H. (1956a). Skarkolinn (*Pleuronectes platessa* L.) í Hamarsfirdi. *Rit Fiskideild.*, **2**: (3) 20 pp.   [177]

EINARSSON, H. (1956b). Frequency and distribution of post-larval stages of herring (*Clupea harengus* L.) in Icelandic waters. *Rit Fiskideild.*, **2**: (4) 39 pp.   [95, 101, 102, 114]

ELLIS, D. V. (1961). Diving and photographic techniques for observing and recording salmon activities. *J. Fish. Res. Bd Can.*, **18**: 1159–66.   [36]

ELLIS, D. V. (1962). Preliminary studies on the visible migrations of adult salmon. *J. Fish. Res. Bd Can.*, **19**: 137–48.   [36]

ELLIS, G. H. (1956). Observations on the shoaling behaviour of cod (*Gadus callarias*) in deep water relative to daylight. *J. mar. biol. Ass. U.K.*, **35**: 415–7.   [149]

ELSON, P. H. (1939). Effects of current on the movement of speckled trout. *J. Fish. Res. Bd Can.*, **4**: 491–9.   [197]

EWART, J. C. (1884). Natural history of the herring. *Rep. Fishery Bd Scotl.*, (2) 61–73.   [91]

EWART, J. C. and BROOK, G. (1885). Observations on the spawning of cod. *Rep. Fishery Bd Scotl.*, (3) appendix F (2) 52–5.   [147]

FABRICIUS, E. (1954). Aquarium observations on the spawning behaviour of the burbot, *Lota vulgaris* L. *Rep. Inst. Freshwat. Res. Drottningholm*, (35) 51–7.   [12]

FAO. (1966). *Yb. Fish. Statist.*, **20**: unpaginated.   [2, 44, 45, 71, 86]

FARRIS, D. A. (1957). A review of paper chromatography as used in systematics. *Spec. scient. Rep. U.S. Fish. Wildl. Serv. Fisheries*, (208) 35–8.   [34]

FAVORITE, F. (1961). Surface temperature and salinity off the Washington and British Columbia coasts, August 1958 and 1959. *J. Fish. Res. Bd Can.*, **18**: 311–9.   [264]

FEDOROV, S. S. (1960). The distribution and migrations of immature and young mature Atlanto-Scandian herring. In *Soviet fisheries investigations in North European Seas*, 341–50. VNIRO/PINRO, Moscow. 468 pp.   [106]

FISHER, K. C. (1958). An approach to the organ and cellular physiology of adaptation to temperature in fish and small mammals. In *Physiological adaptation*, 3–49. ed. by C. L. Prosser. Am. Physiol. Soc., Washington, D.C., 185 pp.   [187]

FLEMING, R. A. (1931). Interim report on experiments with marked fishes during the year 1930. *Rep. Lancs. Sea-Fish. Labs*, 1930, (39) 74–97.   [178]

FLEMING, R. H. (1955). Review of oceanography of the northern Pacific. *Bull. int. N. Pacif. Fish. Commn*, (2) 1–43.   [204, 205]

FOERSTER, R. E. (1934). An investigation of the life history and propagation of the sockeye salmon (*Oncorhynchus nerka*) at Cultus Lake, British Columbia. No. 4. The life cycle of the 1925 year class with natural propagation. *Contr. Can. Biol. Fish.*, **8**: 347–55.   [47]

FOERSTER, R. E. (1936). An investigation of the life history and propagation of the sockeye salmon (*Oncorhynchus nerka*) at Cultus Lake, British Columbia. No. 5. The life history cycle of the 1926 year class with artificial propagation involving the liberation of free-swimming fry. *J. biol. Bd Can.*, **2**: 311–33.   [47]

FOERSTER, R. E. (1937). The return from the sea of sockeye salmon (*Oncorhynchus nerka*) with special reference to percentage survival, sex proportions and progress. *J. biol. Bd Can.*, **3**: 26–42.   [20, 47, 48, 49]

FOERSTER, R. E. (1946). Restocking depleted sockeye salmon areas by transfer of eggs. *J. Fish. Res. Bd Can.*, **6**: 483–90.   [56]

FOERSTER, R. E. (1955). The Pacific salmon (Genus *Oncorhynchus*) of the Canadian Pacific coast, with particular reference to their occurrence in or near freshwater. *Bull. int. N. Pacif. Fish. Commn*, (1) 1–56.   [43]

FONTAINE, M. (1954). Du déterminisme physiologique des migrations. *Biol. Rev.*, **29**: 390–418.   [201]

FORSELIUS, S. (1957). Studies of Anabantid fishes. I, II, and III. *Zool. Bidr. Upps.*, **32**: 93–301, 302–78, and 379–597. [12]

FORSTER, G. R. (1953). The spawning behaviour of plaice. *J. mar. biol. Ass. U.K.*, **32**: 319. [170]

FRAENKEL, G. S. and GUNN, D. L. (1940). *The orientation of animals.* Clarendon Press, Oxford. 352 pp. [4, 187, 188, 190]

FRAENKEL, G. S. and GUNN, D. L. (1961). *The orientation of animals.* Dover Publ. Inc., New York and Lond. 376 pp. [187, 218]

FREEDMAN, W. B. and WALKER, R. (1942). Size, development and innervation of the labyrinth sensory areas in *Squallus. J. comp. Neurol.*, **77**: 667–92. [31]

FRIDLAND, I. G., OSETINSKAYA, I. I., and BERNIKOVA, T. A. (1960). Distribution of herring of the Atlanto-Scandian stock. In *Soviet fisheries investigations in North European Seas*, 379–89. VNIRO/PINRO, Moscow. 468 pp. [104]

FRIDRIKSSON, A. (1944). Nordurlands-sildin. *Rit. Fiskideild.*, (1) 338 pp. [90, 107, 116]

FRIDRIKSSON, A. (1950). On the herring of the North Coast of Iceland during the summer of 1949. *Annls biol., Copenh.*, **6**: 162–7. [111]

FRIDRIKSSON, A. (1952). The marking of fish in Europe during 1927–51. *Rapp. P.-v. Réun. Cons. int. perm. Explor. Mer*, **132**: 55–64. [19]

FRIDRIKSSON, A. (1953). The Icelandic north coast herring in 1952. *Annls biol., Copenh.*, **9**: 164–7. [108]

FRIDRIKSSON, A. (1954). The Icelandic north coast herring in 1953. *Annls biol., Copenh.*, **10**: 143–7. [108]

FRIDRIKSSON, A. (1956). The Icelandic north coast herring in 1954. *Annls biol., Copenh.*, **11**: 114–8. [108]

FRIDRIKSSON, A. (1957). The Icelandic north coast herring in 1955. *Annls biol., Copenh.*, **12**: 158–62. [108]

FRIDRIKSSON, A. (1958a). The tribes in the north coast herring of Iceland with special reference to the period 1948–1955. *Rapp. P.-v. Réun. Cons. perm. int. Explor. Mer*, **143**: (2) 36–44. [107, 114]

FRIDRIKSSON, A. (1958b). The Icelandic north coast herring in 1956. *Annls biol., Copenh.*, **13**: 173–6. [108]

FRIDRIKSSON, A. (1959). The Icelandic north coast herring in 1957. *Annls biol., Copenh.*, **14**: 149–54. [108]

FRIDRIKSSON, A. (1960). The Icelandic north coast herring in 1958. *Annls biol., Copenh.*, **15**: 126–31. [108]

FRIDRIKSSON, A. (1961). The Icelandic north coast herring in 1959. *Annls biol., Copenh.*, **16**: 163–7. [108]

FRIDRIKSSON, A. (1962). The Icelandic north coast herring in 1960. *Annls biol., Copenh.*, **17**: 161–6. [108]

FRIDRIKSSON, A. and AASEN, O. (1952). The Norwegian-Icelandic herring tagging experiments. Report No. 2. *Rit. Fiskideild.*, (1) 54 pp. [20, 108, 116]

FRIDRIKSSON, A. and TIMMERMANN, G. (1951). Herring spawning grounds off the south coast of Iceland during spring 1950. *J. Cons. perm. int. Explor. Mer*, **17**: 172–80. [91]

FRITZ, R. L. (1959). Hake tagging in Europe and the United States. *J. Cons. perm. int. Explor. Mer*, **24**: 480–5. [20]

FROST, W. E. (1963). The homing of charr *Salvelinus willughbii* (Günther) in Windermere. *Anim. Behav.*, **11**: 74–82. [185, 246, 247]

FUKUHARA, F. M. (1955). Japanese high-seas mothership-type drift gill-net salmon fishery 1954. *Comml Fish. Rev.*, **17**: (3) 1–12. [66]

FULTON, T. W. (1897). The currents of the North Sea, and their relation to fisheries. *Scient. Invest. Fishery Bd Scotl.*, (15) *Part III. Scient. Invest.*, (XIII) 334–95. [14]

FULTON, T. W. (1903). Investigations on the abundance, distribution and migrations of the food fishes. *Rep. Fishery Bd Scotl.*, (21) *Part III. Scient. Invest.*, (I) 15–108. [16]

FULTON, T. W. (1906). On the spawning and fecundity of the plaice (*Pleuronectes platessa*). *Rep. Fishery Bd Scotl.*, (24) *Part III. Scient. Invest.*, (X) 281–9. [170]

FULTON, T. W. (1919). Report on the marking experiments on plaice, made by the S.S. 'Goldseeker' in the years 1910–1933. *Scient. Invest. Fishery Bd Scotl.*, (1) 468 pp. [15, 172]

GARROD, D. J. and NEWELL, B. S. (1958). Ring formation in *Tilapia esculenta. Nature, Lond.*, **181**: 1411–2. [28]

GARSTANG, W. (1905a). Report on experiments with marked fish during 1902–3. *Rep. N. Sea Fish. Invest. Comm.*, (1) 1902–1903. 13–43. [171]

GARSTANG, W. (1905b). Provisional report on the natural history of the plaice, based on the work of Committee B in the period ending June 30, 1904. *Rapp. P.-v. Réun. Cons. perm. int. Explor. Mer*, **3**: appendix H. 53 pp. [172]

GARSTANG, W. (1909). The distribution of the plaice in the North Sea, Skagerak and Kattegat, according to size, age, and frequency. *Rapp. P.-v. Réun. Cons. perm. int. Explor. Mer*, **11**: 65–133. [170]

GARSTANG, W. (1912). Report on experiments with marked plaice during 1904 and 1905. *Rep. N. Sea Fish. Invest. Comm.*, (4) 1909. 153–224. [171, 172]

GEMEROY, D. G. (1943). On the relationship of some common fishes as determined by the precipitin reaction. *Zoologica N.Y.*, **28**: 109–23. [34]

GEMEROY, D. and BOYDEN, A. (1961). Preliminary report on precipitin tests with American and European eel sera. *Bull. serol. Mus., New Brunsw.*, (26) 7–8.   [85]

GERKING, S. D. (1953). Evidence for the concepts of home range and territory in stream fishes. *Ecology*, **34**: 347–65.   [245, 248, 249, 255]

GERKING, S. D. (1959). The restricted movements of fish populations. *Biol. Rev.*, **34**: 221–42.   [4, 199, 244, 245]

GIDUMAL, J. L. (1958). A survey of the biology of the grass carp, *Ctenopharyngodon idellus* (Cuv. & Val.). *Hong Kong Univ. Fish. J.*, (2) 1–6.   [12]

GILBERT, C. H. (1914). Contributions to the life-history of the sockeye salmon (No. 1). *Rep. Commnr Fish. Br. Columb.*, 1913, 53–78.   [60]

GILBERT, C. H. (1916). Contributions to the life-history of the sockeye salmon (No. 3). *Rep. Commnr Fish. Br. Columb.*, 1915, 27–64.   [60]

GILBERT, C. H. (1918). Contributions to the life-history of the sockeye salmon (No.   *Rep. Commnr Fish. Br. Columb.*, 1917, 33–80.   [60, 260]

GILBERT, C. H. (1919). Contributions to the life-history of the sockeye salmon. (No. 5). *Rep. Commnr Fish. Br. Columb.*, 1918, 26–52.   [60]

GILHOUSEN, P. (1960). Migratory behavior of adult Fraser River sockeye. *Prog. Rep. int. Pacif. Salm. Fish. Commn*, 78 pp. (mimeo).   [269]

GILIS, C. (1949). Continued observations on the herring concentrations on the Fladen ground, the Gut, and environment, 1948. *Annls biol., Copenh.*, **5**: 71–3.   [130]

GILIS, C. (1950). Concentrations of full herring exploited by the Belgian herring trawlers in 1949. *Annls biol., Copenh.*, **6**: 183–9.   [130]

GILIS, C. (1959). The Belgian herring fisheries in 1957–1958. *Annls biol., Copenh.*, **14**: 182–8.   [90]

GILIS, C. (1960). The Belgian herring fishery in 1958–1959. *Annls biol., Copenh.*, **15**: 176–81.   [90]

GILSON, G. (1939). Spent herring from the Silver Pit. *Rapp. P.-v. Réun. Cons. perm. int. Explor. Mer*, **109**: (3) 88.   [133]

GRAHAM, M. (1924). The annual cycle in the life of the mature cod in the North Sea. *Fishery Invest., Lond.*, Ser. 2, **6**: (6) 77 pp.   [21, 32]

GRAHAM, M. (1926). A precise method for determining the first winter zone in cod scales. *J. Cons. perm. int. Explor. Mer*, **1**: 344–52.   [27]

GRAHAM, M. (1929*a*). On methods of marking round fish with an account of tests in aquaria. *Fishery Invest., Lond.*, Ser. 2, **11**: (4) 25 pp.   [19]

GRAHAM, M. (1929*b*). Studies of age-determination in fish. Part I. A study of the growth-rate of codling (*Gadus callarias* L.) of the Inner Herring-Trawling ground. *Fishery Invest., Lond.*, Ser. 2, **11**: (2) 50 + 32 pp.   [146]

GRAHAM, M. (1929*c*). Studies of age-determination in fish. Part II. A survey of the literature. *Fishery Invest., Lond.*, Ser. 2, **11**: (3) 50 pp.   [28, 31, 32]

GRAHAM, M. (1931). Some problems in herring behaviour. *J. Cons. perm. int. Explor. Mer*, **6**: 252–65.   [93]

GRAHAM, M. (1934). Report on the North Sea cod. *Fishery Invest., Lond.*, Ser. 2, **13**: (4) 160 pp.   [26, 148]

GRAHAM, M. (1956). *Sea Fisheries, their investigation in the United Kingdom*. Arnold, Lond., 487 pp.   [168]

GRAHAM, M. and CARRUTHERS, J. N. (1926). The distribution of pelagic stages of the cod in the North Sea in 1924 in relation to the system of currents. *Fishery Invest., Lond.*, Ser. 2, **8**: (6) 31 pp.   [148]

GRAHAM, M., TROUT, G. C., BEVERTON, R. J. H., CORLETT, J., LEE, A. J., and BLACKER, R. W. (1954). Report on research from the 'Ernest Holt' into the fishery near Bear Island 1949 and 1950. *Fishery Invest., Lond.*, Ser. 2, **18**: (3) 87 pp.   [161]

GRAHAM, T. R. (1962). A relationship between growth, hatching and spawning season in Canadian Atlantic herring (*Clupea harengus* L.). *J. Fish. Res. Bd Can.*, **19**: 985–7.   [93]

GRASSI, G. B. (1896). The reproduction and metamorphosis of the common eel (*Anguilla vulgaris*). *Q. Jl microsc. Sci.*, **39**: 371–85.   [80]

GRAY, J. (1937). Pseudo-rheotropism in fishes. *J. exp. Biol.*, **14**: 95–103.   [193, 194]

GRAY, J. (1953). The Locomotion of fishes. In *Essays in Marine Biology (Richard Elmhirst Memorial Lectures)*, 1–6. ed. by S. M. Marshall and A. P. Orr. Oliver and Boyd, Edinburgh. 144 pp.   [16]

GRAY, J. and SETNA, S. B. (1931). The growth of fish. IV. The effect of food supply on the scales of *Salmo irideus*. *J. exp. Biol.*, **8**: 55–62.   [28]

GRAY, O. (1951). An introduction to the study of the comparative anatomy of the labyrinth. *J. Lar. Otol.*, **65**: 681–703.   [30]

GREGORY, R. W. and FIELDS, P. E. (1962). Discrimination of low water velocities by juvenile silver (*Oncorhynchus kisutch*) and chinook salmon (*Oncorhynchus tshawytscha*). *Univ. Wash. Coll. Fish., Rep. tech. U.S. Army Corps Engrs*, (52) 58 pp. (mimeo). [197]

GRIFFIN, D. R. (1952). Bird navigation, with an Appendix by Ernst Mayr on German experiments on the orientation of migratory birds. *Biol. Rev.*, **27**: 359–400. [4, 199, 209, 212, 213, 214]

GRIFFIN, D. R. (1953). Sensory physiology and the orientation of animals. *Am. Scient.*, **41**: 201–44 (and 281). [3, 4]

GROEN, J. J. (1956). The semicircular canal system of the organs of equilibrium—I. *Physics Med. Biol.*, **1**: 103–17. [30]

GROEN, J. J. and JONGKEES, L. B. W. (1948). The threshold of angular acceleration perception. *J. Physiol.*, **107**: 1–7. [194]

GROOT, C. (1965). On the orientation of young sockeye salmon (*Oncorhynchus nerka*) during their seaward migration out of lakes. *Behaviour*, suppl. (14) 198 pp. [240]

GROOT, C. and WILEY, W. L. (1965). Time-lapse photography of an ASDIC echo-sounder PPI-scope as a technique for recording fish movements during migration. *J. Fish. Res. Bd Can.*, **22**: 1025–34. [240]

GULLAND, J. A. (1956). On the fishing effort in English demersal fisheries. *Fishery Invest., Lond.*, Ser. 2, **20**: (5) 40 pp. [33]

GUNN, D. L., KENNEDY, J. S., and PIELOU, D. P. (1937). Classification of taxes and kineses. *Nature, Lond.*, **140**: 1064. [187]

GUNNING, G. E. (1959). The sensory basis for homing in the longear sunfish, *Lepomis megalotis megalotis* (Rafinesque). *Invest. Indiana Lakes Streams*, **5**: 103–30. [244, 245, 252, 255, 257, 258]

GUNNING, G. E. (1963). The concepts of home range and homing in stream fishes. *Ergebn. Biol.*, **26**: 202–15. [244]

GUNNING, G. E. and SHOOP, C. R. (1962). Restricted movements of the American eel, *Anguilla rostrata* (Le Sueur), in freshwater streams, with comments on growth rate. *Tulane Stud. Zool.*, **9**: 265–72. [244, 245]

GUNNING, G. E. and SHOOP, C. R. (1963). Occupancy of home range by longear sunfish, *Lepomis m. megalotis* (Rafinesque), and Bluegill, *Lepomis m. macrochirus* Rafinesque. *J. Anim. Behav.*, **11**: 325–30. [244, 245]

HACHEY, H. B., HERMANN, F., and BAILEY, W. B. (1954). The waters of the ICNAF convention area. *A. Proc. int. Commn NW. Atlant. Fish.*, **4**: 67–102. [10, 150, 151]

HANSEN, P. M. (1949). Studies on the biology of the cod in Greenland waters. *Rapp. P.-v. Réun. Cons. perm. int. Explor. Mer*, **123**: 1–77. [35, 147, 149, 154, 156, 160]

HANSEN, P. M. (1957). Cod investigations in the coastal waters and on the offshore banks of West Greenland in 1955. *Annls biol. Copenh.*, **12**: 131–6. [154]

HANSEN, P. M. (1958). II. Danish Research Report, 1957. I. Biology. *A. Proc. int. Commn NW. Atlant. Fish*, **8**: 27–36. [146, 154]

HANSEN, P. M., JENSEN, A. S., and TÅNING, Å. VEDEL. (1935). Cod marking experiments in the waters of Greenland 1924–1933. *Meddr Kommn Danm. Fish.-og Havunders.*, Serie: Fiskeri, **10**: (1) 119 pp. [149, 150, 154, 156, 158, 159, 160]

HARDEN JONES, F. R. (1956). An apparent reaction of fish to linear accelerations. *Nature, Lond.*, **178**: 642–3. [193]

HARDEN JONES, F. R. (1957a). Movements of herring shoals in relation to the tidal current. *J. cons. perm. int. Explor. Mer*, **22**: 322–8. [40]

HARDEN JONES, F. R. (1957b). Cross channel echo surveys. *Wld Fishg*, **6**: 38–9. [41]

HARDEN JONES, F. R. (1957c). Rotation experiments with blind goldfish. *J. exp. Biol.*, **34**: 259–75. [194, 215]

HARDEN JONES, F. R. (1959). Echo sounding experiments with single cod. *Fishery Invest., Lond.*, Ser. 2, **22**: (9) 16–21. [39]

HARDEN JONES, F. R. (1960). Reactions of fish to stimuli. *Proc. Indo-Pacif. Fish. Coun., 8th Session, Columbo*. Sect. III, 18–28. [187]

HARDEN JONES, F. R. (1961). The migration of fish. *Biology hum. Affairs*, **26**: (3) 31–9. [72, 83]

HARDEN JONES, F. R. (1962). Further observations on the movements of herring (*Clupea harengus* L.) shoals in relation to the tidal current. *J. Cons. perm. int. Explor. Mer*, **27**: 52–76. [40, 224]

HARDEN JONES, F. R. (1963). The reaction of fish to moving backgrounds. *J. exp. Biol.*, **40**: 437–46. [196, 197, 216, 217, 219, 232]

HARDEN JONES, F. R. (1965). Fish migration and water currents. *Spec. Publ. int. Commn NW. Atlant. Fish.*, (6) 257–66. [207, 219, 230]

HARDEN JONES, F. R. and MCCARTNEY, B. S. (1962). The use of electronic sector-scanning sonar for following the movements of fish shoals: sea trials on R.R.S. "Discovery II". *J. Cons. perm. int. Explor. Mer*, **27**: 141–9. [40, 224]

HARDEN JONES, F. R. and PEARCE, G. (1958). Acoustic reflexion experiments with perch (*Perca fluviatilis* Linn.) to determine the proportion of the echo returned by the swimbladder. *J. exp. Biol.*, **35**: 437–50. [39, 40]

HARDY, A. C. (1924a). The herring in relation to its animate environment. Part I. The food and feeding habits of herring with special reference to the east coast of England. *Fishery Invest., Lond.*, Ser. 2, **7**: (3) 53 pp. [92]

HARDY, A. C. (1924b). Report on the possibilities of aerial spotting of fish. *Fishery Invest., Lond.*, Ser. 2, **7**: (5) 8 pp. [35]

HARDY, A. C. (1936). Part V. The plankton community, the whale fisheries, and the hypothesis of animal exclusion. In *The plankton of the South Georgia whaling grounds, and adjacent waters, 1926–1927*, 273–360. by A. C. Hardy and E. R. Gunther. '*Discovery*' *Rep.*, **11**: 1–456. [3]

HARDY, M. J. (1952). Aircraft as an aid to fishing. *Wld Fishg*, **1**: 171–4. [35]

HARPER, W. G. (1958). Detection of bird migration by centimetric radar—a cause of radar 'angels'. *Proc. R. Soc.*, B., **149**: 484–502. [40]

HARRISON, R. W. (1931). The Menhaden industry. *Investl Rep. U.S. Bur. Fish.*, **1**: (1) 113 pp. [35]

HARTMAN, W. L. and RALEIGH, R. F. (1964). Tributary homing of sockeye salmon at Brooks and Karluk Lakes, Alaska. *J. Fish. Res. Bd Can.*, **21**: 485–504. [251]

HARTT, A. C. (1962). Movement of salmon in the North Pacific Ocean and Bering Sea as determined by tagging 1956–1958. *Bull. int. N. Pacif. Fish. Commn*, (6) 157 pp. [36, 67, 202]

HASHIMOTO, T. and MANIWA, Y. (1956). Experiment of fish-finding at fishing-ground of salmon in the North Pacific Ocean. *Tech. Rep. Fishg Boat*, (8) 131–50. [66]

HASLER, A. D. (1954). Odour perception and orientation in fishes. *J. Fish. Res. Bd Can.*, **11**: 107–29. [187, 259]

HASLER, A. D. (1956). Perception of pathways by fishes in migration. *Q. Rev. Biol.*, **31**: 200–9. [15 187, 259]

HASLER, A. D. (1960). Homing orientation in migrating fishes. *Ergebn. Biol.*, **23**: 94–115. [35, 187, 227, 235, 242, 259]

HASLER, A. D. (1966). *Underwater guideposts*. Univ. Wisconsin Press. 155 pp. [187, 235, 259]

HASLER, A. D., HORRALL, R. M., WISBY, W. J., and BRAEMER, W. (1958). Sun-orientation and homing in fishes. *Limnol. Oceanogr.*, **3**: 353–61. [224, 235, 239, 240, 249, 250]

HASLER, A. D. and WISBY, W. J. (1951). Discrimination of stream odors by fishes and its relation to parent stream behavior. *Am. Nat.*, **85**: 223–38. [259, 260]

HASLER, A. D. and WISBY, W. J. (1958). The return of displaced largemouth bass and green sunfish to a 'home' area. *Ecology*, **39**: 289–93. [249]

HASLETT, R. W. G. (1964). Physics applied to echo sounding for fish. *Ultrasonics*, **2**: 11–22. [39]

HEALEY, E. G. (1957). The nervous system. In *The physiology of fishes*, **2**: 1–119. ed. by M. E. Brown. Academic Press, N.Y., 526 pp. [197]

HEAPE, W. (1931). *Emigration, migration and nomadism*. Heffer, Camb., 369 pp. [2, 4, 199]

HEFFORD, A. E. (1916). Report on sexual differentiation in the biology and distribution of plaice in the North Sea. *Fishery Invest., Lond.*, Ser. 2, **3**: (2) 73 pp. [147, 169]

HEFFORD, A. E. (1931). Report on fisheries for the year ending 31st March 1930. *Rep. Fish. N.Z.*, 63 pp. [17]

HEINCKE, F. (1913). Investigations on the plaice. General report. *Rapp. P.-v. Réun. Cons. perm. int. Explor. Mer*, **17**: 153 pp. [168, 170]

HELDT, H. (1921). La coopération de la navigation aérienne aux pêches maritimes. *Notes Mém. Off. scient. tech. Pêch. marit.*, (12) 8 pp. [35]

HELLAND-HANSEN, B. (1934). The Sognefjord Section. In *James Johnstone Memorial Volume*, 257–74. Univ. Press Liverpool. 348 pp. [101]

HELLAND-HANSEN, B. and NANSEN, F. (1909). The Norwegian Sea. *Rep. Norw. Fishery mar. Invest.*, **2**: (2) 390 pp. [101]

HEMPEL, G. and BLAXTER, J. H. S. (1961). The experimental modification of meristic characters in herring (*Clupea harengus* L.). *J. Cons. perm. int. Explor. Mer*, **26**: 336–46. [94]

HENRY, K. A. (1961). Racial identification of Fraser River sockeye salmon by means of scales and its applications to salmon management. *Bull. int. Pacif. Salm. Fish. Commn*, (12) 97 pp. [60, 68]

HENTSCHEL, E. (1950). Die Nahrung Heringslarven. *Helgoländer wiss. Meeresunters.*, **3**: 59–81. [92]

HERLINVEAUX, R. H. and TULLY, J. P. (1961). Some oceanographic features of Juan de Fuca Strait. *J. Fish. Res. Bd Can.*, **18**: 1027–71. [263]

HERMANN, F. (1953). Influence of temperature on strength of cod year-classes. *Annls biol., Copenh.*, **9**: 31–2. [158]

HERMANN, F. and THOMSEN, H. (1946). Drift-bottle experiments in the northern North Atlantic. *Meddr Kommn Danm. Fisk.-og Havunders.*, Serie: Hydrografi, **3**: (4) 87 pp. [101, 150, 151]

HESSLE, C. (1929). De senare årens fiskmärkningar vid svenska östersjökusten. *Meddn K. Lantbr Styr.*, (278) 37 pp. [207]

HICKLING, C. F. (1927). The natural history of the hake. Parts I and II. *Fishery Invest., Lond.*, Ser. 2, **10**: (2) 100 pp. [21, 33]

HICKLING, C. F. (1928). The Fleetwood exploratory voyages for hake. *J. Cons. perm. int. Explor. Mer*, **3**: 70–89. [103]

HICKLING, C. F. (1931). The structure of the otolith of the hake. *Q. Jl microsc. Sci.*, **74**: 547–61. [31]

HICKLING, C. F. (1938). The English plaice-marking experiments 1929–1932. *Fishery Invest., Lond.*, Ser. 2, **16**: (1) 80 pp. [172]

HICKLING, C. F. (1945). Marking fish with the electric tattooing needle. *J. mar. biol. Ass. U.K.*, **26**: 166–9. [18]

HILDEBRAND, S. F. (1957). Salmon and Salmonidae. *Encyclopædia Britannica*, **19**: 889–90. [42]

HILDEMANN, W. H. (1956). Goldfish erythrocyte antigens and serology. *Science N.Y.*, **124**: 315–6. [34]

HILL, H. W. (1956). Plaice movements off the Cumberland coast. *Rep. Challenger Soc.*, **3**: (8) 20–1. [178]

HJORT, J. (1910a). Eel-larvae (*Leptocephalus brevirostris*) from the central North Atlantic. *Nature, Lond.*, **85**: 104–6. [71, 77]

HJORT, J. (1910b). Report on herring-investigations until January 1910. *Publs Circonst. Cons. perm. int. Explor. Mer*, (53) 174 pp. [89, 102]

HJORT, J. (1914). Fluctuations in the great fisheries of Northern Europe. *Rapp. P.-v. Réun. Cons. perm. int. Explor. Mer*, **20**: 228 pp. [29, 148, 149, 163, 165]

HJORT, J. (1926). Fluctuations in the year classes of important food fishes. *J. Cons. perm. int. Explor. Mer*, **1**: 5–38. [161, 163]

HOAR, W. S. (1951). The behaviour of chum, pink, and coho salmon in relation to their seaward migration. *J. Fish. Res. Bd Can.*, **8**: 241–63. [224]

HOAR, W. S. (1953). Control and timing of fish migration. *Biol. Rev.*, **28**: 437–52. [201]

HOAR, W. S. (1954). The behaviour of juvenile Pacific salmon, with particular reference to the sockeye (*Oncorhynchus nerka*). *J. Fish. Res. Bd Can.*, **11**: 69–97. [224]

HOAR, W. S. (1956). The behaviour of migrating pink and chum salmon fry. *J. Fish. Res. Bd Can.*, **13**: 309–25. [214]

HOAR, W. S. (1959). The evolution of migratory behaviour among juvenile salmon of the genus *Oncorhynchus*. *J. Fish. Res. Bd Can.*, **15**: 391–428. [12]

HOBSON, E. S. (1963). Feeding behaviour in three species of sharks. *Pacif. Sci.*, **17**: 171–94. [218]

HODGSON, W. C. (1925). Investigations into the age, length, and maturity of the herring of the southern North Sea. Part II. The composition of the catches in 1922–1924. *Fishery Invest., Lond.*, Ser. 2, **8**: (5) 48 pp. [125, 126, 137]

HODGSON, W. C. (1926). The herrings of the eastern part of the English channel. *Nature, Lond.*, **117**: 342–3. [139]

HODGSON, W. C. (1927). Size and age composition of the East Anglian autumn herring. *J. Cons. perm. int. Explor. Mer*, **2**: 69–74. [90, 98, 136]

HODGSON, W. C. (1928). Some spawning places of the herring of the southern North Sea. *J. Cons. perm. int. Explor. Mer*, **3**: 224–30. [127]

HODGSON, W. C. (1929). Investigations into the age, length, and maturity of the herring of the southern North Sea. Part III. The composition of the catches from 1923 to 1928. *Fishery Invest., Lond.*, Ser. 2, **11**: (7) 75 pp. [93, 133, 137, 140]

HODGSON, W. C. (1934). *The natural history of the herring of the southern North Sea*. Arnold, Lond., 120 pp. [87, 93, 137, 200]

HODGSON, W. C. (1936). The present state of knowledge concerning the origin and distribution of herring populations in western European waters. The Southern Bight. *Rapp. P.-v. Réun. Cons. perm. int. Explor. Mer*, **100**: (2) 19–20. [138]

HODGSON, W. C. (1950a). Echo sounding and the pelagic fisheries. *Fishery Invest., Lond.*, Ser. 2, **17**: (4) 25 pp. [39]

HODGSON, W. C. (1950b). The East Anglian herring fishery in 1949. *Annls biol., Copenh.*, **6**: 175–7. [112]

HODGSON, W. C. (1957). *The herring and its fishery*. Routledge and Kegan Paul, Lond., 197 pp. [87, 112, 135]

HODGSON, W. C. and FRIDRIKSSON, A. (1955). Report on echo-sounding and asdic for fishing purposes. *Rapp. P.-v. Réun. Cons. int. Explor. Mer*, **139**: 1–49. [39]

HÖGLUND, H. (1955). Swedish herring tagging experiments 1949–53. *Rapp. P.-v. Réun. Cons. perm. int. Explor. Mer*, **140**: (2) 19–29. [22, 24, 130, 132]

HÖGLUND, L. B. (1961). The reactions of fish in concentration gradients. *Rep. Inst. Freshwat. Res. Drottningholm*, (43) 147 pp. [194, 197, 223]

HOLLIDAY, F. G. T. (1958). The spawning of the herring. *Scott. Fish. Bull.*, (10) 11–3. [91]

HOWARD, R. A. (1953). Sun-sand and survival, an analysis of survival experiences in desert areas. *Arctic, desert, tropic information center. Air University, Maxwell Air Force Base, Alabama. ADTIC Publ.* No. D-102. 42 pp. [215]

HOWLAND, H. C. and HOWLAND, B. (1962). The reaction of blinded goldfish to rotation in a centrifuge. *J. exp. Biol.*,
    39: 491–502.   [194]
HUNTSMAN, A. G. (1918). The growth of the scales in fishes. *Trans. R. Can. Inst.*, **12**: 63–101.   [27]
HUNTSMAN, A. G. (1936). Return of salmon from the sea. *Bull. biol. Bd Can.*, (51) 20 pp.   [36]
HUNTSMAN, A. G. (1937*a*). 'Migration' and 'homing' of salmon. *Science N.Y.*, **85**: 313–4.   [61]
HUNTSMAN, A. G. (1937*b*). 'Races' and 'homing' of salmon. *Science N.Y.*, **85**: 582.   [62]
HUNTSMAN, A. G. (1938). Sea behaviour in salmon. *Salm. Trout Mag.*, (90) 24–8.   [62, 64]
HUNTSMAN, A. G. (1939). Races and homing instinct. *Salm. Trout Mag.*, (96) 233–7.   [60, 62, 64, 94]
HUNTSMAN, A. G. (1942). Return of a marked salmon from a distant place. *Science N.Y.*, **95**: 381–2.   [62]
HUNTSMAN, A. G. (1948). Migration of salmon in the sea. *Salm. Trout Mag.*, (123) 153–8.   [64]
HUNTSMAN, A. G. (1950). Factors which may affect migration. *Salm. Trout Mag.*, (130) 227–39.   [64]
HUNTSMAN, A. G. (1952). Wandering versus homing in salmon. *Salm. Trout Mag.*, (136) 186–92.   [64]
HYLEN, A. (1963). The non-returning of fish tags recovered by Norwegian fishermen. *FiskDir. Skr.*, Serie Havun-
    dersøkelser, **13**: (6) 80–7.   [23]
HYLEN, A., MIDTTUN, L., and SAETERSDAL, G. (1961). Torskeundersøkelsene i Lofoten og i Barentshavet 1960. *Fiskets
    Gang*, (5) 101–14.   [165, 166]
ICES. (1913). B. Procès-Verbaux des réuions du Conseil et des sections. Annexe A. Résolutions du Conseil de la
    Séance à Copenhague, septembre 1912. Resolution 10. *Rapp. P.-v. Réun. Cons. perm. int. Explor. Mer*, **15**:
    62.   [71]
ICES. (1962). Mean monthly temperature and salinity of the surface layer of the North Sea and adjacent waters from
    1905 to 1954. *Serv. hydrogr. Cons. perm. int. Explor. Mer*, (no pagination).   [120]
ICES. (1965). The North Sea herring. *Cons. perm. int. Explor. Mer Coop. Res. Rep.*, (4) 57 pp.   [137]
ICNAF. (1954). *Statist. Bull. int. Commn NW. Atlant. Fish.*, **2**: 55 pp.   [154]
ICNAF. (1963). North Atlantic fish marking symposium. *Spec. Publs int. Commn NW. Atlant. Fish.*, (4) 370 pp. [19]
IDELSON, M. (1931). Fish marking in the Barents Sea. *J. Cons. perm. int. Explor. Mer*, **6**: 432–3.   [161]
IDLER, D. R., MCBRIDE, J. R., JONAS, R. E. E., and TOMLINSON, N. (1961). Olfactory perception in migrating salmon.
    II. Studies on a laboratory bio-assay for homestream water and mammalian repellant. *Can. J. Biochem. Physiol.*,
    39: 1575–84.   [259, 260, 265]
ILES, T. D. (1964). The duration of maturation stages in herring. *J. Cons. perm. int. Explor. Mer*, **29**: 166–88.   [89]
ILES, T. D. and JOHNSON, P. O. (1962). The correlation table analysis of a sprat (*Clupea sprattus* L.) year-class to separate
    two groups differing in growth characteristics. *J. Cons. perm. int. Explor. Mer*, **27**: 287–303.   [98]
INNIS, H. A. (1940). *The cod fisheries.* Yale Univ. Press, New Haven. 520 pp.   [144]
INTERNATIONAL NORTH PACIFIC FISHERIES COMMISSION (1961). *Rep. int. N. Pacif. Fish. Commn*, 1960, 118 pp. see
    p. 32.   [19]
IPSFC. (1954). *Rep. int. Pacif. Salm. Fish Commn*, 1953, 37 pp.   [266, 267]
IRIE, T. (1957). On the forming season of annual rings (opaque and translucent zones) in the otoliths of several
    marine teleosts. *J. Fac. Fish. Anim. Husb. Hiroshima Univ.*, **1**: 311–7.   [31]
IRIE, T. (1960). The growth of the fish otolith. *J. Fac. Fish. Anim. Husb. Hiroshima Univ.*, **3**: 203–21.   [31, 32]
ISAEV, A. I. (1961). Acclimatization of Pacific salmon in the Barents and White Seas. *Vop. Ikhtiol.*, **1**: (1) 46–51.
    Transl. ser. Fish. Res. Bd Can., (361) 7 pp. (mimeo).   [59]
ISELIN, C. O'D. (1936). A study of the circulation of the Western North Atlantic. *Pap. phys. Oceanogr. Met.*, **4**: (4)
    101 pp.   [74]
IVERSEN, T. (1934). Some observations on cod in Northern waters. *FiskDir. Skr.*, Serie Havundersøkelser, 4: (8)
    35 pp.   [149, 156, 162, 163, 164]
IVLEV, V. S. (1960). An analysis of the mechanism of distribution of fish in a temperature gradient. *Zool. Zh.*, **39**:
    494–9 (in russian). *Trans. Ser. Fish. Res. Bd Can.*, (364) 8 pp. (mimeo).   [192]
JACOBSEN, J. P. and JOHANSEN, A. C. (1908). Remarks on the changes in specific gravity of pelagic fish eggs and the
    transportation of same in Danish waters. *Meddr Kommn Havunders.*, Serie: Fiskeri, **3**: (2) 24 pp.   [148]
JAKOBSSON, J. (1961). Icelandic driftnet herring tagging experiments. *Rit. Fiskideild.*, **2**: (10) 16 pp.   [108]
JAKOBSSON, J. (1963). The Icelandic herring fishery in 1961. *Annls biol., Copenh.*, **18**: 142–7.   [108]
JAKOBSSON, J. (1964). The Icelandic herring fishery in 1962. *Annls biol., Copenh.*, **19**: 119–24.   [108, 112]
JEAN, Y. (1956). A study of spring and fall spawning herring (*Clupea harengus* L.) at Grande-Rivière, Bay of Chaleur,
    Québec. *Contr. Dép. Pêch., Québ.*, (49) 76 pp.   [90, 92, 93]
JENSEN, A. J. C. (1960). Skagerak, Kattegat, and Baltic Belt Seas. *Annls biol., Copenh.*, **15**: 184–7.   [123]

JENSEN, A. S. (1905). On fish-otoliths in the bottom-deposits of the sea. I. Otoliths of the *Gadus*-species discovered in the Polar Deep. *Meddr Kommn Havunders.*, Serie: Fiskeri, **1**: (7) 14 pp.   [80]

JENSEN, A. S. (1925). On the fishery of the Greenlanders. *Meddr Kommn Havunders.*, Serie: Fiskeri, **7**: (7) 39 pp.   [153]

JENSEN, A. S. (1937). Remarks on the Greenland eel, its occurrence and reference to *Anguilla rostrata*. *Meddr Gronland*, **118**: (9) 8 pp.   [25]

JENSEN, A. S. (1939). Concerning a change of climate during recent decades in the arctic and subarctic regions, from Greenland in the west to Eurasia in the east, and contemporary biological and geophysical changes. *Biol. Meddr*, **14**: (8) 75 pp.   [64, 145]

JENSEN, A. S. and HANSEN, P. M. (1931). Investigations on the Greenland cod (*Gadus callarias* L.), with an Introduction on the History of the Greenland cod fisheries. *Rapp. P.-v. Réun. Cons. perm. int. Explor. Mer*, **72**: 1–41.   [153, 159]

JESPERSEN, P. (1942). Indo-Pacific Leptocephalids of the Genus *Anguilla*. Systematic and biological studies. *Dana Rep.*, **4**: (22) 128 pp.   [85]

JOHANSEN, A. C. (1921). The Atlanto-Scandian spring herring spawning at the Faroes. *Meddr Kommn Havunders.*, Serie: Fiskeri, **6**: (4) 10 pp.   [103]

JOHANSEN, A. C. (1924). On the summer- and autumn-spawning herrings of the North Sea. *Meddr Kommn Havunders.*, Serie: Fiskeri, **7**: (5) 119 pp.   [130]

JOHANSEN, A. C. (1927). On the migrations of the herring. *J. Cons. perm. int. Explor. Mer*, **2**: 3–27.   [36, 91]

JOHNSEN, R. C. (1964). Direction of movement of salmon in the North Pacific Ocean and Bering Sea as indicated by surface gillnet catches, 1959–1960. *Bull. int. N. Pacif. Fish. Commn*, (14) 33–48.   [36]

JOHNSEN, S. (1936). On the variation of fishes in relation to environment. *Bergens Mus. Årb.*, (4) 26 pp.   [25]

JOHNSON, J. H. (1960). Sonic tracking of adult salmon at Bonneville Dam, 1957. *Fishery Bull. Fish Wildl. Serv. U.S.*, **60**: (176) 471–85.   [40]

JOHNSON, W. E. (1961). Aspects of the ecology of a pelagic, zooplankton-eating fish. *Verh. int. Verein. theor. angew. Limnol.*, **14**: 727–31.   [228]

JOHNSON, W. E. and GROOT, C. (1963). Observations on the migration of young sockeye (*Oncorhynchus nerka*) through a large, complex lake system. *J. Fish. Res. Bd Can.*, **20**: 919–38.   [226, 228, 239]

JOHNSTONE, J. BIRTWISTLE, W., and SMITH, W. C. (1922). The fisheries of the Irish Sea. *Rep. Lancs. Sea-Fish. Labs*, 1921, (30) 37–179.   [177]

JONES, J. W. (1959). *The salmon*. Collins, Lond., 192 pp.   [43, 64, 147]

JONES, J. W. and TUCKER, D. W. (1959). Eel migration. *Nature, Lond.*, **184**: 1281–3.   [72, 80]

JONES, R. (1959). A method of analysis of some tagged haddock returns. *J. Cons. perm. int. Explor. Mer*, **25**: 58–72.   [24, 210]

JONES, R. (1966). Manual of methods for fish stock assessment. *F.A.O. Fish. Biol. tech. Pap.*, (51) Suppl. 1. (unpaginated).   [24]

JONES, S. (1940). Notes on the breeding habits and early development of *Macropodus cupanus* (Cuv. and Val.) with special reference to the cement glands of the early larvae. *Rec. Indian Mus.*, **42**: 269–76.   [12]

JONGKEES, L. B. W. and GROEN, J. J. (1946). The nature of the vestibular stimulus. *J. Lar. Otol.*, **61**: 529–41.   [193]

JÓNSSON, J. (1953). Migrations of cod from Iceland to Norwegian waters. *Annls biol, Copenh.*, **9**: 41–3.   [153, 158]

JÓNSSON, J. (1959). Icelandic cod investigations in South-West and South-East Greenland waters, 1957. *Annls biol., Copenh.*, **14**: 115–8.   [153]

JOUBIN, L. (1918). Note sur l'utilisation des hydravions pour la pêche et les recherches océanographique. *Bull. Inst. océanogr., Monaco*, **15**: (349) 4 pp.   [35]

JUDANOV, I. G. (1960). Quelques particularités de la ponte des harengs Atlanto-Scandinaves dans la région des Féroés. *Annls biol., Copenh.*, **15**: 132–5.   [102]

KALLEBERG, H. (1958). Observations in a stream tank of territoriality and competition in juvenile salmon and trout (*Salmo salar* L. and *S. trutta* L.). *Rep. Inst. Freshwat. Res. Drottningholm*, (39) 55–98.   [245, 252]

KALMUS, H. (1964). Comparative physiology: navigation by animals. *A. Rev. Physiol.*, **26**: 109–30.   [215]

KASAHARA, S. (1957). Marking experiments on the glass-eel of *Anguilla japonica*. *Rec. Res. Fac. Agric. Univ. Tokyo*, (6) 66.   [18]

KAUFFMAN, D. E. (1955). Noteworthy recoveries of tagged dogfish. *Fish. Res. Pap. St. Wash.*, **1**: (3) 41–2.   [22]

KELEZ, G. B. (1947). Measurement of salmon spawning by means of aerial photography. *Pacif. Fisherm.*, **45**: (3) 46–51.   [36]

KIILERICH, A. (1943). The hydrography of the West Greenland fishing banks. *Meddr. Kommn Danm. Fisk.-og Havunders.*, Serie: Hydrografi, **3**: (3) 45 pp.   [150, 153, 158, 159]

KIILERICH, A. (1945). On the hydrography of the Greenland Sea. *Meddr Grønland*, **144**: (2) 63 pp.   [150]

KLEEREKOPER, H. (1963). The response to amine 'F' by six species of marine fish. *Am. Zool.*, **3**: 517.   [230]

KLEEREKOPER, H. and CHAGNON, E. C. (1954). Hearing in fish with special reference to *Semotilus atromaculatus atromaculatus* (Mitchill). *J. Fish. Res. Bd Can.*, **11**: 130–52.   [37]

KLEEREKOPER, H. and MOGENSEN, J. (1963). Role of olfaction in the orientation of *Petromyzon marinus*. 1. Response to a single amine in prey's body odor. *Physiol. Zoöl.*, **36**: 347–60.   [230]

KYLE, H. M. (1898). The post-larval stages of the plaice, dab, flounder, long rough dab and common dab. *Rep. Fishery Bd Scotl.*, (16) Part III. *Scient. Invest.*, (VIII) 225–47.   [26]

LAEVASTU, T. (1962). Water types in the North Sea and their characteristics. *Rep. Hawaii Inst. geophys.*, (24) 3 + X pp.   [120]

LAKTIONOV, A. F. (1959). Bottom topography of the Greenland Sea in the region of Nansen's Sill. *Priroda, Mosk.*, **10**: 95–7. *Trans.* (T333R) *by DSIS DRB Can.*, 5 pp. (mimeo).   [99]

LANDSBOROUGH THOMPSON, A. (1942). *Bird migration.* 2nd edition. Witherby, Lond. 192 pp.   [1]

LANGEVIN, P. (1932). Improvements relating to the emission and reception of submarine waves. *British Patent* (145,691).   [38]

LARKINS, H. A. (1964). Direction of movement of salmon in the North Pacific Ocean, Bering Sea and Gulf of Alaska as indicated by surface gillnet catches. *Bull. int. N. Pacif. Fish. Commn*, (14) 49–58.   [36]

LAYRLE, M. (1951). Une intéressante enquête sur la pêche au saumon en mer par les fillets de surface. *Bull. Cons. sup. Pêche Paris*, **5**: 67–70.   [64]

LEA, E. (1910). On the methods used in the herring-investigations. *Publs Circonst. Cons. perm. int. Explor. Mer*, (53) 7–33.   [96]

LEA, E. (1924). Frequency curves in herring investigations. *Rep. Norw. Fishery mar. Invest.*, **3**: (4) 27 pp.   [28]

LEA, E. (1929a). The oceanic stage in the life history of the Norwegian herring. *J. Cons. perm. int. Explor. Mer*, **4**: 3–42.   [105, 106, 107]

LEA, E. (1929b). The herring's scale as a certificate of origin. Its applicability to race investigations. *Rapp. P.-v. Réun. Cons. perm. int. Explor. Mer*, **54**: 20–34.   [29, 94, 105]

LEARY, F. (1965). Search for subs. *Space/Aeronaut.*, Sept. 1965, 58–68.   [273]

LEBOUR, M. V. (1919). The larval and post-larval stages of the pilchard, sprat and herring from Plymouth district. *J. mar. biol. Ass. U.K.*, **12**: 427–57.   [26]

LE CREN, E. D. (1954). A subcutaneous tag for fish. *J. Cons. perm. int. Explor. Mer*, **20**: 72–82.   [18]

LEE, A. J. (1952). The influence of hydrography on the Bear Island cod fishery. *Rapp. P.-v. Réun. Cons. perm. int. Explor, Mer*, **131**: 74–102.   [162, 163]

LEE, A. J. (1960). Hydrographical observations in the Irish Sea. *Fishery Invest., Lond.*, Ser. 2, **23**: (2) 25 pp.   [177]

LEE, A. J. (1962). The effect of the wind on water movements in the Norwegian and Greenland Seas. In *Proceedings of the symposium on mathematical-hydrodynamical methods of physical oceanography. Mitt. Inst. Meeresk. Univ. Hamb.*, (1) 353–74.   [148]

LEE, A. J. (1963). The hydrography of the European arctic and subarctic seas. *Oceanogr. mar. Biol.*, **1**: 47–76.   [10, 100]

LE GALL, J. (1935). Le hareng *Clupea harengus* Linné. I. Les populations de l'Atlantique Nord-Est. *Annls Inst. océanogr., Monaco*, **15**: (1) 215 pp.   [87, 98, 124, 139]

LEIBOWITZ, H. W., MYERS, N. A., and GRANT, D. A. (1955). Radial localization of a single stimulus as a function of luminance and duration of exposure. *J. opt. Soc. Am.*, **45**: 76–8.   [236]

LIAMIN, K. A. (1959). Investigation into the life-cycle of summer spawning herring of Iceland. *Spec. scient. Rep. U.S. Fish Wildl. Serv. Fisheries*, (327) 166–202. (Trans. from Russian).   [90, 91, 95, 98, 102, 111, 114]

LIAMIN, K. A. (1960). On the distribution and migrations of the summer-spawning herring in the Norwegian Sea. In *Soviet fisheries investigations in North European Seas*, 371–7. VNIRO/PINRO, Moscow. 468 pp.   [111]

LIEBERMANN, L. N. (1962). Transmission of energy within the sea: other electromagnetic radiation. In *The Seas*, **1**: 469–75. ed. by M. N. Hill. Interscience Publ., N.Y., 864 pp.   [40]

LIN, S. Y. (1935). Life-history of Waan Ue, *Ctenopharyngodon idellus* (Cuv. & Val.). *Lingnan Sci. J.*, **14**: 129–35 and 271–4.   [12]

LINDROTH, A. (1957). A study of the whitefish (*Coregonus*) of the Sundsvall Bay district. *Rep. Inst. Freshwat. Res. Drottningholm*, (38) 70–108.   [260]

LINDSEY, C. C. (1957). Possible effects of water diversions on fish distributions in British Columbia. *J. Fish. Res. Bd Can.*, **14**: 651–68. [266]

LINDSEY, C. C. (1958). Modification of meristic characters by light duration in kokanee, *Oncorhynchus nerka*. *Copeia*, 134–6. [25]

LINDSEY, C. C. (1961). The bearing of experimental meristic studies on racial analyses of fish populations. *Proc. 9th. Pacif. Sci. Congr.*, **10**: 54–7. [24]

LINDSEY, C. C., NORTHCOTE, T. G., and HARTMAN, G. F. (1959). Homing of rainbow trout to inlet and outlet spawning streams at Loon Lake, British Columbia. *J. Fish. Res. Bd Can.*, **16**: 695–719. [7, 12, 248, 271]

LISSMANN, H. W. (1958). On the function and evolution of electric organs in fish. *J. exp. Biol.*, **35**: 156–91. [252]

LOWE, R. H. (1952). The influence of light and other factors on the seaward migration of the silver eel (*Anguilla anguilla* L.). *J. Anim. Ecol.*, **21**: 275–309. [197]

LÖWENSTEIN, O. (1932). Experimentelle Untersuchungen über den Gleichgewichtsinn der Elritze (*Phoxinus lævis* L.). *Z. vergl. Physiol.*, **17**: 806–56. [193]

LÖWENSTEIN, O. (1957). The sense organs: the acoustico-lateralis system. In *The physiology of fishes*, **2**: 155–86. ed. by M. E. Brown. Academic Press, N.Y., 526 pp. [252]

LÜHMANN, M. and MANN, H. (1958). Wiederfänge markierter Elbaale vor der küste Dänemarks. *Arch. FischWiss.*, **9**: 200–2. [207]

LUMBY, J. R. (1955). The depth of the wind-produced homogeneous layer in the oceans. *Fishery Invest., Lond.*, Ser. 2, **20**: (2) 12 pp. [77]

LUMBY, J. R. and ELLETT, D. J. (1965). Some considerations on oceanographic observations. *J. Cons. perm. int. Explor. Mer*, **29**:–48. 237 [192]

LYON, E. P. (1904). On rheotropism. 1.—rheotropism in fishes. *Am. J. Physiol.*, **12**: 149–61. [193, 194, 223]

LYON, E. P. (1909). On rheotropism. 2. rheotropism of fish blinded in one eye. *Am. J. Physiol.*, **24**: 244–51. [193, 219, 221]

MÅÅR, A. (1947). Über die Aalwanderung im Baltischen Meer auf Grund der Wanderaalmarkierungsversuche im Finnischen und Livischen Meerbusen in den Jahren 1937–1939. *Meddn St. Unders.-o. FörsAnst. SötvattFisk.*, (27) 56 pp. [80, 207]

MACHIN, K. E. and LISSMANN, H. W. (1960). The mode of operation of the electric receptors in *Gymnarchus niloticus*. *J. exp. Biol.*, **37**: 801–11. [195]

MACKAY, B. S. (1954). Tidal current observations in Hecate Strait. *J. Fish. Res. Bd Can.*, **11**: 48–56. [10]

MACKINNON, D. and BRETT, J. R. (1955). Some observations on the movement of Pacific salmon fry through a small impounded water basin. *J. Fish. Res. Bd Can.*, **12**: 362–8. [224, 226]

MACKINNON, D. and HOAR, W. S. (1953). Responses of coho and chum salmon fry to current. *J. Fish. Res. Bd Can.*, **10**: 523–38. [197]

MACKINTOSH, N. A. (1937). The seasonal circulation of the Antarctic macroplankton. '*Discovery*' *Rep.*, **16**: 365–412. [3]

MAFF. (1959). *Fish Stk Rec.*, 1958, 8 pp. + 19 Tables (mimeo). [165]

MAFF. (1965). *Sea Fish. statist. Tabl., Lond.*, 1964, 43 pp. [45, 167]

MAFF. (1967). *Sea Fish. statist. Tabl., Lond.*, 1965, 38 pp. [144, 145, 146, 167]

MANZER, J. I. (1964). Preliminary observations on the vertical distribution of Pacific salmon (genus *Oncorhynchus*) in the Gulf of Alaska. *J. Fish. Res. Bd Can.*, **21**: 891–903. [203, 217, 224]

MARCKMANN, K. (1958). The influence of the temperature on the respiratory metabolism during the development of the sea trout. *Meddr Danm. Fisk.-og Havunders.*, **2**: (21) 20 pp. [79]

MARSHALL, N. B. (1954). *Aspects of deep sea biology*. Hutchinson. Lond. 380 pp. [13]

MARSHALL, S. M. and ORR, A. P. (1955). *The biology of a marine copepod*. Oliver & Boyd, Edinburgh & London. 188 pp. [220]

MARTY, J. J. (1959). The fundamental stages of the life cycle of Atlantic-Scandinavian herring. *Spec. scient. Rep. U.S. Wildl. Serv. Fisheries*, (327) 5–68a. (Trans. from Russian). [33, 35, 64, 91, 93, 105, 107, 108, 109, 110, 207]

MARTY, J. J. and WILSON, P. A. (1960). Migrations of the Atlanto-Scandian herring. In *Soviet fisheries investigations in North European Seas*, 329–40. VNIRO/PINRO Moscow. 468 pp. [107, 110]

MASLOV, N. A. (1944). The bottom fishes of the Barents Sea. *Trudȳ polyar. nauchno-issled. Inst. morsk. rȳb. Khoz. Okeanogr.*, **8**: 3–186. (In Russian; partial trans. held at Fisheries Laboratory, Lowestoft). [145, 149, 161, 166]

MASLOV, N. A. (1960). Soviet investigations on the biology of the cod and other demersal fish in the Barents Sea. In *Soviet fishery investigations in North European Seas*, 185–231. VNIRO/PINRO, Moscow. 468 pp. [162, 163, 164, 206]

MATSUI, I. (1957). On the records of a leptocephalus and catadromous eels of *Anguilla japonica* in the waters around Japan with a presumption of their spawning places. *J. Shimonoseki Coll. Fish.*, **7**: 151–67.   [85]

MATTHEWS, G. V. T. (1966). Book Reviews. *Anim. Behav.*, **14**: 593–4.   [243]

MCALLISTER, C. D. (1961). Zooplankton studies at Ocean Weather Station 'P' in the northeast Pacific Ocean. *J. Fish. Res. Bd Can.*, **18**: 1–29.   [68]

MCINERNEY, J. E. (1964). Salinity preference: an orientation mechanism in salmon migration. *J. Fish. Res. Bd Can.*, **21**: 995–1018.   [218]

M'INTOSH, W. C. and PRINCE, E. E. (1890). On the development and life histories of the teleostean food and other fishes. *Trans. R. Soc. Edinb.*, **35**: 665–944.   [29]

MCKENZIE, R. A. (1940). Nova Scotian autumn cod spawning. *J. Fish. Res. Bd Can.*, **5**: 105–20.   [146]

MCMAHON, V. H. (1948). Lakes of the Skeena River drainage. VII. Morrison Lake. *Prog. Rep. Pacif. Cst Stns*, (74) 6–9.   [226]

MCPHERSON, G. (1957). O- and I-group, Scotland 1954–55. *Annls biol., Copenh.*, **12**: 174.   [103]

MEEK, A. (1915a). Migrations in the sea. *Nature, Lond.*, **95**: 231.   [15]

MEEK, A. (1915b). The migrations of the grey gurnard, *Trigla gurnardus*. *Rep. Dove mar. Lab.*, NS (4) 9–15.   [15]

MEEK, A. (1916a). *The Migrations of Fish*. Arnold, Lond., 427 pp.   [3]

MEEK, A. (1916b). The scales of herring and their value as an aid to investigation. *Rep. Dove mar. Lab.*, NS (5) 11–26.   [26]

MEEK, A. (1924). The development of the cod (*Gadus callarias*, L.). *Fishery Invest., Lond.*, Ser. 2, **7**: (1) 26 pp.   [148]

MENZIES, W. J. M. (1939a). Separate biological races. *Publs Am. Ass. Advmt Sci.*, (8) 86–8.   [59]

MENZIES, W. J. M. (1939b). Some preliminary observations on the migrations of the European salmon. *Publs Am. Ass. Advmt Sci.*, (8) 13–25.   [63]

MESSIATZEVA, E. (1932). Chief results of the fishery research in the Barents Sea in 1930 by the GOIN (State Oceanographical Institute of the U.S.S.R.). *Rapp. P.-v. Réun. Cons. perm. int. Explor. Mer*, **81**: 141–51.   [150, 161]

METEOROLOGICAL OFFICE (1945). *Quarterly surface current charts of the Atlantic Ocean*. M.O. 466, Hydrographic Department, Admiralty, Lond., 26 pp.   [77, 78]

MEYER, A. (1958). German investigations. *Annls biol., Copenh.*, **13**: 137–9.   [156]

MEYER, A. (1959). German investigations on Greenland cod, 1957. *Annls biol., Copenh.*, **14**: 118–21.   [153, 156]

MIDTTUN, L. and HOFF, I. (1962). Measurements of the reflection of sound by fish. *FiskDir. Skr.*, Serie Havundersøkelser, **13**: (3) 18 pp.   [39]

MILNE, D. J. (1957). Recent British Columbia spring and coho salmon tagging experiments, and a comparison with those conducted from 1925 to 1930. *Bull. Fish. Res. Bd Can.*, (113) 56 pp.   [64, 65, 67]

MITSON, R. B. and WOOD, R. J. (1961). An automatic method of counting fish echoes. *J. Cons. perm. int. Explor. Mer*, **26**: 281–91.   [41]

MOLANDER, A. R. (1947). Observations on the growth of the plaice and on the formation of annual rings in its otoliths. *Svenska hydrogr.-biol. Kommn. Skr.*, Serie Biol., **2**: (8) 11 pp.   [31]

MOORE, W. H. and MORTIMER, C. H. (1954). A portable instrument for the location of subcutaneous fish-tags. *J. Cons. perm. int. Explor. Mer*, **20**: 83–6.   [19]

MORTIMER, C. H. (1961). Motion in thermoclines. *Verh. int. Verein. theor. angew. Limnol.*, **14**: 79–83.   [220]

MOULTON, F. R. (1939). The migration and conservation of salmon. *Publs Am. Ass. Advmt Sci.*, (8) 106 pp.   [42, 62]

MUGIYA, Y. (1964). Calcification in fish and shell-fish. III. Seasonal occurrence of a prealbumin fraction in the otolith fluid of some fish, corresponding to the period of opaque zone formation in the otolith. *Bull. Jap. Soc. scient. Fish.*, **30**: 955–67.   [32]

MUGIYA, Y. (1966). Calcification in fish and shell-fish. VI. Seasonal change in calcium and magnesium concentrations of the otolith fluid in some fish, with special reference to the zone formation of their otolith. *Bull. Jap. Soc. scient. Fish.*, **32**: 549–57.   [32]

MUNK, W. (1955). The circulation of the oceans. *Scient. Am.*, **193**: (3) 96–104.   [8]

MURRAY, R. W. (1962). The response of the ampullae of Lorenzini of elasmobranchs to electrical stimulation. *J. exp. Biol.*, **39**: 119–28.   [196]

MUZINIC, R. and RICHARDSON, I. D. (1958). On the appearance of rings on herring scales. *J. Cons. perm. int. Explor. Mer*, **24**: 120–34.   [27]

MUŽINIĆ, S. (1931). Der Rhythmus der Nahrungsaufnahme beim Hering. *Ber. dt. wiss. Kommn Meeresforsch.*, **6**: 62–4.   [92]

MYERS, G. S. (1949). Usage of anadromous, catadromous, and allied terms for migratory fishes. *Copeia*, 89–97. [2, 16]

NDRC. (1946). *The physics of sound in the sea.* Summary Technical Rep. Div. 6, National Defence Research Council, 8. Washington, D.C., 566 pp. [39, 40]

NEAVE, F. (1940). On the histology and regeneration of the teleost scale. *Q. Jl microsc. Sci.*, **81**: 541–68. [26]

NEAVE, F. (1955). Notes on the seaward migration of pink and chum salmon fry. *J. Fish. Res. Bd Can.*, **12**: 369–74. [200, 224, 225]

NEAVE, F. (1964). Ocean migrations of Pacific salmon. *J. Fish. Res. Bd Can.*, **21**: 1227–44. [9, 203, 204, 205, 228]

NEWMAN, M. A. (1956). Social behavior and interspecific competition in two trout species. *Physiol. Zoöl.*, **29**: 64–81. [245]

NIELSEN, J. (1960). Preliminary results of tagging experiments with herring (*Clupea harengus* L.) in Greenland. *J. Cons. perm. int. Explor. Mer*, **26**: 73–9. [101]

NIKOL'SKII, G. V. (1962). On some adaptations to the regulation of population density in fish species with different types of stock structure. *Symp., Br. ecol. Soc.*, (2) 265–82. [92]

NIKOLSKY, G. V. (1963). *The ecology of fishes.* Academic Press, N.Y., 352 pp. [6, 12]

NORTHCOTE, T. G. (1962). Migratory behaviour of juvenile rainbow trout, *Salmo gairdneri* in outlet and inlet streams of Loon Lake, British Columbia. *J. Fish. Res. Bd Can.*, **19**: 201–70. [219, 225]

NYMAN, L. (1965). Inter- and intraspecific variations of proteins in fishes. *K. VetenskSamh. Upps. Årsb.*, (9) 18 pp. [34]

O'ROURKE, F. J. (1959). Serological relationships in the genus *Gadus. Nature, Lond.*, **183**: 1192. [34]

ØSTVEDT, O. J. (1958). Some considerations concerning the homogeneity of the Atlanto-Scandian herring. *Rapp. P.-v. Réun. Cons. perm. int. Explor. Mer*, **143**: (2) 53–7. [115]

ØSTVEDT, O. J. (1960a). Rapport over tokt med F/F 'G. O. Sars' 3/12–17/12, 1959. *Fiskets Gang*, (16) 230–1. [111]

ØSTVEDT, O. J. (1960b). Rapport fra sildeundersøkelser ved Island 2/6–8/7 1960 med F/F 'G. O. Sars'. *Fiskets Gang*, (44) 611–6. [109]

ØSTVEDT, O. J. (1962). Sildeundersøkelser i Norskehavet med F/F 'Johan Hjort' 5–17 desember 1961. *Fiskets Gang*, (17) 258. [111]

PAGET, G. W. (1920). Report on the scales of some teleostean fish with special reference to their method of growth. *Fishery Invest., Lond.*, Ser. 2, **4**: (4) 28 pp. [26, 27]

PARKER, G. H. (1922). *Smell, taste and allied senses in the vertebrates.* Lippincott, Philadelphia and London. 192 pp. [191]

PARKER, R. A. and HASLER, A. D. (1959). Movements of some displaced centrarchids. *Copeia*, 11–8. [4]

PARKER, R. P. and KIRKNESS, W. (1956). King salmon and the ocean troll fishery of southeastern Alaska. *Res. Rep. Alaska Dep. Fish*, (1) 64 pp. [21]

PARRISH, B. B. (1962). Problems concerning the population dynamics of the Atlantic herring (*Clupea harengus* L.) with special reference to the North Sea. *Symp., Br. ecol. Soc.*, (2) 3–28. [87]

PARRISH, B. B. and CRAIG, R. E. (1957). Recent changes in the North Sea herring fisheries. *Rapp. P.-v. Réun. Cons. perm. int. Explor. Mer*, **143**: (1) 12–21. [130]

PARRISH, B. B. and SAVILLE, A. (1965). The biology of the north-east Atlantic herring population. *Oceanogr. mar. Biol.*, **3**: 323–73. [87]

PARRISH, B. B. and SHARMAN, D. P. (1958). Some remarks on methods used in herring 'racial' investigations with special reference to otolith studies. *Rapp. P.-v. Réun. Cons. perm. int. Explor. Mer*, **143**: (2) 66–80. [96]

PARRISH, B. B., BAXTER, I. G., McPHERSON, G., and BUCHAN, J. D. (1960). Scottish fisheries 1958. *Annls biol., Copenh.*, **15**: 160–71. [130]

PARRISH, B. B., BAXTER, I. G., McPHERSON, G., and BUCHAN, J. D. (1961). Scottish fisheries in 1959. *Annls biol., Copenh.*, **16**: 181–91. [130]

PARRISH, B. B., SAVILLE, A., BAXTER, I. G., McPHERSON, G., and BUCHAN, J. D. (1962). Scottish fisheries 1960. *Annls biol., Copenh.*, **17**: 176–88. [130]

PARRISH, B. B., SAVILLE, A., CRAIG, R. E., BAXTER, I. G., and PRIESTLEY, R. (1959). Observations on herring spawning and larval distribution in the Firth of Clyde in 1958. *J. mar. biol. Ass. U.K.*, **38**: 445–53. [91]

PATLAK, C. S. (1953). A mathematical contribution to the study of orientation of organisms. *Bull. math. Biophys.*, **15**: 431–76. [188, 189]

PATTEN, B. C. (1964). The rational decision process in salmon migration. *J. Cons. perm. int. Explor. Mer*, **28**: 410–17. [268]

PAVSHTIKS, E. A. (1959). Seasonal changes in plankton and feeding migrations of herring. *Spec. scient. Rep. U.S. Fish Wildl. Serv. Fisheries*, (327) 104–39a. [92, 108, 109]

PEARSALL, W. H. and ULLYOTT, P. (1934). Light penetration into fresh water. III. Seasonal variations in the light conditions in Windermere in relation to vegetation. *J. exp. Biol.*, **11**: 89–93.   [238]

PENDLETON, R. C. (1956). Uses of marking animals in ecological studies. Labelling animals with radioisotopes. *Ecology*, **37**: 686–9.   [19]

PETERS, H. M. (1947). Über Bau, Entwicklung und Funktion eines eigenartigen hydrostatischen apparates Larvaler Labyrinthfische. *Biol. Zbl.*, **66**: 304–29.   [12]

PETERSEN, C. G. J. (1905). Larval eels (*Leptocephalus brevirostris*) of the Atlantic coasts of Europe. *Meddr Kommn Havunders.*, Serie: Fiskeri, **1**: (5) 9 pp.   [70]

PETTERSSON, O. (1904). On the influence of ice-melting upon oceanic circulation. *Svenska hydrogr.-biol. Kommn. Skr.*, (II) 16 pp.   [206]

PETTERSSON, O. (1926). Currents and fish-migrations in the transition area. *J. Cons. perm. int. Explor. Mer*, **1**: 322–6.   [201]

POLDER, J. J. W. (1961). Cyclical changes in testis and ovary related to maturity stages in the North Sea herring, *Clupea harengus* L. *Archs néerl. Zool.*, **14**: 45–60.   [90, 91]

POSTUMA, K. H. (1960). Vertical migration in the herring. *Archs néerl. Zool.*, **13**: 592–5.   [93]

POSTUMA, K. H. and ZIJLSTRA, J. J. (1958). On the distinction between herring races in the autumn- and winter-spawning herring of the North Sea and English Channel by means of the otoliths and an application of this method in tracing the offspring of the races along the continental coast of the North Sea. *Rapp. P.-v. Réun. Cons. perm. int. Explor. Mer*, **143**: (2) 130–3.   [32, 96, 124, 139]

POSTUMA, K. H., ZIJLSTRA, J. J., and DAS, N. (1965). On the immature herring of the North Sea. *J. Cons. perm. int. Explor. Mer*, **29**: 256–76.   [125]

PRITCHARD, A. L. (1938). Transplantation of pink salmon (*Oncorhynchus gorbuscha*) into Masset Inlet, British Columbia, in the barren years. *J. Fish. Res. Bd Can.*, **4**: 141–50.   [50, 56]

PRITCHARD, A. L. (1939). Homing tendency and age at maturity of pink salmon (*Oncorhynchus gorbuscha*) in British Columbia. *J. Fish. Res. Bd Can.*, **4**: 233–51.   [49, 50, 51]

PRITCHARD, A. L. (1944a). Physical characteristics and behaviour of pink salmon fry at McClinton Creek, B.C. *J. Fish. Res. Bd Can.*, **6**: 217–27.   [50, 225]

PRITCHARD, A. L. (1944b). Return of two marked pink salmon (*Oncorhynchus gorbuscha*) to the natal stream from distant places in the sea. *Copeia*, 80–2.   [62]

PRITCHARD, A. L. (1948a). Efficiency of natural propagation of the pink salmon (*Oncorhynchus gorbuscha*) in McClinton Creek, Masset Inlet, B.C. *J. Fish. Res. Bd Can.*, **7**: 224–36.   [50]

PRITCHARD, A. L. (1948b). A discussion of the mortality in pink salmon (*Oncorhynchus gorbuscha*) during their first period of marine life. *Trans. R. Soc. Can.*, **42**: section V, 125–33.   [51, 53]

PUMPHREY, R. J. (1950). Hearing. *Symp. Soc. exp. Biol.*, **4**: 3–18.   [29]

PYEFINCH, K. A. (1955). A review of the literature on the biology of the Atlantic salmon (*Salmo salar* Linn.). *Freshwat. Salm. Fish. Res.*, (9) 24 pp.   [43, 59]

QASIM, S. Z. (1955). Time and duration of the spawning season in some marine teleosts in relation to their distribution. *J. Cons. perm. int. Explor. Mer*, **21**: 144–55.   [13]

RAINEY, R. C. (1951). Weather and the movements of locust swarms: a new hypothesis. *Nature, Lond.*, **168**: 1057–60.   [208]

RAINEY, R. C. (1960). Applications of theoretical models to the study of flight-behaviour in locusts and birds. *Symp. Soc. exp. Biol.*, **14**: 122–39.   [208]

RAITT, D. F. S. (1961). Otolith studies of southern North Sea herring. *J. Cons. perm. int. Explor. Mer*, **26**: 312–28.   [32, 140]

RAMSTER, J. (1965). Studies with the Woodhead sea-bed drifter in the southern North Sea. *Fish. Lab. Lowest. Leafl.*, (6) 8 pp.   [120]

RASMUSSEN, B. (1953). Norwegian fishery investigations in 1952. *Annls biol., Copenh.*, **9**: 52–3.   [149]

RASMUSSEN, B. (1954). On the Norwegian pelagic long-line fishery in the Holsteinborg Deep 1953. *A. Proc. int. Commn NW. Atlant. Fish.*, 1953–54. 40–8.   [149]

RASMUSSEN, B. (1959). On the migration pattern of the West Greenland stock of cod. *Annls biol., Copenh.*, **4**: 123–4.   [150, 154, 155]

RASMUSSEN, T. (1940). Islandssild i norske kystfarvann. *FiskDir. Skr.*, Serie Havundersøkelser, **6**: (4) 19–22.   [112]

RASS, T. S. (1939). The reproduction and life-cycle of the Murman herring (*Clupea harengus harengus* L.). *Trudȳ polyar. nauchno-issled. Inst. morsk. rȳb. Khoz. Okeanogr.*, **6**: 93–164. (In Russian with English summary. Full translation made by the Office of Technical Services, U.S. Dept. Commerce, Washington D.C. OTS 60-51149 PST Cat. (357) 1961. p. 46–119). [105, 111, 116]

RASS, T. S. (1959). Biogeographical fishery complexes of the Atlantic and Pacific Oceans and their comparison. *J. Cons. perm. int. Explor. Mer*, **24**: 243–54. [13, 87, 144]

REDEKE, H. C. (1905). The distribution of the plaice on the Dutch coast. *Rapp. P.-v. Réun. Cons. perm. int. Explor. Mer*, **3**: appendix H¹. 10 pp. [170]

REGNART, H. C. (1932). The generation of electric currents by water moving in a magnetic field. *Proc. Univ. Durham phil. Soc.*, **8**: 291–300. [196]

RETZIUS, G. (1881). *Das Gehörorgan der Wirbelthiere. I. Das Gehörorgan der Fische und Amphibien.* **1**: Stockholm, 150 pp. [30]

RICH, W. H. (1937a). 'Homing' of Pacific salmon. *Science, N.Y.*, **85**: 477–8. [62]

RICH, W. H. (1937b). 'Races' and 'homing' of Pacific salmon. *Science, N.Y.*, **86**: 122. [59, 62]

RICH, W. H. (1939). Local populations and migrations in relation to the conservation of Pacific salmon in the Western States and Alaska. *Publs. Am. Ass. Advmt Sci.*, (8) 45–50. [42, 59]

RICH, W. H. and HOLMES, H. B. (1929). Experiments in marking young chinook salmon on the Columbia River, 1916–1927. *Bull. Bur. Fish., Wash.*, **44**: 215–64. [45, 57, 59]

RICHARDSON, I. D. (1952). Some reactions of pelagic fish to light as recorded by echo-sounding. *Fishery Invest., Lond.*, Ser. 2, **18**: (1) 20 pp. [93]

RICHARDSON, I. D. (1960). Observations on the size and numbers of herring taken by the herring trawl. *J. Cons. perm. int. Explor. Mer*, **25**: 204–9. [93]

RICKER, W. E. (1938). 'Residual' and Kokanee salmon in Cultus Lake. *J. Fish. Res. Bd Can.*, **4**: 192–218. [42]

RICKER, W. E. (1956). Uses of marking animals in ecological studies: the marking of fish. *Ecology*, **37**: 665–70. [19]

RICKER, W. E. and ROBERTSON, A. (1935). Observations on the behaviour of adult sockeye salmon during the spawning migration. *Can. Fld. Nat.*, **49**: 132–4. [266]

RIDGWAY, G. J. and KLONTZ, G. W. (1961). Blood types in Pacific salmon. *Bull. int. N. Pacif. Fish. Commn*, (5) 49–55. [34]

RIDGWAY, G. J., CUSHING, J. E., and DURALL, G. L. (1958). Serological differentiation of populations of Sockeye salmon, *Oncorhynchus nerka*. *Spec. scient. Rep. U.S. Fish Wildl. Serv. Fisheries*, (257) 9 pp. [34]

RILEY, J. D. (1966). Liquid latex marking technique for small fish. *J. Cons. perm. int. Explor. Mer*, **30**: 354–7. [18]

RIVAS, L. R. (1954). A comparison between giant bluefin tuna (*Thunnus thynnus*) from the Straits of Florida and Gulf of Maine, with reference to migration and population identity. *Proc. Gulf Caribb. Fish. Inst. 7th. A. Sess.*, 1–17. [36]

ROGALLA, E. (1961). The distribution and layering of water masses in the North Sea during June/July 1959. *Annls biol., Copenh.*, **16**: 35. [122]

ROLLEFSEN, G. (1930). Observations on cod eggs. *Rapp. P.-v. Réun. Cons. perm. int. Explor. Mer*, **65**: 31–4. [148]

ROLLEFSEN, G. (1934a). Observations on the propagation of the cod and the plaice. *K. norske Vidensk. Selsk. Forh.*, **7**: 33–4. [147, 148]

ROLLEFSEN, G. (1934b). The cod otolith as a guide to race, sexual development and mortality. *Rapp. P.-v. Réun. Cons. perm. int. Explor. Mer*, **88**: (2) 5 pp. [32, 149]

ROLLEFSEN, G. (1938). Torsken og fiskehavet 1937. 3. Aldersundersøkelser. *FiskDir. Skr.*, Serie Havundersøkelser, **5**: (7) 23–32. [146, 147]

ROLLEFSEN, G. (1954). Observations on the cod and cod fisheries of Lofoten. *Rapp. P.-v. Réun. Cons. perm. int. Explor. Mer*, **136**: 40–7. [160]

ROLLEFSEN, G. (1959). Note on extra rewards for returned tags. *A. Proc. int. Commn NW. Atlant. Fish*, 1958. p. 25. [23]

ROSENTHAL, R. (1963). On the social psychology of the psychological experiment: the experimenter's hypothesis as unintended determinant of experimental results. *Am. Scient.*, **51**: 268–83. [240]

ROSENTHAL, R. and FODE, K. L. (1963). The effect of experimenter bias on the performance of the albino rat. *Behavl Sci.*, **8**: 183–9. [240]

ROUNSEFELL, G. A. and KASK, J. L. (1945). How to mark fish. *Trans. Am. Fish. Soc.*, **73**: 320–63. [19]

RUDAKOVA, V. A. (1959). Data on the food of the Atlantic herring. *Spec. scient. Rep. U.S. Fish Wildl. Serv. Fisheries*, (327) 140–65. [92]

RUNNSTRÖM, S. (1936a). The distribution of the Atlanto-Scandian spring herring. *Rapp. P.-v. Réun. Cons. perm. int. Explor. Mer*, **100**: (2) 24–8. [101, 103]

RUNNSTRÖM, S. (1936*b*). Investigations on Icelandic herrings in 1929–35. *Rapp. P.-v. Réun. Cons. perm. int. Explor. Mer*, **99**: (4) 11 pp. [101]

RUNNSTRÖM, S. (1936*c*). A study of the life history and migrations of the Norwegian spring-herring based on the analysis of the winter rings and summer zones of the scale. *FiskDir. Skr.*, Serie Havundersøkelser, **5**: (2) 103 pp. [92, 105, 106, 107, 115]

RUNNSTRÖM, S. (1941*a*). Racial analysis of the herring in Norwegian waters. *FiskDir. Skr.*, Serie Havundersøkelser, **6**: (7) 110 pp. [90, 92, 93, 104, 105, 106, 111, 114, 115]

RUNNSTRÖM, S. (1941*b*). Quantitative investigations on herring spawning and its yearly fluctuations at the west coast of Norway. *FiskDir. Skr.*, Serie Havundersøkelser, **6**: (8) 71 pp. [91, 93, 111, 116]

RUSSELL, E. S. (1937). Fish migrations. *Biol. Rev.*, **12**: 320–37. [15, 146, 177, 179]

RYLAND, J. S. (1963). The swimming speeds of plaice larvae. *J. exp. Biol.*, **40**: 285–300. [16, 200]

SÆMUNDSSON, B. (1913). Continued marking experiments on plaice and cod in Icelandic waters. *Meddr Kommn Havunders.*, Serie: Fiskeri, **4**: (6) 34 pp. [153, 176]

SAILA, S. B. (1961). A study of winter flounder movements. *Limnol. Oceanogr.*, **6**: 292–8. [209, 210]

SAILA, S. B. and SHAPPY, R. A. (1963). Random movement and orientation in salmon migration. *J. Cons. perm. int. Explor. Mer*, **28**: 153–66. [209, 211, 212]

SASAKI, T., WATANABE, S., OSHIBA, G., and OKAMI, N. (1958). Measurements of angular distribution of submarine daylight by means of new instrument. *J. oceanogr. Soc. Japan*, **14**: 47–52. [237]

SAUNDERS, R. L. and GEE, J. H. (1964). Movements of young Atlantic salmon in a small stream. *J. Fish. Res. Bd Can.*, **21**: 27–36. [245]

SAUNDERS, R. L., KERSWILL, C. J., and ELSON, P. F. (1965). Canadian Atlantic salmon recaptured near Greenland. *J. Fish. Res. Bd Can*, **22**: 625–9. [64]

SAVAGE, R. E. (1937). The food of North Sea herring 1930–1934. *Fishery Invest., Lond.*, Ser. 2, **15**: (5) 57 pp. [92]

SAVILLE, A. (1960). Autumn spawned herring larvae in the northern North Sea. *Annls biol., Copenh.*, **15**: 135–6. [123]

SCATTERGOOD, L. W. (1957). A bibliography of the herring (*Clupea harengus* and *C. pallasii*). *Res. Bull. Dep. Sea Shore Fish. Me*, (26) 108 pp. [87]

SCHAEFFER, A. A. (1928). Spiral movements in man. *J. Morph.*, **45**: 293–398. [215]

SCHEER, B. T. (1939). Homing instinct in salmon. *Q. Rev. Biol.*, **14**: 408–30. [43, 59, 60]

SCHEURING, L. (1929). Die Wanderungen der Fische. *Ergebn. Biol.*, **5**: 405–691. [3]

SCHEURING, L. (1930). Die Wanderungen der Fische. *Ergebn. Biol.*, **6**: 4–304. [3]

SCHMIDT, J. (1906). Contributions to the life-history of the eel (*Anguilla vulgaris*, Flem). *Rapp. P.-v. Réun. Cons. perm. int. Explor. Mer*, **5**: 137–274. [69, 76, 80]

SCHMIDT, J. (1907). Marking experiments on plaice and cod in Icelandic waters. *Meddr Kommn Havunders.*, Serie: Fiskeri, **2**: (6) 23 pp. [153, 176]

SCHMIDT, J. (1909*a*). Remarks on the metamorphosis and distribution of the larvae of the eel (*Anguilla vulgaris*, Turt.). *Meddr Kommn Havunders.*, Serie: Fiskeri, **3**: (3) 17 pp. [76]

SCHMIDT, J. (1909*b*). On the distribution of the fresh-water eels (*Anguilla*) throughout the world. I. Atlantic Ocean and adjacent regions. *Meddr Kommn Havunders.*, Serie: Fiskeri, **3**: (7) 45 pp. [77, 79]

SCHMIDT, J. (1909*c*). The distribution of the pelagic fry and the spawning regions of the gadoids in the North Atlantic from Iceland to Spain. *Rapp. P.-v. Réun. Cons. perm. int. Explor. Mer*, **10**: B. Special Part. (4) 229 pp. [148, 152]

SCHMIDT, J. (1912). Report on the Danish Oceanographical Expeditions, 1908–1910 to the Mediterranean and adjacent seas. I. Introduction. *Rep. Dan. oceanogr. Exped. Mediterr.*, **1**: (1) 49 pp. [72]

SCHMIDT, J. (1913). First report on eel investigations 1913. *Rapp. P.-v. Réun. Cons. perm. int. Explor. Mer*, **18**: 29 pp. [69]

SCHMIDT, J. (1916). Second report on eel investigations 1915. *Rapp. P.-v. Réun. Cons. perm. int. Explor. Mer*, **23**: 24 pp. [81]

SCHMIDT, J. (1917). Racial investigations. I. *Zoarces viviparus* L. and local races of the same. *C.r. Trav. Lab. Carlsberg*, **13**: 279–396. [81, 83]

SCHMIDT, J. (1919). Stations in the Atlantic, etc. 1911–15. *Meddr Kommn Havunders.*, Serie: Fiskeri, **5**: (7) 27 pp. [72]

SCHMIDT, J. (1920). Racial investigations. V. Experimental investigations with *Zoarces viviparus* L. *C. r. Trav. Lab. Carlsberg*, **14**: (9) 14 pp. [81, 82, 83]

SCHMIDT, J. (1922). The breeding places of the eel. *Phil. Trans. R. Soc.*, B, **211**: 179–208. [73, 74, 75, 76]

SCHMIDT, J. (1923). Breeding places and migrations of the eel. *Nature, Lond.*, **111**: 51–4. [76]

SCHMIDT, J. (1924). L'immigration des larves d'Anguille, dans la Méditerranée, par le Détroit de Gibraltar. *C. r. hebd. Séanc. Acad. Sci., Paris*, **179**: 729–33. [79]

SCHMIDT, J. (1925). The breeding places of the eel. *Rep. Smithson. Instn*, 1924, 279–316. [69, 73, 74, 76]

SCHMIDT, J. (1927). Eel larvae in the Faroe Channel. *J. Cons. perm. int. Explor. Mer*, **2**: 38–43. [76]

SCHMIDT, J. (1929). Introduction to the oceanographical reports. *Oceanogrl Rep. 'Dana' Exped.*, **1**: (1) 87 pp. [72, 73, 74]

SCHMIDT, J. (1930). Racial investigations. X. The Atlantic cod (*Gadus callarias* L.) and local races of the same. *C. r. Trav. Lab. Carlsberg*, **18**: (6) 71 pp. [24, 145]

SCHMIDT, J. (1931a). Summary of the Danish marking experiments on cod, 1904–1929, at the Faroes, Iceland and Greenland. *Rapp. P.-v. Réun. Cons. perm. int. Explor. Mer*, **72**: 13 pp. [153, 159]

SCHMIDT, J. (1931b). On the occurrence of the cod (*Gadus callarias* L.) at East Greenland. *Rapp. P.-v. Réun. Cons. perm. int. Explor. Mer*, **72**: 8 pp. [153]

SCHMIDT, J. (1932). *Danish eel investigations during 25 years 1905–1930*. Carlsberg Foundation. 16 pp. [73]

SCHOEN, L. and HOLST, E. VON. (1950). Das Zussamenspiel von Lagena und Utriculus bei der Lageorientierung der Knochenfische. *Z. vergl. Physiol.*, **32**: 552–71. [32]

SCHUBERT, K. (1954). Herring from the 'Otterbank'. *Annls biol., Copenh.*, **10**: 169. [103]

SCHUBERT, K. (1962). Survey of the German commercial herring fisheries in 1960. *Annls biol., Copenh.*, **17**: 188–205. [124, 126]

SCHUBERT, K. (1963). Survey of the German commercial herring fisheries in 1961. *Annls biol., Copenh.*, **18**: 169–83. [130]

SCHUCK, H. A. (1943). Survival, population density, growth, and movement of the wild brown trout in Crystal Creek. *Trans. Am. Fish. Soc.*, **73**: 209–30. [245]

SCHWASSMANN, H. O. and BRAEMER, W. (1961). The effect of experimentally changed photoperiod on the sun-orientation rhythm of fish. *Physiol. Zoöl.*, **34**: 273–86. [235]

SCHWASSMANN, H. O. and HASLER, A. D. (1964). The role of the sun's altitude in sun orientation of fish. *Physiol. Zoöl.*, **37**: 163–78. [235]

SCOTT, A. (1899). Observations on the occurrence and habits of leptocephalae. *Rep. Lancs. Sea-Fish. Labs*, 1898, 17–21. [80]

SCUDDER, N. P. (1883). The halibut fishery.—Davis Strait. *Rep. U.S. Commnr Fish.*, (8) 189–228. [64]

SEYMOUR, A. H. (1958). The use of radioisotopes as a tag for fish. *Proc. Gulf. Caribb. Fish. Inst.*, 10th. A. sess., 118–25. [19]

SHAPOVALOV, L. (1937). Trout and salmon marking in California. *Calif. Fish Game*, **23**: 205–7. [54]

SHAPOVALOV, L. (1941). The homing instinct in trout and salmon. *Proc. 6th. Pacif. Sci. Congr.*, **3**: 317–22. [43]

SHELBOURNE, J. E. (1956). The effect of water conservation on the structure of marine fish embryos and larvae. *J. mar. biol. Ass. U.K.*, **35**: 275–86. [13]

SHEPHERD, C. E. (1910). Comparison of otoliths found in fishes. *Zoologist*, 4th ser., **14**: 292–8. [31]

SICK, K. (1961). Hæmoglobin polymorphism in fishes. *Nature, Lond.*, **192**: 894–6. [34]

SICK, K. (1965). Hæmoglobin polymorphism of cod in the Baltic and Danish Belt Sea. *Hereditas*, **54**: 19–48. [34]

SICK, K. (1966). Hæmoglobin polymorphism of cod in the North Sea and the North Atlantic ocean. *Hereditas*, **54**: 49–73. [34]

SICK, K., WESTERGAARD, N., and FRYDENBERG, O. (1962). Hæmoglobin pattern and chromosome number of American, European and Japanese eels (*Anguilla*). *Nature, Lond.*, **193**: 1001–2. [85]

SIMPSON, A. C. (1959a). The spawning of the plaice (*Pleuronectes platessa*) in the North Sea. *Fishery Invest., Lond.*, Ser. 2, **22**: (7) 111 pp. [169, 170]

SIMPSON, A. C. (1959b). The spawning of the plaice (*Pleuronectes platessa*) in the Irish Sea. *Fishery Invest., Lond.*, Ser. 2, **22**: (8) 30 pp. [177,178]

SINDERMANN, C. J. (1961). Serological techniques in fishery research. *Trans. 26th N. Am. Wildl. Conf.*, 293–309. [34]

SINDERMANN, C. J. and MAIRS, D. F. (1959a). The C blood group system of Atlantic sea herring (abstract). *Anat. Rec.*, **13**: 640. [34]

SINDERMANN, C. J. and MAIRS, D. F. (1959b). A major blood group system in Atlantic sea herring. *Copeia*, 228–32. [34]

11

SMITH, P. F. (1954). Further measurements of the sound scattering properties of several marine organisms. *Deep Sea Res.*, **2**: 71–9.   [39]

SMITH, S. (1957). Early development and hatching. In *The physiology of fishes*, **1**: 323–59. ed. by M. E. Brown. Academic Press, N.Y., 447 pp.   [148]

SNYDER, J. O. (1931). Salmon of the Klamath River, California. *Bull. Dep. Fish. Game St. Calif.*, (34) 129 pp.   [55, 57]

SNYDER, J. O. (1940). The trouts of California. *Calif. Fish Game*, **26**: 96–138.   [43]

SPARLING, S. C. (1945). *Echo sounding engineering*. Marine Instruments Ltd., Lond., 122 pp.   [38]

SQUIRE, J. L. (1961). Aerial fish spotting in the United States Commercial Fisheries. *Comml Fish. Rev.*, **23**: (12) 1–7.   [35]

STEELE, J. H. (1957). The role of lateral eddy diffusion in the northern North Sea. *J. Cons. perm. int. Explor. Mer*, **22**: 152–62.   [120]

STEELE, J. H. (1961). The environment of a herring fishery. *Mar. Res.*, (6) 19 pp.   [122, 218]

STEFÁNSSON, U. (1962). North Icelandic waters. *Rit Fiskideild.*, **3**: (1) 269 pp.   [10, 98, 99, 101, 150, 151]

STEVEN, D. M. (1959). Studies on the shoaling behaviour of fish. I. Responses of two species to changes of illumination and to olfactory stimuli. *J. exp. Biol.*, **36**: 261–80.   [192]

STEVEN, D. M. (1963). The dermal light sense. *Biol. Rev.*, **38**: 204–40.   [197]

STEVENSON, J. C. (1955). The movement of herring in British Columbia waters as determined by tagging, with a description of tagging and tag recovery methods. *Rapp. P.-v. Réun. Cons. perm. int. Explor. Mer*, **140**: (2) 33–4.   [141]

STEVENSON, R. E. (1958). *An investigation of nearshore ocean currents at Newport Beach, California*. Los Angeles, California. 108 pp. (mimeo).   [228]

STOCKS, T. (1950). Die Tiefenverhältnisse des Europäischen Nordmeeres. *Dt. hydrogr. Z.*, **3**: 93–100.   [99, 100, 161, 162, 164]

STORROW, B. (1920). Herring investigations. I. Herring shoals. *Rep. Dove mar. Lab.*, NS (9) 8–82.   [93]

STRUBBERG, A. C. (1913). The metamorphosis of elvers as influenced by outward conditions. Some experiments. *Meddr Kommn Havunders.*, Serie: Fiskeri, **4**: (3) 11 pp.   [76]

STRUBBERG, A. C. (1916). Marking experiments with cod at the Faroes. *Meddr Kommn Havunders.*, Serie: Fiskeri, **5**: (2) 125 pp.   [148]

STRUBBERG, A. C. (1923). Elvers from north and south Europe. *Rep. Dan. oceanogr. Exped. Mediterr.*, **3**: (4) 28 pp.   [76, 77, 80]

STRUBBERG, A. C. (1933). Marking experiments with cod at the Faroes. II. Second report. Experiments in 1923–1927. *Meddr Kommn Danm. Fisk.-og Havunders.*, Serie: Fiskeri, **9**: (7) 36 pp.   [148]

STUART, T. A. (1953). Spawning migration, reproduction and young stages of Loch trout (*Salmo trutta* L.). *Freshwat. Salm. Fish. Res.*, (5) 39 pp.   [206]

STUART, T. A. (1957). The migrations and homing behaviour of brown trout. *Freshwat. Salm. Fish. Res.*, (18) 27 pp.   [252, 254, 255, 258]

STUART, T. A. (1958). Marking and regeneration of fins. *Freshwat. Salm. Fish. Res.*, (22) 14 pp.   [18]

STUART, T. A. (1962). The leaping behaviour of salmon and trout at falls and obstructions. *Freshwat. Salm. Fish. Res.*, (28) 46 pp.   [194]

SULLIVAN, C. M. (1954). Temperature reception and responses in fish. *J. Fish. Res. Bd Can.*, **11**: 153–70.   [187, 192]

SUND, O. (1932). On the German and Norwegian observations on the cod in 1931. *Rapp. P.-v. Réun. Cons. perm. int. Explor. Mer*, **81**: 151–6.   [206]

SUND, O. (1937). North-eastern area committee, Fishing technique. *Rapp. P.-v. Réun. Cons. perm. int. Explor. Mer*, **105**: (2) 10.   [93]

SUND, O. (1938a). Merking av torsk. *FiskDir. Skr.*, Serie Havundersøkelser, **5**: (7) 3–11.   [206]

SUND, O. (1938b). Torskebestanden i 1937. *FiskDir. Skr.*, Serie Havundersøkelser, **5**: (7) 11–22.   [147]

SUND, O. (1939). Torskebestanden i 1938. *FiskDir. Skr.*, Serie Havundersøkelser, **6**: (1) 5–22.   [206]

SVERDRUP, H. U., JOHNSON, M. W., and FLEMING, R. H. (1946). *The Oceans*. Prentice-Hall, N.Y., 1087 pp.   [120]

TAFT, A. C. and SHAPOVALOV, L. (1938). Homing instinct and straying among steelhead trout (*Salmo gairdnerii*) and silver salmon (*Oncorhynchus kisutch*). *Calif. Fish Game*, **24**: 118–25.   [42, 54, 55]

TAGUCHI, K. (1955). The movement of water masses in the seas of West Aleutian Is. and off East Coast of Kamchatka salmon fishing ground—1. Inference from the distribution of water temperature, water colour, and transparency. *Bull. Jap. Soc. scient. Fish.*, **20**: 774–9.   [202]

TAGUCHI, K. (1956). A report of drift-bottle surveies off Kamchatka, USSR in 1940 and 1941. *Bull. Jap. Soc. scient. Fish.*, **22**: 393–99. [202]

TAGUCHI, K. (1957a). The seasonal variation of the good fishing area of salmon and the movements of water masses in the waters of western North Pacific—1. Distribution and movement of water masses. *Bull. Jap. Soc. scient. Fish.*, **22**: 511–4. [202]

TAGUCHI, K. (1957b). The seasonal variation of the good fishing area of salmon and the movements of the water masses in the waters of the western North Pacific—II. The distribution and migration of salmon populations in offshore waters. *Bull. Jap. Soc. scient. Fish.*, **22**: 515–21. [202]

TAGUCHI, K. (1959). On the surface currents in the waters fished by Japanese salmon motherships from the results of drift float experiments. *Bull. Jap. Soc. scient. Fish.*, **25**: 117–21. [202]

TAGUCHI, K. and HIROSE, Y. (1954). Surface currents and oceanographical condition in the Northern Pacific salmon fishing ground. *Bull. Jap. Soc. scient. Fish.*, **20**: 576–80. [202]

TAGUCHI, K. and SHOJI, Y. (1955). The movement of water masses in the seas of West Aleutian Is. and off East Coast of Kamchatka salmon fishing ground—II. Inference after observation by the current meter in two layers. *Bull. Jap. Soc. scient. Fish.*, **20**: 780–2. [202]

TAIT, J. B. (1930). The surface drift in the northern and middle areas of the North Sea and in the Faroe-Shetland Channel. Part II, Section 1: a cartographical analysis of the results of Scottish surface drift-bottle experiments commenced in the year 1910. *Scient. Invest. Fishery Bd Scotl.*, (iv) 56 pp. [120]

TAIT, J. B. (1937). The surface water drift in the northern and middle areas of the North Sea and in the Faroe-Shetland Channel. Part II, Section 3: a cartographical analysis of the results of Scottish surface drift-bottle experiments of the year 1912; with a discussion on some hydrographical and biological implications of the drift-bottle results of 1910, 1911, and 1912, including statement of a theory of the upper water circulation of the northern and middle North Sea. *Scient. Invest. Fishery Bd Scotl.*, (i) 60 pp. [120, 121]

TAIT, J. B. (1952). *Hydrography in relation to fisheries*. Arnold, Lond., 106 pp. [15, 179]

TAIT, J. B. (1957). Hydrography of the Faroe-Shetland channel 1927–1952. *Mar. Res.*, (2) 309 pp. [120]

TÅNING, Å. VEDEL. (1929). Plaice investigations in Icelandic waters. *Rapp. P.-v. Réun. Cons. perm. int. Explor. Mer*, **57**: 134 pp. [176]

TÅNING, Å. VEDEL. (1931a). Fluctuations in the stock of cod in Icelandic waters. *Meddr Kommn Danm. Fisk.-og Havunders.*, Serie: Fiskeri, **9**: (3) 43 pp. [147]

TÅNING, Å. VEDEL. (1931b). Drift-bottle experiments in Icelandic waters. *Rapp. P.-v. Réun. Cons. perm. int. Explor. Mer*, **72**: 20 pp. [153]

TÅNING, Å. VEDEL. (1934a). Marking experiments with plaice in east Icelandic waters. *Rapp. P.-v. Réun. Cons. perm. int. Explor. Mer*, **86**: (iv) 13 pp. [176, 235]

TÅNING, Å. VEDEL. (1934b). Survey of long distance migrations of cod in the North Western Atlantic according to marking experiments. *Rapp. P.-v. Réun. Cons. perm. int. Explor. Mer*, **89**: (3) 5–11. [153, 156]

TÅNING, Å. VEDEL. (1934c). A supposed submarine ridge along the south-east coast of Greenland. *Nature, Lond.*, **133**: 326. [156]

TÅNING, Å. VEDEL. (1936a). Young herring and sprat in Faroese waters. *Meddr Kommn Danm. Fisk.-og Havunders.*, Serie: Fiskeri, **10**: (3) 28 pp. [102]

TÅNING, Å. VEDEL. (1936b). The herring stocks of the Faroes, Iceland and Greenland. *Rapp. P.-v. Réun. Cons. perm. int. Explor. Mer*, **100**: (2) 32–3. [101]

TÅNING, Å. VEDEL. (1937). Some features in the migration of cod. *J. Cons. perm. int. Explor. Mer*, **12**: 1–35. [23, 149, 152, 153, 154, 156, 158]

TÅNING, Å. VEDEL. (1951). Occurrence of herring north-east of the Faroe Islands, in June and August, 1950. *Annls biol. Copenh.*, **7**: 119–20. [108, 109]

TÅNING, Å. VEDEL. (1952a). Experimental study of meristic characters in fishes. *Biol. Rev.*, **27**: 169–93. [24, 83, 84]

TÅNING, Å. VEDEL. (1952b). North-East of the Faroe Islands. Occurrence of herring in June and about 1. December 1951. *Annls biol., Copenh.*, **8**: 140. [108, 111]

TÅNING, Å. VEDEL. (1953). North and North-East of the Faroe Islands. Occurrence of herring. *Annls biol., Copenh.*, **9**: 167. [109, 111]

TÅNING, Å. VEDEL. (1956). North and North-East of the Faroe Islands. Occurrence of herring. *Annls biol., Copenh.*, **11**: 118. [110]

TÅNING, Å. VEDEL. (1957). North and North-East of the Faroe Islands. Occurrence of herring. *Annls biol., Copenh.*, **12**: 169. [109]

TÅNING, Å. VEDEL. (1958). Observations on supposed intermingling or a certain connection between some stocks of boreal and subarctic demersal food fishes of the eastern and western Atlantic. *Spec. Publs int. Commn NW. Atlant. Fish.*, (i) 313–25.   [153]

TATE REGAN, C. (1914). The systematic arrangement of the fishes of the family Salmonidae. *Ann. Mag. nat. Hist.*, **13**: 405–8.   [42]

TATE REGAN, C. (1916). The British fishes of the subfamily Clupeinae and related species in other seas. *Ann. Mag. nat. Hist.*, **18**: 1–19.   [86]

TATE REGAN, C. (1929). Salmon and Salmonidae. *Encyclopædia Britannica*, **19**: 889–90. 14th edition.   [42]

TATE REGAN, C. (1933). Johannes Schmidt (1877–1933). *J. Cons. perm. int. Explor. Mer*, **8**: 145–60.   [72]

TAVOLGA, W. N. and WODINSKY, J. (1963). Auditory capacities in fishes. Pure tone thresholds in nine species of marine teleosts. *Bull. Am. Mus. nat. Hist.*, **126**: 177–240.   [37]

TCHERNAVIN, V. (1938). The absorption of bones in the skull of salmon during their migration to rivers. *Salm. Fish., Edinb.*, (6) 4 pp.   [28]

TCHERNAVIN, V. (1939). The origin of salmon. *Salm. Trout. Mag.*, (95) 120–40.   [42]

TEDD, J. G. and LACK, D. (1958). The detection of bird migration by high-power radar. *Proc. R. Soc. B.*, **149**: 503–10.
                                                                                                                   [40]

TEICHMANN, H. (1959). Über die Leistung des Geruchssinnes beim Aal (*Anguilla anguilla* (L.)). *Z. vergl. Physiol.*, **42**: 206–54.   [191, 192]

TEICHMANN, H. (1962). Die Chemorezeption der Fische. *Ergebn. Biol.*, **25**: 177–205.   [187]

TELKORA, L. P. (1961). Recruitment of the spawning stock of the Atlanto-Scandia herring by the rich 1950 year-class. *ICES CM 1961 Herring Symposium.* (37) 3 pp. (mimeo).   [107]

TEMPLEMAN, W. (1958). How cod spawn—Nielsen's observations. *Rep. Atlant. biol. Stn St Andrews*, (68) 15–6.   [147]

TESCH, J. J. (1928). On sex and growth investigations on the freshwater eel in Dutch waters. *J. Cons. perm. int. Explor. Mer*, **3**: 52–69.   [75]

TESCH, J. J. (1929). Investigations on herring in the southern North Sea. *Rapp. P.-v. Réun. Cons. perm. int. Explor. Mer*, **54**: 56–71.   [124]

TESCH, J. J. (1934). Herring races in the southern North Sea. *Rapp. P.-v. Réun. Cons. perm. int. Explor. Mer*, **89**: (3) 45–52.   [136, 139]

TESCH, J. J. (1937). Racial investigations on herring larvæ in the south-western inlets of Holland. *Rapp. P.-v. Réun· Cons. perm. int. Explor. Mer*, **105**: (3) 7–9.   [96, 124]

TESCH, J. J. (1939). Observations on the herring population in the Flemish Bight and the eastern part of the Channel in the Winter 1938–1939. *Rapp. P.-v. Réun. Cons. perm. int. Explor. Mer*, **109**: (3) 46–50.   [140]

TESTER, A. L. (1937). Populations of herring (*Clupea pallasii*) in the coastal waters of British Columbia. *J. biol. Bd Can.*, **3**: 108–44.   [24, 141, 143]

TESTER, A. L. (1938a). What time of day are herring caught? *Progr. Rep. biol. Stas Nanaimo & Prince Rupert*, (37) 3–6.   [93]

TESTER, A. L. (1938b). Herring, the tide, and the moon. *Progr. Rep. biol. Stas Nanaimo & Prince Rupert*, (38) 10–4.
                                                                                                                  [230]

TESTER, A. L. (1938c). Variation in the mean vertebral count of herring (*Clupea pallasii*) with water temperature. *J. Cons. perm. int. Explor. Mer*, **13**: 72–5.   [24]

TESTER, A. L. (1943). Use of the echo sounder to locate herring in British Columbia waters. *Bull. Fish. Res. Bd Can.*, (63) 21 pp.   [93]

THINES, G. (1955). Les poissons aveugles. (1). *Annls Soc. r. zool. Belg.*, **86**: 1–128.   [252]

THOMPSON, H. (1943). A biological and economic study of cod (*Gadus callarias*, L.) in the Newfoundland area. *Res. Bull. Div. Res. Newfoundld*, (14) 160 pp.   [29, 145, 146, 148]

THOMPSON, W. F. (1959). An approach to population dynamics of the Pacific red salmon. *Trans. Am. Fish. Soc.*, **88**: 206–9.   [7]

THORNTON, W. M. (1932). Electrical perception by deep sea fish. *Proc. Univ. Durham phil. Soc.*, **8**: 301–12.   [196]

THORPE, W. H. (1956). *Learning and instinct in animals.* Methuen, Lond., 493 pp.   [252, 260]

TINBERGEN, N. (1951). *The study of instinct.* Clarendon Press, Oxford, 228 pp.   [187, 190]

TOMASCHEK, H. (1937). Histologische Untersuchungen des Gehörorgans von *Trutta fario*. *Zool. Jb.*, (*Allg. Zool.*), **58**: 159–62.   [31]

TOMCZAK, G. and GOEDECKE, E. (1962). Monatskarten der Temperatur der Nordsee. *Dt. hydrogr. Z.*, Ergänz B (4) (7) 16 pp.   [123, 124]

TREFETHEN, P. S. (1956). Sonic equipment for tracking individual fish. *Spec. scient. Rep. U.S. Fish Wildl. Serv. Fisheries*, (179) 11 pp. [40]

TREFETHEN, P. S., DUDLEY, J. W., and SMYTH, M. R. (1957). Ultrasonic tracer follows tagged fish. *Electronics*, **30**: (4) 156–60. [40]

TROUT, G. C. (1954). Otolith growth of the Barents Sea cod. *Rapp. P.-v. Réun. Cons. perm. int. Explor. Mer*, **136**: 89–102. [31]

TROUT, G. C. (1957). The Bear Island cod: migrations and movements. *Fishery Invest., Lond.*, Ser. 2, **21**: (6) 51 pp. [21, 32, 33, 149, 161, 162, 163, 164, 200, 206, 229]

TROUT, G. C. (1958). Results of English cod tagging in the Barents Sea. *J. Cons. perm. int. Explor. Mer*, **23**: 371–80. [23]

TROUT, G. C., LEE, A. J., RICHARDSON, I. D., and HARDEN JONES, F. R. (1952). Recent echo sounder studies. *Nature, Lond.*, **170**: 71–2. [23]

TRYBOM, F. (1904). Ålmärkningar i Östersjön 1903 och 1904. *Svenska hydrogr.-biol. Kommn. Skr.*, (III) 4 pp. [206]

TRYBOM, F. (1907). Ålmärkningar i Östersjön 1905. *Svenska hydrogr.-biol. Kommn. Skr.*, (III) 6 pp. [206]

TRYBOM, F. and SCHNEIDER, G. (1907). Die im Jahre 1906 in Schweden ausgeführten Versuche mit gekennzeichneten Aalen. *Svenska hydrogr.-biol. Kommn. Skr.*, (III) 2 pp. [207]

TUCKER, D. G. (1959). Electronic sector-scanning asdic. *J. Inst. Navig.*, **12**: 184–9. [40]

TUCKER, D. W. (1959). A new solution to the Atlantic eel problem. *Nature, Lond.*, **183**: 495–501. [72, 74, 80]

TULLY, J. P. (1942). Surface non-tidal currents in the approaches to Juan de Fuca Strait. *J. Fish. Res. Bd Can.*, **5**: 398–409. [264]

TULLY, J. P. (1952). Notes on the behaviour of fresh water entering the sea. *Proc. 7th. Pacif. Sci. Congr.*, **3**: 267–89. [263]

TULLY, J. P. (1958). On structure, entrainment, and transport in estuarine embayments. *J. mar. Res.*, **17**: 523–35. [263]

TULLY, J. P. and BARBER, F. G. (1960). An estuarine analogy in the subarctic Pacific Ocean. *J. Fish. Res. Bd Can.*, **17**: 91–112. [265]

TUNGATE, D. S. (1958). Echo-sounder surveys in the autumn of 1956. *Fishery Invest., Lond.*, Ser. 2, **22**: (2) 17 pp. [41, 202]

TYLER, J. E. (1960). Radiance distribution as a function of depth in an underwater environment. *Bull. Scripps. Instn Oceanogr.*, **7**: 363–412. [237, 238]

TYLER, J. E. (1961). Sun-altitude effect on the distribution of underwater light. *Limnol. Oceanogr.*, **6**: 24–5. [237]

TYLER, J. E. and PREISENDORFER, R. W. (1964). Transmission of energy within the sea. In *The Seas*, **1**: 397–451. ed. by M. N. Hill. Interscience Publ., N.Y. 864 pp. [237]

ULLYOTT, P. (1936). The behaviour of *Dendrocoelum lacteum*. II. Responses in non-directional gradients. *J. exp. Biol.*, **13**: 265–78. [188]

VAN OOSTEN, J. (1929). Life history of the lake herring (*Leucichthys artedi* Le Sueur) of Lake Huron as revealed by its scales, with a critique of the scale method. *Bull. Bur. Fish., Wash.*, **44**: 265–428. [28]

VAN SOMEREN, V. D. (1937). A preliminary investigation into the causes of scale absorption in salmon (*Salmo salar*, Linné). *Salm. Fish., Edinb.*, (2) 12 pp. [28]

VAUX, D. (1965). Current measuring by towed electrodes; observations in the Arctic and North Seas, 1953–59. *Fishery Invest., Lond.*, Ser. 2, **23**: (8) 154 pp. [195]

DE VEEN, J. F. (1961). The 1960 tagging experiments on mature plaice in different spawning areas in the southern North Sea. *ICES CM* 1961, (44) 7 pp. (mimeo). [173, 234]

DE VEEN, J. F. (1962). On the sub-populations of plaice in the southern North Sea. *ICES CM* 1962, (94) 6 pp. (mimeo). [173, 174, 175, 234]

DE VEEN, J. F. (1963). On the phenomenon of soles swimming near the surface of the sea. *ICES CM* 1963, (56) 4 pp. (mimeo). [35]

DE VEEN, J. F. (1967). On the phenomenon of soles (*Solea solea* L.) swimming at the surface. *J. Cons. perm. int. Explor. Mer*, **31**: 207–36. [243]

DE VEEN, J. F. and BOEREMA, L. K. (1959). Distinguishing southern North Sea spawning populations of plaice by means of otolith characteristics. *ICES CM* 1959, (91) 5 pp. (mimeo). [32, 172, 173]

VERHEIJEN, F. J. (1958). The mechanisms of the trapping effect of artificial light sources upon animals. *Archs néerl. Zool.*, **13**: 1–107. [187]

VERHOEVEN, L. A. and DAVIDOFF, E. B. (1962). Marine tagging of Fraser River sockeye salmon. *Bull. int. Pacif. Salm. Fish. Commn*, (13) 132 pp. [67, 261, 269]

VERNON, E. H. (1957). Morphometric comparison of three races of kokanee (*Oncorhynchus nerka*) within a large British Columbia lake. *J. Fish. Res. Bd Can.*, **14**: 573–98.   [25]

VERWEY, J. (1958). Orientation in migrating marine animals and a comparison with that of other migrants. *Archs néerl. Zool.*, **13**: suppl., 418–45.   [179, 187, 215, 224, 227, 269]

VLADYKOV, V. D. (1964). Quest for the true breeding area of the American eel (*Anguilla rostrata* Le Sueur). *J. Fish. Res. Bd Can.*, **21**: 1523–30.   [77]

VOGLIS, G. M. and COOK, J. C. (1966). Underwater applications of an advanced acoustic scanning equipment. *Ultrasonics*, **4**: 1–9.   [40, 207]

DE VRIES, H. (1956). Physical aspects of the sense organs. *Prog. Biophys. biophys. Chem.*, **6**: 208–64.   [29]

WALFORD, L. A. (1938). Effect of currents on distribution and survival of the eggs and larvæ of the haddock (*Melanogrammus æglefinus*) on Georges Bank. *Bull. Bur. Fish., Wash.*, **49**: (29) 73 pp.   [200]

WALKER, T. J. and HASLER, A. D. (1949). Detection and discrimination of odors of aquatic plants by bluntnose minnow (*Hyborhynchus notatus*). *Physiol. Zoöl.*, **22**: 45–63.   [259]

WALLACE, W. (1924). First report on young herring in the southern North Sea and English Channel. *Fishery Invest., Lond.*, Ser. 2, **7**: (4) 84 pp.   [127]

WALLIN, O. (1957). On the growth structure and developmental physiology of the scale of fishes. *Rep. Inst. Freshwat. Res. Drottningholm*, (38) 385–447.   [26, 28]

WATERMAN, T. H. (1954). Polarization patterns in submarine illumination. *Science, N.Y.*, **120**: 927–32.   [237]

WATERMAN, T. H. (1961). The importance of radiance distribution and polarization of submarine daylight for animal orientation. In *Symposium on radiant energy in the sea. Un. geod. geophys. int. Monograph*, (10) 103–7.   [239]

WATERMAN, T. H. and WESTELL, W. E. (1956). Quantitative effect of the sun's position on submarine light polarization. *J. mar. Res.*, **15**: 149–69.   [239]

WENT, A. E. J. (1947). Value of the kelt. *Salm. Trout Mag.*, (119) 41–8.   [54]

WENT, A. E. J. (1964). Irish salmon. A review of investigations up to 1963. *Scient. Proc. R. Dubl. Soc.*, Ser. A, **1**: 365–412.   [55]

WERNER, C. F. (1928). Studien über die Otolithen der Knochenfische. *Z. wiss. Zool.*, **131**: 502–87.   [29]

WHITE, H. C. (1934). A spawning migration of salmon in E. Apple river. *Rep. biol. Bd Can.*, 1933, p. 41.   [59]

WHITE, H. C. (1936). The homing of salmon in Apple River, N.S. *J. Fish. Res. Bd Can.*, **2**: 391–400.   [58]

WHITE, H. C. and HUNTSMAN, A. G. (1938). Is local behaviour in salmon heritable? *J. Fish. Res. Bd Can.*, **4**: 1–18.   [58]

WIBORG, K. F. (1957). Occurrence of herring larvæ in coastal waters of North-Western Norway. *Annls biol., Copenh.*, **12**: 157–8.   [105]

WILIMOVSKY, N. J. and FREIHOFER, W. O. (1957). Guide to the literature on systematic biology of Pacific salmon. *Spec. scient. Rep. U.S. Fish Wildl. Serv. Fisheries*, (209) 266 pp.   [43]

WILKINSON, D. H. (1952). The random element in bird 'navigation'. *J. exp. Biol.*, **29**: 532–60.   [1, 209]

WILLIAMS, G. C. (1957). Homing behaviour of California rocky shore fishes. *Univ. Calif. Publs Zool.*, **59**: 249–84.   [248, 252]

WILSON, A. P. (1958). Tagging experiments. *Annls biol., Copenh.*, **13**: 170–2.   [106]

WIMPENNY, R. S. (1953). *The plaice.* Arnold, Lond., 145 pp.   [168, 170, 172, 179]

WIMPENNY, R. S. (1960). Young plaice hauls off the English East Coast. *Fishery Invest., Lond.*, Ser. 2, **23**: (1) 20 pp.   [170]

WINGE, Ö. (1915). On the value of the rings in the scales of the cod as a means of age determination. *Meddr Kommn Havunders.*, Serie: Fiskeri, **4**: (8) 21 pp.   [28]

WINGE, Ö. (1923). The Sargasso Sea, its boundaries and vegetation. *Rep. Dan. oceanogr. Exped. Mediterr.*, **3**: (2) 34 pp.   [77]

WINN, H. E., SALMON, M., and ROBERTS, N. (1964). Sun-compass orientation by parrot fishes. *Z. Tierpsychol.*, **21**: 798–812.   [224, 240, 241, 242]

WISBY, W. J. and HASLER, A. D. (1954). The effect of olfactory occlusion on migrating silver salmon (*O. kisutch*). *J. Fish. Res. Bd Can.*, **11**: 472–8.   [252, 253, 254, 258]

WISE, J. P. (1958a). Cod and hydrography—a review. *Spec. scient. Rep. U.S. Fish Wildl. Serv. Fisheries*, (245) 16 pp.   [144]

WISE, J. P. (1958b). The world's southernmost indigenous cod. *J. Cons. perm. int. Explor. Mer*, **23**: 208–12.   [145]

DE WIT, G. (1953). Seasickness (motion sickness). *Acta oto-lar.*, **108**: suppl. 56 pp.   [215]

WITHLER, F. C., McCONNELL, J. A., and McMAHON, V. H. (1949). Lakes of the Skeena River drainage. IX. Babine Lake. *Prog. Rep. Pacif. Cst Stns*, (78) 6–10.   [226, 227]

WITTING, R. (1912). Zusammenfassende Übersicht der Hydrographie des Bottnischen und Finnischen Meerbusens und der Nördlichen Ostsee. *Finnl. hydrogr.-biol. Unters.*, (7) 82 pp. [207]

WOOD, A. B. (1941). *A textbook of Sound.* 2nd. Edition. Bell, Lond., 578 pp. [38]

WOOD, H. (1930). Scottish herring shoals, pre-spawning and spawning movements. *Scient. Invest. Fishery Bd Scotl.*, (1) 71 pp. [90, 93, 123, 127, 128]

WOOD, H. (1934). *The natural history of the herring in Scottish waters.* Fishg News, Aberd., 36 pp. [90]

WOOD, H. (1936). Race investigation of the herring population of Scottish waters. *Scient. Invest. Fishery Bd Scotl.*, (3) 52 pp. [90, 103, 125, 133, 135]

WOOD, H. (1937). Movements of herring in the northern North Sea. *Scient. Invest. Fishery Bd Scotl.*, (3) 49 pp. [126, 128, 129, 130, 135]

WOOD, H. and McGEE, G. (1925). Aircraft experiments for the locating of herring shoals in Scottish waters, 1924. *Scient. Invest. Fishery Bd Scotl.*, (1) 20 pp. [35]

WOOD, H., PARRISH, B. B., and McPHERSON, G. (1955). Review of Scottish herring tagging experiments, 1948–1953. *Rapp. P.-v. Réun. Cons. perm. int. Explor. Mer*, **140**: (2) 35–54. [129, 132]

WOOD, H., PARRISH, B. B., BAXTER, I. G., and McPHERSON, G. (1952). Scottish Fisheries. *Annls biol., Copenh.*, **8**: 143–50. [130]

WOOD, R. J. (1959). Investigations on O-group herring. *J. Cons. perm. int. Explor. Mer*, **24**: 264–76. [124]

WOOD, R. W. (1906). Fish-eye views, and vision under water. *Lond. Edinb. Dubl. Phil. Mag.*, **12**: 159–62. [236]

WOOD, R. W. (1934). *Physical Optics.* 3rd. Ed. Macmillan, Lond., 846 pp. [236]

WOODHEAD, A. D. (1959). Variations in the activity of the thyroid gland of the cod, *Gadus callarias* L., in relation to its migrations in the Barents Sea—II. The 'dummy run' of the immature fish. *J. mar. biol. Ass. U.K.*, **38**: 417–22. [163]

WOODHEAD, A. D. and WOODHEAD, P. M. J. (1965). Seasonal changes in the physiology of the Barents Sea cod, *Gadus morhua* L., in relation to its environment. I. Endocrine changes particularly affecting migration and maturation. *Spec. Publs int. Commn NW. Atlant. Fish.*, (6) 691–715. [201]

WOODHEAD, P. M. J. (1965). Effects of light upon behaviour and distribution of demersal fishes of the North Atlantic. *Spec. Publs int. Commn NW. Atlant. Fish.*, (6) 267–87. [224]

WOODHEAD, P. M. J. (1966). The behaviour of fish in relation to light in the sea. *Oceanogr. mar. Biol.*, **4**: 337–403. [187, 224, 235]

WOODS, J. D. and FOSBERRY, G. G. (1967). The structure of the thermocline. *Rep. Underwat. Ass.*, 1966–67, 5–18. [221]

WRIGHT, R. H. (1964). *The science of smell.* Allen & Unwin, Lond., 164 pp. [187]

WRIGHT, W. D. (1938). *The perception of light.* Blackie, London and Glasgow. 100 pp. [238]

WÜST, G. (1964). *Stratification and circulation in the Antillean-Caribbean Basins. Part one. Spreading and mixing of the water types with an oceanographic atlas.* Columbia Univ. Press, 20 pp. [77]

YUDANOV, I. G. (1962). Soviet investigations of the Atlanto-Scandian herring stock. *Annls biol., Copenh.*, **17**: 170–1. [103]

ZIJLSTRA, J. J. (1958). On the herring 'races' spawning in the southern North Sea and English Channel. *Rapp. P.-v. Réun. Cons. perm. int. Explor. Mer*, **143**: (2) 134–45. [93, 96, 136, 138, 139]

ZIJLSTRA, J. J. (1963). On the recruitment mechanism of North Sea autumn spawning herring. *Rapp. P.-v. Réun. Cons. perm. int. Explor. Mer*, **154**: 198–202. [138, 139]

Subject Index

The more important place names and sea areas are listed in the Geographical Index. The main Oceanic currents mentioned in the text are included in the Subject Index under their own name (viz, Irminger Current) and under the general heading Oceanic currents.

Geographical Index

The index includes the more important place names and sea areas (but not Oceanic currents) mentioned in the text. Bold figures indicate pages on which there are maps or charts from which positions can be located.